Global Environmental Assessments

Global Environmental Accord: Strategies for Sustainability and
Institutional Innovation
Nazli Choucri, series editor

(continued at back of book)

Global Environmental Assessments

Information and Influence

edited by Ronald B. Mitchell, William C. Clark,
David W. Cash, and Nancy M. Dickson

The MIT Press
Cambridge, Massachusetts
London, England

MIT Press books may be purchased at special quantity discounts for business or sales promotional use. For information, please e-mail special_sales@ mitpress.mit.edu or write to Special Sales Department, The MIT Press, 55 Hayward Street, Cambridge, MA 02142-1315.

This book was set in Sabon by SNP Best-set Typesetter Ltd., Hong Kong. Printed and bound in the United States of America on recycled paper.

Library of Congress Cataloging-in-Publication Data

Global environmental assessments: information and influence / edited by Ronald B. Mitchell . . . [et al.].
    p.   cm.—(Global environmental accord)
Includes bibliographical references and index.
ISBN-13: 978-0-262-13468-2; ISBN-10: 0-262-13468-3 (alk. paper)
ISBN-13: 978-0-262-63336-9; ISBN-10: 0-262-63336-1 (pbk. : alk. paper)
1. Environmental policy—International cooperation. 2. Environmental protection—International cooperation. 3. Envirronmental impact analysis—Case studies. I. Mitchell, Ronald B. (Ronald Bruce) II. Global environmental accords.

GE170.G55   2006
333.7—dc22

2006041963

10 9 8 7 6 5 4 3 2 1

Contents

Series Foreword

A new recognition of profound interconnections between social and natural systems is challenging conventional constructs and the policy predispositions informed by them. Our current intellectual challenge is to develop the analytical and theoretical underpinnings of an understanding of the relationship between the social and the natural systems. Our policy challenge is to identify and implement effective decision-making approaches to managing the global environment.

The series Global Environmental Accord: Strategies for Sustainability and Institutional Innovation adopts an integrated perspective on national, international, cross-border, and cross-jurisdictional problems, priorities, and purposes. It examines the sources and the consequences of social transactions as these relate to environmental conditions and concerns. Our goal is to make a contribution to both intellectual and policy endeavors.

Nazli Choucri

Preface

This study emerges from the Global Environmental Assessment Project (GEA). The project was launched by William C. Clark, Nancy Dickson, Jill Jäger, Sheila Jasanoff, Robert O. Keohane, and James J. McCarthy in 1995 as an international, interdisciplinary effort directed at understanding the role of organized efforts to bring scientific information to bear in shaping social responses to large-scale environmental change. The focus of the project was the growing number of such efforts—ranging from the periodic reports of the Intergovernmental Panel on Climate Change to the Global Biodiversity Assessment to the Millennium Ecosystem Assessment—that have been conducted in support of international policymaking over the last quarter century. Its central concern was to understand the impacts of environmental assessments on large-scale interactions between nature and society, and how changes in the conduct of those assessments could alter their impacts. The project attempted to advance a common understanding of what it might mean to say that one effort to mobilize scientific information is more "effective" than another. It tried to view such issues from the perspectives of the scientific experts involved in producing assessments, the decision makers at multiple scales who use those assessments, and the societies affected by the assessments. It attempted to embed its research approaches and interpretation of findings in contemporary theoretical frameworks of science studies, policy studies, and international relations. At the same time, the project tried to ensure that its efforts were consistently informed by pragmatic policy considerations and perspectives through a series of workshops that engaged practitioners, users, and scholars of assessments in an off-the-record dialogue that let them compare insights and experiences.

Over the course of the study, the GEA project engaged more than fifty senior scholars, postdoctoral fellows, and students drawn from the natural, social, and policy sciences in an intensive program of training and research. Its series of workshops with assessment practitioners and managers engaged another fifty individuals. The project produced more than forty working papers, many of which have appeared in the peer-reviewed literature. Three synthesis volumes have emerged from the GEA project. *Earthly Politics: Local and Global in Environmental Governance* (MIT Press, 2004), edited by Sheila Jasanoff and Marybeth Long Martello, has been written for scholars concerned about the tensions between political power, governance, and the globally and locally referenced knowledge that is mobilized or marginalized in environmental assessment practice. *Assessments of Regional and Global Environmental Risks: Designing Processes for the Effective Use of Science in Decisionmaking* (Resources for the Future 2005), edited by Alexander E. Farrell and Jill Jäger, is directed toward assessment practitioners and summarizes findings on how the practices of global and regional environmental assessment can be reformed to improve their utility to decision makers. Finally, the present volume, *Global Environmental Assessments: Information and Influence*, is addressed to the community of scholars and institutional designers seeking to understand the interactions of information and institutions in structuring international affairs. A website for the project, at http://www.ksg.harvard.edu/gea/, provides detailed information on its participants, publications, and activities.

Global Environmental Assessments: Information and Influence focuses on what we have learned through our work in the Global Environmental Assessment Project about how institutions that generate, organize, and disseminate scientific knowledge can bring that knowledge to bear on the wide range of global and regional environmental issues currently facing the world. In producing the volume, we have drawn on work from virtually all participants in the project, as well as relevant scholarship of others. The individual contributions that make up the body of the book reflect a subset of GEA case studies we selected as providing particularly rich illumination of institutional issues. The contributors assembled at a workshop to plan this volume in January 2001.

At the workshop, we explored common themes, findings, and synergies from the individual case studies, critiqued a preliminary draft of chapter 1, and defined focal questions for the chapters published here. We hope that the result will be of interest not only to students of global environmental politics and policy, but also to the growing community of scholars seeking to understand the changing role in world affairs of institutions that produce or broker information.

We acknowledge with gratitude the numerous groups that have provided financial and institutional support for the project. Initial support for the Global Environmental Assessment Project was provided by a core grant from the National Science Foundation (Award No. SBR-9521910) to the "Global Environmental Assessment Team." Supplemental financial support for the team was provided by the National Oceanic and Atmospheric Administration's Office of Global Programs, the Department of Energy, and the National Aeronautics and Space Administration. Additional support has been provided by the Department of Energy (Award No. DE-FG02-95ER62122) for the project "Assessment Strategies for Global Environmental Change," the National Institute for Global Environmental Change (Awards No. 901214-HAR, LWT 62-123-06518) for the project "Towards Useful Integrated Assessments," the Center for Integrated Study of the Human Dimensions of Global Integrated Assessment at Carnegie Mellon University (NSF Award No. SBR-9521914) for the project "The Use of Global Environmental Assessments," the European Environment Agency, the Belfer Center for Science and International Affairs at Harvard University's Kennedy School of Government, the International Human Dimensions Programme on Global Environmental Change, Harvard's Weatherhead Center for International Affairs, Harvard's Environmental Information Center, the International Institute for Applied Systems Analysis, the German Academic Exchange Service, the Heinrich Böll Foundation in Germany, the Massachusetts Institute of Technology's Center for Environmental Initiatives, the Heinz Family Foundation, the Heinz Center for Science, Economics and the Environment, and the National Center for Environmental Decision-making Research. Ronald B. Mitchell's work on this project was supported in part by the National Science Foundation (Award No. SES-0318374) for "Analysis of the Effects of Environmental Treaties," by a 2002–2003 Sabbatical Fellowship in the Humanities and Social Sciences from the American Philosophical Society and a 2002 Summer Research Award from the University of Oregon.

Among the many individuals who contributed significantly to the overall project, we owe special thanks to Executive Director Nancy Dickson, whose talents and dedication in fostering international, interdisciplinary research and training programs are simply incomparable and whose contributions to making the GEA project work are acknowledged by her inclusion as an editor of this volume. We also owe a special debt to Frank Alcock, who worked very closely with us in the early stages of formulating this volume, and to Bob Keohane, Barbara Connolly, Lisa Martin, and Oran Young, all of whom generously contributed to our initial development of some of its key ideas. We also drew on insights and case studies of many contributors to the project, whose studies are listed on our website but could not be included here. Finally, we extend our deepest thanks and admiration to J. Michael Hall, who for much of this project was director of the Office of Global Programs at the U.S. National Oceanic and Atmospheric Administration. His vision, wisdom, and commitment sustained us through the GEA effort, and enriched our lives.

Contributors

Institutional Affiliations of Editors and Authors during the Project
(1995–2005)

Numbers identify institutional affiliations from list below, in reverse chronological order.

Editors

David W. Cash 19, 15

William C. Clark 15

Nancy M. Dickson 15

Ronald B. Mitchell 27, 22

Authors

Liliana B. Andonova 4, 6, 12, 15, 17

Frank Biermann 28, 8, 21, 9, 18, 15

Aarti Gupta 29, 5, 15, 30

Susanne C. Moser 20, 24, 16, 15, 3

Anthony G. Patt 1, 21, 15, 11, 17, 2

Noelle Eckley Selin 11, 7, 23, 15, 13

Wendy E. F. Torrance 14, 10, 12, 15, 17

Stacy D. VanDeveer 26, 15, 25, 17

1. Department of Geography and Environment, Boston University

2. Center for International Earth Science Information Network

3. School of Geography, Clark University

4. Department of Government, Colby College

5. Center for Science, Policy and Outcomes, Columbia University
6. Earth Institute, Columbia University
7. European Environment Agency
8. Department of Political Science, Freie Universität Berlin
9. German Advisory Council on Global Change (WBGU)
10. Committee on Degrees in Social Studies, Harvard University
11. Department of Earth and Planetary Sciences, Harvard University
12. Department of Government, Harvard University
13. Environmental Science and Public Policy Program, Harvard University
14. Freshman Dean's Office, Harvard University
15. John F. Kennedy School of Government, Harvard University
16. The H. John Heinz III Center for Science, Economics and the Environment
17. International Institute for Applied Systems Analysis
18. School of International Studies, Jawaharlal Nehru University
19. Massachusetts Executive Office of Environmental Affairs
20. Institute for the Study of Society and the Environment, National Center for Atmospheric Research
21. Potsdam Institute for Climate Impact Research
22. Center for Environmental Science and Policy, Stanford University
23. University of Copenhagen
24. Global Environment Program, Union of Concerned Scientists
25. Department of Government and Politics, University of Maryland
26. Department of Political Science, University of New Hampshire
27. Department of Political Science, University of Oregon
28. Department of Environmental Policy Analysis, Vrije Universiteit Amsterdam
29. Technology and Agrarian Development Group, Wageningen University
30. Department of Forestry and Environmental Studies, Yale University

1

Evaluating the Influence of Global Environmental Assessments

William C. Clark, Ronald B. Mitchell, and David W. Cash

Introduction

Global environmental changes and scientific assessments of those changes have become increasingly common elements in international, national, and even local policymaking and decision making. Do assessments of the causes of, impacts of, and options for dealing with global environmental problems influence how society addresses those problems? How do those assessments influence policy and economic decisions at levels from the global to the local? What conditions foster or inhibit such influence? In what ways can careful design of an assessment increase such influence?

Large-scale environmental problems typify the challenges of complex interdependence facing today's global community (Keohane and Nye 1977/1989). Both understanding and addressing most such problems require cooperation among different countries, between scientists and policymakers, and across the range of concerned and affected actors from the local to the global level (Keck and Sikkink 1998; Ostrom 1990; Betsill and Corell 2001; Young 2002). In response to such problems, organized efforts to mobilize scientific information in support of decision making have become increasingly frequent. The work of the Intergovernmental Panel on Climate Change (IPCC) is perhaps the best known assessment but assessments have been regularly conducted in the past and are planned for the future, with recent ones including the Millennium Ecosystem Assessment, the Global Mountain Biodiversity Assessment, the Global International Waters Assessment, the Comprehensive Assessment of the Freshwater Resources of the World, and a planned Global Marine Assessment (Parris 2003). We sought to build on the emerging literature on the interaction of science and environmental policy (Haas 1992b; Jasanoff 1990; Boehmer-Christiansen 1997; Andresen et al. 2000; Social Learning Group 2001a, 2001b; Grundmann 2001; Parson 2003) by characterizing and trying to explain variation in the influence of a range of global environmental assessments.

In this book, we present results from a multiyear, interdisciplinary, international research program that compared a range of environmental assessments from climate change and water management to biodiversity in an effort to better understand how global environmental assessments operate, when and how they influence policymaking and decision making, and how they can be designed to be more effective.[1] In this chapter, we begin by defining and reviewing the "global environmental assessments" (GEAs) we seek to understand and the challenges and opportunities for using them to inform environmental decision making. We then briefly summarize relevant scholarship from a variety of fields that informed our initial research on the influence of GEAs. There follows an outline of the conceptual framework we developed for this study and a preview of the case studies that constitute the bulk of this volume. Our conclusions on both the design of institutions for carrying out more effective GEAs and on the implications of GEA experience for broader social science scholarship on the influence of information are presented and discussed in the book's final chapter.

What Are Global Environmental Assessments?

Global environmental change, and its human causes and consequences, has become an increasingly prominent dimension of international affairs over the last thirty years (Committee on Global Change Research and National Research Council 1999; Young et al. 1999). Nations have negotiated hundreds of bilateral and multilateral environmental agreements to address transnational problems from climate change and biotechnology to endangered species and nature preservation (Mitchell 2003). Large-scale environmental issues have become linked to globalization, energy, trade, population, and other policy issues. Political and economic decision makers increasingly realize that understanding environmental change and devising strategies to mitigate or adapt to it require appreciation of scientific and social processes, and of how those processes interact at and across levels from the local to the global (Schellnhuber 1999; Steffen et al. 2001; Turner et al. 1990; Clark 2000). This has led to a growing demand for scientific knowledge that can inform and support decision making in ways that acknowledge the large spatial and temporal scale of many environmental problems without ignoring the more delimited information needs of decision makers from local farmers to international negotiators (Carnegie Commission on Science, Technology, and Government 1992; Corell and Bolin 1998; Mahoney 2002).

Scientists often seek to inform public debate on policy issues through publications in the peer-reviewed literature, through the popular media, and through private advice to decision makers. Large-scale international scientific assessments have become another, and increasingly common, arena in which science and policy interact. We call such assessments "global environmental assessments" or GEAs. We define "assessments" as formal efforts to assemble selected knowledge with a view toward making it publicly available in a form intended to be useful for decision making. By "formal," we mean that an assessment is sufficiently organized that such aspects as products, participants, and issuing authority can be identified relatively easily. By "efforts to assemble selected knowledge," we seek to recognize that assessments vary both with respect to how comprehensive they are and whether they involve conducting new, or summarizing and evaluating existing, research. We interpret "knowledge" broadly, treating the question of which kinds of information or expertise a specific assessment chooses to incorporate as an empirical rather than definitional one. We emphasize "publicly available" to distinguish assessments from technical advice prepared for the private use of decision makers.[2] Finally, we use "decision makers" to encompass actors in government, private corporations, research laboratories, nongovernmental organizations (NGOs), and civil society more generally.

The "global" focus of our study also deserves comment. Global environmental assessments have been the subject of less research and that research has been far less conclusive than that on the influence of assessments at national and subnational levels, which themselves remain areas where considerable work remains to be done. Although countries could rely exclusively on national scientific capabilities to understand global problems, most see advantages in pooling scientific expertise and data in "global" assessments. "Global" or transnational assessments such as those listed in table 1.1 can differ from local or national assessments in at least three senses. They may address environmental problems caused by actors in more than one country; they may address problems that have implications for decision makers in more than one country; or they may simply involve participants from more than one country in the assessment. Such assessments are usually undertaken with at least the nominal goal of constructing a science-based account of the problem in a way that decision makers in multiple countries will view as useful. While the primary focus of our analysis was on assessments defined as "global," we understood the importance of exploring the interaction of the global with the national and local. After all, one of the purposes of "global" assessments is to inform national and subnational decision makers. Thus, as described later, several of our cases studies were selected specifically to examine the dynamics of assessment influence in subnational issue domains.

Although no comprehensive catalog of GEAs exists, the number, size, and costs of global environmental assessments is both large and growing. From the mid-1980s to the mid-1990s, two to three GEAs per year were completed on climate change, ozone depletion, and acid rain (Social Learning Group 2001a; Social Learning Group 2001b, chaps. 15, 17). In 2003, large-scale GEAs were underway on at least a dozen issues (Convention on Biological Diversity 2003). The UNEP Global Environment Outlook (GEO) project has produced three comprehensive global state-of-the-environment reports as well as regional, subregional, and national assessments. Some involve ongoing scientific committees created to provide inputs to the processes of environmental management conducted under international treaties, such as by recommending catch quotas to the parties to fisheries agreements. Others involve independent scientific bodies with close ties to policy—for example, the nongovernmental joint wildlife trade monitoring program of the Convention on International Trade in Endangered Species (CITES), the International Institute for Applied Systems Analysis (IIASA) for the Convention on

Table 1.1
Recent global environmental assessments

Assessment	Lead organization	Scope; scale; timetable
Dryland Land Degradation Assessment	FAO	Drylands; global, regional; in development from 2001
Forest Resources Assessment	FAO	Forests; global, regional, national; FRA 2000 every 10 years
Global International Waters Assessment	UNEP	International (transboundary) waters; global, regional; 1999–2002
Global Environment Outlook	UNEP	Environment; global, regional; GEO-3 report 2002, biannual
Intergovernmental Panel on Climate Change	IPCC	Climate change; global, regional; 3rd report 2001
Millennium Ecosystem Assessment	UNEP	Ecosystems—goods and services; global, regional, national, local; 2001–2005
World Resources Report	WRI	Environment (themes); global, regional; biannual
World Water Assessment Programme	UNESCO	Freshwater; global, regional, basins; 2000, 1st report 2003
State of the world's plant genetic resources	FAO	Plant genetic resources; global, regional, national; 1996 (I) and 2007 (II)
State of the world's animal genetic resources	FAO	Animal genetic resources; global, regional, national; 2005, country reports 2003
Comprehensive assessment of the status and trends of agricultural biodiversity	SCBD, FAO, MA	Agricultural biodiversity; global, regional, national; 2007, preliminary assessment 2003, draft full assessment 2005
State of the world's traditional knowledge on biodiversity	CBD	Indigenous knowledge on biodiversity; global; 2003

Source: Adapted from Convention on Biological Diversity 2003.

Long-Range Transboundary Air Pollution (LRTAP), and the Scientific Committee on Antarctic Research (SCAR) for the Antarctic Treaty System. Yet others become primary sources of information for certain policymaking forums even though no formal ties exist, as evident in the International Council for the Exploration of the Sea providing expertise to several fishing agreements or the IPCC informing the UN Framework Convention on Climate Change (UNFCCC). Some GEAs limit themselves to scientific issues while others examine social and economic impacts and possible options for problem resolution. Some involve participants as representatives of governments and NGOs while others require participants to serve in their individual capacities. Some are intended to be ongoing whereas others are intended to disband after producing a single report. Some explicitly focus on one level (purely global), while others focus on multiple levels simultaneously and the interactions across levels.

In short, GEAs have become part of the political landscape at the international, national, and local levels. Scientists, governments, and both nongovernmental and international organizations expend considerable time, effort, and resources supporting them. They create large networks of scientists and focus the attention of numerous scientists on certain environmental issues and not others. Collectively, they have produced innumerable reports and policy recommendations that, in turn, have led to extensive press coverage. The key question for the research presented here was "do they matter?" That is, in what ways have GEAs influenced political, social, and economic choices regarding global environmental issues? And what factors explain why some GEAs are more influential than others?

The Influence of Scientific Information on Policy

Practitioners—the scientists, civil servants, and other advocates and policy advisors engaged in conducting and using GEAs—have learned a great deal about how to design a GEA that works and have shared that with immediate colleagues (Social Learning Group 2001a, 2001b). But few of those lessons have been evaluated and generalized by independent analysts. Some practitioners have thoughtfully reflected on their involvement in one or more assessments (Watson 2002, 1994; Tuinstra,

Hordijk, and Amann 1999; Bolin 2002, 1994; Schoenmaeckers 2000; Houghton 2004; Somerville 1996; Tolba and Rummel-Bulska 1998; Benedick 1998). Others have used their experience to advocate particular assessment methods or approaches (Clark and Jäger 1997; O'Riordan 1997; Kates 1997; Morgan and Dowlatabadi 1996; Dowlatabadi and Morgan 1993; Rotmans 1998; Rotmans and Vellinga 1998; Rotmans and Dowlatabadi 1998; Hordijk and Kroeze 1997; Morgan et al. 1984; Rubin, Lave, and Morgan 1991–1992). Efforts to bring experienced practitioners together, such as the OECD's Megascience Forum, have produced a rich, practice-based literature (Corell and Bolin 1998) with valuable insights "from the trenches" that have not yet been analyzed comparatively to identify lessons that can be confidently applied to other environmental challenges.

Scholars interested in the role of science have just begun to study GEAs. Several studies have examined how technical information in general and formal assessments in particular—have influenced particular issue areas such as marine pollution (Haas 1990), stratospheric ozone depletion (Downing and Kates 1982; Haas 1992a; Parson 2003; Litfin 1994; Grundmann 2001), whaling (Andresen 1989), climate change (Miller 2001), and acid precipitation (Boehmer-Christiansen and Skea 1991; Wettestad 1995; Alcamo, Shaw, and Hordijk 1990). A few teams of scholars have systematically compared a range of assessment experiences within a common analytic framework (Andresen et al. 2000; Social Learning Group 2001a, 2001b; Young 2002), including the two companion volumes emerging from our research program (Jasanoff and Martello 2004; Farrell and Jäger 2005).

Insights from this previous work provided the initial foundation for the research presented here. GEAs have varied considerably in their influence. They also vary considerably in their designs, in their processes, and in the circumstances under which they operate. Numerous propositions have been put forth regarding why science, and particularly GEAs, appear to contribute significantly to environmental progress in some areas but not others. Some have pointed to the importance of context, such as how much attention is paid to the issue, how politically contested it is, and how it is linked to other issues (e.g., Social Learning Group 2001a, 2001b). Others have seen cognitive factors as central, including the maturity of scientific understanding and the degree of consensus about the problem, its causes, and its solutions (e.g., Ravetz 1986; Haas 1990). Yet others have focused on design factors, such as how assessments structure the interactions among scientific and policy communities and how they incorporate information and knowledge from, and disseminate them to, stakeholders at the local, national, and international level (e.g., Farrell and Jäger 2005). One branch of this line of work asserts that polycentric systems that entail nodes of authority across levels and between science and decision making effectively integrate multiple ways of producing and utilizing knowledge (Ostrom 1998; McGinnis 1999). Still another perspective has focused on the construction and use of scientific information as involving social processes in which norms, methods, and agendas are dynamic, interactive, and negotiated elements of social, political, and cultural processes (Jasanoff 2004; Jasanoff and Wynne 1998).

When, why, and how GEAs wield influence constitute special cases of larger questions related to how information influences action at both the domestic and international level. Domestic theorists have posited two competing models of decision making and, hence, of informational influence. A standard, "rational actor," model sees policymakers as undertaking a careful analysis of the costs and benefits of available alternatives, choosing those that best further their objectives given their resource constraints. Policymakers are assumed to desire—and be consistently open to—new information since it helps them better achieve their objectives. Such a model assumes "the breadth and competence of analysis" (Lindblom 1977, 314), with an assumption that decision makers turn to scientists to provide disinterested analysis for use in identifying and evaluating alternative scenarios and options comprehensively in order to make the best possible decisions. Decision makers are assumed to understand the problems they face well enough to ask scientists questions that, once answered, will allow them to decide on the best course of action. In this view, assessments are reports that provide answers to clearly delineated questions from policymakers.

Alternative models view decision makers as facing significant constraints on their time, resources, knowledge, and cognitive abilities, particularly when faced with problems as complex as most global environmental problems. Rather than seeking out information to optimize their decisions across various alternatives, decision makers "satisfice" and make "good enough" decisions by using rules of thumb and other heuristics that reduce the need to collect and process information (Simon 1957, 1982; Kahneman et al. 1982). In such models, decision making entails "muddling through," with scientific information being only one element of "a broad, diffuse, open-ended, mistake-making social or interactive process, both cognitive and political" (Lindblom 1990, 7; also Lindblom 1959). Scientists and decision makers are involved in ongoing and iterative interactions. Rather than knowledge informing decision making, policy choices get made only in conducive contexts in which usually independent streams of problems and solutions come together (Cohen et al. 1972; Kingdon 1984). Policies develop out of ongoing interactions among groups of people and organizations concerned with a given policy issue (Jenkins-Smith and Sabatier 1999, 119, 135). Over time, these interactions can produce shared understandings that a problem exists, how the problem should be defined, that action should be taken, and what is the best choice from the range of possible solutions (Sabatier 1988). Scholars of science studies and constructivism have taken this logic further, arguing that the degree to which science is, and is seen as, separate from other forms of knowledge and from policymaking is "a contextually contingent and interests-driven pragmatic accomplishment drawing selectively on inconsistent and ambiguous attributes" (Gieryn 1995, 393; see also Beck 1992; Wynne 1995; Hajer 1995; Jasanoff 1990). In this view, assessments are iterative social processes in which what questions are being asked about what problem and what information is being collected and analyzed are identified not at the outset but through an ongoing and iterative process between policymakers, scientists, and stakeholders (Jäger, van Eijndhoven, and Clark 2001).

International relations scholars have been particularly skeptical of the influence of scientific information (Susskind 1994, 63; Funtowicz and Ravetz 2001; Haas 2002). National policymakers are unlikely to be swayed by scientific information generated by others because of a deep-seated belief that other governments generate and disseminate information in an effort to manipulate and gain advantage (Morgenthau 1993;

Waltz 1979; Morrow 1994). In an international realm in which competition and the pursuit of power are primary objectives, any information generated by GEAs can be assumed to be simply one more means by which powerful countries seek to manipulate weaker ones (Miles et al. 2002, 472–473). Especially when environmental problems have implications for higher-priority security and economic concerns, international scientific information and ideas are likely to have little independent impact on national behaviors (Goldstein and Keohane 1993). That said, states may be more receptive to new information in situations in which policymakers recognize that they must navigate in a complex and uncertain world in which their own country's welfare depends considerably on the actions of other governments (Keohane and Nye 1977/1989; Jervis 1997). Crises (e.g., oil spills) and scientific breakthroughs (e.g., discovery of the ozone hole) demonstrate that environmental issues are particularly complex and that scientific knowledge is particularly uncertain, limited, and evolving. In response, national policymakers often seek out scientific experts whose engagement with networks of other international scientists allows them to provide better insights into the seriousness and causes of the problem and alternative solutions (Haas 1990, 1992b). Science can prompt intergovernmental negotiations to resolve transnational environmental problems. And the discussions of relevant science such negotiations entail can promote shared understandings, trust, and political consensus that leads, relatively directly, to policy and behavior changes (Kay and Jacobson 1983; Jacobson and Brown Weiss 1998, 525; Risse 2000; Miles et al. 2002). States clarify their goals and the best means of achieving them only through interactions with other states (Ruggie 1998; Checkel 1998). Nominally scientific discussions engage implicit debates over what is "good" or "appropriate" behavior and what it takes to be considered a "green" state or environmental leader (Risse, Ropp, and Sikkink 1999; Checkel and Moravcsik 2001; March and Olsen 1998; Litfin 1994; Katzenstein 1996).

How Should We Evaluate the Influence of GEAs?

These views of the influence of science on policy, and policy on science, provided guidance for examining the influence of GEAs but did not provide specific hypotheses about when we might expect science to influence policy and economic decisions. Given this, we adopted an inductive research strategy in which authors evaluated a set of initial cases that used insights from the practitioner and scholarly literature cited above as investigative starting points. The initial goal was for authors to look at their cases to determine why some assessments appeared to wield considerable influence while others appeared to wield very little. This task required addressing questions about where to look for assessment influence and where to look for its causes.

We initially conceptualized influence as the ability of GEAs to lead governments and substate actors to adopt different policies and behaviors than they would have otherwise. Yet, earlier research on global environmental change (e.g., Social Learning Group 2001a, 2001b) had shown that focusing exclusively on changes in policies and state behaviors would miss much of "the action" in domains—such as global environmental change—characterized by a complex interplay among different actors, interests, ideas, and institutions and in which causal influences may be indirect and take considerable time to become evident. To address this, we broadened our definition of "influence" by looking for changes in what Sabatier and Jenkins-Smith (1999) call "issue domains," defined as arenas in which interested actors seek to address an issue of common concern about which they have different beliefs and policy preferences. To the extent that an assessment ultimately fosters improved environmental quality, such changes must occur through changes in the actors involved in the issue domain, including their relevant goals, interests, beliefs, strategies, and resources; the institutions that enable and constrain interactions among those actors; the framings, discourse, and agenda related to the issue; and the existing policies and behaviors of relevant actors. All these elements of an issue domain are changing over time in response to nonassessment factors such as changes in the attention and resources actors dedicate to the problem, the availability of social and technical solutions, and the norms and discourse regarding behaviors that harm the environment. Thus, authors sought to distinguish changes in issue domains caused by assessments from those caused by other factors. Figure 1.1 illustrates our conceptualization of what constitute issue domains and how assessments influence them.

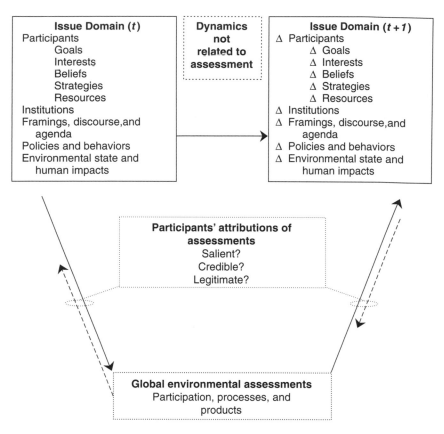

Figure 1.1
The role of scientific assessments in issue development: A conceptual framework

To understand assessment influence, we sought to explore the conditions under which assessments are influential, the design features that foster their influence, and the pathways by which they wield that influence. We sought to identify when GEAs matter—that is, the conditions and external factors that foster or inhibit assessment influence. We started with a strong sense that policymakers and other decision makers sometimes reevaluate their beliefs and alter their behaviors in response to assessments about global environmental problems. At times, cognitive or normative uncertainty seem to create "fluid moments in history" with "openings for rethinking" in which decision makers even seek out new information (Goldstein and Keohane 1993, 16, 26; Ikenberry 1993, 58–59; Kingdon 1984; Lee 1993; Haas 2001; Baumgartner and Jones 1993). But our optimism that assessments can have influence was tempered by knowing they sometimes do not. Decision makers, especially national policymakers addressing global environmental issues, often are unreceptive to new information. Actors ignore new information when they are firmly committed to previously defined goals, options for actions, and the causal connections among them; when the information relates to an issue they do not consider to merit their attention; or when they believe that others will not respond to rational argument but only to power (Hasenclever, Mayer, and Rittberger 1997, 184).

Besides such external conditions of influence, we wanted to know how design choices allow GEAs to take advantage of moments of receptivity. We wanted to know not merely "when" information matters but "what type" of information matters. We were motivated by the knowledge that some assessments released reports that had few apparent impacts on an issue domain, while others, changed the views, policies, and behaviors of far less receptive audiences. We first thought that most variation in GEA influence could be explained by the content of assessment reports and the links between those conducting the assessment and those using it. We were particularly interested in how institutions that produce assessments make those assessments credible. We wanted to know whether assessments were more influential when those producing the assessment had close ties to, or were more distant from, those negotiating and implementing policies. We expected credibility to be an important aspect of assessments but were open to differences in how credibility was achieved and to other facets of assessments that proved important.

Finally, we sought to understand the process that leads decision makers to adopt insights from some GEAs but not others—that is, we tried to understand the causal mechanisms or pathways of GEA influence. Since the influence of GEAs lies only in the information they contain, we recognized that their influence always involves changing actors' beliefs. Precisely because policymakers and decision makers cannot determine for themselves the accuracy of the scientific claims at issue, we sought to understand how assessments gain credibility. We were particularly interested in how assessments balance the desire to involve the "best" scientists in a politically impartial setting and the desire to involve those who may have less scientific expertise but whose views are trusted, and hence more likely to be accepted, by relevant political and economic actors.

After an initial round of research, we sought to make sense of what our team of scholars had discovered about the influence of GEAs and to adjust our research strategy appropriately. Two major insights jumped out of that midterm evaluation of our work. The first insight was that, in almost every case, assessment reports were not the right focus of attention. Thus, proposition 1 became: GEAs are better conceptualized as social processes rather than published products. The right questions were not ones about report content, framing, or components that could be answered by simply reading the report. Rather, the right questions seemed to revolve around the social process of assessment, as well as the products thereof. We came to see assessment as a social process in which scientists, policymakers, and other stakeholders are (or are not) gathering data, conducting analyses, explaining, debating, learning, and interacting with each other around the issue on which the assessment focuses. The process by which information is generated and delivered affects the potential of that information process to influence outcomes. From the time at which a few scientists, policymakers, and/or stakeholders initiate an assessment, it is this process of interactions by which knowledge is created and transmitted among actors that determines whether a GEA will be influential. GEA influence seemed to depend on the characteristics of the extended and extensive social process leading up to as well as coming after an assessment report. It is not merely that these interactions determine how various actors respond to the written products of an assessment, though they certainly do. But it is also that these interactions themselves are important mechanisms by which the assessment influences how and what actors think and, hence, how they behave in response to the information generated. We therefore shifted our focus from evaluating the influence of assessment reports to the influence of assessment processes. We began looking at assessment reports as simply one visible indicator of a larger social process that seemed to be the real source of any assessment's influence.

The second insight from our initial exploratory work was that GEA influence did not just depend on "getting the science right." Building on earlier work of Ravetz (1971), Clark and Majone (1985), and the Social Learning Group (2001a, 2001b), we determined that the credibility of the ideas, information, and knowledge produced and exchanged during an assessment process was only one of three major determinants of GEA influence. Thus, proposition 2 became: to be influential, potential users must view a GEA as salient and legitimate as well as credible. The information produced by an assessment process is salient when potential users believe that the information is relevant to their decision making and is legitimate when they believe that the information was produced by a process that took account of the concerns and insights of relevant stakeholders and was deemed procedurally fair. Not surprisingly, with hindsight, we found that these insights coincided with points raised in the extant literature but that had not been brought together in quite the same way as we were observing them in the global environmental assessment setting. Thus, on salience, analysts are frequently dissatisfied "because they are not listened to," while policymakers are dissatisfied "because they do not hear much they want to listen to" (Lindblom and Cohen 1979; ICSU, ISTS, and TWAS 2002). Decision makers often have little time and attention for any but the most pressing issues; scientists often have little interest in problems that have large policy, but little scientific, import. Equally important, both decision makers and scientists often misperceive the policy-relevant questions to which science can best contribute. On credibility, more has been said, particularly with respect to adapting standard procedures used to gain acceptance of scientific claims to the assessment context. Thus, scientific influence increases by careful attention to issues involving data reliability, methods used, the validity of inferential claims, identification of pitfalls and rival hypotheses, and independent peer review (Ravetz 1971; Underdal 2000, 182). And on legitimacy, scientific information must overcome distrust from those who suspect experts of using information to lead them to adopt behaviors that serve the self-interests of those experts or those to whom they answer. Thus, a tension exists between the desire for science to be simultaneously well informed and well analyzed and to also be democratic (Lindblom 1980, 12). Even those seeking out information are skeptical of claims and arguments made by others unless processes reassure them "that their legitimate interests will be respected" (Hasenclever, Mayer, and Rittberger 1997, 184). Science no longer holds the "numinous" legitimacy accorded to religion and royalty; instead it must gain "civil legitimacy" through freely negotiated agreement among affected parties as to what rules and procedures will govern its meaning and use (Clark and Majone 1985; Ezrahi 1990; Weber 1922/1957; Brickman, Jasanoff, and Ilgen 1985; Jasanoff 1990). We were particularly intrigued by a sense that—in a world of limited resources and time—these three attributions of salience, credibility, and legitimacy were interconnected both in the sense that procedures intended to foster one often undermined another and in the sense that satisfying critical thresholds of all three attributions appeared to be a necessary, but not sufficient, condition for assessment influence.

These insights from the first phase of our research informed the second round reported here in two important ways. The first involved the case-study authors going back to their cases to look more systematically at how assessment processes promote or inhibit an assessment's influence, paying particular attention to how those processes foster perceptions of salience, credibility, and legitimacy and how much those perceptions contribute to assessment influence. Our initial research had demonstrated that different actors perceive the salience, credibility, or legitimacy of any assessment differently. As we returned to our cases, we conceptualized these as attributions that different participants make of assessment processes and products rather than as properties of the assessment per se. This implies both that an assessment's influence on a given actor depends on characteristics of both the actor and the assessment and also that assessment influence varies across different actors. Because actors concerned with an issue differ in their goals, interests, beliefs, strategies, resources, and the local, national, or international scale at which they work, they also tend to differ with respect to what information they will be interested in; what scientific discussions they can actively participate in and understand; how they perceive salience, credibility and legitimacy; and how open they will be to new information and persuasion. We hoped to discover how global environmental assessments foster cooperative resolution of environmental problems by leading actors who come to such problems with different interests and initial policy preferences to share perceptions of an environmental problem and its best solutions. A second, and equally important, change to our research was to incorporate cases, as described below, that allowed us to gain insight into elements of assessment processes that were hinted at but could not be fully developed from our initial cases, most notably the ability of global and large scale assessments to influence local-level action.

Organization of the Book

Our intention for this book was to articulate and explore propositions—rather than test hypotheses—about the conditions under which and processes by which GEAs wield influence. Given the absence of much previous comparative analytic work on their influence, we selected cases that could broaden and deepen our knowledge about GEA influence and that seemed likely to provide a foundation for critical hypothesis testing by subsequent scholars. We sought to include assessments whose influence, if any, would be evident in direct and immediate changes in policies and behaviors at the international level as well as assessments whose influence was at levels below the international and was less direct, less proximate, and less visible. We also sought to capture some variation in the environmental problems being assessed and in the types of actors or potential users that might be influenced by the assessment.

The cases finally included in this volume reflect several perspectives on GEA influence. Some examine a particular global environmental assessment, looking for what influence, if any, that assessment had on particular issue domains. Others start at "the other end of the telescope" and examine particular actors within an issue domain to see what influence, if any, relevant GEAs and intervening institutional arrangements had on them. Yet others illuminate the particular challenges that our initial research showed exist in linking information and action across multiple levels. Most of the cases in this last group do not fit our definition of global environmental assessments, delineated above, but instead are included because they provide "high-resolution" studies at the regional scale that allow close comparisons of how different institutional arrangements affect the ability of assessments to promote cross-scale linkages and provide analogies for examining assessments in international settings.

We have divided the empirical studies into three sections, organized by the scale of the issue domain in which we look for evidence of assessment influence. The first two chapters look at the impact of global assessments on the international policy agenda. Wendy E. F. Torrance examines the sequence of climate change assessments from the 1970s through the 1990s, examining the roles of both political context and assessment content in explaining why a 1985 assessment (the Villach assessment) transformed the issue domain of climate change where previous assessments had failed to do so. Aarti Gupta examines the negotiations over information sharing in the 2000 Cartagena Protocol on Biosafety to the Convention on Biological Diversity. She explores how agreement on procedures for biosafety information production, exchange, and dissemination depends on prior resolution of conflicts over whether—and what type of—an environmental problem exists and, thus, how problem framing affects assessment influence.

The next four chapters look at the impact of global assessments at the national level. Frank Biermann explores why global assessments of climate change and biodiversity had so much less influence in India than in developed countries. Stacy D. VanDeveer, like Torrance, largely links the increasing influence of acid precipitation assessments among Central and Eastern European states to changes in the broader political context rather than changes in those assessments themselves. Liliana B. Andonova explains differences in the responses of Polish and Bulgarian actors to assessments commissioned by the European Union and World Bank as due to variation in assessment processes ranging from collecting data to producing final reports. Noelle Eckley Selin looks at why LRTAP assessments that were European and North American in focus had such significant influence on global negotiations of regulations of persistent organic pollutants.

The final three empirical chapters focus on the influence of assessments on local-level decision makers. GEAs cannot be influential if they only operate at the international level—their influence depends on connecting in meaningful ways to "local" decision makers. Since our initial research demonstrated that bridging barriers of "scale" was important to the influence of many assessments, we sought out cases that would shed light on how knowledge generated at higher levels in the local-national-international hierarchy influenced behavior at lower levels in that hierarchy. Susanne C. Moser explores the different degrees of influence of assessment information in two U.S. coastal states, examining why projections of climate change and sea-level rise had little direct effect on coastal policymaking and management in Maine and Hawai'i but contributed to varying degrees to long-term changes in both states' issue domains. Anthony G. Patt's chapter investigates why some farmers in Zimbabwe directly incorporated global assessments of El Niño/Southern Oscillation events and corresponding rainfall forecasts into their planting decisions while others did not. David W. Cash's investigation of the complex institutional landscape for managing the U.S. High Plains aquifer shows how the influence of aquifer-related information on farmers' water usage depended on the relationships and networks that spanned both the science-action divide and the several informational and regulatory scales involved. While this chapter does not focus on a global assessment, its analysis of cross-level interactions of science and policy examines an analogous case that complements the other chapters.

The final chapter draws two types of conclusions from across these chapters. The first type involve five propositions supported by evidence from most of these cases. First, assessments vary in the type of influence that they have, not just the amount of their influence. Second, assessment influence varies significantly across different audiences or potential user groups and the extent of influence depends significantly on the relationship of the audience to the assessment. Third, that relationship becomes evident in the variation in audiences' attributions of salience, credibility, and legitimacy to an assessment. Fourth, assessment influence is best understood by recognizing that assessments, to be influential, must foster a process of coproduction of knowledge that involves stakeholder participation in ways that build salience, credibility, and legitimacy with many potential users. Finally, achieving those goals depends on building the capacity of various actors to contribute to assessments and to understand the information they produce. These propositions seem to us to have become sufficiently clear from our work that they can be used as the basis for specific hypotheses deserving of rigorous scholarly testing and can also be used, perhaps more tentatively and cautiously, to guide the choices of practitioners trying to improve the influence of assessments.

The second type of conclusions are more speculative propositions for which one or two cases provide tantalizing but anecdotal evidence. These insights might well be artifacts of the constellation of factors and conditions of a particular case—but they may be examples of more generally applicable rules related to successful assessment design. First, we found that the characteristics of the institution responsible for an assessment affect that assessment's influence. Second, attributions of salience, credibility, and legitimacy have particular difficulty traversing from the global to the local scale. Third, an assessment's influence depends on the informational competition it faces. Finally, we found some evidence that assessors can learn to conduct assessments more effectively over time.

We conclude with lessons for practitioners. Our goal in writing this book was to analyze the factors and conditions that lead GEAs to influence policy and decision making but to do so in a way that provides more practical help to those producing global environmental assessments. Those lessons are fivefold:

• Focus on the process, not the report.
• Focus on salience and legitimacy as well as credibility.
• Assess with multiple audiences in mind.
• Involve stakeholders and connect with existing networks.
• Develop influence over time.

We hope this book contributes to a larger process in which both scholars and practitioners learn from the experience of global environmental assessment so that, in the future, individuals and nations around the world committed to learning more about the many global environmental problems we face and how to resolve them can do so more effectively than they have in the past.

Acknowledgments

This chapter reflects ideas developed over five years of collaborative research, working closely with numerous research fellows and with the faculty engaged in the project. We wish to thank all those involved in this project for their helpful insights throughout the project. The authors would like to thank Frank Alcock for his major contributions to the development of this chapter. The ideas in the chapter were influenced early on by work done with Robert O. Keohane and Barbara Connolly, to whom we are indebted. We also wish to thank Liliana Andonova, Frank Biermann, Robert O. Keohane, Susanne Moser, Edward Parson, and Noelle Eckley Selin for helpful comments on earlier drafts of this chapter.

Notes

1. The other two volumes are Jasanoff and Martello 2004 and Farrell and Jäger 2005. All three efforts drew from the Global Environmental Assessment Project.

2. We focus on public advice because earlier work reported by the Social Learning Group (2001a, 2001b) led us to suspect that very different factors may determine the influence of public and private advice.

References

Alcamo, Joseph, Roderick Shaw, and Leen Hordijk, eds. 1990. *The RAINS Model of Acidification: Science and Strategies in Europe.* Dordrecht: Kluwer Academic Publishers.

Andresen, Steinar. 1989, April. Science and politics in the international management of whales. *Marine Policy* 13(2): 99–117.

Andresen, Steinar, Tora Skodvin, Arild Underdal, and Jørgen Wettestad, eds. 2000. *Science and Politics in International Environmental Regimes: Between Integrity and Involvement.* New York: Manchester University Press.

Baumgartner, F. R., and B. D. Jones. 1993. *Agendas and Instability in American Politics.* Chicago: University of Chicago Press.

Benedick, Richard Elliot. 1998. *Ozone Diplomacy: New Directions in Safeguarding the Planet.* Cambridge, MA: Harvard University Press.

Betsill, Michele M., and Elisabeth Corell. 2001, November. NGO influence in international environmental negotiations: A framework for analysis. *Global Environmental Politics* 1(4): 65–85.

Boehmer-Christiansen, Sonja. 1997. Uncertainty in the service of science: Between science policy and the politics of power. In Gunnar Fermann, ed., *International Politics of Climate Change*, 110–152. Oslo: Scandinavian University Press.

Boehmer-Christiansen, Sonja A., and James Skea. 1991. *Acid Politics: Environmental and Energy Policies in Britain and Germany.* London: Belhaven Press.

Bolin, Bert. 1994. Science and policy making. *Ambio* 23(1): 25–29.

Bolin, Bert. 2002. Politics and the IPCC. *Science* 296: 1235.

Brickman, Ronald, Sheila Jasanoff, and Thomas Ilgen. 1985. *Controlling Chemicals: The Politics of Regulation in Europe and the United States.* Ithaca, NY: Cornell University Press.

Carnegie Commission on Science, Technology, and Government. 1992. *International Environmental Research and Assessment: Proposals for Better Organization and Decision Making.* New York: Carnegie Commission on Science, Technology, and Government.

Checkel, Jeffrey T. 1998, January. The constructivist turn in international relations theory. *World Politics* 50(2): 324–348.

Checkel, Jeffrey T., and Andrew Moravcsik. 2001, June. A constructivist research program in EU studies? *European Union Politics* 2(2): 219–249.

Clark, William C. 2000. Environmental globalization. In Joseph S. Nye and John D. Donahue, eds., *Governance in a Globalizing World*, 86–108. Washington, DC: Brookings Institution Press.

Clark, William C., and Jill Jäger. 1997. The science of climate change [Review of IPCC. 1996. "Climate Change 1995"]. *Environment* 39(9): 23–28.

Clark, William C., and Giandomenico Majone. 1985, summer. The critical appraisal of scientific inquiries with policy implications. *Science, Technology, and Human Values* 10(3): 6–19.

Cohen, Michael D., James G. March, and Johan P. Olsen. 1972. A garbage can model of organizational choice. *Administrative Science Quarterly* 17(1): 1–25.

Committee on Global Change Research and National Research Council. 1999. *Global Environmental Change: Research Pathways for the Next Decade.* Washington, DC: National Academy Press.

Convention on Biological Diversity, Subsidiary Body on Scientific, Technical and Technological Advice. 2003. *Dry and Sub-humid Lands Biodiversity: Matters Requested by the Conference of the Parties in Paragraphs 5 and 6 of Its Decision V/23 and Decision VI/4 (Eighth Meeting: Montreal, 10–14 March 2003).* UNEP/CBD/SBSTTA/8/INF/2: Convention on Biological Diversity.

Corell, Robert, and Bert Bolin. 1998. *The OECD Megascience Forum: Workshop on Global Scale Issues.* Saltsjöbaden, Sweden, March 4–6, 1998. Paris: OECD.

Dowlatabadi, Hadi, and Granger M. Morgan. 1993, March 26. Integrated assessment of climate change. *Science* 259(5103): 1813–1815.

Downing, Thomas E., and Robert W. Kates. 1982. The international response to the threat of chlorofluorocarbons to atmospheric ozone. *American Economic Review* 72(2): 267–272.

Ezrahi, Yaron. 1990. *The Descent of Icarus: Science and the Transformation of Contemporary Democracy.* Cambridge, MA: Harvard University Press.

Farrell, Alexander E., and Jill Jäger, eds. 2005. *Assessments of Regional and Global Environmental Risks: Designing Processes for the Effective Use of Science in Decisionmaking.* Washington, DC: Resources for the Future.

Funtowicz, Silvio O., and Jerome R. Ravetz. 2001. Global risk, uncertainty, and ignorance. In Jeanne X. Kasperson and Roger Kasperson, eds., *Global Environmental Risk.* London: Earthscan.

Gieryn, Thomas F. 1995. Boundaries of science. In Sheila Jasanoff, Trevor Pinch, James C. Petersen, and Gerald E. Markle, eds., *Handbook of Science and Technology Studies*, 393–443. Thousand Oaks, CA: Sage.

Goldstein, Judith, and Robert O. Keohane. 1993. Ideas and foreign policy: An analytic framework. In Judith Goldstein and Robert O. Keohane, eds., *Ideas and Foreign Policy: Beliefs, Institutions, and Political Change*, 3–30. Ithaca, NY: Cornell University Press.

Grundmann, Reiner. 2001. *Transnational Environmental Policy: The Ozone Layer.* New York: Routledge.

Haas, Peter M. 1990. *Saving the Mediterranean: The Politics of International Environmental Cooperation.* New York: Columbia University Press.

Haas, Peter M. 1992a, winter. Banning chlorofluorocarbons. *International Organization* 46(1): 187–224.

Haas, Peter M. 1992b, winter. Epistemic communities and international policy coordination. *International Organization* 46(1): 1–35.

Haas, Peter M. 2001. Policy knowledge and epistemic communities. In Neil J. Smelser and Paul B. Baltes, eds., *International Encyclopedia of the Social and Behavioral Sciences.* New York: Elsevier.

Haas, Peter M. 2002. Science policy for multilateral environmental governance. Paper presented at the International Workshop on "The Multilateral Environmental Governance Regime: Structural Integration and the Possibility of a World Environment Organization," United Nations Headquarters, New York, Mach 26–27, 2002.

Hajer, Maarten A. 1995. *The Politics of Environmental Discourse: Ecological Modernization and the Policy Process.* Oxford: Oxford University Press.

Hasenclever, Andreas, Peter Mayer, and Volker Rittberger. 1997. *Theories of International Regimes.* Cambridge: Cambridge University Press.

Hordijk, Leen, and C. Kroeze. 1997. Integrated assessment models for acid rain. *European Journal of Operational Research* 102(3): 405–417.

Houghton, John. 2004. *Global Warming: The Complete Briefing.* Cambridge: Cambridge University Press.

ICSU, ISTS, and TWAS. 2002. *Science and Technology for Sustainable Development: Consensus Report and Background Document for the Mexico*

City Synthesis Workshop on Science and Technology for Sustainable Development, 20–23 May 2002. ICSU Series on Science for Sustainable Development, No. 9. Paris: International Council for Science, Initiative on Science and Technology for Sustainability, and Third World Academy of Sciences.

Ikenberry, G. John. 1993. Creating yesterday's New World Order: Keynesian "New Thinking" and the Anglo-American Postwar Settlement. In Judith Goldstein and Robert O. Keohane, eds., *Ideas and Foreign Policy: Beliefs, Institutions, and Political Change,* 57–86. Ithaca, NY: Cornell University Press.

Jacobson, Harold K., and Edith Brown Weiss. 1998. Assessing the record and designing strategies to engage countries. In Edith Brown Weiss and Harold K. Jacobson, eds., *Engaging Countries: Strengthening Compliance with International Environmental Accords,* 511–554. Cambridge, MA: MIT Press.

Jäger, Jill, Josee van Eijndhoven, and Clark William C. 2001. Knowledge and action: An analysis of linkages among management functions for global environmental risks. In Social Learning Group, ed., *Learning to Manage Global Environmental Risks, Volume 2: A Functional Analysis of Social Responses to Climate Change, Ozone Depletion, and Acid Rain.* Cambridge, MA: MIT Press.

Jasanoff, Sheila. 1990. *The Fifth Branch: Science Advisers as Policy-Makers.* Cambridge, MA: Harvard University Press.

Jasanoff, Sheila. 2004. *States of Knowledge: The Co-production of Science and Social Order.* New York: Routledge.

Jasanoff, Sheila, and Marybeth Long Martello, eds. 2004. *Earthly Politics: Local and Global in Environmental Governance.* Cambridge, MA: MIT Press.

Jenkins-Smith, Hank C., and Paul A. Sabatier. 1999. The advocacy coalition framework: An assessment. In Paul A. Sabatier, ed., *Theories of the Policy Process,* 117–166. Boulder, CO: Westview Press.

Jervis, Robert. 1997. *System Effects: Complexity in Political and Social Life.* Princeton, NJ: Princeton University Press.

Kahneman, Daniel, Paul Slovic, and Amos Tversky. 1982. *Judgment under Uncertainty: Heuristics and Biases.* New York: Cambridge University Press.

Kates, Robert W. 1997. Impacts, adaptations, and mitigation. [Review of IPCC. 1996. "Climate Change 1995"]. *Environment* 39(9): 29–34.

Katzenstein, Peter, ed. 1996. *The Culture of National Security: Norms and Identity in World Politics.* New York: Columbia University Press.

Kay, David A., and Harold K. Jacobson, eds. 1983. *Environmental Protection: The International Dimension.* Totowa, NJ: Allanheld, Osmun & Co.

Keck, Margaret E., and Kathryn Sikkink. 1998. *Activists beyond Borders: Advocacy Networks in International Politics.* Ithaca, NY: Cornell University Press.

Keohane, Robert O., and Joseph S. Nye. 1977/1989. *Power and Interdependence: World Politics in Transition.* Boston: Little, Brown.

Kingdon, John W. 1984. *Agendas, Alternatives, and Public Policies*. Boston: Little, Brown.

Lee, Kai N. 1993. *Compass and Gyroscope: Integrating Science and Politics for the Environment*. Washington, DC: Island Press.

Lindblom, Charles E. 1959. The science of "muddling through." *Public Administration Review* 19: 79–88.

Lindblom, Charles E. 1977. *Politics and Markets: The World's Political Economic Systems*. New York: Basic Books.

Lindblom, Charles E. 1980. *The Policy-Making Process*. Englewood Cliffs, NJ: Prentice-Hall.

Lindblom, Charles E. 1990. *Inquiry and Change: The Troubled Attempt to Understand and Shape Society*. New Haven, CT: Yale University Press.

Lindblom, Charles E., and David K. Cohen. 1979. *Usable Knowledge: Social Science and Social Problem Solving*. New Haven, CT: Yale University Press.

Litfin, Karen T. 1994. *Ozone Discourses: Science and Politics in Global Environmental Cooperation*. New York: Columbia University Press.

Mahoney, James (Assistant Secretary of Commerce for Oceans and Atmosphere and Director, U.S. Climate Change Science Program). 2002, December 3. Purpose and structure of the U.S. Climate Change Science Program. Paper presented at the U.S. Climate Change Science Workshop. Available at http://www.climatescience. gov/Library/workshop2002/openingsessions/mahoney-3dec2002.htm.

March, James, and Johan Olsen. 1998, autumn. The institutional dynamics of international political orders. *International Organization* 52(4): 943–970.

McGinnis, Michael D. 1999. *Polycentric Governance and Development: Readings from the Workshop in Political Theory and Policy Analysis*. Ann Arbor: University of Michigan Press.

Miles, Edward L., Arild Underdal, Steinar Andresen, Elaine M. Carlin, Jon Birger Skjærseth, and Jørgen Wettestad. 2002. Epilogue. In Edward L. Miles, Arild Underdal, Steinar Andresen, Jørgen Wettestad, Jon Birger Skjærseth, and Elaine M. Carlin, eds., *Environmental Regime Effectiveness: Confronting Theory with Evidence*, 467–474. Cambridge, MA: MIT Press.

Miller, Clark. 2001. Hybrid management: Boundary organizations, science policy, and environmental governance in the climate regime. *Science, Technology and Human Values* 26(4): 478–500.

Mitchell, Ronald B. 2003, November. International environmental agreements: A survey of their features, formation, and effects. *Annual Review of Environment and Resources* 28: 429–461.

Morgan, Granger M., and Hadi Dowlatabadi. 1996. Learning from integrated assessment of climate change. *Climatic Change* 34: 337–368.

Morgan, Granger M., Samuel C. Morris, Max Henrion, Deborah A. L. Amaral, and William R. Rish. 1984. Technical uncertainty in quantitative policy analysis: A sulfur air pollution example. *Risk Analysis* 4: 201–216.

Morgenthau, Hans Joachim. 1993. *Politics among Nations: The Struggle for Power and Peace.* New York: McGraw-Hill.

Morrow, James D. 1994, summer. Modeling the forms of international cooperation: Distribution versus information. *International Organization* 48(3): 387–423.

O'Riordan, Timothy. 1997. Economics and social dimensions. [Review of IPCC. 1996. "Climate Change 1995"]. *Environment* 39(9): 34–37.

Ostrom, Elinor. 1990. *Governing the Commons: The Evolution of Institutions for Collective Action.* Cambridge: Cambridge University Press.

Ostrom, Elinor. 1998. Scales, polycentricity, and incentives: Designing complexity to govern complexity. In L. D. Guruswamy and J. A. McNeely, eds., *Protection of Biodiversity: Converging Strategies.* Durham, NC: Duke University Press.

Parris, Thomas. 2003. Global forest assessments. *Environment* 45(10): 3.

Parson, Edward A. 2003. *Protecting the Ozone Layer: Science and Strategy.* Oxford: Oxford University Press.

Ravetz, Jerome R. 1971. *Scientific Knowledge and Its Social Problems.* Oxford: Clarendon Press.

Risse, Thomas. 2000, winter. "Let's argue": Communicative action in world politics. *International Organization* 54(1): 1–39.

Risse, Thomas, Stephen C. Ropp, and Kathryn Sikkink, eds. 1999. *The Power of Human Rights: International Norms and Domestic Change.* Cambridge: Cambridge University Press.

Rotmans, Jan. 1998. Methods for IA: The challenges and opportunities ahead. *Environmental Modelling and Assessment* 3(3): 155–179.

Rotmans, Jan, and Hadi Dowlatabadi. 1998. Integrated assessment of climate change: Evaluation of methods and strategies. In S. Rayner and E. Malone, eds., *Human Choice and Climate Change: An International Social Science Assessment.* Columbus, OH: Battelle Press.

Rotmans, Jan, and Pier Vellinga, eds. 1998. Challenges and opportunities for integrated environmental assessment. *Environmental Modelling and Assessment* 3(3), special issue.

Rubin, Edward S., Lester B. Lave, and M. Granger Morgan. 1991–1992, winter. Keeping climate research relevant. *Issues in Science and Technology* 8(2): 47–55.

Ruggie, John Gerard. 1998, autumn. What makes the world hang together? Neo-utilitarianism and the social constructivist challenge. *International Organization* 52(4): 855–885.

Sabatier, Paul A. 1988. An advocacy coalition framework of policy change and the role of policy-oriented learning therein. *Policy Sciences* 21(1): 123–127.

Schellnhuber, Hans Joachim. 1999, December 2. "Earth system" analysis and the second Copernican revolution. *Nature* 402: C19–C23.

Schoenmaeckers, Baud. 2000. Interview with Bert Bolin. *Change* 50: 5–8.

Simon, Herbert A. 1957. *Models of Man, Social and Rational: Mathematical Essays on Rational Human Behavior in a Social Setting.* New York: Wiley.

Simon, Herbert Alexander. 1982. *Models of Bounded Rationality.* Cambridge, MA: MIT Press.

Social Learning Group, ed. 2001a. *Learning to Manage Global Environmental Risks, Volume 1: A Comparative History of Social Responses to Climate Change, Ozone Depletion, and Acid Rain.* Cambridge, MA: MIT Press.

Social Learning Group, ed. 2001b. *Learning to Manage Global Environmental Risks, Volume 2: A Functional Analysis of Social Responses to Climate Change, Ozone Depletion, and Acid Rain.* Cambridge, MA: MIT Press.

Somerville, Richard. 1996. *The Forgiving Air: Understanding Environmental Change.* Berkeley: University of California Press.

Steffen, Will, Peter Tyson, Jill Jäger, Pamela Matson, Berrien Moore III, Frank Oldfield, Katherine Richardson, Hans Joachim Schellnhuber, Bill Turner II, and Robert Wasson. 2001. Global change and the earth system: A planet under pressure. IGBP Science 4. Stockholm: International Geosphere-Biosphere Programme.

Susskind, Lawrence. 1994. *Environmental Diplomacy: Negotiating More Effective Global Agreements.* New York: Oxford University Press.

Tolba, Mostafa Kamal, and Iwona Rummel-Bulska. 1998. *Global Environmental Diplomacy: Negotiating Environment Agreements for the World, 1973–1992.* Cambridge, MA: MIT Press.

Tuinstra, Willemijn, Leen Hordijk, and Markus Amann. 1999. Using computer models in international negotiations. *Environment* 41(9): 33–42.

Turner, B. L., II, William C. Clark, Robert W. Kates, John F. Richards, Jessica T. Mathews, and William B. Meyer. 1990. *The Earth as Transformed by Human Action: Global and Regional Changes in the Biosphere over the Past 300 Years.* Cambridge: Cambridge University Press with Clark University.

Underdal, Arild. 2000. Comparative conclusions. In Steinar Andresen, Tora Skodvin, Arild Underdal, and Jørgen Wettestad, eds., *Science and Politics in International Environmental Regimes: Between Integrity and Involvement,* 181–201. Manchester: Manchester University Press.

Waltz, Kenneth. 1979. *Theory of International Politics.* Reading, MA: Addison-Wesley.

Watson, Robert T. 1994. The stratospheric ozone debate: Global research that led to achieving scientific consensus. *Abstracts of Papers of the American Chemical Society* 208, part 1, 172.

Watson, Robert T. 2002. The future of the Intergovernmental Panel on Climate Change. *Climate Policy* 2(4): 269–271.

Weber, Max. 1922/1957. *The Theory of Social and Economic Organization.* Glencoe: Free Press.

Wettestad, Jørgen. 1995, summer. Science, politics and institutional design: Some initial notes on the Long-Range Transboundary Air Pollution Regime. *Journal of Environment and Development* 4(2): 165–183.

Wynne, Brian. 1995. Public understanding of science. In Sheila Jasanoff, Trevor Pinch, James C. Petersen, and Gerald E. Markle, eds., *Handbook of Science and Technology Studies*, 361–388. Thousand Oaks, CA: Sage.

Young, Oran R. 2002. *The Institutional Dimensions of Environmental Change: Fit, Interplay, and Scale.* Cambridge, MA: MIT Press.

Young, Oran R., Arun Agrawal, Leslie A. King, Peter H. Sand, Arild Underdal, and Merrilyn Wasson. 1999. *Institutional Dimensions of Global Environmental Change (IDGEC) Science Plan.* IHDP Report No. 9. Bonn: IHDP.

2

Science or Salience: Building an Agenda for Climate Change

Wendy E. F. Torrance

Introduction

Between 1985 and 1990 the climate change issue domain changed significantly. An issue that had been the domain of climatologists, oceanographers, and scientific bureaucracies moved rapidly into the world of international policy analysts, the public, environment ministers, presidents, and prime ministers. By 1988, the issue had reached the international agenda (Jäger and O'Riordan 1996, Mintzer and Leonard 1994; Social Learning Group 2001). Most accounts of the transition of the climate-change issue from the international science agenda to the international policy agenda note the importance of a series of international assessments organized and carried out by the International Council of Scientific Unions (ICSU), the World Meteorological Organization (WMO), and the United Nations Environment Programme (UNEP) between 1985 and 1987. In particular, the work of scientists and policymakers at meetings in Villach, Austria, is often singled out for attention.

A group meeting in 1985, relying on an assessment of the SCOPE committee of ICSU, determined that "substantial warming" would occur as a result of a doubling of CO_2, and noted that increases in CO_2 "were attributable to human activities." They urged governments to "consider future predictions about climatic change in decision-making about water resource management, agriculture, coastal engineering and energy planning." They called for governments to pay attention to the scientific conclusions presented by the group, urged dissemination of public information on greenhouse gases, and urged further research. They argued that policies on energy, the use of fossil fuels, and greenhouse gas emissions could vastly affect the rate and degree of future warming. Finally, international agencies such as UNEP, WMO, and ICSU were encouraged to initiate consideration of a global convention (WMO 1986, 7).

The conclusions of the Villach meetings have been referred to as the consensus that set the climate issue on the road to the international agenda (Paterson 1996, 13). Indeed, within three years, the international community was paying significant attention to the issue. The climate case is often used as an example of scientific consensus creating the persuasive power necessary to achieve success in bringing about policy change (see Chapter 1, this volume). Most accounts of the development of the international policy agenda emphasize that Villach coincides with the burst of international interest in climate change but offer few reasons for attributing importance to these assessments. Such accounts, while providing excellent histories, rarely identify how, if at all, these assessments influenced the policymaking process (see, for example, Bodansky 1993; Social Learning Group 2001; Hecht and Tirpak 1995; Pomerance 1989; Boehmer-Christiansen 1994a, 1994b).

Conventional wisdom about the importance of the assessments of the mid-1980s is captured by Jill Jäger and Tim O'Riordan (1996, 14), who wrote about the Villach 1985 meeting: "Scenarios for future emissions of all of the significant greenhouse gases, not just CO_2, were considered and an international scientific consensus about the potential seriousness of the problem was achieved. The problem of anthropogenic climate change was moved at this point onto the political agenda." Such observations suggest several explanations for linking Villach to the development of an international agenda for climate change. First, these observations suggest that the consensus at Villach presented credible causal arguments and agreement about the relationship between human activities and changes to the earth's climate that drove the decision to take action. Second, the addition of greenhouse gases heightened the salience of these scientific problems for other actors in the international arena. Third, the international composition of this group allowed it to portray itself as a legitimate advocate for international policy change.

This chapter evaluates claims about credibility, salience, and legitimacy, with a view to understanding the extent to which these attributions of the Villach process contributed to its influence on the international arena. The chapter argues that the scientific conclusions reached at Villach were not significantly more credible than those of previous assessments, although years of consistent evidence contributed to the confidence of scientists and analysts in the information. The increased emphasis on greenhouse gases in addition to CO_2 was important, though the centrality of this finding was driven by perceptions on the part of assessors that the time might be ripe to emphasize the need for policy action on climate change. Events in the international arena, including the increased salience of environmental issues in general, and ozone depletion in particular, served to magnify the potential for climatic change for the scientists gathered at Villach, and led to particular efforts to identify climate change as the next salient issue for the international arena. At this task Villach largely succeeded. Villach became the voice for action as climate change entered an international arena that was receptive to statements on the subject. How important was the fact that the information came from an international group? Was Villach a legitimate source of scientific information? The answer to this question is largely yes, though this changes over time. As the climate issue became more salient (a process to which Villach contributed), the new actors in the issue domain began to make specific choices about the legitimacy of various assessment processes. While a process institutionally similar to Villach continued to provide information into the 1990s, new participants in the international arena, primarily states and their negotiators, turned to the Intergovernmental Panel on Climate Change, a new scientific assessment institution, for their scientific information.

This chapter contributes, along with chapters 5 and 7 to an understanding of how changes in the salience of an assessment propels information previously disregarded by policymakers (or groups of policymakers) into a position of persuasion and influence. The chapter also highlights, along with chapter 3, the key role of salience as an issue develops and the subsequent shift to concerns about legitimacy as an issue becomes established on the international agenda.

Change in the Issue Domain

As noted above, an issue that was largely in the domain of scientists doing primary research or working on national scientific panels moved rapidly (in three years) to the agenda of national governments and the United Nations. Starting in 1985, the participants interested in the climate issue dramatically changed, policy statements called for international cooperation to reduce CO_2 and greenhouse gas emissions, and the institutional organization of scientific information was transformed. Although it is difficult to track precisely the new additions to the climate discussion, the path of Villach's conclusions can be traced through several initiatives undertaken by the United Nations during this time period.

What evidence demonstrates that the issue domain had been transformed by 1988? In 1987, the United Nations General Assembly adopted several resolutions, including one that stipulated that

international cooperation for the monitoring of the accumulation of carbon dioxide and other greenhouse gases and of their impacts on climate and sea levels must be strengthened to encompass both the conclusion of international agreements and the formulation of industrial strategies to mitigate the environmental, economic, and social impacts of potential changes. (A/RES/42/186, 96th plenary meeting, December 11, 1987)

Events in 1988 mark particularly significant changes in the issue domain. A conference held in Toronto in June brought together over 300 delegates, including politicians, senior government officials, scientists, industry representatives, and environmental activists representing over 40 countries and 24 international organizations. Although not officially governmental, the conference brought many new actors into the issue domain. The Toronto Conference concluded by urging "immediate action . . . to counter the ongoing degradation of the atmosphere. . . . An Action Plan for the Protection of the Atmosphere needs to be developed, which includes an international framework convention, [and] encourages other standard-setting agreements and national legislation to provide for the protection of the global atmosphere" (WMO, 1989, 296). The mostly widely cited conclusion of the conference was the need to "reduce CO_2 emissions by approximately 20% of 1988 levels by the year 2005 as an initial global goal" (WMO 1989, 296).

The Toronto Conference has been widely cited as a watershed that met a growing public demand for information. In 1988, the United Nations General Assembly (UNGA) resolved to establish the Intergovernmental Panel on Climate Change (IPCC) and urged initiation of climate negotiations, specifying elements to be considered in a possible convention. In 1989, both the Group of Seven industrialized nations and the Group of Seventy-Seven developing states issued communiqués calling for action to "limit emissions of carbon dioxide and other greenhouse gases" (Markham 1989, 1). By the end of 1989, a Declaration adopted at Noordwijk, the Netherlands, by a Ministerial Conference attended by representatives of over fifty countries, noted that there was a "growing awareness among the world population and their political leaders that action is needed" (Noordwijk Conference Report 1989, 19). In December 1989, the UNGA authorized "the Executive Director of the United Nations Environment Programme, in cooperation with the Secretary-General of the World Meteorological Organization, to begin preparations for negotiations on a framework convention on climate" (UNGA 44/207, December 22, 1989).

Other indicators also suggested that international attention to the issue had increased. International media attention to the problem of climate change began a steep rise in 1987–1988, peaking in 1990 (Social Learning Group 2001). In December 1990, the UNGA established the Intergovernmental Negotiating Committee for a Framework Convention on Climate Change (INC/FCCC) to prepare an effective framework convention on climate change. The INC held five sessions between February 1991 and May 1992. "During these meetings," according to an online summary, "participants from over 150 states discussed the issues of binding commitments, targets and timetables for the reduction of carbon dioxide emissions, financial mechanisms, technology transfer, and 'common but differentiated' responsibilities of developed and developing countries" (http://www.iisd.ca/linkages/climate/fcccintro.html, 3/19/99). The Framework Convention on Climate Change was delivered to the United Nations Conference on Environment and Development in the summer of 1992. By that year, a variety of participants in addition to states—including nongovernmental organizations and industry lobbyists—had vastly increased their participation on the issue, mounting publicity campaigns, lobbying national governments, and participating in the international negotiations.

Scientific Credibility

The development of scientific consensus often receives considerable attention in accounts of the development of international polices on environmental issues, as chapter 1 of this volume notes. Richard Cooper's (1989, 180–181) account of the development of international public health guidelines from the nineteenth century illustrate his claim that "so long as costs are positive and benefits are uncertain, countries are not likely to cooperate systematically with one another; and so long as sharply differing views are held on the relationship between actions and outcomes, at least some parties will question the benefits alleged to flow from any particular proposed course of action." Haas (1990) and Benedick (1991) also emphasize this in the cases of the Mediterranean Plan and Montreal Protocol, respectively.

Observers of the development of the climate-change issue also suggest that it received serious attention in the 1980s because of the "maturity" of science. Although the evidence presented at the first World Climate Conference in 1979 "was scary," it took several years for scientists to come up with more evidence. But by the mid-1980s, according to conference participants, "the science was solid" and "the pot was boiling." These claims suggest that the conclusions reached at Villach represented greater agreement than had hitherto been present in the international scientific community.

For more than three decades prior to 1985, international initiatives to evaluate the science of climate change had been underway. The history of climate science has been well documented (Ausubel 1983; Clark and Dickson 2001; Jäger and O'Riordan 1996; Kellogg 1987; Moomaw 1990; Paterson 1996). Beginning in the nineteenth century, several scientists presented theories about the effects of carbon dioxide on the atmosphere. In the mid- to late 1950s, more scientists began to address the possible effects of carbon dioxide on the atmosphere. By the late 1970s, a considerable body of scientific evidence concerning climate change and the effects of carbon dioxide had developed. During the

International Geophysical Year (July 1957–December 1958), Charles Keeling had begun regular measurements of CO_2 at Mauna Loa and by the 1970s they clearly demonstrated steadily increasing concentrations of CO_2 in the atmosphere (Paterson 1996, 22). Atmospheric scientists were beginning to generate general-circulation models of the atmosphere that could estimate the response to a doubling of CO_2 concentrations from its preindustrial values (Jäger and O'Riordan 1996). Scientists and scientific reports were increasingly reaching scientific conclusions about the climate change problem, including

Projected temperature warming due to a doubling of CO_2

Date by which this warming is expected to occur

Relative contribution of CO_2 and other gases

Comparisons of predictions over time suggest that the conclusions reached in 1985 were not significantly different from those that came before them. First, the predicted range of temperature change in response to a doubling of CO_2 had remained very steady at 1.5°C to 4.5°C from a 1979 United States National Academy of Sciences report "up to and including the 1994 IPCC assessment" (Jäger and O'Riordan 1996, 14). Indeed, the SCOPE report and Villach's presentation of it *widened* the range of uncertainty and projected a slower pace than the earlier Villach conclusions (World Climate Programme 1981). Table 2.1 summarizes both international and national (U.S.) assessment conclusions, showing that scientific information related to CO_2, warming rates, and time frames remained quite stable over time.

However, other greenhouse gases are reported to have been significant during the deliberations that took place at Villach in 1985. Some analyses have argued that Villach was a "catalytic event" in reshaping the debate over climate change, particularly in the United States; "Villach's reframing of the climate issue allowed it to be amplified through independently increasing concerns over stratospheric ozone depletion" (Clark and Dickson 2001, 269). Did Villach represent a significant change, presenting policy recommendations that emphasized greenhouse gases, or did international opportunity present an incentive to emphasize the role of greenhouse gases in a way that they had not been before? Was this the triumph of new information that reshaped views of the need

Table 2.1
Comparing scientific conclusions

Organization	Range[1]	Year	CO_2 vs. other
National Research Council, 1979	3 ± 1.5	By 2050[2]	
Department of Energy, 1979	2–3	By 2050[3]	
National Research Council, 1983	1.5–4.5	By 2050[4]	Will contribute[5]
Environmental Protection Agency, 1983	3 ± 1.5	By 2050[6]	May contribute[7]
Department of Energy, 1985 "State of the Art" Reports	1.5–4.5	By 2075[8]	May contribute[9]
SCOPE/Villach, 1985	1.5–5.5	2050–2100[10] 2030[11]	Can contribute
Environmental Protection Agency, 1989	1.5–4.5	By 2030[12]	Can contribute
Intergovernmental Panel on Climate Change	1.5–4.5		

1. Warming range based on a doubling of CO_2 or CO_2 equivalent.
2. "Have assumed a rate of CO_2 increase that would lead to a doubling of airborne concentrations by some time in the first half of the twenty-first century" (National Research Council 1979, 1).
3. "Reach double the present value some time around the middle of the next century" (Department of Energy 1979, 143).
4. Estimate that it will pass 660 ppm (nominal doubling) in the 3rd quarter of the next century (National Research Council 1983, 2).
5. "Several other gases besides CO_2 that can affect the climate appear to be increasing as a result of human activities; if we project increases in all these gases, climate changes can be expected significantly earlier than if we consider CO_2 alone" (National Research Council 1983, 2).
6. Doubling of preindustrial levels (EPA 1983).
7. "Several gases in the atmosphere exhibit the properties of a greenhouse gas. Carbon dioxide is the most abundant and best known. Other potential significant greenhouse gases include methane, nitrous oxide, and chlorofluorocarbons" (EPA 1983, 2–2).
8. Doubling of current levels (Department of Energy, 1985 "State of the Art" Reports).
9. "If increases in their concentrations continue, these trace gases could have significant effects on climate" (Department of Energy, 1985 "State of the Art" Reports, 193).
10. Low- to middle-range scenarios (SCOPE/Villach 1985).
11. When contributions of other greenhouse gases are considered, "equivalent of CO_2 doubling" (SCOPE 1986, xxvii and WMO 1986).
12. "Several other gases besides CO_2 that can affect the climate appear to be increasing as a result of human activities; if we project increases in all these gases, climate changes can be expected significantly earlier than if we consider CO_2 alone" (EPA 1989).

for action or was information simply being viewed through a new lens, one that increased its salience?

More Salience Than Science

Several scientists have noted that evidence regarding the role of other gases in climate change led them to realize that significant global warming could occur within their lifetime (or at least in the lifetimes of their children). Including non-CO_2 greenhouse gases in climate models led to projections of major climate change within thirty to fifty years, rather than late in the next century. For them, this meant that climate change was not a problem that could wait to be addressed. Bert Bolin highlighted this new perspective in recounting the process of preparing the SCOPE report:

An important paper by Ramanathan et al. became available towards the end of the assessment, in which the role of other greenhouse gases in enhancing the greenhouse effect was pointed out. These other gases proved to be as important as CO_2. Suddenly, the climate change issue became much more urgent. The radiative forcing of the atmosphere, corresponding to a doubling of the CO_2 concentration, was anticipated by about 2030 rather than during the latter part of next century. (WMO, 1986, 26)

As Jim Bruce, chair of the Villach conference, observed, the finding that other greenhouse gases had the radiative equivalence of CO_2 made greenhouse gases "the biggest buzz of the conference." The written record suggests that the addition of other greenhouse gases to the climate change calculus was an essential consideration for the participants of this conference. Mostafa Tolba of UNEP and Donald Smith of WMO mention the contribution of greenhouse gases as a factor that tipped the balance in favor of action to stem global climate change. Noted Tolba, "It is now estimated that by adding in the warming effect of other trace gases the equivalent of such a [CO_2] doubling may occur as early as 2030. Trace gases seem to be playing a much larger role in bringing about a greenhouse effect than was earlier expected" (WMO 1986, 11).

Although great attention is often paid to the publication of these findings by Ramanathan et al. in 1985, the Villach conference was not the first time this finding had been presented. The claim had been made in the scientific and assessment literature for years. Others noted the potential contribution of other greenhouse gases. National scientists reported on it via the National Research Council in 1983, as well as through the U.S. government over the years (Department of Energy in 1979 and 1985; Environmental Protection Agency 1983).

In fact, the NRC report made a very compelling argument for the idea that CO_2 should not remain the sole focus of research efforts, or, more importantly, the sole focus of the formulation of solutions. However, the NRC noted that its primary focus was on CO_2, with a bit of attention paid to other greenhouse gases, for reasons having explicitly to do with the mandate and sponsor of the assessment: the U.S. government. As Tom Schelling put it,

The protagonist of this study has been carbon dioxide. The research has been motivated by concern that atmospheric carbon dioxide is increasing and may increase faster as the use of fossil fuels continues to grow and by the known potential for a "greenhouse effect" that could generate worldwide changes in climate. The group responsible for the report is the Carbon Dioxide Assessment Committee; the study was authorized by an act of Congress concerned with carbon-intensive fuels; and the agency principally charged with managing the research is the Department of Energy. The topic is usually referred to as "the carbon dioxide problem," a global challenge to the management of energy resources. (National Research Council, 1983, 450)

The NRC report concluded that scientific uncertainties surrounding projection of future CO_2 emissions were sufficiently great that no statements of the certainty of future climatic changes, or the consequences thereof, could or should be made. As such, they suggested further research, rather than quick policy action to address fossil-fuel use.

The U.S. Department of Energy cautioned that further research was needed, and that the time was not right for extensive action on climate change. The 1983 conclusions of the Environmental Protection Agency wistfully hoped for international cooperation, but deemed it a "distant prospect," concluding that the development of national adaptive strategies was probably the only tenable approach. These observations suggest that salience levels were not sufficient for these assessment groups; the likelihood of getting policy action on climate change on the international agenda was very low. Thomas Malone, the chair of the 1983 NRC report, testified before Congress in 1984 about the need for "caution not panic," elaborating the uncertainties in climate science.[1] In concluding remarks to the Villach conference, Malone noted that "as a reversal of a position I held a year or so ago, I believe it is timely to start on the long, tedious and sensitive task of framing a CONVENTION on greenhouse gases, climate change, and energy" (WMO 1986, 33). Malone (who had also participated in a 1975 WMO Panel on Climate) noted as well that the most important development of the last decade was "the finding that increases in the 'other' greenhouse gases ... have contributed about one half of any equilibrium temperature change that might be ascribed to the increase in CO_2," and these findings moved the date of potentially serious environmental consequences forward by several decades (WMO 1986, 33).

However, careful readers will recall that Malone's report did include other greenhouse gases in its analysis, yet it advocated caution. For Malone, and perhaps for others, there is more to the story of the decision for action. Malone cited several other developments of the latest decade, including improvements in climate models and attention to the impact of climate change on ecosystems.

However, he ultimately concluded that a decision to initiate contact between scientists and policymakers was timely. He noted that there had been a growing perception that there was a wide range of human activities that could "produce changes on a global scale." The ozone agreement, he suggested, was indicative of this change in perception. This stands in stark contrast to the conclusion that the NRC report reached about the likelihood of achieving international agreement on climate change. In 1983, the NRC report concluded that

given the need for widespread, long-term commitment, a CO_2 control strategy could only work if major nations successfully negotiated a global policy. While such an outcome is possible, there are few examples where a multinational environmental pact has succeeded, the nuclear test ban treaty being the most prominent. Other clearly recognized problems—whale fisheries, acid rain, undersea mining, the ozone layer—emphasize how time on the order of decades is required to achieve even modest progress on international management strategies. (National Research Council 1983, 70)

By March 1985 the Vienna Convention for the Protection of the Ozone Layer had been adopted. UNEP, and Tolba in particular, were encouraged by their success in negotiating the ozone agreement, and had determined that a convention on climate change could be their next endeavor. Peter Usher, a major representative of UNEP in the ozone negotiations, notes that as a result of the success of negotiating the Vienna Convention, UNEP had found a niche as a broker of conventions, and it was a role that UNEP wanted to continue. Tolba and the scientists involved in the Villach meetings saw a window of opportunity through which they could push climate change. Like Malone, they viewed the ozone agreement as a breakthrough in the treatment of global environmental issues.

Most, if not all, of those who made formal statements to the Villach gathering mentioned the connections that needed to be drawn between climate change and other environmental issues, particularly ozone depletion. James Bruce's remarks emphasized the connections between acid rain, ozone depletion, and climate change. William Clark's account of the practical implications of increasing greenhouse gas emissions noted that the problem of greenhouse gases was "intimately linked to other problems." The general thrust of the remarks was that tackling one global atmospheric issue necessitated consideration of a spate of others.

The SCOPE report, together with the Villach conference, differed from prior assessments. The conclusions reached about the need for action were different from those reached by other agents during the same (and slightly earlier) period. The most significant difference concerns recommendations for policy response. The SCOPE report (1986, 7) was the first to state that "substantial warming" would occur as a result of a doubling of CO_2, to note that increases in CO_2 "were attributable to human activities," and to recommend a variety of specific policy actions. Interestingly, despite the emphasis on other greenhouse gases, the statements of the Villach conference still underscored the important role of CO_2, as do most subsequent policy statements.

Compared to previous international and national reports, the final 1985 Villach report made bolder statements about the implications of the scientific findings for policymaking. It urged more significant steps toward international cooperation and called for governments to recognize that future climate change could be stemmed by attention to policies concerning fossil-fuel use, energy conservation, and greenhouse gas emissions. These conclusions stand in contrast to those reached by WMO, UNEP, and ICSU, gathered in Villach in 1981. These organizations concluded that

the probability that potentially serious impacts may be realized is sufficiently great that an international commitment to a programme of cooperation in research is required to illuminate the issues and to reduce uncertainties so that the dimensions and time scale of the problem can be more reliably ascertained. (World Climate Programme 1981, 2)

Writing for the Environmental Protection Agency in 1983, Seidel and Keyes concluded:

In the absence of growing international consensus on this subject, it is extremely unlikely that any substantial actions to reduce CO_2 emissions could or would be taken unilaterally. Adaptive strategies undertaken by individual countries appear to be a better bet (p. ix). Given these competing interests [conflicts between developed and developing countries], the future of any international accord remains, at best, a distant prospect. (chap. 5, 18)

Salience and opportunity were perhaps more important than greenhouse gases in driving these conclusions. However, greenhouse gases did provide a handy link to other issues in active negotiation.

Salience and the Issue Domain

The Villach gathering provided an opportunity for climate scientists to acknowledge internationally the importance of climate change, as a scientific matter, but more critically, as a policy matter. They discussed this significance with one another, and began to highlight these features to policy-relevant actors at home, just as PHARE and World Bank representatives did in the case study presented by Andonova (chapter 6, this volume). They concluded:

Many important economic and social decisions are being made today on long-term projects . . . all based on the assumption that past climatic data, without modification, are a reliable guide to the future. This is no longer a good assumption since the increasing concentrations of greenhouse gases are expected to cause a significant warming of the global climate in the next century. (WMO 1986, 1)

Anecdotally, Steve Schneider notes that it was in the 1970s that media stories about the "human impact on the global climate first started appearing" (1989, 191). These stories gradually made their way onto the front pages of newspapers and magazines, particularly in the 1980s (Schneider 1988; 1989, 194). Businesses and other institutions were increasingly discussing climate issues. Many of the Villach participants connected the conclusions they reached at the conference to initiatives that were developing at home.

As was the case for LRTAP and POPs, the rising salience of the issue brought a new audience (see chapter 7, this volume). The group gathered at Villach included not only those scientists who had been concerned with questions related to climate change, atmospheric chemistry, and meteorology, but those who were biologists and other natural scientists who had not been principally concerned with climate, as well as engineers. It was a group that was more inclined to consideration of the practical implications of scientific findings, by virtue of their capacities in government bureaus. These government scientists had not been deeply involved with climate science and were surprised by the findings, as well as by the implications for the speed with which changes in climate change could occur. For example, Pier Vellinga—a seacoast engineer who joined the Villach process shortly after 1985—said the findings of Villach forced him to realize that even the lower bounds of climate-change predictions would necessitate a transformation of his whole field. Jim Bruce, then assistant deputy minister for the Atmospheric Environment Service in Canada, was approached by a representative of the government of the province of Alberta. The official wanted to know if they were "throwing good money after bad" when they bailed out drought-stricken farms, asking whether the area was simply going to be a dry area in the future. These scientists returned home with the messages from Villach, and continued with international initiatives.

The creation of the Advisory Group on Greenhouse Gases (AGGG) was intended to further examine the science and its implications for policy and make recommendations on the development of a climate convention. This group met in Villach in July 1986. The experts (nongovernmental scientists) were nominated (two each) by UNEP, WMO, and ICSU. The AGGG approved a plan for a conference to be organized under its auspices. Discussions at the first meeting of the AGGG led Gordon Goodman (the Beijer Institute), Michael Oppenheimer (Environmental Defense Fund), and George Woodwell (Woods Hole Research Center) to organize a set of workshops designed to address questions of policy response to climate change (Jäger 1990).

The 1987 Villach/Bellagio meeting was the first meeting of the AGGG and provided an opportunity for the activist scientists to begin an initiative to pursue further links to policy. This conference emphasized that the scientific consensus reached at the Villach 1985 conference, along with the conclusions reached at the Villach meeting, should be used as a starting point for both of the 1987 workshops. The basic conclusions of the workshop differed very little from those of Villach 1985. According to Michael Oppenheimer, one of the organizers of the 1987 meetings, "The sponsors of the Villach and Bellagio workshops in 1987 hoped to provide a bridge between the 1985 Villach conference, which found that the issue of climatic change merited the attention of policy-makers, and the actual elaboration of specific measures to limit or adapt to warming" (Oppenheimer 1989, 3).

This group reflected carefully on the uncertainties that faced both climate scientists and policymakers in evaluating the effects of green house gases and climatic changes. They concluded that "a coordinated international response seems inevitable and rapid movement towards it is urged" (World Climate Programme 1988, 37). The group advocated the prompt approval and ratification of the ozone protocol, examination of national energy policies, consideration of the issue of deforestation, evaluation of non-CO_2 greenhouse gases and limitation of the growth of their concentrations in the atmosphere, careful consideration of policies to manage sea-level rise, and continued scientific research. They concluded that the report should be used by the AGGG to further scientific and policy research, and to inform the discussion about the development of an international agreement on climate change.

The information conveyed by the Villach and Bellagio conferences had observable connections to the international scientific information environment and the international policymaking community. The statements issued at Villach and Bellagio were used to inform the deliberative process of the Toronto Conference in 1988 and the UNGA decision to initiate climate negotiations, via the 1987 World Commission on Environment and Development or "Brundtland Commission" report. All nations, the report notes, face suffering caused by "releases by industrialized countries of carbon dioxide and of gases that react with the ozone layer, and from any future war fought with the nuclear arsenals controlled by those nations" (World Commission on Environment and Development 1987, 22). The Commission consulted with thousands of individuals from around the world, heard hours of testimony in public hearings, and read numerous submissions. On the issue of climate change, the report noted that, based on the scientific evidence, particularly in light of the many complexities and uncertainties, "it is urgent that the process [of taking action] start now" (p. 176). Specifically, how did Villach come to be reflected in the Brundtland Commission report?

Gordon Goodman, key Villach participant and member of the AGGG, was directly involved in the work of the Brundtland Commission. He served as part of a "Group of Special Advisers" on Energy; several observers of climate science, including Bert Bolin, credit him with drafting the sections of the report concerned with climate change. Indirect consultations between the Commission and others who contributed to the Villach conclusions is likely, but no direct trail is apparent.[2]

The report's discussion of climate change draws almost exclusively on the Villach findings, frequently citing or paraphrasing the Villach 1985 text. The Brundtland Commission and its report enjoyed a high profile; the report was reprinted numerous times and raised the profile of many global environmental issues. The Commission report was presented to the UNGA in 1987, and the conclusions about climate change were used to underpin their resolutions establishing an intergovernmental science advisory panel and, more importantly, to initiate intergovernmental negotiations on the subject.

In 1988, when the UNGA resolved to establish the IPCC and urged the initiation of climate negotiations even more seriously, it drew directly on the Brundtland Commission report and the conference at Villach. The UNGA recognized the contribution that these works had made to the "emerging evidence [which] indicates that continued growth in atmospheric concentrations of 'greenhouse' gases could produce global warming with an eventual rise in sea levels, the effects of which could be disastrous for mankind if timely steps are not taken at all levels" (UNGA 43/53).

The Brundtland Commission report and the Villach/Bellagio conclusions came together in another venue as well. The Canadian Atmospheric Environment Service (AES) and the Canadian government had an interest in establishing a leadership position for Canada on global environmental issues. The AES used the public hearings of Brundtland to offer to host a major international conference on the global atmosphere: climate change was proposed as the first topic to be considered. The conference was timed to occur after the release of the Brundtland report.

The conclusions of the Villach process informed the conference through a background paper, written by Jill Jäger, who edited accounts of both the 1985 Villach and 1987 Villach/Bellagio conferences. The background paper was intended to provide a common point of departure for conference participants. The conference organizers brought working-group chairs to Toronto in advance to do briefings based on this background document. The document reiterated many, if not most, of the arguments put forward by the Villach groups concerning the seriousness of the climate problem and the urgency of action. Recommendations for policy action echoed the Villach/Bellagio 1987 conclusions. The background paper advocated the development of a law of the atmosphere, which could "incorporate and build on other conventions and protocols such as the 1987 Montreal Protocol" (WMO 1989, 401).

When the Villach group was tapped for a contribution to the Toronto Conference in early 1987, neither that group nor the Toronto Conference planners could have foreseen the high profile that the Toronto Conference would enjoy in June 1988. By 1988, the climate change issue had moved from scientific circles and specialized agencies of the United Nations to the UNGA, and to the government and legislative offices of a number of countries. What happened in the summer of 1988 was an identifiable leap to the public arena, the highest levels of national governments, and the international agenda beyond the United Nations. These events greatly increased the salience of the Toronto conclusions.

By the time the Toronto Conference was convened in June 1988, a serious heat wave had occurred in the United States, and the media, accustomed to using "weather hooks" (Schneider 1989) to write about climate change, had provided extensive coverage of the extreme weather and of its connections to climate change. The June heat wave was just the beginning. The summer was to be one of the hottest on record, and droughts occurred in many places in the United States. However, the June heat wave was enough to bring considerable attention to the Toronto Conference. As Steve Schneider (1989, 194) noted, "An international gathering in Toronto at the end of June attracted so many reporters that extra press rooms had to be added to handle the hordes of descending journalists." International media attention to the problem of climate change began a steep rise in 1987–1988, peaking in 1990 (Social Learning Group 2001).

At the 1988 Toronto Conference, the international work of scientists at the 1985 Villach and 1987 Villach/Bellagio meetings finally coalesced with a growing public demand for information and growing media attention. The effect of this nexus was to make it difficult for national leaders to avoid the issue.

Legitimacy and the Issue Domain

When the international arena, first in the form of the Brundtland Commission, began to seek a voice on the importance of climate change, Villach was the only *international* voice available on the subject, and it had a message that the international arena was ready to hear. This independent group of international scientists was able to make recommendations that their colleagues involved in prior, and even subsequent, national assessments were unable to make. As Frank Alcock (2001) observes: when assessments are presented by organizations (in this case, the U.S. government with an interest in limiting obligations to reduce CO_2 emissions), the assessment information may harmonize with the goals of the organization.

The absence of domestic political constraints on the conclusions reached by this body cannot be underestimated as a source of leeway in reaching policy conclusions. As with scientists participating in SCOPE work and other ICSU meetings (Greenaway 1996), the scientists attending the Villach conference attended in their personal capacities, not as representatives of their governments. They were selected by the three partner agencies. If UNEP and WMO selected them, they were likely to be government scientists, or scientists on contract to government. If selected by ICSU, they were mostly academic scientists. Although they came to the conference from eighty-nine countries, chair James Bruce asked that they "shed their national policy perspectives" and to address the global issues in as comprehensive a way as possible. This admonition applied particularly to those scientists with governmental affiliations.

Participants in several assessments during the early 1980s observed that it was time for an international assessment. Bert Bolin (1994, 26) observed that "international assessment was necessary in order to establish the global importance of the issue." The 1986 SCOPE report noted that while "a number of assessments of [the possibility of climatic change] have been made by national groups, notably in the United States . . . the problem is clearly an international one and an assessment at the international level therefore seems desirable to serve as a basis for discussion and possibly, at some stage, for the development of an action plan" (SCOPE 1986, xv).

The task of this conference was not to assess the climate problem with a view to identifying policy actions that would be in the best interests of a particular country. Rather, the perspective was a global one. The conclusions reached by this conference were not accountable to national agencies, or legislative bodies that would be charged with implementing such conclusions. The mandate handed to the group came from two intergovernmental organizations (UNEP and WMO) and a nongovernmental organization (ICSU). As James Bruce noted, the call for policy recommendations was strongly made by the sponsoring agencies. Tolba urged the participants to recommend the establishment of an international coordinating committee on greenhouse gases, and to discuss in greater detail the options being placed before the world's leaders, encouraging a "wider debate on such issues as the costs and benefits of a radical shift away from fossil fuel consumption" (WMO 1986, 12). It was the hope of James Dooge, speaking on behalf of ICSU, that this conference would "provide a first approach to a sound foundation and appropriate guidelines for the development of the necessary policies at the national and international level" (WMO 1986, 17). Indeed, the Villach conference made recommendations consonant with the goals of its organizational sponsors (continuing global climate research and policy advice for a global accord on the control of greenhouse gases).

However, by 1990, neither Villach nor the AGGG was cited for scientific information. The 1990 IPCC assessment soon became the primary source of scientific information for the international community as it contemplated a framework convention on climate change (Paterson 1996; Bodansky 1993; Agrawala 1997). The 1990 Second World Climate Conference referenced the IPCC report, not the Villach reports (Bodansky 1993, 469; Jäger and Ferguson 1990, 535). Declarations at the negotiations on a climate convention, which began in February 1991, identified the findings of the IPCC as evidence of the need for global attention to the matter of climatic change.

A history of the development of scientific consensus in the climate issue could highlight the role of scientists in international politics by noting the importance of the experts at Villach/Bellagio, and subsequently, the IPCC (see, for example, Paterson 1996; Lunde, cited in Paterson). Those who identify science and scientists as players in the development of international environmental policy might see the IPCC as a continuation of a story that features scientists as crucial contributors of information. It is, however, important to note the significant institutional shift, which highlights the importance of legitimacy as states began to participate in international negotiations at the highest level (see also Gupta, chapter 3, this volume).

The IPCC, established in 1988, was a new institution with a selection process and review mechanisms that were more legitimate to key actors as they began to negotiate an international agreement to limit human-induced changes to the global climate (Agrawala 1997).

Had the AGGG been subsumed by the IPCC? In fact, no. Further work of the AGGG was planned in November 1988. A four-volume report was issued in 1990. These volumes reflected the work of three working groups,[3] and were published just before the Second World Climate Conference in 1990. This group distinguished itself very clearly from the IPCC, noting that "the IPCC reports have been generated by an intergovernmental process. By contrast, the AGGG-related output appearing herc is nongovernmental and produced by invited experts working in their private capacities" (Jäger 1990, 4). In addition, the funding for this endeavor was much smaller. Yet "despite these distinctions, both sets of Reports are not in any sense seen as 'competing' with each other. In fact the approach to the problem has been quite different in each case and in several instances, the same specialists have been involved in both studies" (Jäger 1990, 4). The first part of this observation suggests that the independent status of the AGGG is what distinguished it from the IPCC. The second part suggests that the specialists were the same. Both of these points merit consideration.

An essential feature of the design of the IPCC was that the panel would be constituted of nationally nominated scientists. This was a feature championed by the United States to remove the scientific momentum from the nongovernmental scientists, given the likelihood that intergovernmental negotiations on climate change would be initiated soon (Hecht and Tirpak 1995). Some of the attention Villach received stemmed from the fact that it had successfully approached the problem from a global and nongovernmental perspective, without regard to the interests of particular nations. As Agrawala observes, the AGGG did not have any "formal requirements for the group to report on its activities, or to seek direction from, even the governing bodies of the three sponsoring organizations, let alone national governments" (Agrawala 1997).

The observation that both the IPCC and the AGGG shared expert contributors would lend credence to the notion that states chose a governmental process of assessment over a nongovernmental one. In fact, several of the experts involved in scientific information provision during the 1980s became leaders of and contributors to the IPCC. However, not all participants in the pre-1988 communication of scientific information were incorporated into the IPCC process. Legitimacy, in the form of IPCC mechanisms, began to be important.

AGGG committee members included B. Bolin (Meteorological Institute in Sweden), W. C. Clark (Harvard University), W. Degefu (Ethiopia, National Meteorological Services Agency), H. Ferguson (AES, Environment Canada), G. Goodman (Stockholm Environment Institute, formerly the Beijer Institute), F. K. Hare (University of Toronto), J. Jäger (Germany), M. Oppenheimer (Environmental Defense Fund), C. C.

Wallen (WMO), and G. Woodwell (Woods Hole Research Center). Bolin's prominence in the IPCC is unmistakable; he was appointed its first chair. His presence in the IPCC might lead one to believe that the SCOPE/Villach/Bellagio scientists were incorporated into the IPCC process. This is not, however, an accurate perception. Of the AGGG steering committee members, only Bert Bolin and W. Degefu were contributors to the 1990 IPPC assessment, while Oppenheimer was a reviewer for Working Group I, the scientific assessment.

Those who funded and organized the Villach/Bellagio conferences, helped to communicate those conclusions, and provided background information and conclusions about targets and timetables in Toronto can also be connected to the AGGG in the 1990s, including Jäger, Goodman, and Oppenheimer. Moreover, the sponsors as well as the nongovernmental scientists that participated are nearly identical to those that organized and led initiatives from Villach and Bellagio. Sponsorship came from the Stockholm Environment Institute, the Environmental Defense Fund, and the Rockefeller Brothers Fund for all of these initiatives (Jäger 1990, i). Both Goodman and Oppenheimer became active participants in NGO initiatives once negotiations on a framework convention were underway. For this group, however, the international audience that was available prior to 1990 was largely unavailable.

Conclusion

Some have argued that the Villach assessment was a "catalytic event" that marked important developments in science (see Social Learning Group 2001, 269). As such, this assessment is an important one in this volume. Villach was an assessment process widely identified with great success in affecting policy outcomes. What contributed to its apparent success? This chapter has focused on the extent to which attributions of credibility, salience, and legitimacy contributed to the influence of the assessment. Central questions included: Did Villach represent a significant change in science, legitimacy, salience, or credibility? What factors independent of the assessment may have contributed to the vast distribution of its conclusions?

The chapter has argued that the scientific conclusions reached at Villach were not altogether novel, nor were they significantly more credible than those of previous assessments. Villach was not the first assessment to mention the role of other greenhouse gases in enhancing the greenhouse effect, though evidence for a greenhouse effect had mounted over the years. Indeed, the scientists used scientific conclusions about the contributions of greenhouse gases to press climate change onto the international arena, but the reasons for their influence had largely to do with the fact that the conclusions they generated resonated with developments in the international arena, including increased attention to environmental issues in general and ozone depletion in particular.

The assessment process did derive legitimacy from its international perspective, as well as from its nongovernmental status. The international arena needed an international messenger for the importance of addressing climate change. Villach findings informed the deliberations of the Toronto Conference and set the international agenda.

As climate change moved onto the international agenda, however, new actors in the issue domain began to make specific choices about the legitimacy of various assessment processes. While a scientific assessment process continued to inform international debate, the IPCC is a process that is distinct from Villach and the AGGG. Concerns about legitimacy have driven the careful crafting of a process of appointing scientists, reviewing reports, and producing policymaking summaries. The politicization of the issue brought concerns about legitimacy to the forefront.

This chapter's findings highlight the role that political developments can play in increasing issue salience. This suggests that even where it looks like spectacular scientific findings and novel approaches are influencing the agenda, factors unrelated to the attributes of the assessment can affect the influence these findings have.

Moreover, the chapter suggests that care should be taken in highlighting the role of scientists or assessments in the history of an issue domain. These processes, and the participants in them, change over time in important ways. Concerns about legitimacy drove states to seek advice from a very different assessment process once the issue was on the international agenda. The Villach group and the AGGG found their voices diminished in the new issue domain where states were seeking information in the face of negotiations on a climate convention.

However, there is little doubt that the Villach assessment and the scientists that participated it in played a crucial role in developing an agenda for climate change. In 1987, Willliam Kellogg lamented that despite considerable increases in scientific knowledge and a scientific consensus that increases in atmospheric concentrations of CO_2 were warming the earth and that humans were to blame, "We have yet to see an important governmental or industrial decision that actually acknowledged the climate change factor" (p. 131).

Acknowledgment of the "climate change factor" was encouraged by a group of scientists who recognized connections between the problem of climate change and developments in the international arena. Within several months of Kellogg's lament new developments suggested that serious efforts would be made to reach international agreements on measures to protect the climate. Scientific concern had translated into myriad international declarations and movement toward policy action.

Acknowledgments

This chapter draws on research largely completed under the auspices of the Global Environmental Assessment (GEA) Project. The author thanks the editors and the many colleagues in the GEA project for their discussions and feedback over the years. The author gratefully acknowledges the comments of several anonymous reviewers. At Harvard University the Department of Government, the Belfer Center for Science and International Affairs at the Kennedy School of Government, the Weatherhead Center for International Affairs, and most recently the Freshman Dean's Office and the Committee on Degrees in Social Studies provided the author with institutional homes and valuable support. This chapter builds on work presented previously by the author under the name Wendy E. Franz. This includes a working paper at the Kennedy School of Government and a doctoral dissertation titled *Changing the Climate: Non-State Actors in International Environmental Politics*, presented to the Department of Government at Harvard University.

Interviews with W. E. Franz listed at the end of the chapter were conducted by the author.

Notes

1. I am grateful to Clark Miller for bringing Malone's 1984 testimony to my attention.

2. This conclusion is based on a list of contributors to hearings, communications, and reports for the Commission (World Commission on Environment and Development 1987, 366–387). None of the following people or organizations appear in the report: Villach, Villach Chair J. Bruce, Villach cochairs G. S. Golitsyn, R. Herrera, J. Rasmussun, editors of the SCOPE 29 report including B. Bolin, B. Doos, R. Warrick, J. Jäger, the Advisory Group on Greenhouse Gases, Michael Oppenheimer, and George Woodwell.

3. Analysis of Limitation Strategies, Indicators of Climatic Change, Performing Assessments of Adaptation and Limitation Strategics.

References

Agrawala, S. 1997, June. Explaining the evolution of the IPCC structure and process. ENRP Discussion Paper E-97-05. Cambridge, MA: Kennedy School of Government, Harvard University.

Alcock, Frank. 2001. *Embeddedness and Influence: A contrast of assessment failure in New England and Newfoundland.* Belfer Center for Science and International Affairs (BCSIA) Discussion Paper 2001–19. Cambridge, MA: Environment and Natural Resources Program, Kennedy School of Government, Harvard University.

Ausubel, J. H. 1983. Historical Note. In National Research Council, *Changing Climate.* Washington, DC: National Academy Press.

Benedick, R. E. 1991. *Ozone Diplomacy: New Directions in Safeguarding the Planet.* Cambridge, MA: Harvard University Press.

Bodansky, D. 1993. The United Nations Framework Convention on Climate Change: A Commentary. *Yale Journal of International Law* 18(2): 451–558.

Boehmer-Christiansen, S. 1994a. Global climate protection policy: The limits of scientific advice / Part 1. *Global Environmental Change* 4(2): 140–159.

Boehmer-Christiansen, S. 1994b. Global climate protection policy: The limits of scientific advice / Part 2. *Global Environmental Change* 4(3): 185–200.

Bolin, B. 1994. Science and policy making. *Ambio* 23(1): 25–29.

Clark, W. C., and N. Dickson. 2001. Civic science: America's encounter with global environmental risk. In Social Learning Group, ed., *Learning to Manage Global Environmental Risks, Volume 1: A Comparative History of Social*

Responses to Climate Change, Ozone Depletion, and Acid Rain. Cambridge, MA: MIT Press.

Cooper, R. N. 1989. *Can Nations Agree? Issues in International Economic Cooperation.* Washington, DC: Brookings Institution.

Department of Energy. 1979. *Workshop on Environmental and Societal Consequences of a Possible CO_2-Induced Climate Change.* Annapolis, MD, April 2–6, 1979. Washington, DC: National Technical Information Service.

Department of Energy. 1985a. *Detecting the Climatic Effects of Increasing Carbon Dioxide.* MacCracken, M. C. and F. M. Luther, eds., DOE/ER-0235. Washington, DC: Department of Energy.

Department of Energy. 1985b. *Glaciers, Ice Sheets and Sea Level: Effect of a CO_2-Induced Climatic Change.* DOE/ER/60235-1. Washington, DC: Department of Energy.

Department of Energy. 1985c. *Projecting the Climatic Effects of Increasing Carbon Dioxide.* MacCracken, M. C., and F. M. Luther, eds., DOE/ER-0237. Washington, DC: Department of Energy.

Environmental Protection Agency. 1983. (*See* Seidel and Keyes.)

Environmental Protection Agency. 1989. *The Potential Effects of Global Climate Change on the United States.* J. B. Smith and D. Tirpak, eds. Washington: US EPA, Office of Policy, Planning and Evaluation.

Franz, W. E. 1997, August. *The Development of an International Agenda for Climate Change: Connecting Science to Policy.* ENRP Discussion Paper E-97-07. Cambridge, MA: Kennedy School of Government, Harvard University.

Franz, W. E. 2000. *Changing the Climate? Non-State Actors in International Environmental Politics.* Doctoral dissertation, Department of Government, Harvard University.

Greenaway, F. 1996. *Science International: A History of the International Council of Scientific Unions.* Cambridge: Cambridge University Press.

Haas, P. M. 1990. *Saving the Mediterranean.* New York: Columbia University Press.

Hecht, A. D., and D. Tirpak. 1995. Framework Agreement on Climate Change: A scientific and policy history. *Climatic Change* 29: 371–402.

Jäger, J., ed. 1990. *Responding to Climate Change: Tools for Policy Development.* Stockholm: Stockholm Environment Institute.

Jäger, J., and H. L. Ferguson, eds. 1990. *Climate Change: Science, Impacts and Policy: Proceedings of the Second World Climate Conference.* Cambridge: Cambridge University Press.

Jäger, J., and T. O'Riordan. 1996. The history of climate change science and politics. In J. Jäger and T. O'Riordan, eds., *Politics of Climate Change: A European Perspective.* London: Routledge.

Kellogg, W. W. 1987. Mankind's impact on climate: The evolution of an awareness. *Climatic Change* 10(2): 113–136.

Markham, J. M. 1989, July 17. Paris group urges "decisive action" for environment. *New York Times*, sec. A, p. 1, col. 6.

Mintzer, I., and J. A. Leonard, eds. 1994. *Negotiating Climate Change: The Inside Story of the Rio Convention*. Cambridge: Cambridge University Press.

Moomaw, W. 1990. Scientific and international policy responses to global climate change. *Fletcher Forum of World Affairs* 14(2): 249–261.

National Research Council. 1979. *Carbon Dioxide and Climate: A Scientific Assessment Report of an Ad Hoc Group on Carbon Dioxide and Climate. Woods Hole, MA July 23–27. Assembly of Mathematical and Physical Sciences, Climate Research Board*. Washington, DC: National Academy Press.

National Research Council. 1983. *Changing Climate*. Washington, DC: National Academy Press.

Noordwijk Conference Report. 1989, November. *Ministerial Conference on Atmospheric Pollution and Climatic Change*. Noordwijk, the Netherlands.

Oppenheimer, M. 1989. Greenhouse gas emissions: Environmental consequences and policy responses. *Climatic Change* 15(1/2): 1–4.

Paterson, M. 1996. *Global Warming and Global Politics*. London: Routledge.

Pomerance, R. 1989. The dangers from climate change: A public awakening. In D. E. Abrahamson, ed., *The Challenge of Global Warming*, 259–269. Washington, DC: Island Press.

Schneider, S. 1988. The greenhouse effect and the U.S. summer of 1988: Cause and effect or a media event? / An editorial. *Climatic Change* 13: 113–115.

Schneider, S. 1989. *Global Warming: Are We Entering the Greenhouse Century?* San Francisco: Sierra Club Books.

SCOPE (Scientific Committee on Problems of the Environment). 1986. The Greenhouse Effect, Climatic Change and Ecosystems. SCOPE 29. Bolin, B., B. R. Doos, R. A. Warrick, and J. Jäger, eds. Chichester: Wiley and Sons.

Seidel, S., and D. Keyes. 1983. *Can We Delay a Greenhouse Warming?: The Effectiveness and Feasibility of Options to Slow a Build-Up of Carbon Dioxide in the Atmosphere*. Washington, DC: Environmental Protection Agency.

Social Learning Group, ed. 2001. *Learning to Manage Global Environmental Risks, Volume 1: A Comparative History of Social Responses to Climate Change, Ozone Depletion, and Acid Rain*. Cambridge, MA: MIT Press.

WMO. 1979. *The World Climate Conference: A Conference of Experts on Climate and Mankind, Geneva, Switzerland, February 1979*. Geneva: Secretariat of the WMO.

WMO. 1986. *Report of the International Conference on the Assessment of the Role of Carbon Dioxide and of Other Greenhouse Gases in Climate Variations and Associated Impacts*. Villach, Austria, 1985, WMO, UNEP, and ICSU.

WMO. 1989. The Changing Atmosphere: Implications for Global Security. Conference proceedings from Toronto, Canada, 27–30 June, 1988. Geneva: WMO Secretariat.

World Climate Programme. 1981. *On the Assessment of the Role of CO_2 on Climate Variations and Their Impact*. Villach, Austria, November 1980. Geneva: WMO, UNEP, and ICSU.

World Climate Programme. 1984. *Report of the Study Conference on Sensitivity of Ecosystems and Society to Climate Change*. Villach, Austria, September 1983, Geneva: WMO, UNEP, and ICSU.

World Climate Programme. 1988. *Developing Policies for Responding to Climatic Change: A Summary of the Discussions and Recommendations of the Workshops Held in Villach, Austria, September–October 1987, and Bellagio, November 1987*. WMO, UNEP, and Beijer Institute.

World Commission on Environment and Development. 1987. *Our Common Future*. Oxford: Oxford University Press.

Interviews

Except as indicated, all interviews were with W. E. Franz.

B. Bolin. Chair, Intergovernmental Panel on Climate Change. Interview with S. Agrawala as part of Global Environmental Assessment Project, 1997.

J. P. Bruce. Chair, 1985 Villach Conference. Telephone interview with W. E. Franz and S. Agrawala, April 1997.

W. C. Clark. Harvey Brooks Professor of International Science, Public Policy, and Human Development, Kennedy School of Government, Harvard University. Vienna, Austria, January 1997.

J. Jaeger. Deputy Director, International Insitute for Applied Systems Analysis, Vienna, Austria. Vienna, Austria, February 1997.

R. Torrie, R. Torrie Smith Associates, Ottawa, Ontario, Canada. Telephone interview, August 1995.

P. Usher. Former Chief, United Nations Programme, Atmospheric Unit. Bonn, Germany, March 1997.

P. Vellinga, Professor, Department of Hydrology and Geo-environmental Sciences, Vrije University. Telephone interview, February 1997.

3

Problem Framing in Assessment Processes: The Case of Biosafety

Aarti Gupta

In areas of intense political and scientific controversy, problem framing is the key site where diverse perspectives on the nature of a problem are voiced, mediated, elevated, or marginalized, with consequences for the effectiveness of governance. Particular ways of framing, or drawing boundaries around the nature of a problem, serve to mobilize different interests and actor coalitions, legitimize distinct kinds of knowledges and expertise, and validate certain solutions while excluding others.

This chapter focuses on problem framing in scientific assessment processes. It uses a controversial new global governance challenge: biosafety, or the safe use of biotechnology, to show how problem framing is central to the perceived legitimacy, salience, and credibility of information and scientific assessment processes that may underpin governance. In illustrating this, I focus on the Cartagena Protocol on Biosafety (henceforth biosafety protocol), a global treaty governing transfer and use of genetically modified organisms (GMOs) (CP 2000).

The biosafety protocol was negotiated between 1996 and 2000 under the auspices of the Convention on Biological Diversity, which is concerned with the conservation and sustainable use of biodiversity (CBD 1992). The protocol calls for the "advance informed agreement" of an importing country prior to trade in certain GMOs (CP 2000, Article 7). Unlike other environmental issues such as climate change or ozone depletion, governance of biosafety has not been accompanied or preceded by a global-level biosafety assessment—that is, by a formal state-of-the-art synthesis of knowledge about the safety aspects of GMO use in various sectors of human activity.

Nonetheless, scientific assessment processes lie at the heart of the new global biosafety regime, through two means. First, the biosafety protocol calls for the sharing of existing national-level biosafety assessments between GMO exporting and importing countries, to facilitate importer decisions about whether to accept traded GMOs. Second, it calls for importing countries to undertake additional context-specific biosafety assessments domestically, as necessary, prior to decisions about permitting or restricting GMO trade. Thus biosafety assessment processes, and the exchange of biosafety information between countries, are key elements of this regime.

As this analysis makes clear, the scope of such biosafety assessment processes, as well as the methods through which information is to be shared, are intimately related to how the problem of biosafety has been framed within this global context. The analysis also explores the rationales (legal, scientific, ethical) relied on by different groups to justify broader or narrower understandings of biosafety.

I examine problem framing during initial regime creation, culminating in adoption of the Cartagena Protocol in January 2000. The focus is on regime creation because the framing of biosafety at this early stage continues to shape evolution of this global regime, underway since the biosafety protocol entered into force in 2003.[1] The analysis in this chapter is based on participant observation of biosafety protocol negotiations from 1998 to 2000, analysis of primary documents, and interviews with government and major group representatives.

Problem Framing in Assessment Processes

Much recent research in international conflict resolution, as well as within the Global Environmental Assessment Project, has pointed to the importance of framing, or drawing boundaries around complex nature-society interactions, in analyzing governance efforts (Jasanoff, Miller, and McCarthy 1998; Miller et al. 1997). Studies of global environmental governance have also examined how and why particular frames gain ascendancy or dominance over others in the environmental realm, as well as the consequences of frame changes for governance (Mitchell 1998; Iles 1998). As a study on social learning in the management of environmental risk notes, such changes can be in the direction of complexification of frames, or a broadening of the spectrum of cause-effect scenarios that merit concern and action (Clark et al. 2000). Frame complexification can be confined to quantitatively assessable phenomena, or it can transcend such phenomena to include the social and ethical dimensions of a governance challenge.

In the case of biosafety, distinct and competing frames, articulated by multiple actors, have been coexistent from the start, with none dominant. Conflicts over framing have centered on how narrowly or broadly to understand the problem of biosafety. Is ensuring "safe use of biotechnology" primarily an ecological and/or a human health issue? Or does it also include potential social, political, or ethical dimensions of the use of modern biotechnology in sectors such as agriculture and health? This depends centrally on how broadly or narrowly the term *safety* is defined by different actors, and whether broader or narrower understandings of the term can acquire legitimacy and salience in different contexts.

In examining conflicts over framing, the analysis here thus also sheds light on a key question at the heart of assessing the influence of global environmental assessments: whether "technicalization" of an issue, via problem framings that emphasize scientifically assessable risk and safety (over other aspects), can confer legitimacy in politically controversial areas in a manner that nontechnical arguments cannot. Such a mediating role for an ostensibly value-neutral science has been subject to sustained critique, also within the Global Environmental Assessment Project (Sarewitz 2000; Wynne 1994; Jasanoff 1996; Jasanoff and Long-Martello 2004; Gupta 2004; Jansen and Roquas 2005).

In a similar vein, the analysis of problem framing in this chapter shows that, in normatively contested areas such as biosafety, diverse perceptions of the legitimacy (fairness) and salience (relevance) of particular problem framings and, flowing from that, the salience of biosafety assessments and information, remain at the center of conflict. This suggests that technical credibility (often called sound science) cannot mediate conflicts over salience and legitimacy, which are fundamentally political. It also raises the question, moreover, whether perceptions of credibility are separable from those of legitimacy and salience.

The analysis further highlights the key role of institutional context in problem framing. The chapter shows how the perceived legitimacy of various biosafety problem framings must also contend with the institutional context within which such framing occurs, as well as its links to other relevant institutional contexts. In the case of biosafety, the synergies or conflicts between the Cartagena Protocol and the World Trade Organization (WTO) have played a key role in problem framing within the protocol, with implications for the scope of its biosafety assessment processes and information-sharing obligations.

The sections below discuss further the contested issue domain of biosafety in general, and then the specific conflicts over biosafety framings within the institutional context of the Cartagena Protocol.

Biosafety: A Highly Contested Issue Domain

Modern biotechnology involves the process of inserting genes from one source into another, using molecular techniques (McHughen 2000; CP 2000). A growing array of resulting "transgenic" products are being transferred across the globe. Debates over the risks posed by such products have been underway since at least the 1980s, and show little sign of abating.

A variety of ecological, health-related, socioeconomic, and ethical concerns are voiced by different actors (Nuffield Council on Bioethics 1999). The concerns include, for example, the potential for adverse ecological consequences as a result of novel gene flow from transgenic plants to weeds or wild relatives (Rissler and Mellon 1993). Human health and food-safety concerns relate to the toxicity or allergenicity potential of novel proteins introduced into transgenic crops and foods (Nottingham 1998). In addition to ecological and health risks, a wide range of social, economic, and ethical concerns surround the use of transgenic technology, particularly in agriculture (Asfaw and Egziabher 1997). These can include concern about monopoly control over privatized transgenic seed or disruption of traditional (nontransgenic) agricultural export markets, given commingling of transgenic and nontransgenic crops (Paarlberg 2001).

Even as the potential adverse impacts resulting from traded GMOs is driving demands, by some, for global regulation, the economic stakes for producers of transgenic products from potentially restrictive global regulation are high: in agriculture, a growing percentage of trade in key globally traded commodity crops (such as corn, soybean, cotton, and canola) contains genetically modified varieties (James 1998, 2000). Uses of such traded transgenic commodities can range from seed (for planting), to animal feed, to use as ingredients in a wide variety of processed foods. Conflicts over framings of biosafety, in various forums and by various actors, occurs within such a context.

The governance challenge is further complicated by the fact that claims of both benefits and risks from transgenics are characterized by a high degree of scientific uncertainty. There is as yet insufficient empirical experience with many products of modern biotechnology, especially in developing countries. Most field testing of transgenic crops in agriculture, for example, began only in the 1990s. Thus most claims about ecological and human health risks (or lack thereof) remain scientifically disputed. Added to this are a growing set of (equally disputed) political, economic, and practical concerns over the need to monitor, label, and segregate GMOs from non-GMOs (also to maintain the future option of a nontransgenic agriculture) as well as the lack of human, technical, and financial capacities to do so, especially in developing countries. Disputes over transgenics continue to turn most broadly on their potential impact on food security, market access, and the meeting of agricultural needs and priorities in developed and developing countries alike.

Biosafety thus remains in many respects an anticipatory governance challenge, one where the concerns center around "imponderable features such as irreversible consequences, threats to the resilience of social units, impacts on 'silent' groups (e.g., future generations, biota) . . . where the shape of the problem we should be managing, and even the outcomes we want are often unclear" (Fischhoff et al. 1981, 2). Drawing boundaries around biosafety, or framing the problem, remains therefore a key site of conflict.

Although attempts to govern safe transfer and use of products of modern biotechnology have been underway in a variety of global forums, the Cartagena Protocol is the first legally binding global regime that focuses exclusively on regulating GMO trade. However, as seen further below, these negotiations, and the framing of biosafety within them, have been fundamentally shaped by global trade rules of the WTO, which have as their raison d'être the facilitation of trade and the removal of potential nontariff barriers to trade (with domestic health and safety regulations seen as potential nontariff barriers to trade).

The interlinkages between these two global institutional contexts, and their relevance for biosafety governance, has been the subject of much recent analysis (Isaac and Kerr 2003; Safrin 2002; Gupta 2002). Of most direct relevance here is the WTO's Agreement on the Application of Sanitary and Phytosanitary Measures (SPS Agreement), which requires that potential ecological or health risks posed by traded GMOs be scientifically assessed (or assessable) before they can serve as a valid basis for restricting trade (SPS 1994). Nonscientifically assessable socioeconomic impacts from GMO trade, for example, are not permissible criteria on which to restrict GMO trade under the WTO-SPS Agreement. Conflicts over problem framing within the biosafety protocol have occurred under the shadow of this technicalized risk-based understanding of safety within the WTO.

The sections below address, first, the actors involved with framing biosafety in protocol negotiations. How biosafety has been framed within this global forum is then analyzed via the lens of two concrete axes of conflict in regime creation: the scope of its assessment and information-sharing obligations, and the means for information sharing.

Framing Biosafety within the Cartagena Protocol: The Actors

During negotiation of the biosafety protocol, diverse perspectives on the biosafety problem were articulated by five negotiating alliances. These were the Miami Group of GMO-producing countries (including Argentina, Australia, Canada, Chile, the United States, and Uruguay); the European Union; the Like-Minded Group of developing countries; Eastern European countries in transition; and a Compromise Group of OECD countries who were neither members of the European Union nor the Miami Group (this group included key countries such as Japan,

Mexico, Norway, Singapore, South Korea, Switzerland, and New Zealand).

During protocol negotiations, the countries of the Miami Group were at the forefront of developing and commercializing transgenic crops, with the United States as the leader, followed by Argentina, Canada, and Australia.[2] This group thus represented GMO-exporting-country concerns, with an interest in defining the problem of biosafety as narrowly as possible, in order to minimize exporter obligations to share information prior to trade in GMOs. As primary producers of transgenic crops, a particular concern of this group was to minimize restrictions on the bulk agricultural commodity trade, including transgenic varieties of globally traded crops such as soybeans, corn, and canola (BSWG 1999; Ex-COP 2000; Gupta 2000b). This group also demanded, in particular, that the scope of the protocol's biosafety information-sharing and importer agreement rules should not conflict with the trade rules and obligations of the WTO.

In contrast to the Miami Group, the European Union negotiated the protocol from the perspective of potential GMO importers, especially during the latter stages of the negotiations. This period coincided with rising domestic consumer opposition within the European Union to use of biotechnology in agriculture and, in particular, to transgenic crop imports. As the "Eurobarometer" surveys of European attitudes toward agricultural biotechnology consistently showed, "Europeans have become increasingly opposed to genetically modified foods" (Gaskell et al. 2000, 935).

This increasing public opposition to transgenic crops and foods in the European Union has been accompanied by an escalating trade conflict between the United States and the European Union over the last half decade (Brack, Falkner, and Goll 2003). The European Union has had a de facto moratorium in place against import of transgenic crop varieties since 1999, as the European Community debated amendments to its regional GMO directives, and halted new approvals until such amendments were in place. Although the moratorium was lifted in 2004, the conflict endures, as is evident from a case recently brought by the United States in the WTO against the European Union's regional and national policies regulating GMO trade.

The concerns of the third negotiating alliance in protocol negotiations, the Like-Minded Group of developing countries, were also, as with the European Union, those of current or potential future importers of GMOs. Developing countries were at the forefront of demanding a biosafety protocol, given their concern about the spread of potentially novel hazards to their countries and their lack of capacity and regulations to manage such hazards (Rajan 1997). Thus they argued for the broadest scope for a global biosafety regime, covering the widest possible range of potential adverse impacts and products (ENB 1998; Gupta 2000a, 2000b).

The fourth negotiating alliance, consisting of countries of Central and Eastern Europe, had similar concerns to those of developing countries with regard to their limited capacity to monitor entry and use of GMOs, but they also supported problem framings articulated by the European Union, given the future prospect of integration into the EU and the eventual need for harmonization with EU regulatory approaches.

The fifth and final negotiating alliance, the Compromise Group, consisted of OECD countries that were neither members of the Miami Group nor of the EU. This group reflected a mix of the interests and concerns voiced by the Miami Group and the European Union, since it included important OECD agricultural importers such as Japan, as well as leaders in biotechnology research such as Switzerland (Bail, Falkner, and Marquard 2002; Gupta 2000b).

In addition to these negotiating alliances, a Global Industry Coalition of agricultural, food, and pharmaceutical companies supported the Miami Group in pushing for a "workable" protocol with a narrow scope (Global Industry Coalition 1999a, 1999b). In contrast, an informal coalition of environmental and consumer safety advocates (henceforth green groups) supported developing-country calls for the broadest possible framing of biosafety to facilitate the greatest oversight over the flow of GMOs across the globe (Greenpeace 1999, 2000; TWN 2000).

These actor-coalitions' diverse concerns, deriving in large part from their positioning with regard to import or export of transgenic crops, were reflected in the battles to draw boundaries around, or frame, the problem of biosafety. In doing so, these groups evoked a variety of rationales (legalistic, moral, economic, scientific) to justify their particular problem framing within this global context.

These conflicts over framing both shaped, and were revealed in, concrete negotiations over two elements of the biosafety assessment and information-sharing system developed by the protocol. These two elements include, first, the scope of information sharing—that is, information sharing about *what*. The key question here was which GMOs were to be regulated by the protocol. The second component was the *breadth* of biosafety information to be shared and the *means* by which to share it. These two aspects, and their links to problem framing, are explored further below.

Problem Framing and Scope of Information Sharing

The earliest framing battles over potential adverse impacts from transnational transfers of GMOs took place during negotiation of the Convention on Biological Diversity (CBD) itself, completed in 1992 (under which the Cartagena Protocol was subsequently negotiated). Agreement on a biosafety provision within the CBD contains within it an initial framing of the biosafety problem. This provision calls on Parties to

consider the need for and modalities of a protocol setting out appropriate procedures, including, in particular, advance informed agreement, in the field of the safe transfer, handling and use of any living modified organism resulting from biotechnology that may have adverse effect on the conservation and sustainable use of biological diversity. (CBD 1992, Article 19.3)

This language resulted from extensive negotiation in the Convention on Biological Diversity over the need for global regulation of GMOs within this global environmental agreement (Rajan 1997; McConnell 1996; Gupta 1999). As seen above, GMOs are called "living modified organisms" or LMOs in the Cartagena Protocol, in a striking reflection of fundamental conflict over whether a biosafety problem even existed. The change from "genetically modified organism" to "living modified organism" in the provision above was at the insistence of the United States, which argued that genetic engineering did not pose unique hazards, and did not need to be singled out for regulation. When this proved to be a minority position, the United States pushed for the change in terminology to deflect attention away from *genetic* modification as the focus of global regulatory attention (Rajan 1997, interviews).

The CBD's Article 19.3, as seen above, provided an initial framing of biosafety within this forum, as a concern with "adverse effect on the conservation and sustainable use of biological diversity." However, such a framing left unresolved, at the time, whether and how potential human health effects or socioeconomic effects of LMO use were also part of an understanding of biosafety (ENB 1994; Gupta 1999).

The implications of broader or narrower problem framings were clear: associating biosafety only with adverse impacts on biodiversity would justify information sharing and generation about ecological effects alone, and only for those LMOs that were likely to come into contact with an importing country's environment and biodiversity (although the concern with sustainable use left room for interpretation on this point). However, if adverse impacts on human health are also to be included within a framing of biosafety, then a broader set of genetically modified entities could legitimately be regulated by this global regime, and additional information about human health impacts would also have to be generated, assessed, and shared. Furthermore, going beyond human health concerns, inclusion of a variety of socioeconomic impacts of LMO transfers would further broaden the regime's regulatory reach, as well as the information and assessments on which LMO importer decisions could legitimately be based.

Once the Cartagena Protocol negotiations were launched under the CBD in 1996, these conflicts over problem framing found reflection in debates over the scope as well as the means of its biosafety information-sharing and consent obligations. These debates turned on whether and how the protocol would regulate trade in five categories of LMOs. These included LMOs transferred for deliberate release into the environment; LMOs transferred for intended use as food, feed, or processing (also known as agricultural commodities); LMOs transferred for contained use; the finished or processed products derived from LMOs (called "products thereof"); and LMO-based pharmaceuticals (BSWG 1999; Ex-COP 2000; Gupta 1999).

The distinctions between five categories of LMOs (and their products) were derived from a framing of biosafety as a problem primarily relating to adverse ecological effects and, by implication, contact with an importing country's environment. Thus, of these five categories, only LMOs for deliberate release into the environment were admitted by all negotiating alliances as both salient and legitimate to include within the protocol's most stringent "advance informed agreement" obligation, given the potential for adverse impact on an importing country's biological diversity.

Inclusion or exclusion of the other categories of LMOs (and even the distinctions and boundaries drawn between them) remained the subject of sustained conflict and controversy (Greenpeace 1999, 2000; Ex-COP 2000; Gupta 1999, 2000). These turned, partly, on whether and how human health and socioeconomic concerns were part of biosafety in this context.

Developing countries and environmental groups argued that an understanding of biosafety that excluded consideration of human health impacts was not legitimate (i e., not fair in its inclusion of different priorities) and not salient (i.e., not relevant to the spectrum of biosafety-related concerns within such countries). Equally, then, in their view, an information-sharing system that excluded a broad category of LMOs based on a narrow framing of biosafety as "adverse effects on biodiversity" would also flounder on grounds of salience and legitimacy.

The Like-Minded Group of developing countries, supported by environmental groups, thus argued for the broadest possible framing of biosafety and, related to that, for all five categories of LMOs to be covered by the protocol's information-sharing system. They offered two primary rationales to support this view: first, a risk-based rationale, arguing that uncertain yet potentially novel risks from LMOs to biodiversity *and* human health could result from transnational transfers of all five categories of LMOs; and second, a normative rationale, arguing for the need for importer choice (ENB 1998; Ex-COP 2000; TWN 2000).

In their risk-based rationale, developing countries and environmental groups emphasized that all five categories of LMOs posed uncertain and potentially novel human health risks, hence such risks were as salient to this group as a concern with biodiversity. Furthermore, they argued that human health considerations were not only salient but also legitimate to include within an understanding of biosafety in this institutional context, since humans were not separate but an integral component of biodiversity. For these groups, the Convention on Biological Diversity was thus an appropriate forum for regulating human health impacts of LMOs, under the umbrella concept of biosafety (COP-CBD 1995b).

In contrast, LMO-exporting countries of the Miami Group, supported by industry, argued for exclusion of all LMOs, other than those transferred for deliberate release, from the protocol's stringent advance informed agreement obligations, on grounds that these additional categories of LMOs were unlikely to come into contact with an importing country's biodiversity (e.g., Australia 1998). In framing biosafety as a concern with adverse effects on biodiversity, these countries could not question the *salience* of a broader concern with human health impacts to different countries, or the desire to regulate additional categories of LMOs. Many OECD countries already regulated, domestically, the potential human health impacts of LMOs (Gottweis 1998), thus precluding the argument that human health concerns associated with GMO use were not salient and legitimate concerns.

Instead, the Miami Group, supported by the European Union (on the important question of health impacts), chose to argue that inclusion of human health impacts within an understanding of biosafety was inappropriate in this particular institutional forum. They suggested that only adverse impacts on biodiversity were relevant to include in a biosafety protocol being negotiated under the Convention on Biological Diversity, and that human health considerations associated with GMO use were more suitably addressed in other global forums, such as the World Health Organization, or the Codex Alimentarius Commission, an international food safety standard-setting body whose standards have been endorsed by the WTO (ENB 1998; Gupta 1999).

This rationale was offered most strongly by these groups for LMO-based pharmaceuticals. In making these arguments, the key rationale was hence a legal (rather than a "no-risk") one, which questioned the appropriateness of the protocol as the institutional context for regulating human health aspects. In addition, however, the Miami Group and the EU also argued that free flows of LMO-based pharmaceuticals were particularly essential for developing countries. In putting forward this "need-based" rationale as well, they were strongly supported by the pharmaceutical industry. As the pharmaceutical company Rhône-Poulenc Rorer (1999) stated, excluding LMO-pharmaceuticals from the protocol's information-sharing obligations was essential to "preserve access to medical treatments . . . [and avoid] . . . significantly complicating deliveries of medical goods" to those in need.

Similar framing conflicts shaped decisions over exclusion or inclusion of finished products made from LMOs ("products thereof"), such as canola oil or processed foods, within the protocol's information-sharing obligations. Again, some developing countries and green groups demanded information-sharing obligations on exporters for this category of LMO products as well, given that they saw such inclusion as salient and legitimate (TWN 1999). They argued, for example, that risks or lack thereof associated with products containing novel genetically modified ingredients remained uncertain or unknown, given the lack of empirical testing of their long-term impacts. As stated by an environmental-group position paper:

Neither processing nor ingestion destroy biological activity of transgenes. Therefore, "products thereof" cannot be assumed to have no biological impact. To the contrary, scientific findings as well as the precautionary principle demand the inclusion of "products thereof" in the Biosafety Protocol. (Steinbrecher 1999)

These groups evoked first and foremost, therefore, a science- and risk-based argument for inclusion of this category of LMOs within the regime. However, since claims about the presence or absence of risk remained heavily contested, these groups also chose to emphasize the legal argument that the biosafety protocol's overall mandate to address the "safe transfer, handling and use" of living modified organisms meant that all uses, including uses of LMOs in processed products, were appropriate and legitimate to include within the regime and its information-sharing system (TWN 1999).

Countries of the Miami Group and industry countered these risk-based and legal rationales, arguing that such entities were unlikely to come into contact with biodiversity and hence should not be subject to regulation under the Convention on Biodiversity. As the Japanese delegation stated, "Products from LMOs containing non-viable genetic material should be kept outside the scope of the protocol . . . as their genetic components cannot be transmitted to other living organisms in the recipient environment under natural conditions" (Japan 1999).

Again, an important corollary to the risk rationale was an emphasis on ensuring the implementability of the biosafety regime's information-sharing obligations. The Grocery Manufacturers of America, speaking for the U.S. food and beverage industry, questioned the ability of importing countries to usefully process information about a wide variety of finished products containing genetically modified ingredients (they offered examples such as paper napkins from modified timber, to make their point). Inclusion of "products of LMOs" in the biosafety regime would, according to this group, overwhelm the capacity of importing countries to respond to and process such information, and would "impede the economic development of countries without any compensatory environmental benefit" (GMA 1999).

These conflicts over problem framing, and the resultant scope of the protocol's information-sharing obligations, came to a head in debates over the most contested LMO category: LMOs intended for food, feed, or processing (LMO-FFPs), or bulk agricultural commodities containing transgenic varieties.

The conflict here centered on the fact that this category of LMOs was biologically identical to those intended for deliberate release into the environment. The only difference was in their "intended use" for food, feed, or processing, as opposed to release into the environment (BSWG 1999,7, Article 5.2). Thus, for example, a genetically modified variety of corn could be planted as seed, or be used for direct consumption as food, for animal feed, or for processing into corn oil.

Agricultural commodity producers of the Miami Group, supported by industry, pushed for the distinction between LMOs for deliberate release, and those intended for food, feed, and processing. They argued for this latter category, LMO-FFPs (also called agricultural commodities), to then be exempt from the protocol's stringent advance informed agreement obligations. Their rationale was that LMOs transferred for direct consumption, feed, or processing would not come into contact with an importing country's environment, thus posing no risk to biodiversity (Informal Group on Commodities 1999). The dominant framing of biosafety as a concern with risk to biodiversity, given that the protocol was being negotiated under the CBD, was again central to the justifications offered to defend this position.

At the same time, in an acknowledgment of the centrality of the economic stakes underlying such a framing of biosafety, these groups also evoked a rationale of implementability, as an important corollary to the risk-based rationale they offered for making this distinction. Thus, they argued that the structure of the global agricultural commodity trade precluded stringent pretrade information sharing about LMO-FFPs with potential importers, on cost and logistical grounds (Global Industry Coalition 1999c). According to industry, LMOs in bulk agricultural commodity shipments were commingled with non-LMOs, making it difficult to identify particular LMOs in a given shipment and hence to share specific biosafety information about them with recipient countries. They also argued that the commodity trade was structured in such a way that there remained no business link between the farmer and the final exporter, making it difficult to comply with specific information-sharing requirements (Global Industry Coalition 1999c).

In contesting these risk-based and implementability rationales, developing countries and green groups pointed to the arbitrariness of distinguishing between biologically identical LMOs (which, hence, posed the same theoretical risk to biodiversity) based solely on their intended use. They argued that excluding biologically viable LMOs from the protocol's advance informed consent procedure on the basis of intended use was unacceptable, since intentions could never be categorically enforced or guaranteed not to change, especially in developing-country contexts where seed exchanges are informal and difficult to regulate (Informal Group on Commodities 1999). These debates also highlighted that both "risk" and "ensuring safety" are context specific and cannot be separated from particular social contexts.

In most conflicts over the scope of biosafety information sharing, the Miami Group and the European Union had similar perspectives (they diverged substantially over the precautionary principle and the relationship of the protocol to the WTO) (for detailed analyses, see Gupta 1999, 2000b; Safrin 2002). However, in one critical conflict between the EU and the Miami Group over information sharing for agricultural commodities, the EU did demand that information about different LMO varieties and their unique characteristics be provided along with each agricultural commodity shipment (in contrast to the *advance* notification and agreement demanded by developing countries). For the EU, information, along with the transfer, about the specific transgenic varieties contained in particular bulk agricultural commodity shipments was important and highly salient, given that it would facilitate domestic labeling of LMO-based products within the Union (Ex-COP 2000).

More generally, the disputes over inclusion or exclusion of various categories of LMOs from the protocol's information-sharing obligations brought to the fore another key difference between OECD and developing countries: relating to whether socioeconomic impacts of LMO trade were appropriate to include within a framing of biosafety in this context.

Although, as seen above, developing countries invoked a variety of science- and risk-based rationales in arguing for a broad understanding of bisoafety, and a broad scope for information-sharing obligations, they also argued that their decisions about LMO transfers necessarily transcended concerns over scientifically assessable human and ecological harm, and included a variety of socioeconomic concerns (Egziabher 1999; Asfaw and Egziabher 1997; Greenpeace 2000; see also Stabinksy 2000). These included privatization and concentration of ownership by a few multinational corporations over biological knowledge, commodity crops, and seed, which could result in potentially new forms of dependencies in these critical areas of food production. Equally, these countries were concerned about impacts on their nontransgenic traditional agricultural exports from unintentional comingling with transgenic varieties. Finally, it became clear that even a focus on safety of traded LMOs had an important socioeconomic dimension, in that it required monitoring, assessment, labeling, segregation, and traceability capacities, all of which were legitimate to take into account in deciding whether to permit entry of LMOs, regardless of known risk, or even intended use.

Again, the Miami Group and industry could not contest the salience of various socioeconomic concerns to developing countries. Rather, they chose to argue that such concerns were more suitably addressed at the national level through domestic rules, rather than through a global biosafety regime. Their main justification was that socioeconomic concerns relating to LMO transfers varied from country to country, hence their inclusion in the protocol would prevent harmonized rules for LMO transfers and would conflict with WTO rules. As the Global Industry Coalition (1999a) put it, "Introduction of socioeconomic considerations would create unnecessary and unavoidable conflicts with WTO obligations, and be disruptive of trade."

In response, developing countries and green groups noted the ironic disjuncture between the perceived legitimacy of considering socioeconomic benefits from movement of LMOs across national boundaries (a basic premise of the multilateral trade regime) but the perceived illegitimacy (in the view of those arguing for narrow framings) of considering socioeconomic harms from transnational LMO movements.

The finalized Cartagena Protocol "resolves" these conflicts over problem framing, and the related battles over scope of information sharing, by associating biosafety with a concern over "adverse effects on the conservation and sustainable use of biological diversity" (CP 2000, Article 1), as did the earlier CBD provision. It further addresses the conflict over inclusion of human health by adding a phrase in the protocol's objectives stating that countries should address potential adverse effects on biodiversity "taking also into account the risks to human health" (CP 2000, Article 1). In agreeing to this, both the Miami Group and the European Union suggested that they were making a major concession to developing-country demands on this particular point.

However, while this phrase is scattered throughout the finalized protocol, it remains open to different interpretations. Thus, it can be interpreted to mean both direct impacts on human health from LMO transfers and use, as understood and argued for by developing countries and environmental groups, or indirect impacts on human health arising from impacts on biodiversity, as argued by the Miami Group and the EU (at least during regime creation—the situation is now evolving, with the transatlantic EU-U.S. divide on LMO regulation growing wider on all fronts).

Furthermore, in its resolution of the issue of socioeconomic impacts, the Cartagena Protocol clearly separates such impacts from biosafety risk assessments, which are to consider ecological (and, potentially, human health) impacts from LMO use. It allows, in addition, for a limited consideration of socioeconomic impacts in importer decisions prior to LMO transfers. Specifically, it allows countries to "take into account, consistent with their international obligations, socioeconomic considerations arising from the impact of LMOs on the conservation and sustainable use of biological diversity" (CP 2000, Article 26).

This formulation explicitly links the socioeconomic impacts that can be considered by importing countries in their decision making to those arising from impacts on biodiversity, and builds in a further requirement of consistency with other international obligations, with an eye to the WTO.

The protocol's final obligations for information sharing for the different categories of LMOs flow from this legally circumscribed (based on institutional context) and narrower risk-based framing of biosafety. These final obligations are summarized in table 3.1.

As the table shows, the protocol calls for mandatory advance informed agreement for LMOs intended for deliberate release. Other categories of LMOs (i.e., those for contained use, LMO-FFPs, and LMO products) have less stringent information-sharing obligations. LMO-based pharmaceuticals are excluded from the Cartagena Protocol's regulatory purview altogether, as long as they are being addressed in other international forums (CP 2000, Articles 4–7).

Regarding rationales to justify particular framings of biosafety, the discussion above shows that, despite the dominant risk framing in the protocol, both those arguing for broader and narrower problem framings had to rely on justifications that went beyond risk and safety alone. In some instances, this was because certain risk-based rationales were hard to defend, if they were based on contested distinctions between viable and nonviable genetic material, or between impacts on biodiversity versus humans. In making nonrisk arguments, those supporting narrower problem framings most often evoked a rationale of implementability, while those supporting broader framings evoked the rationale of choice and autonomy, also so as to be able to consider the specific social context for particular LMO use.

Table 3.1
Information-sharing obligations for different categories of LMOs

Category of LMOs	Exporter obligations for information-sharing/soliciting importer agreement
LMOs transferred for intentional introduction into the environment	*In advance:* Notification and solicitation of agreement from importing party prior to transfer; detailed information about the LMO to be provided with this notification. *With transfer:* Documentation that clearly identifies them as LMOs, and specifies their identity and relevant traits and/or characteristics; requirements for safe handling, use and storage; contact point for further information; declaration that transfer is in accordance with exporter's protocol obligations.
LMOs transferred for food, feed, or processing (agricultural commodities)	*In advance:* Instead of country by country, notification to a centralized Biosafety Clearing-House (BCH) of domestic approvals of LMOs that may enter international trade in the future. Information to be supplied to the BCH includes approved domestic uses of the LMO and a risk assessment report done in order to secure domestic approval. *With transfer:* Documentation that clearly identifies that unsegregated bulk agricultural commodity shipments "may contain" LMOs; and that they are not meant for intentional introduction into the environment; contact point for information. This is subject to further negotiations.
LMOs transferred for contained use	*In advance:* No obligations. *With transfer:* Documentation that clearly identifies them as LMOs; requirements for safe handling, transfer, and use; contact point for further information.
Transfers of processed products deriving from LMOs	*In advance:* No obligations. *With transfer:* No obligations. *Where appropriate,* an obligation on all parties to provide regulatory information or summary risk assessments about LMO products to Biosafety Clearing-House.

Source: Compiled by the author from the Cartagena Protocol (CP 2000).

The extent to which the protocol's information-sharing obligations will influence domestic biosafety decision making requires detailed analysis as the Cartagena Protocol is implemented.[3] The analysis above reveals, however, that conflicts over the scope of biosafety information sharing within this global forum centered, first and foremost, around perceptions of salience and legitimacy, as logically prior to technical credibility. This can be seen clearly from the fact that the first-order conflicts were over whether biosafety information, including scientific risk assessments, were to be provided or generated for a broader or narrower set of regulated products (the various categories of LMOs and their intended uses), and whether they were to include consideration of a broader or narrower set of adverse impacts (ecological, health, socioeconomic). Few conflicts focused, at this stage, on whether the information to be shared via the global regime would be credible. This is also evident in the second axis of conflict, discussed below, around means of information sharing.

Problem Framing and Means of Information Sharing

In addition to scope, the *means* for sharing biosafety information was a related axis of conflict, and was also shaped by battles over biosafety framing. Table 3.1 also summarizes the protocol's distinct mechanisms for information sharing. The conflicts over means of information sharing about the five categories of LMOs turned on whether each required full-fledged "advance informed agreement" or whether other methods and avenues of information sharing should be pursued. As stated above, although LMOs transferred for deliberate release require advance informed agreement of an importing country (CP 2000, Article 7), all other LMOs either require specific information to accompany a transfer, or require information sharing through a centralized data source.

The means of information sharing is significant because the accessibility and salience of information is greater to an importing country if information is shared via the advance informed agreement procedure, which requires prior notification of an intended transfer by an exporter to the competent authority of an importing country. This notification has to include specific information about the LMO that may be transferred. Such information includes the taxonomic status and characteristics of the parental and host organisms for an LMO, the genetic modifications made, the intended use of the LMO, an existing risk assessment, and the regulatory status of the LMO in the country of export (CP 2000, Annex I). Importing countries have 90 days to acknowledge receipt of the notification and 270 days to make a decision (CP 2000, Articles 7–10). If an import is permitted, information about the LMO has to accompany the first transfer.

The consequence of this means of information sharing is to place the burden of responsibility for providing biosafety information on those in possession of it. This shift in the burden of responsibility (from those desiring it to those in possession of it) was a consequence of a problem framing that acknowledged, as a minimum, the potential risks to biodiversity from transfers of LMOs intended for release into the environment.

In contrast, the final compromise for the contested category of LMOs for food, feed, or processing (agricultural commodities) is to share some information prior to a transfer, but through a centralized source rather than via advance informed agreement of an importing country. LMO producer countries are required to notify a centralized Biosafety Clearing House (to be established under the Secretariat of the Convention on Biological Diversity) of domestic approval of a new LMO variety within fifteen days of the approval being granted domestically. The information to be provided to the Biosafety Clearing House is similar to that required in the case of LMOs transferred for deliberate release (CP 2000, Annex II). It includes information about approved domestic uses of the LMO and a risk assessment on which the domestic approval is based. A potential importing country can avail itself of this information to decide whether to restrict import of a particular LMO variety that may enter the international commodity trade in the future (CP 2000, Article 11). In one of the few instances where concern over credibility of information came to the fore at this early stage of regime creation, there is an obligation on exporting countries to have domestic mechanisms in place to ensure the "accuracy" of the information provided (CP 2000, Article 11, paragraph 2).

These obligations for LMO commodities do place the onus on producers of LMOs to provide certain information, if not to individual countries, then at least to a centralized locus of information sharing. However, a key difference between this means of information sharing, and advance informed agreement, is that the responsibility to seek out information remains with the importing country, a scenario that developing countries had sought to avoid. The responsibility rests with an importing country to ascertain which LMOs, of those notified by a producer country to the centralized Biosafety Clearing House, are likely to be of concern within their particular national context, and whether such LMOs may at some point be transferred to their countries via bulk agricultural commodity trade (see Africa Group 2000; Lin 2000). Again, this difference in means of information sharing was partly justified via a problem framing that succeeded in placing ecological impact and contact with the environment at the heart of biosafety as understood within this global forum.

As a first-order concern, however, the salience of information is reduced if countries are unable to either access information from centralized sources, or assess its relevance to their particular context. Lim Li Lin of the Third World Network describes potential limitations of such an information-sharing approach, with implications for its perceived salience:

[Centralized information sharing about] a domestic approval by one country shifts the onus onto all other countries to decide whether or not they will accept LMO-commodities, when countries do not even know whether [or when] such commodities might be exported to their country. (Lin 2000, 3)

In addition, reliance on Internet-based information dissemination through the Clearing House exacerbates the concerns of some countries about the lack of domestic capacity to effectively access and utilize such information, with implications for its salience. As stated by an Africa Group communiqué, under the revealing heading "equity and access",

The BCH [Biosafety Clearing House] should not be the mechanism that further divides the technology "have-nots" from the technology "haves" . . . the Africa Group wishes to emphasize the need for capacity building, especially the enhancement of technological capabilities of countries . . . [especially since information sharing through] the BCH is a cornerstone for the implementation of the Protocol. (Africa Group 2000, paragraphs 1, 9)

As reflected here, the salience and hence influence of information on national decisions will depend on whether countries have the institutional wherewithal to utilize the information provided to the centralized Biosafety Clearing House. Since salience of information will depend on the capacity to access and process it, the Cartagena Protocol also encourages capacity building to aid importing countries to access information and assess its relevance to their national context, in taking decisions (CP 2000, Article 22).

Countries of the Miami Group, industry, and international organizations have enthusiastically embraced the call for capacity building for potential importer countries, given their interest in facilitating harmonized biosafety decision-making processes and approaches worldwide (UNEP and GEF 2000; Global Industry Coalition 2000). It remains to be seen if such capacity-building initiatives become vehicles for the transfer of contested producer perspectives on biosafety to potential importer countries, as some fear, or serve, instead, to geniunely augment importer country choice.

Information as Influence? The Case of Biosafety

The analysis here suggests that, during regime creation and initial problem framing, and especially in areas of scientific uncertainty and normative conflict, concerns over legitimacy and salience are logically prior to concerns over credibility, in shaping the influence of information in global governance. The case of biosafety reveals that the credibility of technical information (contained, for example, in a risk assessment of a particular LMO) was a second-order concern during problem framing and negotiation of the Cartagena Protocol, taking a backseat to conflicts over a salient and legitimate scope and methods for biosafety information sharing.

This suggests that a push for "sound" (i.e., technically rigorous) science will carry little weight as long as the fundamental conflicts relate to a legitimate and salient framing of biosafety, and, related to that, to a fair and relevant scope for global biosafety information-sharing obligations.

Paradoxically, however, it is precisely in areas of extreme normative conflict, such as biosafety, that calls for "sound" (i.e., objective and value-free) technical information as a way to mediate political conflict continue to be heard. The Cartagena Protocol also gives credible science a prominent place, by calling for national biosafety decisions to be based on "scientifically sound" risk assessments, and by separating socioeconomic considerations from such risk assessments (CP 2000; Gupta 2001). As revealed in this analysis, however, given first-order conflicts over the legitimacy and salience of problem framing and scope of information sharing, seeking elusive agreement on the technical "soundness" of biosafety information is more likely to be a lightening rod for conflict than a means to resolve it.

More broadly, such a privileging of science-based importer choice suggests a key gap in the global biosafety governance architecture, whereby few systematic and institutionalized mechanisms exist to allow consideration of the social dimensions of LMO use. This differs from another highly contested global environmental issue, climate change, where the social and economic impacts of climate change do indeed form an official part of the scientific assessment process.

In the biosafety realm, one implication of the exclusion of the social dimension, broadly understood, is that the wider range of concerns about the use of biotechnology in agriculture may increasingly have to be articulated in the language of technical risk, harm, and safety. This can entail getting on a testing treadmill, the implications of which need to be explored, particularly for developing countries. This could be either a saving grace or a fatal flaw of global biosafety governance. Under such conditions, in particular, an emphasis on "sound" science as a basis for governance raises the inevitable question of "sound for whom," and the perceived credibility of technical information becomes more closely intertwined with perceptions of its salience and legitimacy.

Acknowledgments

The author thanks the editors of this volume as well as Frank Biermann, Daniel Sarewitz, and two anonymous reviewers for comments on earlier drafts. Financial support is acknowledged from Harvard University's

Global Environmental Assessment Project, Yale University's Center for International and Area Studies, Resources for the Future in Washington, D.C., and the Heinz Family Foundation.

Notes

1. For a detailed discussion of key implementation challenges facing the Cartagena Protocol, now that it has come into force, see Falkner and Gupta 2004.

2. During protocol negotiations, the worldwide area devoted to transgenic crops in 1998 was 27.8 million hectares. Of this area, the United States contributed 74 percent, Argentina 15 percent, Canada 10 percent, and Australia 1 percent. Mexico, Spain, France, China, and South Africa constituted the remainder, each with less than 1 percent. By 2000, this global area had increased to 44.2 million hectares, of which the United States contributed 68 percent, Argentina 23 percent, Canada 7 percent, China 1 percent, and Australia and South Africa over 100,000 hectares. The main crops grown in 1998 were soybeans (consisting of 52 percent of the global area), corn (constituting 30 percent), as well as cotton, canola, and potatoes. The main genetic modifications were for herbicide tolerance (71 percent of all genetic modification) and insect resistance (21 percent). Global sales from transgenics were estimated at $75 million in 1995, $235 million in 1996, $670 million in 1997, and $1.2–$1.5 billion in 1998 (James 1998, 2000).

3. This is the focus of a MacArthur Foundation–funded research project on biotechnology regulation in China, South Africa, and Mexico, being undertaken jointly by the author with Robert Falkner (see Gupta and Falkner 2006; for an early analysis of the protocol's relevance for India, see Gupta 2000a).

References

Africa Group. Undated [2000]. *Working Group: Information Sharing—Pilot Phase of the Biosafety Clearinghouse Mechanism.* Montreal: Africa Group.

Asfaw, Zemede, and Tewolde B. G. Egziabher. 1997. Possible adverse socioeconomic impacts of genetically modified organisms. In K. J. Mulongay, ed., *Transboundary Movement of Living Modified Organisms Resulting from Modern Biotechnology: Issues and Opportunities for Policy-Makers.* Geneva: International Academy of the Environment.

Australia. 1998. *Statement by Australia at the 5th Meeting of the Open-Ended Ad Hoc Working Group on Biosafety.* Montreal: August 17–28, 1998.

Australia. Undated [1998]. *Importer-Based Advance Informed Agreement: A Non-Paper.* Montreal: Australian Delegation Statement.

Bail, Christoph, Robert Falkner, and Helen Marquard, eds. 2002. *The Cartagena Protocol on Biosafety.* London: Royal Institute of International Affairs.

Biermann, Frank. 2001. The rising tide of green unilateralism in world trade law: Options for reconciling the emerging North-South conflict. *Journal of World Trade* 35(3): 421–448.

Brack, Duncan, Robert Falkner, and Judith Goll. 2003. *The Next Trade War? GM Products, the Cartagena Protocol and the WTO.* London: Royal Institute of International Affairs (Chatham House).

BSWG [Open-Ended Ad Hoc Working Group on Biosafety]. 1998. *Revised Consolidated Text of the Draft Articles.* Note by the Secretariat. UNEP/CBD/BSWG/5/Inf.1 of 23 February.

BSWG. 1999. *Protocol on Biosafety: Draft Text Submitted by the Chair of the Working Group.* UNEP/CBD/BSWG/6/L.2/Rev.2. Issued for the Sixth Meeting of the Open-Ended Ad Hoc Working Group on Biosafety, Cartagena, Colombia, February 14–19, 1999.

Canada. Undated [2000]. *Biosafety Clearing House Pilot Phase* (ICCP-1 Position Paper).

CBD [Convention on Biological Diversity]. 1992. Done Rio de Janeiro, 5 June, in force 29 December 1993, in: 31 *International Legal Materials* 818.

Clark, William, J. Jäeger, J. Cavender-Bares, and N. M. Dickson, eds. 2000. *Learning to Manage Global Environmental Risks.* Cambridge, MA: MIT Press.

COP-CBD. 1994. [Conference of the Parties to the Convention on Biological Diversity]. *Medium-Term Programme of Work of the Conference of the Parties. Decision 1/9.* The Bahamas.

COP-CBD 1995a. *Decision II/5 on Agenda Item 4: Consideration of the Need for and Modalities of a Protocol for the Safe Transfer, Handling and Use of Living Modified Organisms.* UN Doc. UNEP/CBD/COP/2/19.

COP-CBD. 1995b. *Report of the Open-ended Ad Hoc Group of Experts on Biosafety.* UN Doc. UNEP/CBD/COP/2/7 of 3 August.

COP-CBD. 1995c. *Terms of Reference for the Open-Ended Ad Hoc Working Group.* UN Doc. UNEP/CBD/COP/2/CW/L.22.

CP [Cartagena Protocol]. 2000. *The Cartagena Protocol on Biosafety to the Convention on Biological Diversity: Text and Annexes.* Montreal: CBD Secretariat.

Egziabher, Tewolde Berhan G. 1999, June. Safety denied. *Our Planet.* http://www.ourplanet.com/imgversn/102/viewpoint.html.

ENB. 1994. The Conference of the Parties to the Convention on Biological Diversity: A summary report of the first meeting. *Earth Negotiations Bulletin.* 9(28). Canada: International Institute for Sustainable Development.

ENB. 1998. Report of the Fourth Session of the Open-Ended Ad Hoc Working Group on Biosafety. *Earth Negotiations Bulletin.* 9(28). Canada: International Institute for Sustainable Development.

Ex-COP [Extraordinary Session of the Conference of the Parties to the Convention on Biological Diversity]. 2000. *Report of the Extraordinary Meeting of the Conference of the Parties to the Convention on Biological Diversity for Adoption of the Protocol on Biosafety.* UN Doc. UNEP/CBD/ExCOP/1/3.

Falkner, Robert, and Aarti Gupta. 2004. *Implementing the Cartagena Protocol: Key Challenges.* Sustainable Development Programme Briefing Paper SDP BP 04/04. Royal Institute of International Affairs (Chatham House), London. November.

Fischhoff, Baruch, Sarah Lichtenstein, Paul Slovic, Stephen L. Derby, and Ralph L. Keeney. 1981. *Acceptable Risk.* Cambridge: Cambridge University Press.

Gaskell, George, Nick Allum, Martin Bauer, John Durant, Agnes Allansdottir, Heinz Bonfadelli, Daniel Boy. 2000. Biotechnology and the European public. *Nature Biotechnology* 18: 935–938.

Global Industry Coalition. 1999a, February. *Basic Requirements for a Successful Biosafety Protocol.* Cartagena.

Global Industry Coalition. 1999b, February. *Biodiversity Jeopardized in Cartagena Biosafety Negotiations.* Cartagena.

Global Industry Coalition. 1999c, February. *Impact Analysis: An Application of AIA to Agricultural Commodities.* Cartagena.

Global Industry Coalition. 2000, September. Capacity building: The biotechnology industry perspective. BIOTECanada.

GMA [Grocery Manufacturers of America]. 1999, February. *Commonly-Asked Questions and Answers about the Inclusion of "Products Thereof" in the Biosafety Protocol as It Relates to Food, Beverages and Consumer Products.* Cartagena: Grocery Manufacturers of America.

Gottweis, Herbert. 1998. *Governing Molecules: The Discursive Politics of Genetic Engineering in Europe and the United States.* Cambridge: MIT Press.

Greenpeace. 1999, February. Greenpeace International's comments on the draft negotiating text. Prepared for the Sixth Meeting of the Open-Ended Ad Hoc Working Group on Biosafety, Cartagena.

Greenpeace. 2000. Biosafety protocol: The ten key elements. Prepared for the Resumed Session on the First Extraordinary Meeting of the convention of the Parties to the Convention on Biological Diversity to Finalize and Adopt a Protocol on Biosafety. Montreal, 24–28 January.

Gupta, Aarti. 1999. *Framing Biosafety in an International Context: The Biosafety Protocol Negotiations.* ENRP Discussion Paper E-99-10. Cambridge, MA: Kennedy School of Government, Harvard University.

Gupta, Aarti. 2000a. *Governing Biosafety in India: The Relevance of the Cartagena Protocol.* ENRP Discussion Paper 2000-24. Cambridge, MA: Kennedy School of Government, Harvard University.

Gupta, Aarti. 2000b. Governing trade in genetically modified organisms: The Cartagena Protocol on Biosafety. *Environment* 42(4): 23–33.

Gupta, Aarti. 2001. Advance Informed Agreement: A shared basis to govern trade in genetically modified organisms? *Indiana Journal of Global Legal Studies* 9(1): 265–281.

Gupta, Aarti. 2004. When global is local: Negotiating safe use of biotechnology. In Sheila Jasanoff and Marybeth Long-Martello, eds., *Earthly Politics: Local and Global in Environmental Governance*, 127–148. Cambridge, MA: MIT Press.

Gupta, Aarti, and Robert Falkner. 2006. The Cartagena Protocol and domestic implementation: Comparing Mexico, China and South Africa. Sustainable Development Programme Briefing Paper. London: Royal Institute of International Affairs (Chatham House).

Iles, Alistair. 1998. *The Evolution of Acidification Impact Frames in Europe: Assessment of Forest conditions*. ENRP Discussion Paper E-98-19. Cambridge, MA: Kennedy School of Government, Harvard University.

Informal Group on Commodities. 1999, February. *Deliberations of the Informal Group on Commodities*. Cartagena.

Isaac, Grant E., and William A. Kerr. 2003. Genetically modified organisms at the World Trade Organization: A harvest of trouble. *Journal of World Trade* 37(6): 1083–1095.

James, Clive. 1998. Global review of commercialized transgenic crops: 1998. *ISAAA Briefs No. 8*. Ithaca: ISAAA.

James, Clive. 2000. Global status of commercialized transgenic crops: 2000. *ISAAA Briefs No. 21, Preview*. Ithaca: ISAAA.

Jansen, Kees, and Esther Roquas. 2005. Absentee expertise: Science advice for biotechnology regulation in developing countries. In Melissa Leach, Ian Scoones, and Brian Wynne, eds., *Science and Citizens: Globalization and the Challenge of Engagement*, 142–154. London: Zed Books.

Japan. 1999, February. Position of the Japanese government toward a Protocol on Biosafety. Cartagena, Columbia.

Jasanoff, Sheila. 1996. Science and norms in global environmental regimes. In Fen Osler Hampson and Judith Reppy, eds., *Earthly Goods: Environmental Change and Social Justice*, 173–197. Ithaca: Cornell University Press.

Jasanoff, Sheila, and Marybeth Long-Martello, eds. 2004. *Earthly Politics: Local and Global in Environmental Governance*. Cambridge, MA: MIT Press.

Jasanoff, Sheila, Clark Miller, and James McCarthy. 1998. *Assessing Impacts: Framing, Communication, Credibility*. Impacts Working Group Theme Draft Paper. Cambridge, MA: Global Environmental Assessment Project, Harvard University.

Lin, Lim Li. 2000. *Capacity Building in Developing Countries to Facilitate the Implementation of the Cartagena Protocol*. Penang, Malaysia: Third World Network.

McConnell, Fiona. 1996. *The Biodiversity Convention: A Negotiating History.* Dordrecht: Kluwer Law International.

McHughen, Alan. 2000. *Pandora's picnic basket: The Potential and Hazards of Genetically Modified Foods.* Oxford: Oxford University Press.

Miller, Clark, Sheila Jasanoff, Marybeth Long, William Clark, Nancy Dickson, Alastair Iles, and Tom Parris. 1997. Shaping Knowledge, Defining Uncertainty: The Dynamic Role of Assessments. In Global Environmental Assessment Team, eds., *A Critical Evaluation of Global Environmental Assessments* Global Environmental Assessment Project, pp. 79–104. Calverton, MD: IGES/CARE.

Mitchell, Ronald B. 1998. Forms of discourse, norms of sovereignty: Interests, science and morality in the regulation of whaling. In K. Litfin, ed., *The Greening of Sovereignty in World Politics.* Cambridge, MA: MIT Press.

Nottingham, Stephen. 1998. *Eat Your Genes: How Genetically Modified Food Is Entering Our Diet.* London: Zed Books.

Nuffield Council on Bioethics. 1999, May. Genetically modified crops: The ethical and social issues. Report by the Nuffield Council on Bioethics. Available at http://www.nuffieldbioethics.org/fileLibrary/pdf/gmcrop.pdf.

Paarlberg, Robert. 2001. *The Politics of Precaution: Genetically Modified Crops in Developing Countries.* Baltimore: John Hopkins University Press.

Rajan, Mukund Govind. 1997. *Global Environmental Politics: India and the North-South Politics of Global Environmental Issues.* Delhi: Oxford University Press.

Rhône-Poulenc Rorer. 1999, February. *Statement on Biosafety Protocol.* Cartagena.

Rissler, Jane, and Margaret Mellon. 1993. *Perils among the Promise: Ecological Risks of Transgenic Crops in a Global Market Place.* Cambridge: Union of Concerned Scientists.

Safrin, Sabrina. 2002. Treaties in collision? The Biosafety Protocol and the World Trade Organization agreements. *American Journal of International Law* 96: 606.

Sarewitz, Daniel. 2000. Science and environmental policy: An excess of objectivity. In R. Frodemen, ed., *Earth Matters: The Earth Sciences, Philosophy and the Claims of Community.* Upper Saddle River, NJ: Prentice Hall.

SPS Agreement. 1994. *Agreement on the Application of Sanitary and Phytosanitary Measures. Annex IA to the Final Act Embodying the Results of the Uruguay Round of Multilateral Trade Negotiations.* Marrakesh, April 15.

Stabinksy, D. 2000. Bringing social analysis into a multilateral environmental agreement: Social impact assessment and the biosafety protocol. *Journal of Environment and Development* 9(3): 260–283.

Steinbrecher, Ricarda A. 1999. Updating Biosafety Assumptions: *Why We Need "Products Thereof."* Penang, Malaysia: Third World Network.

TWN [Third World Network]. 2000. *Open Letter to Delegates to the Resumed Session of the First Extraordinary Meeting of the Conference of the Parties to the Convention on Biological Diversity.* Penang, Malaysia: Third World Network.

TWN [Third World Network]. Undated [1999]. *"Products Thereof" Are Legally within the Scope of the Protocol.* Penang, Malaysia: Third World Network.

UNEP and GEF [Global Environmental Facility]. 2000. *Building Capacity for Safe and Effective Use of Biotechnology.* Nairobi: UNEP/GEF Pilot Biosafety Enabling Activity Project.

Wright, Susan. 1994. *Molecular Politics: Developing American and British Regulatory Policy for Genetic Engineering, 1972–1982.* Chicago: University of Chicago Press.

Wynne, Brian. 1994. Scientific knowledge and the global environment. In Michael Redclift and Ted Benton, eds., *Social Theory and the Global Environment.* London: Routledge.

4

Whose Experts? The Role of Geographic Representation in Global Environmental Assessments

Frank Biermann

Introduction

Global environmental assessments are often hailed as the collective effort of the entire "global scientific community," with thousands of the world's best scientists participating. In part, this claim is true, as much of this book shows. On the other hand, however, participation is strikingly unbalanced in almost all assessments once geographic representation is taken into account. If one asks *whose experts* are participating, one will inevitably find—in particular regarding older assessments—that the vast majority of the members of the world's "invisible college" reside in just a few countries in the rich and highly industrialized Northern Hemisphere.

This has led to a fair amount of friction between North and South in the past. The history of the global scientific assessments in the 1980s and 1990s can be characterized as a prolonged struggle by developing countries to gain influence and increase their participation in the process. The early climate assessments, for example, had been undertaken with almost no participation from developing countries. The 1985 Villach conference, which became one of the most influential climate assessments of the 1980s (see Torrance, chapter 2, this volume), involved no experts from the South; all twenty-two participants came from only seven industrialized countries, even though the meeting was held under the auspices of the United Nations Environment Programme (UNEP) and the World Meteorological Organization (WMO) and could thus flaunt the banner of UN approval and support (Agrawala 1998a, 1998b).

In the succeeding Intergovernmental Panel on Climate Change (IPCC), set up in 1988 by UNEP and WMO, Southern governments sought to strengthen the participation of their experts, arguing that if developing countries do not have access to IPCC, its very legitimacy would be jeopardized. Yet participation of Southern experts remained low. In the second IPCC assessment report (IPCC 1996a, 1996b, 1996c), the percentage of Southern "contributing lead authors," "lead authors," and "contributing authors" in IPCC working groups ranged from 5.1 percent (for Working Group I, the "science of climate change") to 25.0 percent (for Working Group III). Likewise, the percentage of Southern peer reviewers in the working groups was small, reaching from 8.5 (Working Group III) to 11.1 percent (Working Group I) and 14.9 percent (Working Group II) (Dingwerth 2001).

Conflicts over participation are also known from the scientific assessment of biological diversity. In 1992, UNEP initiated the Global Biodiversity Assessment (1995). When this assessment was released in 1995, UNEP praised the report as the product of "over 1,500 scientists and experts from all parts of the world" (UNEP 1995). Indeed, experts from every continent and most larger countries participated in one or more working groups of the assessment. Yet a glance at the list of participants reveals that again, the vast majority came from the North.

As much of this book shows, participation in global environmental assessments has become a major analytic problem because of the consequences that different forms of participation may entail for the salience, credibility, and legitimacy of the information compiled and distributed. This crucial role of participation in assessments has already been analyzed for several national and subnational networks (for example, Cash, chapter 10, this volume; Jaeger 1998; Jung 2000; Farrell and Keating 1998; Keating and Farrell 1998; Mitchell 1998; Moser, chapter 8, this volume; Social Learning Group 2001), as well as for Eastern European states (Andonova, chapter 6, this volume). In these studies, broadening the participation in assessments is often seen as a way to increase their credibility, legitimacy, and salience for stakeholders.

But what are the consequences of low participation of developing countries in global environmental assessments for the salience, credibility, and legitimacy of the information and for its influence in the South? How does asymmetric participation in global assessments affect the influence of the information they produce on countries that are underrepresented? Do global environmental assessments influence scientific research and policymaking in the South at all? In other words, do experts and decision makers in developing countries use the conclusions of the assessments as a basis for decision making?

These are the guiding questions of this research, which analyzes the history of global environmental assessments on climate and biodiversity in the 1980s and 1990s from the North-South perspective. I look at both elements in the causal chain that may affect the influence of an assessment in a developing country: the *content* of the information as it is likely to be influenced by varying degrees of participation from experts with different regional backgrounds; and the *salience, credibility,* and *legitimacy* that this information can then muster in different developing countries.

While the content of assessments can be evaluated from a textual critique of assessment reports—in particular by means of counterfactual reasoning that assumes different constellations of participation (e.g., suppose 90 percent of IPCC authors were Africans)—the analysis of the perception of this information in developing countries requires detailed field studies. For this part of the analysis, I will thus focus on only one developing country, India. A study of India is particularly promising since the country has considerable scientific capabilities and an active environmentalist community, which makes it the most likely case for scientific information to find fertile ground. Any differences in the influence of assessments in India as compared to industrialized countries can thus be expected a fortiori in other, less endowed developing countries.

The study draws on primary sources from India and on a series of in-depth interviews and informal discussions with representatives of the Indian governmental bureaucracy, environmental and business organizations, and scientific community. (Given the sensitivity of the matter, it was agreed with interviewees beforehand that their name would not be disclosed with specific quotations; the list of all experts interviewed has been included at the end of this chapter.)

Global Environmental Politics in India

Before analyzing the salience, credibility, and legitimacy that global environmental assessments could muster in India, I will first lay out the political arena of global environmental issues in India, which would have to be influenced by assessments. It is hardly surprising that global environmental issues are significantly less important for decision makers in developing countries than in industrialized countries. In India, this relative marginalization of global environmental problems is generally explained by widespread poverty and the relatively low degree of economic development, which makes long-term issues such as climate change less salient in public debate than food security or industrialization.

Illustrative for this is a study that compared the perception of global environmental issues in India and Britain. This study concluded that

in global terms, the north south divide is a harsh reality when trying to define environmental problems. Those in the northern developed world believe that most environmental problems occur elsewhere—in Eastern and developing countries. Those in the South regard climate change and ozone holes as difficulties the Northern nations face. (Chapman 1997, 1; Chapman et al. 1997)

Most Indians surveyed by that study considered "development" their core project and the debate on global environmental policy, brought up by the North, rather as a new form of neocolonialism. For most Indian voters, the global debate seemed "irrelevant and unintelligible" (Chapman 1997).

Given this limited interest in global environmental issues in developing countries, it thus appears unlikely from the outset that assessments will have much influence. Parliamentarians in the world's largest democracy, for instance, need not bother about global environmental problems such as climate change since neither voters nor media do (own interviews; Jakobsen 1998, 14). In 1997–1998, to give one example, 373 questions to the Ministry of Environment and Forests (MoEF) on environmental issues had been brought forward in parliament by individual members, yet almost all of these questions were related to vehicular pollution, industrial pollution, or deforestation (MoEF 1998, 143).

Regarding global environmental politics, the Indian parliament is more a forum for the ministry to inform on foreign environmental policy than a locus of deliberation, debate, and decision making (own interviews; MoEF 1999, 63–65; Rajan 1997, 16).

Likewise, environmentalists remain focused on national and local issues, from the plight of peasants affected by pesticides to urban problems caused by hazardous fumes from local industry (own interviews; Jasanoff 1993). While Greenpeace International runs one of the most visible transnational campaigns on climate change and ozone depletion, its Indian branch focuses exclusively on local issues and devotes all its energies to toxic waste and pollution by the burgeoning shipwrecking industry in India (own interviews; Greenpeace 1998).

Regarding industry associations, at least in India they are on distribution lists of UNEP and other UN bodies, and their environmental officers are aware of global environmental assessments. Still, they do not pay much attention to these issues for lack of incentives, since generally no legislation is pending and consumers do not care about corporate responses to global environmental problems (own interviews). Only biodiversity is a national issue of concern, and different branches of industry, from agriculture to biotechnology, have a stake in this issue. And yet the Global Biodiversity Assessment appears to be irrelevant since it does not contain much information that industry would need for its decision making or its lobbying activities vis-à-vis the government's foreign environmental policy (own interviews).

Of course, a number of Indian experts are concerned about these issues and are part of global networks, especially the leading Indian scientists and some environmentalists. This embraces, however, only a small group of individuals and research institutes. It is open for debate to what degree this small group has any influence in the national political decision-making system: it might wield some influence in defining the appropriate policy within the issue domain, but hardly any in raising the importance of the issues themselves. Economic and development concerns remain decisive, and global environmental negotiations are generally seen in this context, with special regard to North-South imbalances in wealth and power. This is hardly a fertile ground for global environmental assessments.

The Influence of Global Environmental Assessments

Given this situation, assessments both on climate and biodiversity have further reduced their chance of extending and influencing the global environmental issue domain in India when they offered information that lacked salience, credibility, and legitimacy for a Southern audience. These limitations can be partly explained by asymmetric participation in the processes that were shaped by experts from industrialized countries. I will first elaborate on the question of salience, and then turn to credibility and legitimacy.

Salience

The salience of the information offered by international assessments was often restricted because it did not fully account for the particular situation and problems of developing countries and for their socioeconomic context (Biermann 2000). Such socioeconomic concerns of developing countries are, to name a few, the specific vulnerability of developing countries (now being addressed in the IPCC); technology transfer (which is also now being addressed by the IPCC; see IPCC 2000) and the technological independence of the South; equity issues; intellectual property rights and Northern "biopiracy" (in the case of India, for example, Northern patents on basmati rice and neem-tree products); or the safety of genetically modified organisms transferred into developing countries (see Gupta, chapter 3, this volume; Gupta 2000). Almost all experts interviewed in India claim that the Global Biodiversity Assessment and the IPCC have tended to neglect these issues (own interviews).

I focus here on a few examples of the Global Biodiversity Assessment, because I found this study to be a particularly illustrative case of an assessment with little use in providing valuable information on salient questions in India. From the outset, the Global Biodiversity Assessment is viewed in India as framed too strongly in the flora-and-fauna-protection paradigm, without paying sufficient attention to the situation of people living in the centers of biodiversity, for "you cannot think about biodiversity without thinking about people" (own interviews). According to Indian experts, the Global Biodiversity Assessment has conceptualized agriculture too much as mere production system and neglects local farmers and their traditional methods. It could be hypothesized that a Southern framing of a global biodiversity assessment would begin with the human person and analyze the biophysical world from this starting point. It would focus much more, for instance, on questions such as, to name a few, the role and relevance of traditional knowledge and seed varieties of local farmers and indigenous communities, or the debate on trade-related intellectual property rights and Northern patents on Southern knowledge and biological diversity.

The assessment's chapter on biotechnology serves as an interesting example. All of its ten lead authors and the coordinators came from industrialized countries. The peer review was done almost exclusively in the North: of twenty-two peer reviewers, only three came from developing countries. Considering this lack of Southern participation, it is hardly surprising that particular Southern concerns were not addressed, and that the assessment remains oblivious of the social, economic, and environmental repercussions of an increased reliance on biotechnology in developing countries (see Gupta 2000 and chapter 3, this volume; Shiva 1993). Biotechnology promises a new, second Green Revolution with production increases, but also raises the specter of the problems of the first Green Revolution, including costly investments in capital-intensive, high-tech applications and growing dependence on Northern suppliers, local wholesale traders, and frail agricultural monocultures. If, for example, progress in genetic engineering allows companies to create new seeds that farmers can no longer reproduce but must buy each spring anew, this will have a tremendous influence on social structures and local markets in the South. Many actors in developing countries fear that they might find themselves in a new form of dependence on multinational companies—a dependence that is not inevitable since indigenous and cheaper alternatives to biotechnology products often exist in developing countries.

In this range of different perceptions, the Global Biodiversity Assessment clearly takes sides. It dismisses traditional practices as disadvantageous without discussing further economic and social aspects as emphasized by Southern critics (Global Biodiversity Assessment 1995, 689). "Indirect impacts" of biotechnology are mentioned but not discussed. Moreover, the focus is on impacts on biodiversity, not on humans. Only the chapter's last page is devoted to "moral/ethical debates." Even here, the assessment's authors seem more afraid that "the debate . . . will lead to delays and restrictions on the use of genetic resources." The last paragraph of the biotechnology chapter finally addresses "disadvantaged groups," who are seen as the "relative losers [that] are seldom discussed" (Global Biodiversity Assessment 1995, 707). Yet the assessment itself did not discuss disadvantaged groups, except for three sentences that suggest that the real danger posed by disadvantaged groups will be a further loss of biodiversity, since the losers could feel compelled "to degrade their environment further" (Global Biodiversity Assessment 1995, 707).

The biotechnology revolution entails different social and economic benefits and risks for developing countries than for developed countries, and the failure of the Global Biodiversity Assessment to address these benefits and risks explains much of its lack of salience. At least one source of this neglect was the participation of lead authors exclusively from Northern countries. This is just one example: there are a number of quite similar examples in which global environmental assessments failed to gain salience in the South due to a negligence of specific Southern concerns (see in more detail Biermann 2000).

Credibility and Legitimacy

A related problem is the question of how actors in developing countries *perceive* the information offered by global environmental assessments in which they have been considerably underrepresented. Is the information viewed as *credible* (that is, authoritative and believable in its technical dimensions) and *legitimate* (that is, politically and ethically acceptable, for example because it results from a fair and open process)?

Regarding Indian expert communities, most actors are fairly critical of global environmental assessments, though their degree of criticism varies. For some, it is essentially "only science," but this appears to be a minority view. Many are wary of prejudices in the framing of assessments. Some watch the IPCC, for example, with "great suspicion." They argue that the IPCC is a "political-scientific" institution with little transparency and inherent Northern intellectual supremacy (own interviews). Also, the degree of Southern participation influences Indian perceptions of global environmental assessments ("you want to find Southern names on the list"). However, there is little confidence in the prospect of single Southern experts altering an assessment's agenda, for "the entire conceptualization has been done in the North, and Southern experts are often mere observers" (own interviews).

To many Indian experts, the Northern viewpoint in the IPCC and the Global Biodiversity Assessment seems "overwhelming" (own interviews). This is explained by financial dominance of industrialized countries, by quantitative preponderance of Northern experts, along with a relative lack of knowledgeable, eloquent, and energetic Southern experts capable of structuring and determining the scientific agenda from a minority position. Some Indian experts feel simply "outnumbered by the North," since "when we write one paper, they write ten" (own interviews). Such perception extends to the international literature that global environmental assessments purport to review and to synthesize. Some Indian scientists felt that peer reviewers in the North "operated on an entirely different wavelength" (own interviews). It is not surprising that extreme anti-Southern frames, such as the "value of life" debate within the IPCC, are received with considerable disapproval by many experts in the South.

A somewhat critical perception of global environmental assessments extends even to natural scientists. For atmospheric scientists, though cooperation with Northern institutes is important and Northern models and data are accepted and used in India, some admit a credibility gap inasmuch as "one has to keep an eye on the numbers" (own interviews). Northern researchers are not suspected of deliberate biases, since "all scientists are fair" (own interviews). It is anticipated, though, that data from the North are easily misleading if merely extrapolated to the South, and occasional linkages between Northern national interests and Northern science seem to be anticipated. It has not gone unnoticed, for example, that many industrialized countries have been changing the method for calculating their carbon dioxide sink capacity over the years, which resulted in overall "growth" of sink capacity of the major greenhouse gas emitters.

One example in which overwhelming participation of Northern scientists helped to shape an assessment in a way that led to sharp criticism by Southern experts, is the dichotomous framing of "anthropogenic" versus "natural" sources of greenhouse gas emissions in the second IPCC report (IPCC 1996c; see Biermann 2000). At the core of this debate stands the question of different responsibilities that individual nations bear for global environmental problems. While this responsibility is not necessarily linked to the outcome of political bargaining, high or low degrees of responsibility may well serve as potent arguments in international negotiations if and when universally accepted. To ascribe responsibility for global warming, numerous boundaries are to be negotiated, starting from ethical assumptions to more technical details of time horizons and sink capacities.

To illustrate this point, consider two expert statements, one from the North and one from the South, both exemplifying ethical judgments typical for either hemisphere. From a Northern perspective, it is typically suggested that the anthropogenic greenhouse effect is "the result of normal, not aberrant, human behavior involving uncountable, independent decisions in daily life by individuals, by industry, and by governments all over the globe" (Skolnikoff 1993, 184).

From a Southern perspective, however, this "take" on the problem is problematic. First, the notion of "all over the globe" is often seen as obfuscating the fact that Northern per capita emissions are much higher than in the South, since "the problem of global warming is caused not by emissions of greenhouse gases as such, but by excessive levels of per capita emissions of these gases." From a Southern perspective, "The accumulation in the earth's atmosphere of [greenhouse] gases is mainly the result of the gargantuan consumption of the developed countries, particularly the United States" (Agarwal and Narain 1991, 1). Southern experts argue that "if all countries had the living standards similar to those in India and China, there would not have been concentrations accumulated as of today" (Parikh 1994, 2943).

Second, the notion of "normal" behavior can also be seen differently from the Southern perspective. If "normal" is understood empirically as "everybody does it," the term hides, in the Southern view, that it is the emissions of a minority of the world's population that have created the need for international action. If "normal behavior" is defined as "legitimate behavior," this provides a normative justification for greenhouse gas emissions in the North, which are seen as "excessive" in the South. Some Southern experts and politicians, in their assessment of the causes of climate change, have therefore framed this dichotomy in terms of "basic," "subsistence," or "survival" emissions—that is, normal and indispensable behavior—versus "excessive" or "luxury" emissions, that is, superfluous and "aberrant" behavior (Agarwal and Narain 1991; Parikh et al. 1991; Chatterjee 1999a, 1999b). This basic distinction has been supported by the governments of India, China, and other developing countries.

How did the IPCC react to this clash of perspectives? When the first assessment was conceptualized, the Northern perspective prevailed. All emissions related to human activities were placed into one category of "anthropogenic" emissions with no further differentiation as to distinct human uses and values (for example, IPCC 1996c). The IPCC perspective thus remained restricted to a Northern framing with a natural science and technical approach to social activities. Technically, IPCC could have easily differentiated further. Although computer models must include all gases to forecast future climate change and to evaluate policy options, this could have been done by creating categories in addition to, or replacing, the simple dichotomy of "natural versus anthropogenic emissions" adopted by the IPCC. It is not inevitable, for example, that emissions from rice plants or digestive systems of certain animals are defined as "anthropogenic" and that essential activities such as food production are placed on the same level as emissions from automobiles, airplanes, or air-conditioners. If Southern views and interests had been given more consideration, the IPCC could have chosen, for example, a threefold approach, defining (1) "natural emissions," (2) "emissions accruing from food production (rice and livestock)," and (3) "other (luxury) anthropogenic emissions." No further efforts would have been needed since data for single sources of emissions are available.

Yet the IPCC did not distinguish between different types of emissions and thus effectively ignored the discussion of "luxury" versus "survival" emissions advanced by Southern actors, by commingling instead Southern rice farmers and Northern suburbanites into one category of "human-caused climate change." The result is a more equal sharing of responsibility for global warming between North and South, between Northern high per capita levels of fossil-fuel consumption and the Southern larger share of subsistence emissions from rice growing and animal husbandry.

The IPCC's way of framing emissions eventually had political consequences, because the approach of including all "anthropogenic" greenhouse gases, weighted only by their "global warming potential," has made its way into the climate regime and forms the basis for the Kyoto commitments of the North. The specific frame of IPCC might thus turn out to be its most crucial impact on the political process, at least with a view to North-South relations. The overwhelming participation of Northern experts in international networks has influenced the political bargaining outcome by framing the climate issue in a way that includes subsistence farming and animal husbandry in a legally binding regime set up to solve a problem that has not been caused, as Southern experts would argue, by the subsistence farmers themselves. By influencing the way gains and losses are politically distributed, IPCC may have thus evolved into a source of "soft power" (Keohane and Nye 1998) in international relations: the power of dominating the international processes of problem definition and assessment. This again might have reduced the overall legitimacy of the assessment reports in the South.

Other legitimacy problems in assessments often arise out of different perceptions of equity considerations, which most Southern actors see at the center of global environmental negotiations. Both the 1992 UN Framework Convention on Climate Change and the 1992 Convention on Biological Diversity mention the need for "equity," as a "principle" of all climate policy or in the context of the "equitable sharing of benefits" of the utilization of genetic resources (Biermann 1999; Harris 1997). Yet what equity does mean in practice is a question very much open to debate. In the beginning, IPCC had not considered notions of "equity" in global warming policy, such as the debate on "fair" entitlements to emissions. The second assessment report of 1995 includes some legal analysis of equity, yet there was not much of a link between this chapter and the overall assessment design, and equity was dealt with as a fringe issue. Southern experts and representatives of nongovernmental organizations have repeatedly complained about this treatment of equity in the assessment process.

After the participation of experts from developing countries in the IPCC had significantly increased during the third assessment cycle, equity concerns gained importance. In February 1999, for example, a clash among Southern and Northern IPCC authors occurred, when several economists from industrialized countries openly impugned a "crosscutting chapter" on equity, sustainability, and development written by a World Bank scientist from Sri Lanka, demanding that this text not be included. Clearly, IPCC's extensive peer-review system is designed to reject papers that do not meet scientific criteria for credibility: but when a chapter on equity and climate change by a Southern scientist is rejected by a group of Northern economists, this suggests a clash between Northern and Southern perspectives on global warming, on economics, and maybe on the general role of science.

Equity concerns of the South were marginalized in the Global Biodiversity Assessment as well, which may have reduced its legitimacy. For example, the assessment has largely ignored the issue of sharing of benefits from biotechnology. For a Northern audience, questions of benefit sharing may not fit into a chapter on new technologies, since technological innovation and progress generally benefit rich industrialized countries, both their citizens who can afford to purchase new products and their companies that have the financial means to pursue cutting-edge research or to buy patents and licenses. For developing countries, however, the situation is generally different.

Added to this comes the Southern concern that the biotechnological revolution relies heavily on genetic resources from developing countries that are processed into products protected by Northern patent laws. Developing countries therefore pressed hard to have the biodiversity convention require that benefits be equitably shared and that genetic resources be accepted as part of the sovereign resources of a country. Article 1 of the 1992 convention hence states three objectives of equal rank: conservation of biological diversity, sustainable use of its components, and fair and equitable sharing of benefits arising out of the utilization of genetic resources. For developing countries, the second and third objectives were crucial conditions for joining a treaty regime that they see as involving developmental as well as environmental concerns (Mugabe et al. 1996, 1997; Henne 1997).

However, these three principles of the convention are not equally covered by the Global Biodiversity Assessment. The overall framing of the assessment centers on the convention's first objective, conservation of biological diversity. The second objective, sustainable use of its components, is discussed, yet annexed to the conservation theme. The convention's third fundamental objective, the "fair and equitable sharing of the benefits" of the use of biodiversity, is almost entirely ignored. Only a few lines have been devoted to the question of benefit sharing, suggesting that the claim of developing countries and the convention's third objective were not ethical in a "conventional sense" (Global Biodiversity Assessment 1995, 707). In sum, this neglect of Southern concerns has significantly limited the perception of legitimacy of the assessment in developing countries such as India.

Issue Development through Global Environmental Assessments

Nonetheless, global environmental assessments could influence issue development to some degree in spite of these salience, credibility, and legitimacy gaps perceived in India (Biermann 2001, 2002). First, direct participation of Indian scientists in the global environmental assessments has led to some capacity building, by increasing the information available to Indian scientists, by establishing contacts between Northern and Indian researchers, and by providing financial and technological support to Indian scientists. For example, the IPCC Trust Fund supports participation of developing countries in IPCC meetings, since most Southern researchers cannot afford to participate in international conferences unless international or foreign donors reimburse the costs. At least one developing-country participant for each IPCC writing team meeting is now usually supported financially (own interviews; Agrawala 1998b, 630). This capacity building is small but still makes a difference: without the international assessment, communication between Southern and Northern scientists would be even more limited.

Second, issue development in India was affected by Northern assessments to the extent that Indian scientists responded with "counterassessments" meant to verify or refute data believed to have negative political consequences for India. A widely known example is the Indian Methane Campaign (own interviews; Kandlikar and Sagar 1999). Developing countries account for a proportionately larger share of global emissions of methane—a potent greenhouse gas—than of global carbon dioxide emissions, because a substantial amount of methane is emitted by agrarian activities, notably animal husbandry and rice farming. In 1990, the U.S. Environmental Protection Agency (EPA 1990) published a study that suggested that India alone would account for more than one-third of global methane emissions from rice paddies—a result that would, if not contested, certainly have influenced climate negotiations. On publication of this Northern assessment, Indian national research institutions launched a focused global environmental assessment, the "Indian Methane Campaign." More than fifty researchers from sixteen Indian institutions joined the "Campaign." Its result indicated that Indian methane emissions from rice paddies were roughly a tenth of what the EPA had suggested, and that global methane emissions were accordingly lower too. This reactive assessment process has broadened into assessing all greenhouse gases to provide the national communications required under Article 12 of the climate convention, and in a sense, the Northern debate has helped to increase communication and cooperation among Indian scientists on climate-related issues (own interviews; Kandlikar and Sagar 1999).

Third, global environmental assessments have influenced issue development by pointing out particular problems for India or by raising concerns about issues that have then been the focus of Indian research. The effect of shaping research agendas by global environmental assessments seems to be particularly strong in developing countries, since in the South, lack of resources places stricter constraints on researchers. In particular, scientists at the national research institutions in India concentrate their work on issues that they perceive as particularly relevant for the national interest and that are not sufficiently covered by global environmental assessments. While most IPCC research addresses general climate modeling and mitigation options, Indian scientists have directed most of their scarce resources on assessing adverse effects of climate change on India. The Working Group on Environment for the Ninth Five-Year Plan

(1997), for example, expressly included in their terms of reference the assessment of adverse impacts of climate change on India.

Fourth, issue development in India has been influenced by global environmental assessments inasmuch as Indian institutes are often partly funded by foreign foundations, foreign governments, and international organizations. International bodies such as the Global Environment Facility, the World Bank, UNDP or UNEP, or foreign foundations, are often closely linked with global environmental assessments, and the IPCC or the Global Biodiversity Assessment play some role in their policy development. Insofar as domestic decisions are made with a view to the availability of foreign funding, some impacts of global environmental assessments on shaping the domestic debate can thus be assumed.

Because the initiative for projects is usually taken by Indian counterparts, the *direct* impact of foreign funding on details of the Indian research and assessment agenda appears limited and is often not seen as such, in particular when donors' interests and the institute's agenda converge. On the other hand, issues that are not financed cannot be analyzed for lack of resources, since private organizations "have to earn money" and "any assessment must be financially viable" (own interviews).

Addressing Participation in Institutional Design

Taken together, the influence of global environmental assessments on issue development in India has been limited. Regarding climate change and biodiversity, India's politics and policies changed little in response to the information offered by global environmental assessments. In climate change, the issue domain was small and issue development in its early stages. Biodiversity protection had already been disputed in public and parliament before the Global Biodiversity Assessment was initiated. Still, global environmental assessments had some effects on issue development. They influenced the research priorities of Indian scientists and helped build some research capacities. They were probably also crucial in raising concerns about the climate problem by initiating research on possible climate-related monsoon changes and sea-level rise, which emphasized India's precarious vulnerability to global warming (Biermann

2001). By and large, this fed back into assessment processes within the Indian government, yet with little effect on negotiating strategies.

This limited influence of global environmental assessments in India seems to differ from other countries studied in this book. It appears that assessments, in order to have any influence in developing countries such as India, have to meet different thresholds to effect changes in developing countries. Global environmental assessments have to provide information that can compete with the pressing short term concerns that dominate much of the policy agenda in the South to gain salience among decision makers and the general public.

The same holds for credibility and legitimacy. Global environmental assessments, largely relying on Northern expertise, need to meet special standards of trustworthiness to be perceived as legitimate and credible in the South, given a general context of fierce contestation between both hemispheres about political solutions to environmental problems. The issue domain in India, and probably in other developing countries too, reveals an inherent suspicion about how global environmental issues are framed and what concerns are addressed. The still relatively small influence of global environmental assessments in India can be explained, among other factors, by the overwhelming participation of experts from industrialized countries. This asymmetry in participation resulted in a specific compilation of information that was often perceived as having little credibility, legitimacy, or salience in countries like India.

The relatively low participation of Indian scientists also restricted the possibility of direct links through the exchange of researchers. Eventually, this limits the sense of ownership of assessments among decision makers, who often see assessments as not being fully reflective of the information needs, socioeconomic context, and political interests of developing countries. Global environmental assessments are thus often viewed as something foreign that is imposed on India by the North. Not surprisingly, this confines the influence of such processes compared to their influence in industrialized countries.

One way to redress this situation would be to increase the participation of Southern experts. This call for increased participation is not new. Already by 1989 the IPCC plenary had agreed to establish a Special Committee on the Participation of Developing Countries based on parity representation, which means that five of the committee's members came from developing and five from industrialized countries (Agrawala 1998b). This committee presented to the IPCC plenary in 1990 several factors that limited Southern participation in the IPCC process.

The IPCC has since then taken a number of actions to remove obstacles that impair developing-country participation, and over the years, the number of developing-country participants has increased (Agrawala 1998b). This could be interpreted as successful "learning" of an assessment institution, which has become the focus of much research interest recently (Siebenhüner 2002a, 2002b). For example, to increase the communication of scientific knowledge and IPCC findings, major documents are now translated into all six UN languages, and the IPCC takes more account of geographic representation as well as representation of the views of environmental and business organizations (own interviews; IPCC 1997). Current IPCC rules of procedure require each working group to be chaired by one developed- and one developing-country scientist. Each chapter of assessment reports must have at least one lead author from a developing country. Participation of developing-country scientists in the most recent assessment cycle of the IPCC thus appears much more visible than in previous rounds. Most strikingly, India now provides, with Rajendra K. Pachauri of The Energy and Resources Institute in Delhi, the chair of IPCC.

Nonetheless, financing remains a problem. Government-funded research institutes in developing countries normally lack funds to send their scientists to professional conferences abroad. This has been attenuated for direct participation in IPCC working groups. Still, general communication between Indian and foreign scientists is scarce compared to transatlantic or intra-European cooperation. Moreover, traveling and communicating alone are not sufficient to enable developing-country experts to write or review chapters for international assessments, since working time in itself is a scarce and costly resource. In particular, private institutes are sometimes unable to permit their staff to devote their time to (unpaid) international assessments if this is not accompanied by project funds (own interviews). The difficult financial situation in India thus privileges participation of researchers with sufficient financial support to widely communicate on a regular basis with Northern scientific communities. Added to this is the general lack of interest in global environmental issues within the government, which submitted too late, for example, the list of Indian experts suitable for participation in the third assessment cycle. Some Indian researchers also felt poorly informed about the recruitment process for the IPCC's third assessment cycle and complained of a lack of transparency on the side of the government, of the better-connected Indian institutes, and of the IPCC (own interviews).

Unlike the IPCC with its series of reports, the Global Biodiversity Assessment has been produced only once. The scientific assessment of the state of global biodiversity has its place in the framework of the convention organs, notably the Subsidiary Body on Scientific, Technical, and Technological Advice. This body has evolved, however, into an overtly political body that some observers have likened to a "miniature" Conference of the Parties, with little influence from scientists. In this context it has been argued, for instance by the German Advisory Council on Global Change (2001), that the scientific assessment of the threats to biodiversity should be conducted in a more science-based body, for example in the form of an Intergovernmental Panel on Biological Diversity, which might be structured along the lines of the IPCC. If such a body is set up, participation of developing countries will be a disputed issue again, and given the special nature of biological diversity and its various uses and threats, balanced geographic representation in this issue area could be more important than in the case of the IPCC. The Millennium Assessment has shown, however, that assessment managers have learned from the shortcomings of the Global Biodiversity Assessment and have opted from the very outset for a more geographically balanced approach.

Eventually, the need to increase participation of Southern experts will require enhancing the endogenous research capacity in the South (see also Agrawala 1998b, 632; Kandlikar and Sagar 1999). Two ways of doing this are conceivable. One would be increasing the funds of the IPCC or of a future global biodiversity assessment to enable them not only to reimburse travel costs of developing-country participants at the IPCC but to organize Southern contributions as commissioned papers— that is, to pay for them. At least in the Indian context, this would help to achieve a more balanced participation of Indian scientists and would assist in building up more endogenous capacities within the Indian national research institutes. If Indian scientists, for example, could base their assessments and statements to their government less on Northern data than on global circulation models that have been developed and are used within India itself, this might influence the perception of these data in the Indian decision-making system. A second possibility would be to provide more research capacities directly, for instance through the Global Environment Facility, with similar effects.

After all, merely increasing the participation of developing-country experts in global environmental assessments might not suffice. Even a balanced geographic representation of views in the assessments does not help to overcome the geographic imbalance in the underlying scientific capacities between North and South. Since global environmental assessments are only meant to collect and evaluate existing knowledge, even assessments with equal representation cannot change the inequalities in the global research community. This, however, calls for more than adjusting the design of global environmental assessments: it calls for a fundamental reform of the way science in North and South is conducted.

Acknowledgments

This chapter has benefited from valuable comments on earlier versions from William C. Clark, Carsten Helm, Jill Jäger, Milind Kandlikar, Robert O. Keohane, Ronald Mitchell, Ambuj Sagar, Eileen Shea, Bernd Siebenhüner, Udo E. Simonis, and the 1998–1999 Research Fellows of the Global Environmental Assessment Project, Harvard University. The study would not have been possible without financial support from the German Academic Exchange Service (DAAD) and from the Belfer Center for Science and International Affairs, Harvard University, as well as institutional support from Jawaharlal Nehru University, New Delhi. I owe a considerable debt to Professor Rahmatullah Khan, (then) Rector and Jawaharlal Nehru Chair in Environmental Law, Jawaharlal Nehru University, for welcoming me as a visiting scholar at the School of International Studies, thus enabling this research in India. Also, I wish to thank all interviewees, without whom the present study would not have been possible.

References

Agarwal, Anil, and Sunita Narain. 1991. *Global Warming in an Unequal World: A Case of Environmental Colonialism*. New Delhi: Centre for Science and Environment.

Agrawala, Shardul. 1998a. Context and early origins of the Intergovernmental Panel on Climate Change. *Climatic Change* 39: 605–620.

Agrawala, Shardul. 1998b. Structural and process history of the Intergovernmental Panel on Climate Change. *Climatic Change* 39: 621–642.

Biermann, Frank. 1999. Justice in the greenhouse: Perspectives from international law. In Ferenc L. Tóth, ed., *Fair Weather? Equity Concerns in Climate Change*, 160–172. London: Earthscan.

Biermann, Frank. 2000. *Science as Power in International Environmental Negotiations: Global Environmental Assessments between North and South*. ENRP Discussion Paper E-2000–17. Cambridge, MA: John F. Kennedy School of Government, Harvard University. Available at http://environment.harvard.edu/gea.

Biermann, Frank. 2001. Big science, small impacts—in the South? The influence of global environmental assessments on expert communities in India. *Global Environmental Change* 11(4): 297–309.

Biermann, Frank. 2002. Institutions for scientific advice: Global environmental assessments and their influence in developing countries. *Global Governance* 8(2): 195–219.

Chapman, Graham. 1997. *Environmentalism, the Mass Media and the Global Silent Majority*. Global Environmental Change Programme Briefings No. 15. Brighton: University of Sussex.

Chapman, Graham, Keval Kumar, Caroline Fraser, and Ivor Gaber. 1997. *Environmentalism and the Mass Media: The North-South Divide*. London: Routledge.

Chatterjee, Kalipada. 1999a. Climate change and ozone layer protocols (part I). *Development Alternatives* 9(2): 5–7.

Chatterjee, Kalipada. 1999b. COP [Conference of the Parties] 4 in Buenos Aires: The city of good airs. *Development Alternatives* 9(1): 8–13.

Dingwerth, Klaus. 2001. *Die Wissenschaft in der internationalen Klimapolitik: Partizipation, Kommunikation und Effektivität* [The science in international climate politics: Participation, communication, and effectiveness]. Berlin: Freie Universität Berlin, mimeo (on file with author).

EPA [U.S. Environmental Protection Agency]. 1990. *Methane Emissions and Opportunities for Control*. Washington, DC: EPA.

Farrell, Alexander, and Terry Keating. 1998. *Multi-Jurisdictional Air Pollution Assessment: A Comparison of the Eastern United States and Western Europe.* ENRP Discussion Paper E-98-12. Cambridge, MA: John F. Kennedy School of Government, Harvard University. Available at http://environment.harvard.edu/gea.

German Advisory Council on Global Change. 2001. *World in Transition: Reforming International Environmental Institutions.* London: Earthscan. Full text available at www.wbgu.de.

Global Biodiversity Assessment. 1995. V. H. Heywood, ed., and R. T. Watson, chair, *Global Biodiversity Assessment.* Published for the United Nations Environment Programme. Cambridge: Cambridge University Press.

Global Environment Facility. 1994. *Instrument for the Establishment of the Restructured Global Environment Facility,* 16 March 1994, reprinted in 33 International Legal Materials 1273 (1994).

Greenpeace. 1998. *Ships for Scrap: Steel and Toxic Wastes for Asia: The Health and Environmental Hazards in Recipient States—A Fact-Finding Mission to the Indian Shipbreaking Yards in Alang and Bombay in October 1998.* Hamburg: Greenpeace.

Gupta, Aarti. 2000. Governing trade in genetically modified organisms: The Cartagena Protocol on Biosafety. *Environment* 42(4): 23–33.

Harris, Paul G. 1997. Environment, history, and international justice. *Journal of International Studies* (Tokyo) 40: 1–33.

Henne, Gudrun. 1997. "Mutually agreed terms" in the Convention on Biological Diversity: Requirements under public international law. In John Mugabe, Charles Victor Barber, Gudrun Henne, Lyle Glowka, and Antonio La Viña, eds., *Access to Genetic Resources: Strategies for Sharing Benefits,* 71–91. Nairobi: African Centre for Technology Studies Press.

IPCC [Intergovernmental Panel on Climate Change]. 1996a. *Climate Change 1995: Economic and Social Dimensions of Climate Change.* Cambridge: Cambridge University Press.

IPCC [Intergovernmental Panel on Climate Change]. 1996b. *Climate Change 1995: Impacts, Adaptations and Mitigation of Climate Change.* Cambridge: Cambridge University Press.

IPCC [Intergovernmental Panel on Climate Change]. 1996c. *Climate Change 1995: The Science of Climate Change.* Cambridge: Cambridge University Press.

IPCC [Intergovernmental Panel on Climate Change]. 1997. *The IPCC Third Assessment Report Decision Paper.* Approved at the XIIIth session of the IPCC, 21–28 September 1997, Republic of the Maldives. Available at http://www.ipcc.ch.

IPCC [Intergovernmental Panel on Climate Change]. 1998. In Robert T. Watson, Marufu C. Zinyowera, and Richard H. Moss, eds., *The Regional Impacts of*

Climate Change: An Assessment of Vulnerability. IPCC Working Group II special report. Cambridge: Cambridge University Press.

IPCC [Intergovernmental Panel on Climate Change]. 2000. In B. Metz, O. R. Davidson, J.-W. Martens, S. N. M. van Rooijen, and L. V. W. McGrory, eds., *Methodological and Technological Issues in Technology Transfer.* IPCC Working Group III special report. Cambridge: Cambridge University Press.

Jäger, Jill. 1998. Current thinking on using scientific findings in environmental policy-making. *Environmental Modeling and Assessment* 3: 143–153.

Jakobsen, Susanne. 1998. *India's Position on Climate Change from Rio to Kyoto: A Policy Analysis.* CDR Working Paper 98.11. Copenhagen: Center for Udviklingsforskning (Center for Development Research).

Jasanoff, Sheila. 1993. India at the crossroads in global environmental policy. *Global Environmental Change* 3(1): 32–52.

Jung, Wolfgang. 2000. *Expert Advice in Global Environmental Decision-Making: How Close Should Science and Policy Get?* ENRP Discussion Paper 99–14. Cambridge, MA: John F. Kennedy School of Government, Harvard University.

Kandlikar, Milind, and Ambuj Sagar. 1999. Climate change research and analysis in India: An integrated assessment of a South-North divide. *Global Environmental Change* 9(2): 119–138.

Keating, Terry, and Alexander Farrell. 1998. *Problem Framing and Model Formulation: The Regionality of Tropospheric Ozone in the United States and Europe.* ENRP Discussion Paper E-98-11. Cambridge, MA: John F. Kennedy School of Government, Harvard University. Available at http://environment.harvard.edu/gea.

Keohane, Robert O., and Joseph S. Nye, Jr. 1998. Power and interdependence in the information age. *Foreign Affairs* 77(5): 81–94.

Mitchell, Ronald B. 1998. Sources of transparency: Information systems in international regimes. *International Studies Quarterly* 42(1): 109–130.

MoEF [Ministry of Environment and Forests, Government of India]. 1998. *Annual Report 1997–1998.* New Delhi: Environmental Information System, Ministry of Environment and Forests, Government of India.

MoEF [Ministry of Environment and Forests, Government of India]. 1999, January. *New Initiatives, New Programmes: First 300 Days of Government.* New Delhi: Environmental Information System, Ministry of Environment and Forests, Government of India.

Mugabe, John, Charles Victor Barber, Gudrun Henne, Lyle Glowka, and Antonio La Viña. 1996. *Managing Access to Genetic Resources: Towards Strategies for Benefit-Sharing.* Nairobi and Washington, DC: African Centre for Technology Studies and World Resources Institute.

Mugabe, John, Charles Victor Barber, Gudrun Henne, Lyle Glowka, and Antonio La Viña, eds. 1997. *Access to Genetic Resources: Strategies for Sharing Benefits.* Nairobi: African Centre for Technology Studies Press.

Parikh, Jyoti. 1994, November 5–12. North-South issues for climate change. *Economic and Political Weekly* (Mumbai), pp. 2940–2943.

Parikh, Jyoti, Kirit Parikh, Subir Gokarn, J. P. Painuly, Bibhas Saha, and Vibhooti Shukla. 1991. *Consumption Patterns: The Driving Force of Environmental Stress*. Report prepared for the United Nations Conference on Environment and Development. Bombay [now Mumbai]: Indira Gandhi Institute of Development Research.

Rajan, Mukund Govind. 1997. Global environmental politics: India and the North-South politics of global environmental issues. Delhi: Oxford University Press.

Ravenhill, John. 1990. The North-South balance of power. *International Affairs* 66(4): 731–748.

Shiva, Vandana. 1993. *Monocultures of the mind: Perspectives on biodiversity and biotechnology*. Penang: Third World Network.

Siebenhüner, Bernd. 2002a. How do scientific assessments learn? Part 1. Conceptual framework and case study of the IPCC. *Environmental Science and Policy* 5: 411–420.

Siebenhüner, Bernd. 2002b. How do scientific assessments learn? Part 2. Case study of the LRTAP assessment and comparative conclusions. *Environmental Science and Policy* 5: 421–427.

Skolnikoff, Eugene B. 1993. *The Elusive Transformation: Science, Technology, and the Evolution of International Politics*. Princeton, NJ: Princeton University Press.

Social Learning Group. 2001. *Learning to Manage Global Environmental Risks: A Comparative History of Social Responses to Climate Change, Ozone Depletion, and Acid Rain*. Cambridge, MA: MIT Press.

UNEP [United Nations Environment Programme]. 1995. *UNEP Releases First Global Biodiversity Assessment Report*. UNEP Press Release HE/916 of 14 November 1995.

Working Group on Environment for the Ninth Five Year Plan, Government of India. 1997. *Report to the Planning Commission, Government of India, for the Ninth Five Year Plan (1997–2002)*. New Delhi: Government of India. Unpublished.

Interviews

If not stated otherwise, all interviews were conducted by the author in New Delhi or Mumbai from January to March, 1999.

Anil Agarwal, Director, Centre for Science and Environment, New Delhi.

V. Asthana, Professor, School of Environmental Sciences, Jawaharlal Nehru University, New Delhi.

Tarun Bose, Professor, Jadavpur University, Calcutta.

Kalipada Chatterjee, Manager, Global Environmental Systems Group, Development Alternatives, New Delhi.

Hemant Datye, Fellow, Indira Gandhi Institute of Development Research, Mumbai.

Uma Garud, Additional Secretary, Federation of Indian Chambers of Commerce and Industry, New Delhi.

Nirmala Karunan, Greenpeace International, New Delhi.

Rahmatullah Khan, (then) Rector and Jawaharlal Nehru Chair in Environmental Law, School of International Studies, Jawaharlal Nehru University, New Delhi.

Murari Lal, Chief Scientific Officer, Centre for Atmospheric Sciences, Indian Institute of Technology, New Delhi; Convening Lead Author, Intergovernmental Panel on Climate Change.

V. S. Mani, Professor, School of International Studies, Jawaharlal Nehru University, New Delhi; Secretary-General, Indian Society of International Law.

Abraham P. Meachinkara, Ministry of Environment and Forests, Government of India.

Sunita Narain, (then) Deputy Director, Centre for Science and Environment, New Delhi.

Rajendra K. Pachauri, Director, Tata Energy Research Institute, New Delhi; (then) Vice Chair Intergovernmental Panel on Climate Change [today IPCC Chair].

P. H. Parekh, Advocate Supreme Court of India, President of Supreme Court Advocates on Record Association; Chairman of Consumer Education and Research Centre, Ahmedabad; Secretary-General of the International Institute of Human Rights, New Delhi.

Jyoti K. Parikh, Professor and Acting Director, Indira Gandhi Institute of Development Research, Mumbai.

Kirit S. Parikh, Professor and Founder Director, Indira Gandhi Institute of Development Research, Mumbai.

The Honourable Shri Suresh Prabhakar Prabhu, (then) Union Cabinet Minister of Environment and Forests, Government of India, New Delhi.

Lakshmi Raghupathy, Joint Director, Ministry of Environment and Forests, Government of India.

P. S. Ramakrishnan, Professor, School of Environmental Sciences, Jawaharlal Nehru University, New Delhi.

Shikhar Ranjan, International Legal Studies Division, School of International Studies, Jawaharlal Nehru University, New Delhi, and Affiliate, Greenpeace International, New Delhi.

K. Vinayak Rao, (then) Research Affiliate, School of International Studies, Jawaharlal Nehru University, New Delhi; former Senior Policy Analyst with Centre for Science and Environment and Fellow at Tata Energy Research Institute, both New Delhi.

Pia Sethi, Research Associate, Tata Energy Research Institute, New Delhi.

T. P. Singh, Fellow, Tata Energy Research Institute, New Delhi.

Sharmila B. Srikanth, Area Convenor, Tata Energy Research Institute, New Delhi.

Robert T. Watson, (then) Chair of the Intergovernmental Panel on Climate Change. Interview with GEA Project Participants, Harvard University, December 1998.

5

Assessment Information in European Politics: East and West

Stacy D. VanDeveer

Introduction

The science and policymaking of European cooperation on air pollution remains dominated by the continent's divisions between East and West. International science cannot be separated from international politics when pan-European consensus positions are constructed primarily by Western European scientific and technical experts. Western European expertise, state interests, and resource dedication drive policymaking and scientific agendas associated with transboundary air pollution in Europe. As outlined below, the initial framing of transboundary air pollution problems in Europe—primarily in terms of acid rain—involved little participation from state officials or scientists from Central and Eastern European countries.

The Long-Range Transboundary Air Pollution (LRTAP) Convention and its related activities, situated within the United Nations Economic Commission for Europe (UNECE), organize European air pollution assessment and policymaking. International environmental policymaking around acidification and related international scientific assessments are driven largely by leading states and scientific communities in Northern and Western Europe. Scientific research and the interests of lead states simultaneously drive assessment and multilateral policymaking agendas. These leaders framed the initial transboundary pollution issue around acidification and "venue shopped" to locate assessment efforts within multilateral organizations that could garner greater international attention, such as the Organization for Economic Cooperation and Development (OECD) and the 1972 United Nations Conference on the

Human Environment (UNCHE). Later, officials from lead countries pushed to move assessment processes to the UNECE, where they could be explicitly linked to state-controlled policymaking authority and where participation in assessment and policymaking could be expanded to include individuals and states from the Eastern Bloc.

This chapter draws attention to unequal participation in assessment processes and policymaking between Western and Eastern European state officials and scientific and technical experts. Asymmetric participation, driven by such factors as the organizational venue of assessment and unequal distribution of scientific capabilities among states, involves a risk of biases in favor of those participating. Access to scientific capabilities enables states to define agendas and fashion agreements more suited to their needs, with science becoming "politics by other means" (Harding 1991, 10). Many recent analyses of scientific and technical information—in domestic and international settings—view scientific and technological information, including most "facts," as socially constructed (e.g., Haas 1992; Jasanoff 1990; Jasanoff and Wynne 1998). Such knowledge is viewed as contingent on participants' views, organizations, and the social institutions involved in its creation. Participation-related issues are important factors in the credibility and legitimation of knowledge (Andonova, chapter 6, this volume).

The argument presented here is based on documentary research as well as fieldwork in eight European countries and over fifty personal interviews with over three dozen current and former LRTAP participants (governmental and nongovernmental) and Central and Eastern European (CEE) environmental policymakers and researchers (see the list at the end of the chapter).

Initial framing of transboundary acidification issues and subsequent development of LRTAP assessment agendas and policy outcomes have been driven largely by Western European participation and interests. Most of the extensive literature on the international and domestic politics of LRTAP has not focused on Central and Eastern European states' behavior or the role of assessment information in these states (Connolly 1997; Levy 1993; McCormick 1997, 1998; Munton 1998; Selin 2000; Social Learning Group 2001a, 2001b; Underdal and Hanf 2000; Victor, Raustiala, and Skolnikoff 1998; Wetstone and Rosencranz 1983;

Wettestad 1997, 2002). This chapter analyzes the influence of LRTAP assessment on CEE scientific and technical research and on domestic environmental policy. It shows that, although the credibility of Western-driven research and assessment remained relatively high, the salience of acidification issues and policy remained low among CEE officials. Increased EU policymaking activity, also driven by interests of Western Europe's environmental policy leaders, has broadened the frame of transboundary air pollution issues well beyond acidification concerns. CEE responses to these changes demonstrate the multiple sources of issue salience for state officials. Transboundary pollution issues have rarely been inherently salient to CEE officials, but have been salient when linked to various types of political power and "nonenvironmental" interests. The concluding section of the chapter demonstrates the importance of participation patterns and strategic choices regarding the organizational venues of multilateral assessment and policymaking.

Acid Rain and Western Europe

The burning of fossil fuels releases sulfur dioxide and nitrogen oxides into the air that can be deposited up to hundreds of miles from their sources. Sulfur and nitrogen oxides form acids that can damage terrestrial and aquatic ecosystems as well as human materials. This section reviews the near-simultaneous emergence of the long-range transboundary air pollution issues onto international scientific and political agendas and the framing of such pollution primarily in terms of acidification. Discussion of various multinational assessments illustrates the importance of the interrelated factors of participation patterns, organizational venue, and the perceived interests of leaders within the issue domain. These leaders controlled the initial framing of the transboundary pollution issue by "venue shopping" to locate assessment efforts within existing multilateral organizations—such as the OECD and the UNCHE—that could garner acidification issues international attention. Later, officials from lead countries pushed to move assessment processes to the UNECE where they could be explicitly linked to state-controlled policymaking authority and where participation in assessment and policymaking could be expanded to include individuals and states from the Eastern Bloc.

The Acid Rain Issue Emerges

Acidification science and politics, and formal assessment efforts, prior to the establishment of LRTAP were driven by Scandinavian nationals concerned that their countries' environments were victims of transboundary pollution. These initial concerns prompted international assessment efforts and assessment participation patterns that framed European transboundary air pollution discourse in terms of acidification. The most active "early movers" around transboundary air pollution and acidification were Swedish scientists and public officials (Cowling 1982; Bäckstrand and Selin 2000). Swedish scientists, including Svante Oden, began to argue that a link existed between increasing levels of pollution in precipitation and the environmental damage observed by others in fields such as limnology, atmospheric chemistry, forestry, and agriculture (Oden 1967, 1968; Cowling 1982; McCormick 1997). In both the popular press and scientific journals, Oden claimed that a "chemical war" was being waged among European countries, creating a flurry of popular and scientific interest in acid rain in the Nordic states (Cowling 1982). Prior to Oden's work, published attempts to raise scientific and public awareness of acidification went unnoticed. Oden served as an information producer and an information framer, brokering knowledge "so that questions of value were rendered as questions of fact," increasing public interest and, in turn, the dedication of public resources to further research (Litfin 1995, 255). Once preliminary scientific studies suggested that acidifying substances could travel long distances and were doing so, downwind states introduced acid rain issues to the international agenda, calling for multilateral research, data gathering, analysis, and policymaking. Thus, the states that worked to "internationalize" issues associated with long-range transboundary air pollution were those in which ill effects had already been observed.

Early Assessment: Framing Acid Rain

Three arenas of scientific and political cooperation and consensus building framed the issue domain of acid rain in Europe prior to negotiation of LRTAP: (1) the Air Management Research Group (AMRG), sponsored by the OECD in the late 1960s; (2) the 1972 UNCHE in Stockholm; and (3) the data gathering, analysis, and scientific assessment activities over the course of the 1970s done by the OECD and the Norwegian Interdisciplinary Research Programme (the so-called SNSF Project). All three of these pre-LRTAP cooperation arenas included formal assessment processes as central aspects of their work (see box 5.1). None involved significant Central and Eastern European participation.

As box 5.1 demonstrates, pre-LRTAP assessment processes on transboundary air pollution were connected to policymaking debates. Formal assessment processes were largely "science for policy" from the beginning. Long-range transboundary air pollution issues were generally framed by overlapping Scandinavian scientific assessment and policymaking communities. The members of these communities, and their respective governments, came to perceive their countries as the victims of damage from the long-range transport of pollutants. LRTAP's initial focus on acid rain issues resulted in large part from the persistent interest in these issues among Scandinavian scientific researchers and public officials.

The OECD research raised awareness among many Western European policymakers and segments of the public and helped delegitimize denials of the occurrence of transboundary pollution transport. A preliminary report on the OECD program stated: "One conclusion which is certain is that pollution travels between countries to a greater or lesser extent" (Reed 1976, 202). Wetstone and Rosencranz (1983, 135) noted that "it was OECD's groundbreaking research and monitoring work that made many national and international policy-makers aware, for the first time, of the extent and importance of transboundary air pollution in Europe." OECD data gathering and assessment work was well received within scientific communities and increased the salience of acid rain issues with policymakers and the public. Air pollution issues contributed to general public environmental concern in Northern Europe, further increasing the salience of the issue to public officials.

State officials found the OECD an attractive forum for a transboundary air pollution research program because it is a "talk shop" whose advisory reports, recommendations, and pronouncements are frequently ignored by policymakers. The OECD was an attractive home for assessment precisely because it was not a forum for official interstate treaty

Box 5.1
Three pre-LRTAP arenas for international assessment

Arena 1: The Air Management Research Group

Beginning in 1968, the OECD sponsored an Air Quality Research Group (AMRG) that helped to build the initial political networks and discursive foundation for OECD involvement in multilateral efforts to assess and address air pollution issues throughout the 1970s, producing a foundation for negotiation of the LRTAP Convention and for early LRTAP programs. The AMRG surveyed OECD member states regarding air pollution policy interests and research needs, established international networks of state officials and experts, and surveyed the state of knowledge among participant states regarding air pollution measurement as well as management and control technologies (see OECD 1968). The AMRG encouraged and facilitated interstate information sharing around air pollution issues. Among Europeans, only Westerners were involved in the AMRG.[1] Non-OECD states were not invited to participate. All individual AMRG participants were designated by their national OECD representative and most were employed within state bureaucracies (or international organizations).[2] The AMRG survey of OECD states found a "majority interest in ten areas" (OECD 1968, 3).[3] AMRG members grouped these areas into three categories: (1) research on measurement of air pollution, (2) research on effects of air pollution, and (3) research on control technology and planning. These three areas were designated "areas selected for immediate study and evaluation" and participants agreed to survey national research programs (and progress) in these areas and report to the group.

The AMRG established working groups of experts—designated by OECD delegations—on measurement research and on research on desulfurization of fuel and flue gases. For the latter topic, "national experts from France, Germany, Sweden, United Kingdom and United States" met and reported "on research in progress and planned on desulphurization of fuels and flue gasses" (OECD 1968, 3). The AMRG participants worked to establish an international network of "national experts" on air pollution issues from OECD states. The AMRG's efforts produced a glossary of air pollution terminology "of terms used in France, the FRG, Italy, United Kingdom and United States" (OECD 1968, 6). The glossary was intended to begin to standardize terminology across borders in order to facilitate data and information exchange. In fact, the term "long-range transboundary air pollution" (or "LRTAP") appears to have been coined and brought to prominence by AMRG. Thirty years later, LRTAP incorporates separate groups and organizational structures for things like the effects of pollution, measurement of pollution, modeling, and control technologies in much the same way the AMRG organized its work.

Box 5.1
(continued)

Arena 2: The 1972 Stockholm UNCHE

Swedish officials pushed air pollution and acidification issues at the 1972 UNCHE in Stockholm.[4] Delegates from the Soviet Union and Eastern Europe participated in preparatory meetings and drafting sessions prior to the conference; however, the USSR led an East Bloc boycott of the 1972 Stockholm conference over the lack of Western formal diplomatic recognition of the German Democratic Republic (GDR). Swedish officials commissioned a study, which became "Sweden's Case Study for the United Nations Conference on the Human Environment: Air Pollution across National Boundaries" (Bolin 1972). Swedish UNCHE participants led calls for the multilateral data gathering and research programs to test, and attempt to demonstrate, Scandinavian claims that sulfur dioxide was traveling long distances across Europe, depositing in Nordic counties and causing ill effects vis-à-vis aquatic and terrestrial ecosystems.

Principle 21 of the UNCHE final declaration asserts the following:

States have, in accordance with the Charter of the United Nations and the principles of international law, the sovereign right to exploit their own resources pursuant to their own environmental policies, and the responsibility to ensure that activities within their jurisdiction or control do not cause damage to the environment or other states or of areas beyond the limits of national jurisdiction.

East Bloc officials, absent in Stockholm, did not officially assent to Principle 21. Nor did they have the opportunity to engage and publicly address the air pollution issues put forth in Stockholm. Their absence, for geopolitical reasons, set the stage for their nonparticipation in multilateral air pollution–related data gathering and analysis activities throughout the 1970s under OECD and Norwegian auspices.

Arena 3: Overlapping Norwegian and OECD assessments

Increased scientific, governmental, and public awareness of acid rain issues in the early 1970s produced the Norwegian Interdisciplinary Research Programme (the SNSF Project) titled "Acid Precipitation: Effects on Forests and Fish," and an OECD research program (from 1973 to 1975) focusing on the long-range transport of pollutants across Europe. Many individuals participated in both programs, and the latter was pushed and led by Nordic officials. The SNSF project focused on determining, to the degree possible, the effects of acidic deposition on terrestrial and aquatic ecosystems. The OECD study (OECD 1977) "confirmed the idea that pollutants are transported long distances and showed that the air quality in each European country is measurably effected from all other European

Box 5.1
(continued)

countries" (Cowling 1982, 116A). Eleven West European states participated in the study by submitting emission data and setting up monitoring
stations. The OECD study made claims about pollution dispersion and
national imports and exports of pollution for Eastern and Western European countries. However, only Western countries had representatives in
the design and execution of the study, and emission data were reported
only by (Western) OECD members (OECD 1973, 1979). Emissions were
estimated for East Bloc countries. Despite large error margins for many
aspects of the OECD study (e.g., emissions, transport, and deposition), the
program's conclusions and its rather precise numerical estimates of
national importing and exporting of sulfur pollutants were widely cited.

1. In 1968, the AMRG's thirty-four participants included twenty-four individuals from fifteen states (Austria, Belgium, Canada, Denmark, the Federal Republic of Germany, Finland, France, Italy, Japan, the Netherlands, Spain, Sweden,
Switzerland, the United Kingdom, and the United States) and seven people from
five international organizations (Council of Europe, World Health Organization,
World Meteorological Organization, European Communities, and OECD Secretariat). In addition, there was one "consultant" and two staff persons.
2. It remains unclear whether such reports were made public. The meeting documents are labeled "Restricted." See OECD 1968, documents DAS/CSI/A.66.96
and DAS/CSI/A.66.70.
3. The ten areas are as follows: "(a) Research on the technology of emission
control in respect of air pollution from industrial sources; (b) Research on the
technology of emission control in respect of pollution from motor vehicles; (c)
Research on the measurement of direct effects of specific pollutants on human
health; (d) Research on the measurement of direct effects of specific pollutants
on vegetation; (e) Research on the development of automatic systems for the
monitoring of air pollution, including their implications for warning and control;
(f) The use of planning techniques in respect to the location of industry; (g)
Research on long-term effects of air pollution on the environment, for example
ecological changes and regional climate changes; (h) Research on methods of
measurement for specific ambient air pollutants; (i) Measurement of background
levels of pollution outside the urban region; and (j) Research to understand the
meteorological factors affecting dispersion and removal of pollutants in the
atmosphere" (OECD 1968, 3)
4. In fact, Sweden initially proposed, within the United Nations, that such a conference be organized. The UN General Assembly adopted Sweden's proposal in
1968, beginning four years of preparatory work for the UNCHE.

and policy negotiations. The OECD had "earned itself a key role as a think-tank and data development center" across many economic and social areas (Wetstone and Rosencranz 1983, 135). This reputation helped legitimize its data gathering methods, delineation of areas of inquiry, and the individuals and organizations involved in its air pollution studies. Although the organizational venue of LRTAP-related international scientific and technical assessment changed, many of the organizational, methodological, participatory, and discursive patterns established in the OECD work would continue.

Assessment processes under the OECD had limitations. Since Communist Bloc states were not members of the OECD, they were not involved in OECD-sponsored assessment processes. Western assessment participants estimated CEE emissions rather than requesting data submission. The absence of data or participation from Central and Eastern Europe weakened both the scientific credibility and the political legitimacy of these early assessment efforts. All three assessment arenas noted that CEE countries such as Poland and Czechoslovakia were significant sources of sulfur emissions, so their failure to participate was scientifically and politically problematic. To circumvent such limitations, the OECD program on the long-range transport of pollutants was made independent of the OECD in 1978. The retitled Cooperative Program for Monitoring and Evaluation of the Long-Range Transmission of Air Pollution in Europe (EMEP) sought to increase Soviet and CEE participation in monitoring, data gathering, and assessment of transport and deposition patterns.

Given the OECD's organization and membership rules, an international convention around air pollution issues would have to be negotiated in a different international organization. State officials selected the United Nations Economic Commission for Europe (UNECE) as host for LRTAP negotiations and its secretariat, because it was the only existing organization with both environmental and economic interests that also had members from both East and West. Thus, the selection of UNECE addressed some legitimacy concerns associated with the OECD's exclusively Western membership. The notion that the UNECE operated on the basis of consensus was also attractive to many state officials (East and West), generally protective of sovereign independence.

In short, the arenas of cooperation prior to the LRTAP negotiations framed the European transboundary air pollution debate largely in terms of the concerns about "acid rain" among Scandinavian researchers and officials with virtually no Eastern and Central European participation. The pre-LRTAP assessment activities coined the term *long-range transboundary air pollution* and worked to standardize air pollution terminology across borders. They built and expanded the initial networks connecting scientific, technical, and air pollution policy experts from various research and policy communities. The participation patterns within early international assessment efforts set the stage for LRTAP's near-exclusive focus on acidification issues in the 1980s and early 1990s, in effect making "long-range transboundary air pollution" a euphemism for acidification concerns. Over time, this frame, LRTAP's assessment, and policymaking activities built relatively high levels of salience, legitimacy, and credibility among relevant Northern European political and scientific communities.

The acidification frame reflected the beliefs within Northern European scientific and technical communities and it shaped the policy preferences of Northern European policymakers. Scandinavian scientists and policymakers built scientific credibility through organized international assessment activities that expanded the network of researchers and broadened scientific consensus regarding acidification problems (see, e.g., Schneider 1986, 1992). Northern European policymakers linked assessment information to policy debates by engaging international organizations such as the OECD and the UNCHE to increase awareness of acidification issues among policymakers and publics. Such "venue shopping"[1] by environmental policy leaders was employed again as Northern European policymakers turned from the OECD to the UNECE to expand national participation in acidification cooperation efforts and develop acidification-related treaties.

Western-Driven LRTAP Growth

The policymaking and scientific and technical assessment agendas within LRTAP have been driven by Northern/Western European officials and assessment participants. Early advocates of international cooperation on transboundary air pollution faced a host of challenges common to other international environmental problems. These challenges include political obstacles to interstate cooperation (such as Cold War divisions), the frequent lack of transnational organizations and networks for scientific and technical cooperation, the lack of scientific and technical consensus regarding "problem definition" and potential "solutions," and the absence of international organizations in which to negotiate multilateral policies (VanDeveer 2000).

Since the signing of the LRTAP Convention, the cooperation regime has grown in terms of state membership, the number of treaties completed, and organizational size and complexity. Environmental "leaders" among LRTAP states, national scientific communities, scientific and environmental organizations, and individuals have worked to broaden and deepen interstate and transnational environmental cooperation around acidification and, eventually, other transboundary air pollution issues. Assessment processes are supported by environmental lead countries, and assessment information is used by officials from these states in their pursuit of stronger multilateral environmental policy. Central, Eastern, and Mediterranean countries remain largely on the periphery of LRTAP's activities (VanDeveer 2005).

LRTAP was the joint result of developments within Cold War politics and international environmental cooperation around acid rain issues (Chossudovsky 1989). The Convention on Long-Range Transboundary Air Pollution was negotiated between 1977 and 1979 and entered into force in March 1983. Negotiations took place largely between Nordic states (Sweden, Norway, Denmark, and Finland) on the one hand, and other more reluctant Western Europeans, including West Germany and the United Kingdom, on the other (Chossudovsky 1989; Wetstone and Rosencranz 1983). Generally speaking, Eastern and Central Europeans and the USSR played a minor role in the negotiation process. The Central and Eastern Europeans were understood to be following the Soviet lead, taking no public or negotiating position not in accord with that of the USSR. For their part, the Soviets signaled their willingness to sign a framework convention early in the LRTAP negotiating process. To date, forty-nine states and the EU Commission are parties to LRTAP. As a framework convention LRTAP spelled out no specific, binding pollution control or reduction commitments. It merely established an institutional basis for research and information sharing regarding environmental conditions, natural science, policy development, and control technologies. Yet international negotiators were not unanimous about the value of transnational information sharing, or about what type of information should be exchanged. Soviet and CEE officials remained unwilling to share emission data, claiming that sensitive economic, security, and energy-related secrecy would be compromised. Instead, they agreed to report "transboundary fluxes" of pollutants—an estimate of the amount of sulfur crossing their borders in both directions.

In 1981 and 1982, Swedish officials pushed for further international action, using the tenth anniversary of UNCHE in Stockholm to host an international "Conference on Acidification of the Environment." The Swedish government, hoping to raise public and official awareness of acid rain across Europe and to pressure governments to ratify LRTAP, organized two meetings. In one, experts attended representing themselves. The other was a ministerial meeting at which official government positions were articulated. The experts "scrutinized the scientific evidence of the causes, transport and effects of transboundary air pollutants, and the information available on strategies and methods (including costs) for the control of emissions" (McCormick 1997, 64). Among other things, they agreed that sulfur and nitrogen compounds released via anthropogenic activity were primarily to blame for acid deposition and that commercially available technologies for significant reductions of sulfur emissions were available. At their meeting, ministers agreed that the Convention needed to be brought into force and that substantive work must begin at the international level to commit states to sulfur emission reductions (using available technologies). Many CEE countries, including the major sulfur emitters, were not at the conference.

The first substantive agreement to be negotiated under the LRTAP framework was a financing mechanism for EMEP.[2] This required parties to pay mandatory contributions (and invited voluntary contributions) to cover the costs of the international technical EMEP centers that monitor air pollutants and report data. EMEP was assured ongoing funding for its activities, while LRTAP was provided with a source of information viewed as credible and legitimate by state officials. In addition to the EMEP Protocol, LRTAP delegates have produced seven pollution-reduction protocols. Table 5.1 lists the protocols, briefly describes their major provisions, and includes information on the number of signatories and parties to each agreement. In 1983, when LRTAP entered into force, work began on creating a sulfur agreement calling for a flat emission cut of 30 percent. When scientific research and assessment identified nitrogen as an important contributor to acidification, it was added to the Convention's agenda, producing a nitrogen protocol in 1988. Because volatile organic compound (VOC) emissions from fuels, solvents, cleaners, and a number of other volatile chemicals were partly linked to acidification issues and the formation of ground-level ozone, a protocol on VOCs was negotiated between 1989 and 1991. The obsolescence of the first sulfur protocol led to its replacement by a second sulfur protocol in 1994. Signaling a shift from mainly environmental protocols to pollutants with a stronger human health dimension, agreements on heavy metals and persistent organic pollutants (POPs) were developed during the 1990s and signed in 1998 (Selin 2000).[3]

Despite these efforts, it was believed in the mid-1990s that pollution levels of sulfur, nitrogen, and VOCs remained above levels safe for ecosystems and humans. Simultaneously addressing this set of environmental concerns would take into account the close relationship between emission sources, their receptors, and the transboundary nature of the pollutants. For that purpose, a multieffect/multipollutant protocol on acidification, eutrophication, and ground-level ozone was developed and adopted in Gothenburg in 1999, setting national emission-reduction targets for each pollutant for each state (Wettestad 2002). Going a step beyond the general flat-rate cuts of the first protocols, the Gothenburg Protocol is based on a critical-load concept first used in the 1994 Second Sulfur Protocol. The concept of critical load denotes an attempt to establish a critical environmental level below which no harmful effects occur. Regulations are said to be guided by nature's tolerance limits and emission reductions are divided among countries on a regional basis in an attempt to minimize the costs for the region as a whole. Relevant environmental data is gathered within the EMEP monitoring system and critical-load maps are made on outputs generated by the Regional Air Pollution Information and Simulation (RAINS) model developed at the International Institute for Applied Systems Analysis (IIASA).

Table 5.1
The LRTAP Convention and its protocols

1979 *LRTAP Convention*	Framework convention, states agree to try to limit and/or reduce air pollution using best-available technologies and to share scientific, technical, and environmental policy information. (Adopted in Geneva, 13 November 1979; entry into force, 16 March 1983; 49 parties)
1984 *EMEP Protocol*	Creates a multilateral trust fund for the long-term financial support of EMEP activities. (Adopted in Geneva, 28 September 1984; entry into force, 28 January 1988; 41 parties)
1985 *Sulphur Protocol*	States agree to reduce sulphur emissions or their transboundary fluxes by 30%, from 1980 levels, by 1993. All parties in compliance by 1998. (Adopted in Helsinki, 8 July 1985; entry into force, 2 September 1987; 22 parties)
1988 NO_x *Protocol*	States commit to freezing NO_x emissions (at 1987 or earlier levels) by the end of 1994, and to future cooperation to further reduce NO_x emissions and establish critical loads. Eighteen of the Protocol's first 25 parties complied with the terms of the freeze. Twelve West European states went farther, aiming to reduce NO_x emissions by 30% by 1998. (Adopted in Sophia, 31 October 1988; entry into force, 14 February 1991; 29 parties)
1991 *VOCs Protocol*	States agree to reduce VOC emissions by 30% from a chosen baseline year between 1984 and 1990. Most countries chose 1988. By 2000, only seven states had achieved the targeted reductions, while four more had documented reductions between 16% and 21%. (Adopted in Geneva, 18 November 1991; entry into force, 29 September 1997; 21 parties)
1994 *Second Sulphur Protocol*	Replaces the expired 1985 Sulphur Protocol. Retaining 1980 levels as a baseline and using an "effects-based" approach setting "target loads" based on calculated critical loads, states agreed to different emission reductions by 2000, 2005, and 2010—representing a 60% reduction in the difference between existing deposition levels and critical loads. By the late 1990s, 19 states had either achieved their 2000 target levels or appeared to be on track to do so. (Adopted in Oslo, 14 June 1994; entry into force 5 August 1998; 25 parties)

Table 5.1
(continued)

1998 *Heavy Metals Protocol*	States commit to reduce emissions of lead, cadmium, and mercury below 1990 levels (or an alternate year between 1985 and 1995). Aims to cut emissions from industrial and combustion sources and from waste incineration. Sets limit values for stationary sources, suggests numerous BAT standards, and requires phaseout of lead in qasoline. (Adopted in Århus, Denmark, 24 June 1998; entry into force, 29 December 2003; 25 parties)
1998 *POPs Protocol*	States pledge to eliminate discharges, emissions, and losses of POPs. Sixteen POPS are covered. Various restrictions (i.e., bans, use criteria, and emission-reduction targets) are applied to various POPs. (Adopted in Århus, Denmark, 24 June 1998; entry into force, 23 October 2003; 23 parties)
1999 *Protocol to Abate Acidification, Eutrophication, and Ground-level Ozone*	States agree on national emission ceilings for 2010 for sulfur, nitrogen, VOCs, and ammonia. If fully implemented, Europe's sulfur emissions will be cut by at least 63%, nitrogen emissions by 41%, VOC emissions by 40%, and ammonia emissions by 17% compared to 1990. (Adopted in Gothenburg, Sweden, 30 November 1999; entry into force, 17 May 2005; 17 parties)

Note: Status information as of May 2005.
Source: LRTAP website: http://www.unece.org/env/lrtap/.

LRTAP participants' acceptance of the critical-load concept and the RAINS integrated assessment model constituted a significant breakthrough for international cooperation. State negotiators adopted the RAINS model because, of three available models, most scientists thought it the most developed, the most credible (because of its development within an organization with East-West membership), and the most responsive to negotiators' requests (Tuinstra, Hordijk, and Amann 1999; Hordijk interviews). The model was technically credible to many assessment participants, legitimate across the East-West divide, and salient to officials conducting the negotiations. The critical-load approach and the RAINS model allowed state officials to accommodate and justify differential national emission-reductions commitments, allowing negotiators to frame policy in response to differential costs and variance in states' willingness to pay. This helped them overcome least-common-denominator outcomes.

The LRTAP organization structure has changed over the years. As the focus of work under the Convention has shifted, new subsidiary bodies have been created and existing ones have been given new work tasks (and new names) or abolished. LRTAP's organizational structure, like many international cooperation arrangements, retains policymaking control for state officials (see figure 5.1). Operating under the Executive Body are the EMEP Steering Body, the Working Group on Effects, the Working Group on Strategies and Review, and the Working Group on Abatement Techniques. The EMEP Steering Body oversees the activities of the EMEP programs on collection of emission data, measurement of air and precipitation quality, and modeling of atmospheric transport and deposition of air pollution. The Working Group on Effects provides information on impacts on human health and the environment of air pollutants. The Working Group on Strategies and Review is the political negotiation committee where the parties conduct formal negotiations on pollution-specific agreements and review progress. Under the main bodies, one or several International Cooperative Programs and Technical and Scientific Centers can be established on an ad hoc basis, either to supervise continuing programs or prepare technical and scientific reports. The Executive Body established the Implementation Committee in 1997 to aid in review of compliance by parties.[4] LRTAP's "driver" countries (Germany, the Netherlands, Norway, Sweden, and the UK) host the vast majority of cooperative programs and task forces. Of coordinating and synthesizing centers, seven of nine are located in the big five countries.

Generally, individual states take lead administrative roles for each area of assessment. Assessment as practiced within LRTAP does not focus on a "final report" or "final product." There are few glossy reports for analysts to mistake for "the assessment" of issues associated with air pollution and related economic, technological, and policy questions. Occasionally, issue-specific "state of the art" reports are issued. Regular reports of task force meetings and activities are presented in brief summaries. The details of debates, differences, and social learning processes

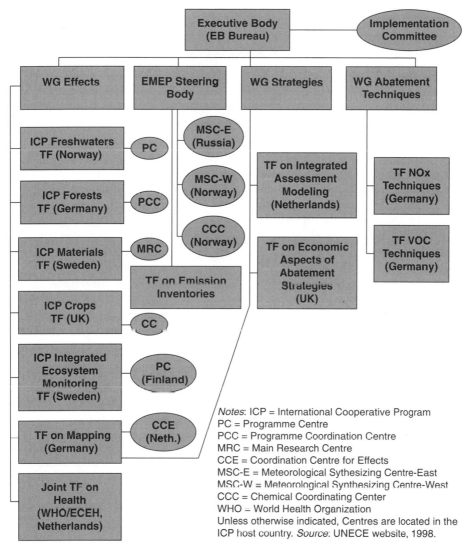

Figure 5.1
LRTAP organizational structure

among task force members remain largely hidden from view. New research, not all of it formally peer reviewed prior to inclusion, is used during assessment, but new research is rarely commissioned by LRTAP bodies. The formal modeling work done by individuals at IIASA serves as a partial exception (Hordijk and Amann interviews, 1998). LRTAP assessment is explicitly policy relevant, often driven by requests to participating individuals and task forces by the policymaking LRTAP bodies. Although such requests are usually formal—made by an administrative body as a whole and issued publicly—informal requests prior to important meetings and official negotiations are not uncommon.

Green Leadership in LRTAP Politics and Assessment

Germany supported Nordic pressures for LRTAP assessment and negotiation after discovering acid rain's impact on its own forests (Social Learning Group 2001a, 2001b). In contrast, the United Kingdom—often a LRTAP skeptic—agreed to a Convention only reluctantly and refused to sign the first Sulphur Protocol. Thus, the "big players" include Sweden, the Netherlands, Norway, the UK, and Germany, with nationals on virtually all LRTAP bodies. These countries are major sponsors of LRTAP-related multilateral bodies and programs—usually with state funds. Furthermore, they have frequently hosted large scientific, technical, and political conferences and research institutes. The "green leaders" were usually joined in international negotiations by Austria, Denmark, Finland, and Switzerland.[5] The UK frequently relied on southern European (and at times North American) support for its less environmentally ambitious policy positions. Western European states have ratified more protocols, and in more timely fashion, than other states. CEE states, significant sources of transboundary air pollution, have generally poor ratification records (VanDeveer 2005).

Levy (1993) argues that a "Tote-Board" effect drove many states' policies on LRTAP, with states competing to keep up with each other's announced emission-reduction goals. However, this effect was influential almost exclusively among the wealthier, democratic Western European states with significant domestic environmental constituencies. The tote-board effect was frequently driven by domestic environmental demand, which produced stringent domestic environmental policy independent of

LRTAP. Environmental "leaders" such as Norway, Sweden, and Germany, for example, reduced sulfur emissions in advance of LRTAP commitments (Levy 1993, 76). These "green leaders" sought to "internationalize" their comparatively stringent (and costly) environmental standards in hopes of reducing their importation of acidifying substances from other states and reducing any competitive disadvantages resulting from their higher regulatory standards. These states also had, by all accounts, the largest and most politically active groups of scientific and technical researchers focused on the effects of acid precipitation. The tote-board effect expanded the number of states willing to sign on to larger emission-reduction targets. It drove consensus among many Western European states with domestic "green" constituencies. Other states' willingness to agree to substantial emission-reduction goals also emerged, at least in part, from "accidental" emission reductions resulting from energy and industrial restructuring. Such states included France, Spain, and the United Kingdom (see Farrell and Keating 1998; Farrell 1998).

Environmental "leaders" among LRTAP states, national scientific communities, scientific and environmental organizations, and individuals have broadened and deepened interstate and transnational environmental cooperation around acidification and, eventually, other transboundary air pollution issues. Acidification-related assessment information also entered public consciousness and domestic political debate in much of Western Europe (Social Learning Project 2001a, 2001b). For most Western European policymakers, the perceived salience, credibility, and legitimacy of acidification science and assessment were mutually reinforcing over time. Assessment was salient to policymakers in "downwind" states because it framed them as victims of other countries' pollution. Ongoing research and iterated assessment continued to reinforce this view. As public environmental concern grew across much of Europe in the 1980s and early 1990s, acidification damage gained greater political salience for state officials. Policymakers felt the need to respond to public environmental demands.

Regarding the credibility of LRTAP assessment, participating researchers consistently included much of the relevant expertise from across Western Europe. The scientific and technical network, its foundations emerging from the pre-LRTAP assessment efforts outlined above, incorporated ongoing research and developed around periodic acidification conferences. Since Western European policymakers drove the agendas of both assessment and policymaking in LRTAP, it is not surprising that they saw these processes and their outcomes as legitimate. Europe's "green leaders" drove acidification assessment and policymaking, determining what questions got asked and what programs got funded. Furthermore, in the 1970s and 1980s, many European government officials saw East-West cooperation as a good in itself. Thus, organizational venues such as UNECE and IIASA—both built as forums for pan-European cooperation—appear to have added to the sense of legitimacy of LRTAP processes and information. Nevertheless, Central European countries, like Southern Europeans, remained largely on the periphery of LRTAP's activities. It is to this issue I now turn.

Pushing LRTAP East

LRTAP assessment and policymaking have played out differently in Eastern Europe and the former Soviet Union than in Western Europe. With few exceptions, transition-country officials and scientists were usually reactive to Western European environmental science, technology, and politics. Central and Eastern Europeans played minor roles in shaping the LRTAP protocols relative to Western states. What influence they had was generally used in calls to weaken commitments or allow exceptions to targets, timetables, and information sharing.

Prior to 1989–1990, international assessment information had little influence on domestic environmental policy within the Communist Bloc. CEE states followed the Soviet lead when expressing their policy preferences in international forums. Central and Eastern European countries were developing widely varying domestic environmental policies, which one might expect to yield variance in international environmental policy positions. But the USSR dominated Eastern Bloc foreign policy positions, occasionally "correcting" CEE officials during negotiating sessions. Long-time LRTAP participants tell stories of CEE officials rapidly changing their policy preferences at the behest of the Soviets. In addition,

Western negotiators and the secretariat officials generally viewed Soviet negotiating positions as de facto expressions of CEE preferences.

LRTAP Assessment and Policy in Post-Communist Europe
First, let us consider the relative influence in CEE of acidification research agendas developed in Western Europe and North America.[6] Western European scientific, technical, and political activity related to trans-boundary air pollution stimulated some research in CEE countries and the Soviet Union (Toth and Hizsnyik 2001; Sokolov and Jäger 2001). This suggests that CEE and Soviet scientific and technical researchers greeted the Western acidification research agenda as scientifically credible. Academic researchers and meteorological services, for example, picked up the trend toward greater interest in air pollution issues and dynamics, incorporating these topics into their research. However, there was little institutional development linking domestic air pollution research to domestic or foreign policymaking in these countries. CEE environmental researchers were given little latitude to pursue their interests absent constraints from the state in the Communist period. Only Poland and Hungary—arguably the most open Soviet bloc states—appear exceptional in this regard. Established meteorological organizations and communities, with ambient air quality monitoring capabilities that predated the socialist regimes, produced larger communities of air pollution researchers with relatively wide latitude in research design.

Furthermore, in the absence of a political/policymaking prioritization of long-range transboundary air pollution issues, state funding for such research did not increase dramatically as it did in the 1970s and 1980s in Western Europe. Policymakers in Eastern Europe did not view trans-boundary air pollution as particularly salient and did not prioritize research funding, leading acidification science and technical research in these countries to lag behind Western research. Where scientific research is dependent on public funding, an issue's salience among policymakers has important ramifications for the quantity and quality of scientific and technical research.

EMEP programs, particularly those providing deposition and transport data for regular air quality monitoring, are frequently cited as crucial to cooperation with LRTAP. Researchers at the International Institute for Applied Systems Analysis (IIASA) played a particularly important role in legitimizing and refining research, modeling, and visual representations of transboundary air pollution across Europe (VanDeveer 2004). IIASA, established to bridge the East-West divide, has a long history of interest in air pollution issues. The institute's researchers have been very strategic in selling their RAINS models of atmospheric transport and deposition of pollution in Europe to policymakers across the continent (Alcamo, Shaw, and Hordijk 1990). They held demonstrations of the model and workshops with policymakers and non-IIASA researchers and modelers at the UNECE secretariat, at IIASA, and in various capitals. When U.S.-driven export bans constrained Eastern European access to modern computers, the RAINS developers designed the program to run on simpler machines that were available in CEE states and the Soviet Union. Leen Hordijk, the first leader of IIASA's Transboundary Air Pollution Project that developed the RAINS model, believes that demonstrations of RAINS to Soviet and CEE officials were centrally important for their acceptance of the model and the critical-load concept within the LRTAP framework. Numerous IIASA alumni, using personal and professional networks established there, worked with or for LRTAP's Integrated Assessment Modeling Task Force, becoming central to the development of critical-load concepts, models, and maps. These individuals formed the core of a science-policy network doing applied, policy-related scientific and technical work on long-range air pollution. The network contains many densely connected "nodes" among Scandinavian, Austrian, German, and UK researchers, with fewer participants on the European periphery. Like spokes on a wheel, CEE participants are generally connected to the Western European network by one or more "nodes" in Western Europe.

Many participants in LRTAP assessment bodies believed the RAINS model gained legitimacy relative to "national" models from its association with IIASA and its multinational, particularly East-West, character. IIASA's involvement in RAINS development and IIASA modelers' campaign to "sell" the model contributed to capacity building around acidification research in a number of CEE countries, including Czechoslovakia, Hungary, Poland, and the USSR. However, this capacity appears to have remained largely within national technical communities, not spilling over into the policymaking bureaucracy. Domestic policy remained largely unaffected by this work, although greater understanding of the model likely contributed to CEE countries' acceptance of the RAINS model for use within LRTAP assessment and negotiations.

Numerous CEE LRTAP negotiators and domestic environmental policy officials (and the consultants they hire) do use information generated within LRTAP (and EMEP) data gathering and assessment processes when they attempt to assess national prospects for compliance with LRTAP protocols. Regarding LRTAP assessment processes and products, however, domestic CEE officials are recipients and users of assessments—generally *after* international policies and standards have been agreed on within LRTAP negotiations. This is similar to the processes whereby CEE officials harmonized domestic environmental policies with EU policies—policies they did not participate in making—before the 2004 enlargement of EU membership to include eight CEE states (Carmin and VanDeveer 2005).

In general, CEE policy officials and assessment practitioners report focusing on two basic questions: (1) What, if any, domestic legal and regulatory changes would be required to achieve compliance with a given protocol? and (2) How much would such changes cost and who would pay for them? When the answers to the first question constitute little or no change to existing policies and the costs of these changes are perceived to be small, CEE governments tend to support ratification. Such instances have been rare in post-Communist countries. When this is not the case, prospects for ratification dim and/or environmental officials search for other justifications in support of joining a specific protocol. By the late 1990s, such justifications included the perceived requirements for accession to membership in the European Union. There is currently little domestic political pressure in support of LRTAP protocol ratification (specifically) or for more stringent domestic environmental policy (in general). Since the mid-1990s, the questions above have been salient only in reference to harmonization with EU policies and accession to EU memberships. CEE environmental policymakers want to know the extent to which EU air pollution policy and LRTAP standards are mutually compatible. Such harmonization was necessary for EU membership. In turn, the EU Commission recognizes that "CLRTAP is the main forum through which the European Community and the Member States can influence and promote emission reductions in non-member countries. Further action in some of those countries has proven generally to be highly cost-effective."[7]

LRTAP Assessment in an EU-Centered Europe

Because CEE domestic and foreign politics have changed so dramatically in the post–Cold War period, increased understanding of the contemporary influence of assessment processes and information requires a focus on recent LRTAP activities. In 1998, two LRTAP protocols concerning heavy metals and persistent organic pollutants (POPs) were completed. CEE negotiators and domestic environmental policy officials reported using LRTAP information and contacts to follow the technical and policy debates between Western states during negotiations. CEE and Russian negotiators expressed strong preferences in negotiating sessions only over regulatory provisions they believed to be too costly to achieve in their countries within the time frames proposed. In most cases, these "countries with economies in transition" were granted broad exemptions. CEE officials announced their intention to commission detailed national-level assessments of the prospects and costs for implementation of these two new protocols *after* the texts were finalized. Such national-level assessments invariably use LRTAP-generated information.

CEE officials saw developments in negotiating and assessment bodies similarly—as indications of where Western environmental policy officials (particularly EU policymakers and "green leaders") were going vis-à-vis European environmental policy. LRTAP assessment processes communicate the direction of policy desired for the whole of Europe by the states and societies that drive the processes. Thus, CEE officials contended that Western European state officials and assessment participants used assessment processes and information strategically to shape international policy agendas. CEE officials reported on LRTAP activities and developments to individuals and groups involved in EU accession negotiations. Likewise, by the late 1990s, LRTAP Secretariat officials and participating state policymakers expected EU members to shape LRTAP's multieffect/multipollutant protocol to suit the acidification-related directives negotiated within the EU (Selin and VanDeveer 2003).

In the 1990s, both LRTAP and the EU expanded regulatory scope by increasing the number of pollutants and emission sources they regulate and strengthened their regulations by setting more ambitious reduction targets (Wettestad 2002). Furthermore, the EU Commission has become increasingly active in LRTAP, seeking to establish and maintain common EU policy positions within LRTAP. Over the course of the 1990s, LRTAP cooperation bodies and EU air pollution policy have become increasingly linked in terms of their institutions, organizational and individual actors, and the information used.[8] By 1998, for example, LRTAP negotiators readily acknowledged that the time frames and content of EU air pollution policy negotiations were increasingly driving LRTAP's work on the multieffect/multipollutant protocol.[9]

Environmental leader states often exercise influence by sponsoring technical and scientific activities around particular policy issues. Such action often greatly influences the direction of policy and technical debates. "Lead states" marshal scientific and technical expertise and resources that often are used in both forums. The same states are generally lead states in both LRTAP and the EU, coupling political will with technical and scientific capability to push air pollution policy (Botcheva 2001). Despite the growing importance of linkages between LRTAP and EU policy, many states fail to coordinate national delegates and experts at LRTAP and EU meetings. Only Sweden, Denmark, Germany, and the UK consistently send the same representatives to Geneva and Brussels (Selin and VanDeveer 2003). As a result, policy tools such as the RAINS model and technical and scientific aspects of the critical-load/level approach have been explained and debated in both Geneva and Brussels.

Increasingly, LRTAP and EU air policy are linked through the common use of scientific and technical ideas, such as the concept of critical load (Selin and VanDeveer 2003; VanDeveer 2004). As discussed above, IIASA developed the critical-load concept and the RAINS model. While the EU Commission initially was skeptical of the feasibility of a Community critical-load strategy, technical and scientific work on critical loads since the mid-1990s has been conducted with the goal of its being used in LRTAP and the EU. Thus, both forums formulate policy based on the same technical and scientific assumptions and assessments of environmental quality. EU incorporation of the critical-load concept and the RAINS model was facilitated by previous acceptance of these ideas by EU member states and the EU Commission within LRTAP.[10] Environmental policy leaders perceived the use of RAINS and critical loads to be in their interests, while EU environmental "laggard" states had already accepted their use. Furthermore, the RAINS model and the critical-load approach had established scientific credibility, and developing alternatives would be more time consuming and costlier. Using inputs from LRTAP provided consistency in terms of data and models as well as common data.[11]

Both LRTAP and the EU use IIASA's network of experts and RAINS modeling techniques. Both also use LRTAP's EMEP data to grapple with the complex challenges of combating tropospheric ozone pollution, acidification, and eutrophication at the same time. While most European states have domestic monitoring systems, EMEP builds and maintains a regional European monitoring and environmental data analysis system. EMEP is the only pan-European monitoring and data gathering analysis of this kind. From the Commission's perspective, "There is an increasingly large overlap in both policy and geographical terms between CLRTAP and EU air quality policy, and enhanced cooperation with CLRTAP will therefore be essential. . . . Cooperation and coordination at the technical level will thus be the key to exploiting synergies and avoiding duplication."[12]

In addition, the use of the RAINS model within EU policy has lead to the increased inclusion of IIASA alumni and other RAINS model users in EU policymaking circles. Such experience is an asset for those seeking to participate in policymaking. The ongoing development of EU air pollution policy in cooperation with LRTAP is fostering and being fostered by an increasing interchange of scientists and technical experts between the two forums (Selin and VanDeveer 2003).

Conclusions: Assessment Information East and West

The overarching "East-West" European political context has significantly influenced the conduct and content of scientific and technical assessment—particularly in terms of problem framing and assessment participation. As much of the literature on LRTAP suggests, transnational scientific networks have exercised increased influence in European air pollution politics over the past decade within LRTAP cooperation and among the Western European "lead" states. Such networks have been central to development of the critical-load concept, to putting POPs and heavy metals on the LRTAP agenda, and to ensuring that separate POPs and heavy-metal protocols were adopted. The development of a common assessment methodology has created linkages between LRTAP and the EU, facilitating the goal of both institutions to harmonize assessment methodologies. The adoption by EU institutions of LRTAP's assessment bodies, data gathering and calibration organizations, and critical-load concepts and RAINS modeling techniques are testaments to the high level of their salience, credibility, and legitimacy in Western Europe.

LRTAP information had different levels of salience, credibility, and legitimacy in Central and Eastern Europe than in Western Europe. Understanding these attributions by CEE states regarding LRTAP information requires attention to the links between East-West politics and transboundary air pollution. For example, although CEE countries had serious transboundary air pollution problems—including relatively high levels of pollution importation—official attention to these issues and related policies was shaped primarily by Soviet power in the early days of LRTAP. Furthermore, because CEE officials and scientific experts were excluded from pre-LRTAP assessment efforts, there was little domestic-expert concern (or interest) when LRTAP was established. Early framings of pollution as a transboundary problem did not resonate in CEE countries, where the emerging environmental concern was more often focused on the severe effects of urban and local pollution. Thus, political dynamics and participation patterns in early assessment efforts mutually reinforced an initially low level of salience.

LRTAP information became salient to CEE officials primarily in the form of domestic cost and feasibility assessments related to ratification and implementation of LRTAP protocols. Because of low issue salience, however, CEE officials were not willing to incur the costs of implementing LRTAP protocols. By the late 1990s, LRTAP became salient to CEE officials mainly in response to the desire to join the EU. LRTAP's assessment and policymaking agenda helped clarify the direction and content of EU environmental policies. Such information helps CEE officials identify the policies, and costs, of EU membership. This chapter demonstrates that salience may be directly associated with the organized information and its perceived effects, as in most Western European states, or it may rest on links between the environmental issue and broader political interests.

LRTAP-related assessment information was generally credible to CEE scientific experts. It has been widely used in research and domestic assessment efforts (Botcheva 1998). Furthermore, it has gone largely unchallenged among CEE experts and within CEE environmental bureaucracies. CEE officials and technical experts interviewed for this research reported few reasons to doubt the quality of LRTAP information. Similarly, they regarded the RAINS modeling work sponsored by IIASA as exceptional. CEE officials tended to regard organizations with which they were familiar or in which they felt represented as both credible and legitimate (see Andonova, chapter 6, this volume).

Credibility and legitimacy of information are closely linked. Many CEE air policy officials and researchers spent time at IIASA or have colleagues who have done so. Furthermore, IIASA's East-West membership and its explicit efforts to include CEE participants in its modeling and research programs over the years lend the organization credibility. IIASA has built credibility by working with CEE officials and researchers, making models available and useful to them, and familiarizing policymakers in both East and West. This has helped IIASA models gain acceptance within LRTAP assessment bodies and policy negotiations and in EU policymaking.

Regarding legitimacy, the most common complaints from CEE technical experts and policymakers relate to the costs associated with participating in international forums. Often CEE experts can participate in the technical meetings, assessment bodies, and international conferences usually held in Western Europe, only if their costs are covered by an international or Western European organization. Such funds are often unavailable. Support for cutting-edge research is often unavailable to CEE scientists. As a result, asymmetric participation has persisted in international forums well beyond the collapse of Communist-era restrictions (VanDeveer 2005).

Two important and interrelated determinants of salience, credibility, and legitimacy are highlighted by this study: participation patterns and the organizational venue of assessment and policymaking. National asymmetries in participation, some driven by the choice of venue, shaped the initial framing of transboundary acidification. The transboundary acidification frame produced information quite salient to the Northern European "downwind" states. The lack of CEE participation resulted, at least in part, from the OECD's membership rules and from the boycott of the UNCHE by the Eastern Bloc.

The "venue shopping" of environmental policy leaders illustrates the importance of strategic choices regarding organizational venues. The OECD helped Scandinavian leaders push their air pollution assessment agenda within a multilateral research organization that included Western European pollution exporters. The UNECE allowed Northern European states to engage Eastern Bloc countries and to link assessment of transboundary pollutants to multinational policymaking. Unlike Western European states, CEE states participated in these venues largely due to their geopolitical position in relation to the Soviet Union, and later to the EU.

As the EU's membership expands and its environmental policymaking authority grows, one sees a parallel growth in EU dominance of LRTAP-related agenda setting and policymaking. LRTAP is being transformed into a body increasingly operating as a vehicle for "Europeanization" of environmental governance across the continent. Yet LRTAP bodies retain important roles. EU policymaking is folding LRTAP environmental policy institutions and organizations into its policy development and environmental monitoring and assessment systems. Once LRTAP's assessment institutions and information were regarded as salient, credible, and legitimate by Western European officials, Northern European environmental policy leaders pushed for the use of these institutions within more enforceable EU policymaking. Incorporating LRTAP's established and accepted assessment processes is likely more efficient than attempting to duplicate them with EU institutions, thus taking advantage of the assessment capacity constructed over time within

LRTAP bodies (Farrell, VanDeveer, and Jäger 2002). Because CEE officials wanted membership in the EU (achieved for eight CEE states in 2004) and EU officials wanted stronger CEE environmental policies, they could not be seen as obstructionist in international environmental policymaking venues such as LRTAP.

After thirty years of multilateral air pollution assessment efforts, CEE policymakers and scientific and technical experts remain in a reactive position. While the credibility of LRTAP-related assessment information appears similar across East and West, the East-West differences in issue and information salience reflect the East-West differences in policy outcomes. In short, LRTAP protocols remain largely unratified and unimplemented in CEE countries and the other transition states—despite dramatic air pollution policy changes in CEE states engendered by EU harmonization. While environmental leader states and scientific communities have demonstrated the ability to drive the LRTAP assessment and policymaking agenda, they have been largely unable to significantly and directly influence Eastern European domestic air pollution policy outcomes. Pushing environmental "laggards" with assessment information and international legal agreements has had limited policy results. CEE states' efforts to harmonize domestic law and regulation with that of the EU yielded massive domestic environmental policy change. Thus, it is EU membership, not assessment information, that increased the salience of air pollution policy across Eastern Europe.

Acknowledgments

For their time, interest, and comments on earlier drafts, the author would like to thank Liliana Andonova, William C. Clark, Barbara Connolly, Alex Farrell, Peter M. Haas, Leen Hordijk, Jill Jäger, Sheila Jasanoff, Terry Keating, Robert O. Keohane, Marc A. Levy, Ronald B. Mitchell, Kate O'Neill, Ambuj Sagar, Henrik Selin, Henning Wuester, and many individuals who gave up scarce time and allowed themselves to be interviewed. Thanks also to Nancy Dickson, Jarek Krol, Rebecca Storo, Eniko Szabo, and Trevor Wysong for their assistance, as well as John Beale, Bill Harnett, and Mary Gorjance for allowing me to observe the work of the LRTAP Working Group on Strategies. This research was funded by the Global Environmental Assessment Project at the Belfer Center for Science and International Affairs with the assistance and support of the International Institute for Applied Systems Analysis in Laxenburg, Austria. As usual, the author is responsible for any errors herein.

Notes

1. For a review of "venue shopping," see Pralle 2003.

2. On EMEP, see di Primio 1998.

3. Heavy metals include such substances as lead, mercury, and cadmium. POPs include pesticides such as aldrin, chlordane, chlordecone, DDT, dieldrin, endrin, heptachlor, hexachlorobenzene (HBC), mirex, toxaphene, and hexachlorocyclohexane (HCH) (including lindane); industrial chemicals such as hexabromobiphenyl and polychlorinated biphenyls (PCBs); and byproducts and/or contaminants such as dioxins, furans, and polycyclic aromatic hydrocarbons (PAHs).

4. For more information on the role and procedures of the Committee, see UNECE, ECE.EB.AIR/53. 19 December 1997. Decision 1997/2 Concerning the Implementation Committee, Its Structure and Functions and Procedures for Review of Compliance.

5. For one example of these important negotiating coalitions, see Patt 1998 on the adoption of the "critical-load" concept for use within LRTAP negotiations.

6. This section draws heavily on the author interviews listed at the end of the chapter.

7. Commission of the European Communities, Proposal for a Directive of the European Parliament and the Council on National Emission Ceilings for Certain Atmospheric Pollutants/Proposal for a Directive of the European Parliament and the Council Relating to Ozone in Ambient Air, Brussels, 9 June 1999, COM(1999) 125: 39.

8. This section draws heavily from Selin and VanDeveer 2003.

9. Author interviews with state representatives to the LRTAP Working Group on Strategies, February 1998, Geneva.

10. Interviews with Markus Amman, Director of the Transboundary Air Pollution Project, IIASA, February 1998.

11. Commission of the European Communities, Proposal for a Directive of the European Parliament and the Council on National Emission Ceilings for Certain Atmospheric Pollutants/Proposal for a Directive of the European Parliament and the Council Relating to Ozone in Ambient Air, Brussels, 9 June 1999, COM(1999) 125: 10.

12. Communication from the Commission, The Clean Air for Europe (CAFE) Programme: Towards a Thematic Strategy for Air Quality, Brussels 04.05.2001 COM (2001) 245, sec. 5.9.1.

References

Agrawal, A., and S. Narain. 1991. *Global Warming in an Unequal World: A Case of Environmental Colonialism*. Delhi: Center for Science and Environment.

Agrawal, Shardul. 1997. *Explaining the Evolution of the IPCC Structure and Process*. Working paper. Cambridge, MA: Belfer Center for Science and International Affairs, Harvard University.

Alcamo, Joseph, Roderick Shaw, and Leen Hordijk, eds. 1990. *The RAINS Model of Acidification: Science and Strategies for Europe*. Dordrecht: Kluwer Academic Publishers.

Bäckstrand, Karin, and Selin, Henrik. 2000. Sweden—a pioneer of acidification abatement. In Arild Underdal and Kenneth Hanf, eds., *International Environmental Agreements and Domestic Politics: The Case of Acid Rain*. Aldershot: Ashgate.

Bolin, Bert, ed. 1972. *Sweden's Case Study for the United Nations Conference on the Human Environment: Air Pollution across National Boundaries*. Stockholm: Norstadt and Sons.

Botcheva, Liliana. 1998. *Information, Credibility, and Cooperation: The Use of Economic Assessment in the Approximation of EU Environmental Legislation in Eastern Europe*. Working paper. Cambridge, MA: Belfer Center for Science and International Affairs, Harvard University.

Botcheva, Liliana. 2001. Expertise and international governance: Eastern Europe and the adoption of European Union environmental legislation. *Global Governance* 7(3): 197–224.

Carmin, JoAnn, and Stacy D. VanDeveer. 2005. *EU Enlargement and the Environment: Institutional Change and Environmental Policy in Central and Eastern Europe*. London: Routledge.

Chossudovsky, Evgeny. 1989. *East-West Diplomacy for the Environment in the United Nations: The High Level Meeting within the Framework of the ECE on the Protection of the Environment*. New York: UNITAR.

Connolly, Barbara Mary. 1997. *Organizational Choices for International Cooperation: East-West European Cooperation on Regional Environmental Problems*. Doctoral dissertation, University of California, Berkeley.

Cowling, Ellis B. 1982. Acid precipitation in historical perspective. *Environmental Science and Technology* 16(2): 110A–123A.

di Primio, Juan Carlos. 1998. Data quality and compliance control in the European air pollution regime. In David Victor, Kal Raustiala, and Eugene B. Skolnikoff, eds., *The Implementation and Effectiveness of International Envi-*

ronmental Commitments: Theory and Practice, 283–303. Cambridge, MA: MIT Press.

Farrell, Alex. 1999. *Environmental policy in an industrializing, democratizing nation: Air pollution in Spain*. Paper presented at the annual meetings of the American Political Science Association, Atlanta, Georgia, September 2–5.

Farrell, Alex, and Terry Keating. 1998. *Multi-Jurisdictional Air Pollution Assessment: A Comparison of the Eastern United States and Western Europe*. Working paper. Cambridge, MA: Belfer Center for Science and International Affairs, Harvard University.

Farrell, Alex, Stacy D. VanDeveer, and Jill Jäger. 2002. Environmental assessments: Four under-appreciated elements of design. *Global Environmental Change* 1: 311–333.

Haas, Peter M., ed. 1992. Knowledge, Power and International Policy Coordination. *International Organization* 46(1), special issue.

Harding, Sandra. 1991. *Whose Science? Whose Knowledge? Thinking from Women's Lives*. Buckingham, UK: Open University Press.

Jasanoff, Sheila. 1990. *The Fifth Branch: Science Advisors as Policy-Makers*. Cambridge, MA: Harvard University Press.

Jasanoff, Sheila, and Brian Wynne. 1998. Science and decision-making. In Steve Rayner and Elizabeth L. Malone, eds., *Human Choices and Climate Change, Volume 1: The Societal Framework*, 1–88. Columbus, OH: Battelle Press.

Kandlikar, Milind, and Ambuj Sagar. 1999. Climate change research and analysis in India: An integrated assessment of a South-North divide. *Global Environmental Change* 9(2): 119–138.

Levy, Marc. 1993. European acid rain: The power of toteboard diplomacy. In Peter M. Haas, Robert O. Keohane, and Marc A. Levy, eds., *Institutions for the Earth*, 75–133. Cambridge, MA: MIT Press.

Litfin, Karen T. 1995. Framing science: Precautionary discourse and the ozone treaties. *Millennium* 24(2): 251–277.

McCormick, John. 1997. *Acid Earth*. 3rd ed. London: Earthscan.

McCormick, John. 1998. Acid pollution: The international community's continuing struggle. *Environment* 40(3): 17–20, 41–45.

Munton, Don. 1998. Dispelling the myths of the acid rain story. *Environment* 40(6): 4–7, 27–34.

Oden, Svante. 1967, October 24. Dagens Nyheter.

Oden, Svante. 1968. The acidification of air and precipitation and its consequences in the natural environment. *Ecology Community Bulletin No. 1*. Stockholm: Swedish National Science Research Council.

OECD. 1968. *Air Management Research Group. Decisions and Conclusions of the 1st Session*. Document DAS/CSI/A.68.96.

OECD. 1973. *Long Range Transport of Air Pollutants: A Cooperative Programme*. Report from the specialists meeting on the atmospheric dispersion of air pollutants, Lillehammer, Norway. Kjeller, Norway: Norwegian Institute for Air Research.

OECD. 1977. *The OECD Programme on Long-Range Transport of Air Pollutants*. Paris: OECD.

OECD. 1979. *The OECD Programme on Long Range Transport of Air Pollutants: Measurement and Findings*. 2nd ed. Paris: OECD.

Patt, Anthony. 1998. *Analytic Frameworks and Politics: The Case of Acid Rain in Europe*. Working paper. Cambridge, MA: Belfer Center for Science and International Affairs, Harvard University.

Pralle, Sarah B. 2003. Venure shopping, political strategy, and policy change: The internationalization of Canadian forest advocacy. *Journal of Public Policy* 23(3): 233–260.

Reed, Leslie. 1976. The long-Range Transport of Air Pollutants. *Ambio* 5(5–6): 202.

Ringius, Lasse. 2001. *Radioactive Waste Disposal at Sea: Public Ideas, Transnational Entrepreneurs, and Environmental Regimes*. Cambridge, MA: MIT Press.

Schneider, T. 1986. *Acidification and Its Policy Implications*. Proceedings of an international conference, Amsterdam, May 5–9, 1986. Amsterdam: Elsevier.

Schneider, T. 1992. *Acidification Research: Evaluation and Policy Applications*. Proceedings of an international conference, Maastricht, October 14–18, 1991. Amsterdam: Elsevier.

Selin, Henrik. 2000. *Towards international chemical safety: Taking action on persistent organic pollutants (POPs)*. Linköping Studies in Arts and Sciences, No. 211. Linköping University.

Selin, Henrik, and Stacy D. VanDeveer. 2003. Mapping institutional linkages in European air pollution politics. *Global Environmental Politics* 3(3): 14–46.

Social Learning Group, ed. 2001a. *Learning to Manage Global Environmental Risks, Volume 1: A Comparative History of Social Responses to Climate Change, Ozone Depletion, and Acid Rain*. Cambridge, MA: MIT Press.

Social Learning Group, ed. 2001b. *Learning to Manage Global Environmental Risks, Volume 2: A Functional Analysis of Social Responses to Climate Change, Ozone Depletion, and Acid Rain*. Cambridge, MA: MIT Press.

Sokolov, Vassily, and Jill Jäger. 2001. Turning points: The management of global environmental risks in the Soviet Union. In Social Learning Group, ed., *Learning to Manage Global Environmental Risks, Volume 1: A Comparative History of Social Responses to Climate Change, Ozone Depletion, and Acid Rain*, 139–166. Cambridge, MA: MIT Press.

Toth, Ferenc L., and Eva Hizsnyik. 2001. Catching up with the international bandwagon. In Social Learning Group, ed., *Learning to Manage Global Environmental Risks, Volume 1: A Comparative History of Social Responses to Climate Change, Ozone Depletion, and Acid Rain*, 167–190. Cambridge, MA: MIT Press.

Tuinstra, W. L. Hordijk, and Marcus Amman. 1999. Using computer models in international negotiations: Acidification in Europe. *Environment* 41(9): 32–42.

Underdal, Arild, and Hanf, Kenneth, eds., 2000. *International Environmental Agreements and Domestic Politics: The Case of Acid Rain.* Aldershot: Ashgate.

VanDeveer, Stacy D. 1997. *Normative Force: The State Transnational Norms and International Environmental Regimes.* Doctoral dissertation, University of Maryland, College Park.

VanDeveer, Stacy D. 2000. Protecting Europe's seas: Lessons from the last 25 years. *Environment* 42(6): 10–26.

VanDeveer, Stacy D. 2004. Ordering environments: Organizing knowledge and regions in European international environmental cooperation. In Sheila Jasanoff and Marybeth Long-Martello, eds., *Earthly Politics: Local and Global in Environmental Governance.* Cambridge, MA: MIT Press.

VanDeveer, Stacy D. 2005. European politics with a scientific face: Framing, asymmetrical participation and capacity in LRTAP. In Alex E. Farrell and Jill Jäger, eds., *Assessments of Regional and Global Environmental Risks: Designing Processes for Effective Use of Science in Decision-Making.* Washington, DC: Resources for the Future Press.

Victor, David G., Kal Raustiala, and Eugene B. Skolnikoff, eds. 1998. *The Implementation and Effectiveness of International Environmental Commitments: Theory and Practice.* Cambridge, MA: MIT Press.

Wetstone, Gregory S., and Armin Rosencranz. 1983. *Acid Rain in Europe and North America: National Responses to an International Problem.* Washington, DC: Environmental Law Institute.

Wettestad, Jørgen. 1997. Acid Lessons? LRTAP implementation and effectiveness. *Global Environmental Change* 7(3): 235–249.

Wettestad, Jørgen. 2002. *Clearing the air: European advances in tackling acid rain and atmospheric pollution.* Aldershot: Ashgate.

Interviews

Serena Adler, Director, Directorate for European Integration and International Relations, (Romanian) Ministry of Waters, Forests and Environmental Protection, Bucharest, Romania, March 5, 1998.

Christer Agren, Director, Swedish NGO Secretariat on Acid Rain (formerly with the European Commission), Cambridge, Massachusetts, April 13–14, 1998.

Markus Amann, Project Leader, Transboundary Air Pollution Project, IIASA, Laxenburg, Austria, various dates, January 1998.

Ewa Anzorge, Head, Department of European Integration and International Cooperation, (Polish) Ministry of Environmental Protection, Natural Resources and Forestry, Warsaw, Poland, February 26, 1998.

Tibor Asboth, Hungarian Academy of Sciences, Laxenburg, Austria, January 28, 1998.

John Beale, Head, U.S. delegation to LRTAP WGS, U.S. EPA, Geneva, various dates, February 9–13, 1998.

Lars Björkbom, Chairman, LRTAP WGS, Swedish Environmental Protection Agency, Laxenburg, Austria, February 12–13, 1998.

Peter Borrell, Scientific Secretary, EUROTRAC, Laxenburg, Austria, January 23, 1998.

Laszlo Bozo, (Hungarian) Meteorological Service, Budapest, Hungary, January 30, 1998.

Radovan Chrast, Secretary of the Working Group on Effects, LRTAP Secretariat, UNECE, Geneva, February 12, 1998.

Anton Eliassen, Director, Norwegian Meteorological Institute and Director, EMEP Meteorological Synthesis Center (EMEP-West), Laxenburg, Austria, January 20, 1998.

Tibor Farago, (Hungarian) Ministry for Environment and Regional Policy, Budapest, Hungary, January 29, 1998.

Janos Gacs, Acting Project Leader, Economic Transition and Integration Project, IIASA, Laxenburg, Austria, various dates, January 1998.

Ramon Guardans, Spanish Delegate to LRTAP WGS, DIAE/CIEMAT, Geneva, February 12, 1998.

Leen Hordijk, Director, Wageningen Institute for Environment and Climate Research, former Head of IIASA's Transboundary Air Pollution Project and former chair of the LRTAP Task Force on Integrated Assessment Modeling, Laxenburg, Austria, February 4–6, 1998, and Cambridge, Massachusetts, various dates, April—May, 1998.

Boleslaw Jankowski, Vice President, "EnergSys" (Environmental Consulting), Warsaw, Poland, February 25, 1998.

Eugeniusz Jedrysik, Environmental Policy Department, (Polish) Ministry of Environmental Protection, Natural Resources and Forestry, Warsaw, Poland, February 26, 1998.

Terry Keating, U.S. Environmental Protection Agency, various locations and dates, 1998–2000.

Ger Klassen, Economic Analysis and Environmental Forward Studies, European Commission, DG XI-Environment, Nuclear Safety and Civil Protection, Laxenburg, Austria, January 21, 1998.

Maria Klokocka, Environmental Policy Department, (Polish) Ministry of Environmental Protection, Natural Resources and Forestry, Warsaw, Poland, February 26, 1998.

Endre Kovacs, Deputy Head, Department of Integrated Pollution Control, (Hungarian) Ministry for Environment and Regional Policy, Budapest, Hungary, January 29, 1998.

Milan Lapin, Chair, Department of Meteorology and Climatology, Comenius University, Bratislava, Slovak Republic, February 3, 1998.

Eija Lumme, Secretary of the Steering Body to EMEP, LRTAP Secretariat, UNECE, Geneva, February 12, 1998.

Martin Lutz, Expert—Urban Environment, European Commission, DG XI-Environment, Nuclear Safety and Civil Protection, Laxenburg, Austria, January 21, 1998.

Olga Majercakova, Department of Hydrology, Slovak Hydrometeorological Institute, Bratislava, Slovak Republic, February 3, 1998.

Katarina Mareckova, Slovak Hydrometeorological Institute, Bratislava, Slovak Republic, February 3, 1998.

Dumitu Mihu, Romanian Delegate to LRTAP WGS and Technical Assistant, (Romanian) National Center for Sustainable Development, Bucharest, Romania, March 3, 1998.

Jeffrey Miller, Executive Director, Lead Industries Association (U.S.), Geneva, February 9–10.

Ivan Mojik, Director, Department of Air Protection, Ministry of the Environment of the Slovak Republic, Bratislava, Slovak Republic, February 3, 1998.

Brian Muehling, Member of U.S. delegation to LRTAP WGS, U.S. Environmental Protection Agency, Geneva, various dates, February 9–13, 1998.

Teodor Ognean, Expert, (Romanian) Ministry of Waters, Forests and Environmental Protection, Bucharest, Romania, March 5, 1998.

Krystyna Panek, Deputy Director, Department of European Integration and International Cooperation, (Polish) Ministry of Environmental Protection, Natural Resources and Forestry, Warsaw, Poland, February 26, 1998.

Ryszard Purski, Chief Specialist, (Polish) Ministry of Environmental Protection, Natural Resources and Forestry, Warsaw, Poland, February 26, 1998.

Henrik Selin, doctoral candidate and observer of LRTAP WGS, Linkoping University, Sweden; Geneva, various dates, February 11–13, 1998.

Janos Sudar, Head, Section for European Integration, Ministry for Environment and Regional Policy, Budapest, Hungary, January 29, 1998.

Tajthy Tihamer, Energy and Environmental Consultant, Budapest, Hungary, January 29, 1998.

Robert Toth, Meteorologist and Hungarian Delegate to the LRTAP WGS, Department for Integrated Environmental Protection, (Hungarian) Ministry for Environment and Regional Policy, Geneva, February 11–12, 1998.

Ewa Wesolowska, Department of European Integration and International Cooperation, (Polish) Ministry of Environmental Protection, Natural Resources and Forestry, Warsaw, Poland, February 26, 1998.

Henning Wuester, Secretary to the working Group on Strategies, LRTAP Secretariat, UNECE, Laxenburg, Austria, January 26, 1998, and Geneva, various dates, February 9–13, 1998.

Dusan Zavodsky, Associate Professor, Slovak Hydrometeorological Institute, Bratislava, Slovak Republic, February 3, 1998.

Nandor Zoltai, Head, Department for European Integration and International Relations, Budapest, Romania, January 29, 1998.

Ivan Zuzula, Deputy Director, Slovak Hydrometeorological Institute, Bratislava, Slovak Republic, February 3, 1998.

6

Structure and Influence of International Assessments: Lessons from Central and Eastern Europe

Liliana B. Andonova

Introduction

After the collapse of Communist regimes in 1989, multiple frameworks of East-West environmental cooperation were established in Europe. The Environment for Europe process was the first prominent pan-European forum for discussion and policy assistance. Issue-specific cooperation within international organizations also continued in areas such as acid rain, global climate change, biodiversity, and access to environmental information. The requirement to adopt the environmental regulations of the European Union (EU) as a condition for membership created another international dimension in the environmental reforms of Central and Eastern European states.[1]

International assessments[2] have been an important aspect of East-West environmental cooperation. Technical assessments were intended to strengthen the capacity for environmental management in transition states, which had a great deal of scientific expertise but little experience in environmental management or in the open use of information as a basis for decision making. Advisory institutions and projects were expected to identify multiple options for policy change and facilitate the adoption of cost-effective environmental instruments. Assessments also represented a conscious effort by donors to increase the transparency of interaction and to ensure that financial assistance was justified and used adequately (Connolly, Gutner, and Bedarff 1996; World Bank 1994).

Expertise-building projects, however, have often been criticized in Central and Eastern Europe as involving a large expenditure of resources that mainly went to international consultants but had little practical effect on policymaking and environmental change (Connolly, Gutner, and Bedarff 1996). Such criticisms have prompted questions about the effectiveness of international assessments that seek to generate and communicate expertise across boundaries and societies. After more than ten years of active East-West cooperation, when most Central and Eastern European states have made significant strides in advancing environmental policy objectives, we can step back and evaluate the impact of assessments and draw lessons about characteristics that determine their effect. This case study uses the context of environmental cooperation in Central and Eastern Europe to shed light on the central issue addressed by the book: what conditions allow some international environmental assessments but not others to influence national policy domains.

This chapter examines the impact of economic assessments of the cost of alternative policy instruments for compliance with European sulfur emission standards on the development of the acid rain issue domain in two Central and Eastern European countries, Bulgaria and Poland. While other chapters in this book focus on the role of expertise in shaping environmental cooperation and transfer of expertise in the context of the European acid rain regime (VanDeveer, chapter 5, this volume; Selin, chapter 7, this volume), the analysis here shifts the focus to domestic actors and issue development. The chapter evaluates four assessments, contrasting two assessments that affected in visible ways the development of the acid rain issue in Poland with equally prominent and technically sound assessments that had little influence in Poland and Bulgaria. This research design provides an opportunity to examine what structural characteristics enable some assessments to build consensual knowledge that facilitates agreement (Haas 1992).

The cases are selected to control for many of the contextual factors that may influence the uptake of expertise. In both Bulgaria and Poland, the adoption of international air emission standards has been a highly contested issue, associated with high cost for the electricity industry, strong international pressure, and uneven power relations with the West. At the same time, the selection of four assessments that had equally high levels of technical expertise allows us to control for the quality of expertise, clearly an important characteristic of assessments when we are studying the relation between assessment structure and its impact on an issue domain. The analysis identifies the institutional characteristics of assessment processes that facilitate the uptake and influence of expertise across international and domestic environmental policy arenas. It looks closely at the expertise-policy interface to determine through what mechanisms, if at all, technical information provided by assessment institutions affected the management of acid rain in these two states. The study draws on extensive field research, interviews, and examination of policy documents and assessment reports, conducted mostly in 1998 and updated in 2000.

The analysis reveals that in a context characterized by a high level of policy contestation and uneven power distribution, some form of stakeholder representation, although not necessarily direct involvement, is necessary for the uptake of information. In the more influential assessments considered here, stakeholder involvement enhanced all three attributes identified by this volume as important for the effectiveness of expertise: the perceived salience, legitimacy, and credibility of information. The participatory structure of these institutions facilitated closer dialogue among actors with divergent interests, influenced the strategies of powerful groups, and provided credible policy-relevant options for more fine-tuned bargains domestically and internationally.

The legitimizing and credibility-strengthening role of wider political involvement in global environmental assessments is one of the central findings of this book (Biermann, chapter 4, this volume; Clark, Mitchell, and Cash, chapter 1, this volume). While it is logical to expect that a participatory structure of assessments would increase the salience and legitimacy of information communicated, the finding that stakeholder participation also enhanced the credibility of expertise is surprising. After all, the "neutrality" and political detachment of science are traditionally seen as essential for the credibility of technical information in the policy arena. The involvement of nonscientists in an assessment process is typically expected to harm the technical credibility of information. The case studies presented here examine the tensions between political involvement and credibility, and on the basis of the empirical material, identify institutional mechanisms through which participation can enhance the credibility of information while guarding the integrity of expertise. The analysis thus traces how a participatory institutional structure enhances the three assessment attributes—credibility, salience, and legitimacy—identified by the volume as key determinants of information influence.

The chapter is structured as follows. The first section describes the issue domain of acid rain cooperation in Europe and the requirements for policy adjustment in Bulgaria and Poland. The second section examines the structure of the two international assessments that successfully influenced the Polish context and specifies the mechanisms of that influence. The third section contrasts the success stories with several prominent assessments, whose institutional structure did not allow for adequate stakeholder involvement and thus limited the opportunities for influence. I conclude by identifying broader implications for global environmental issues and the role of assessments in international cooperation.

The Issue Domain: Acid Rain Cooperation and Policies in Bulgaria and Poland

Cooperation between East and West to combat transboundary air pollution dates back to the 1975 Conference on Security and Cooperation in Europe. In the late 1970s, the goal of Soviet Union to use environmental issues as a forum to advance the process of détente presented an opportunity for acid rain cooperation in Europe. The Geneva Convention on Long-Range Transboundary Air Pollution (LRTAP) was signed in 1979 under the auspices of the United Nations Economic Commission for Europe (UNECE), as the first East-West environmental agreement. The treaty established no specific regulatory provisions, but provided a framework for monitoring, scientific research, and the negotiations of more precise protocols to control acidification (Levy 1993). Scientific data and technical expertise were thus established as essential components of European cooperation to curb transboundary air pollution (Levy 1993; Alcamo, Shaw, and Hordijk 1990).

In the course of the 1980s and the 1990s, a number of protocols to the LRTAP convention were signed. The First Sulfur Protocol (1985) committed parties to a uniform 30 percent reduction of SO_2 emissions. Negotiators of the Second Sulfur Protocol agreed to differential national emission-reduction targets that took into account the notion of "critical loads" of acid depositions embedded in the RAINS integrated assessment model of the International Institute for Applied Systems Analysis (IIASA). The Second Sulfur Protocol also set limit values for combustion sources, and a requirement to use best-available technology not entailing excessive costs (BATNEC).

Other protocols under the convention include the 1988 Protocol on NO_x, the 1991 Protocol controlling emissions of volatile organic compounds (VOCs), the 1998 Protocols on Heavy Metals and Persistent Organic Pollutants, and the 1999 Protocol to Abate Acidification, Eutrophication, and Ground-Level Ozone. The 1999 Protocol to Abate Acidification, Eutrophication, and Ground-Level Ozone addresses several environmental problems on the basis of improved scientific understanding of the interaction between air pollutants and their multiple effects. It specifies new reduction targets for sulfur, nitrogen oxides, ground-level ozone, and ammonia.

Before the end of the Cold War, Central and Eastern European states signed LRTAP agreements to advance other strategic objectives without much consideration for their actual implementation. In the 1990s, however, as a consequence of democratization and more substantial East-West environmental cooperation, Central and Eastern European countries became increasingly concerned with the cost of air emission reductions and their ability to comply with international commitments. Questions about the cost of compliance became especially acute in the negotiations of the Second Sulfur Protocol, which established tight emission ceilings and technology standards (Andonova 2004).

International pressure on Central and Eastern European states to reduce sulfur emissions intensified with the beginning of preparations for EU accession negotiations. Key EU proponents of enlargement such as Sweden, Denmark, Germany, Finland, and Austria receive large amounts of acidifying emissions from Central and Eastern Europe and are advocates of proactive environmental policy in the Union. Membership in the

EU thus implies a strong commitment for accession candidates to comply with LRTAP protocols and EU directives that deal with air pollution (Andonova 2004; VanDeveer, chapter 5, this volume).

Compliance with the Second Sulfur Protocol and with the EU Large Combustion Plant Directive (LCPD),[3] in particular, presented the most difficult challenge for countries such as Poland and Bulgaria during the 1990s. These countries have been among the heaviest sulfur emitters in Europe. The Second Sulfur Protocol mandates significant reductions of sulfur dioxide emissions by these two states, while both the protocol and the LCPD require that combustion sources meet specific emission and technology standards. Achieving international standards was politically difficult for economies in transition because it imposes high costs on the electricity sector and other influential industrial lobbies.

Assessments of the cost of different options for compliance with European standards were viewed as mechanisms to facilitate policy change in Central and Eastern Europe. Cost information was needed to allow countries to develop a realistic implementation schedule, to facilitate compliance with international standards, and to serve as a credible basis for agreement with the EU on realistic implementation schedules. In some cases, industrial actors and national governments produced such assessments to inform their position. A number of cost assessments were also produced with the support of international donors to facilitate the adoption of European acid rain standards in Central and Eastern Europe and to serve as an instrument for capacity building and cooperation.

In Bulgaria and Poland alone, at least fifteen international cost assessments have been carried out during the 1990s, examining the options for compliance with the Second Sulfur Protocol and the LCPD (Botcheva 2001). Rather than describing all these information institutions, this chapter focuses first on two assessments, both conducted for Poland, that stand out as particularly successful in influencing the acid rain issue domain to examine what structural characteristics of these institutions enhanced the uptake of expertise and its influence. These success stories are then juxtaposed to two other assessments that were sponsored by the same institutions, but that had little impact on the issue domain in Bulgaria or Poland.

Success of Assessments: Engaging Audiences

The two assessments that successfully influenced the acid rain issue domain in Poland shared one important characteristic: institutional structure that facilitated direct or indirect involvement of interested actors. In both cases, a participatory assessment procedure was part of a deliberate strategy targeting consensus building and informational outreach.

The first assessment, "Development of Cost Methodology and Evaluation of Cost-Effective Strategies for Achieving Harmonization with EC Environmental Standard" (1996), was one of the early cost assessments sponsored by the EU's Poland and Hungary Assistance for Restructuring of Economies (PHARE) program and carried out by the Krakow Academy of Economics. The assessment process engaged relevant audiences by anchoring the study within a domestic institution, the Krakow Academy of Economics, which had a strong reputation and good relations with government and industry, and had linkages to the NGO sector. The project involved several direct consultations with stakeholders. For example, an analysis of the political feasibility of a tradable permit scheme for SO_2 reductions was based on consultations with virtually all relevant actors: the Ministry of the Environment, the Polish Power Grid Company, the Ministry of Trade, Members of Parliament, managers of individual power plants, and representatives of advocacy organizations (Krakow Academy of Economics and Grontmij Consulting Engineers 1996).

The second assessment, "Compliance with EU Air Emission Standards: Cost of Alternative Strategies for Reducing Sulfur Emissions" (1998), was sponsored by the World Bank and also created expanded institutional linkages between experts, government bodies, industry, and societal actors. EnergySys, the organization that carried out the analysis, included experts associated with the highly reputable Polish Academy of Science. The team had previously undertaken studies both for the Polish Power Grid Company and for the Ministry of the Environment, establishing contact and reputation with these key institutions in the acid rain issue domain. The EnergySys analysis built on previous studies and models done for the energy sector. The preliminary results of the assessment were also subject to a broader discussion at a special seminar, which hosted members of other scientific institutions, government officials, enterprise representatives, and representatives of environmental organizations actively engaged in air pollution issues.[4]

The outreach and participatory component in the structure of each assessment enhanced the perceived salience, legitimacy, and credibility of assessment results. The very exercise of engaging audiences enhanced the salience of these assessments and ensured that the questions asked corresponded to the policy concerns of stakeholders. In studying the development of air pollution policies, my research found that the PHARE and World Bank assessments are widely cited and referred to in policy documents, in specialized journals, and by public advocates in Poland. This indicates that the two assessments were perceived as scientifically credible independent of the extent to which they might have been used to inform policy. The backing of the World Bank and EU funds further strengthened the prominence and visibility of the two assessments internationally (Council of Ministers of the Republic of Poland 2000; World Bank 1997; EkoFinanse 1997).[5]

The participatory design of the projects also enhanced tremendously the perceived legitimacy of technical advice communicated by these institutions. This, in turn, greatly increased the likelihood of information influence. In a context characterized by strong international pressure, uneven power distribution, and high costs of compliance with international standards, the perceived legitimacy of international assessments is crucial for their successful presence in the domestic policy arena. This point had been emphasized on many occasions by policymakers as well as by NGOs and industry groups in reference to international studies and in relation to the World Bank and PHARE cost assessments in particular.[6]

The head of the EU approximation unit at the Polish Ministry of the Environment, Natural Resources and Forestry, for example, underscored that what makes the World Bank study useful for the Ministry is that "it involves a lot of Polish specialists, and builds on work that was done before in Poland. . . . It uses and cites analyses that were done by the Polish Power Grid Company, as well as the study of the Krakow Academy of Economics. . . . In fact, the World Bank report was prepared by some of the same experts involved in earlier Polish studies."[7] Similarly, a prominent economic advisor to the Ministry of the Environment identified the report completed by the Krakow Academy of Economics as "an example of a very good study, funded by the PHARE, but undertaken by excellent Polish economists, who have solid knowledge of previous work done in Poland, adequate access to data, and understanding of the political objectives of policy-makers."[8]

The iterated consultation with industry and societal representatives enhanced the legitimacy of assessment results within these groups as well. The Polish Power Grid Company, representing the interests of the single most powerful industrial actor in the acid rain issue debate, had no reason to challenge the legitimacy of the World Bank and PHARE studies, which had consulted analytic work done by the sector and had been structured to incorporate industry's feedback.[9] The involvement of environmental NGOs active in the acid rain issue domain through the seminars organized as part of the World Bank's assessment and through the personal contacts of the economic team conducting the PHARE study, also established these two assessments as legitimate reference points for environmental groups in their policy actions.

What remains most surprising is that the participatory structure of the World Bank and the PHARE assessments, intended to bring greater legitimacy to the process, also strengthened the perceived technical credibility of information—a characteristic that is essential for information influence. The finding that stakeholder involvement could increase the credibility of technical advice may seem counterintuitive. Scientists often seek to build technical credibility by insulating expertise from politics to ensure the "neutrality" of technical assessments. While political involvement may seem a commendable way to enhance the legitimacy of assessments in a transnational context, such political vetting may incur costs in terms of the perceived scientific integrity of the assessment. In what ways, then, did the participatory aspect of the two assessment institutions examined here simultaneously enhance their credibility as well as their legitimacy?

The main way in which the World Bank and the PHARE assessments advanced their credibility was by centering the process within institutions with high academic reputations established independently of the assessment process. The economists engaged in the studies were affiliated with prestigious academic institutions, maintained high publishing and peer-review standards, and had successfully competed in national competitions for research funding. The high reputation built outside the assessment processes contributed to the credibility of the assessments despite the close involvement of interested actors. The reports produced by these assessment processes were also subject to peer review, further strengthening the confidence in the quality of analysis.

The involvement of stakeholders with different preferences furthermore decreased the likelihood of a deliberate self-serving bias in the results being reported and increased the confidence in the technical accuracy of assessments. As a consequence, the results of these assessments were not subject to "deconstruction"—they were not challenged on technical and scientific grounds for purely political reasons. By maintaining high scholarly standards as well as iterated dialogue with diverse actors in the acid rain issue domain, the World Bank and PHARE assessments guaranteed high technical standards as well as clear recognition of these standards by key audiences.

The participatory aspect of these assessment institutions also enhanced their technical credibility by improving access to the data that is crucial for credible cost estimates under different scenarios and enhancing the quality of that data, an observation confirmed by the role of international climate assessments in India (Biermann, chapter 4, this volume) and domestic resource issues in the United States (Cash, chapter 10, this volume). The credibility of data and energy scenarios used was of crucial importance for the electricity industry in Poland, which had an interest in using reliable, accurate cost estimates to inform its strategy and bargaining position.[10] The use of prior industry analyses increased the reliability of information presented by the World Bank and PHARE assessments and thus the perceived accuracy of the scenarios. Instead of damaging the quality of analysis, therefore, the participatory aspect of the World Bank and PHARE assessments strengthened their credibility by diminishing the likelihood of bias in the reporting of results and by improving the quality of the data on the basis of which cost projections are made.

While it is possible to discern the legitimacy, salience, and credibility of assessment information using interviews and documents, the ultimate policy influence of assessments is more difficult to disentangle. Multiple political, economic, and institutional forces shape policy choice, and the imprint of technical assessments and expertise is rarely direct. The concept of issue domain is, therefore, analytically useful precisely because it allows us to trace the development of the domain toward specific policy choices and to understand the more subtle and precursor mechanisms of information influence.

The World Bank and PHARE assessments affected the policy process in Poland in a number of indirect ways by virtue of being perceived as credible, legitimate, and salient. The very structure of these assessments, which emphasized interaction and consultation of relevant actors, created a close network that facilitated discussion and agreement among groups with differential interests. In the course of the 1990s, economic expertise and concepts became an essential part of environmental policymaking, especially in issue domains such as air pollution and wastewater treatment, which required costly adjustment to international standards. Visible and credible assessments such as the World Bank and PHARE studies provided a focal point of discussion and increased the transparency of interaction.

Participatory economic assessments not only contributed to closer interaction among relevant actors, but also introduced a number of options for policy change considered salient and credible. However, although many of these cost-minimizing options had high levels of public acceptance, they did not have a direct imprint on policy because of political factors unrelated to the assessment process. The tradable permit scheme examined by the PHARE project provides a good example. The PHARE assessment demonstrated that such a scheme would have a considerable cost advantage if integrated in Polish air pollution policies for curbing total air emissions, and was perceived as an appropriate policy mechanism by industry, experts, and some environmental organizations (Krakow Academy of Economics and Grontmij Consulting Engineers 1996). Despite the high-level of acceptance of this policy instrument in Poland, however, it was never seriously considered in the process of regulatory reforms since such a scheme would have been difficult to reconcile with EU and LRTAP requirements for source-specific emissions and technology standards. Direct links between policy choice and the options advocated by this credible and legitimate assessment are therefore difficult to establish. Still, the fact that key actors in Poland accepted several policy options as legitimate and credible mechanisms for adopting international standards was nevertheless of enormous significance for moving the air pollution agenda forward (Andonova 2004).

The credibility of cost-minimizing policy options advanced by the World Bank and PHARE studies, together with other political factors, helped to shift the framing of the debate and the bargaining strategies of important actors. In the early 1990s, the question raised by industry was whether Poland can comply with international standards for the reduction of SO_2 emissions and, consequently, the industry's strategy was to oppose any agreement on compliance (Andonova 2004; Karaczun 1996; Levy 1993). In the late 1990s, the only question seriously asked was how Poland would achieve this compliance, within what time frame, and at what cost to industry (EkoFinanse 1997; Council of Ministers of the Republic of Poland 2000).[11] The strategy of the electricity industry moved away from blocking policy change toward a sophisticated bargaining about cost-minimizing instruments and compensation (Andersson 1999; Andonova 2004; EkoFinanse 1997; Council of Ministers of the Republic of Poland 2000). Factors such as growing pressure from the EU accession and the availability of government support for investment in pollution-abatement technology contributed significantly to this shift of the debate and the bargaining strategy of the power industry. However, the availability of commonly accepted assessments such as the PHARE and the World Bank studies, which provided widely accepted references to the cost of compliance, was an important condition for formulating the new position of industrial interests and facilitating an agreement with the government.[12]

Finally, studies such as the World Bank costing analysis were important for justifying and lending international credibility to Poland's negotiation position on sulfur emission standards and to its preferred course of gradual adaptation to EU and LRTAP standards with special emphasis on the capacity of industrial actors to implement new regulations.

A Ministry of the Environment, Natural Resources and Forestry official noted:

The Commission points out in the *Opinion* that it does not expect associated countries to fulfill all elements of European legislation by the time of accession, but expects to have a realistic and credible implementation program. The EU has underscored several times the need for credible commitment to meeting the environmental requirements of membership. By undertaking a plan and a study of the cost of complying with the Second Sulfur Protocol, we are signaling a credible commitment. This is part of our integration strategy.[13]

In sum, while it is hardly possible to find a direct imprint of the World Bank and PHARE assessments on air pollution policies in Poland, these assessment processes were an important part of a critical mass of economic expertise that has played an influential role in shaping the acid rain issue domain and facilitating an agreement among interested parties. What distinguishes these two assessments was their high salience as well as perceived legitimacy and technical quality with all relevant audiences. The importance of these characteristics for the uptake of expert advice is further demonstrated by examples of assessment institutions that lack these attributes. The next section briefly considers two assessments—a World Bank assessment for Bulgaria similar to the one conducted in Poland and an EU-sponsored assessment that covers all accession countries. Both failed to generate sufficient legitimacy and credibility to influence the development of the issue domain.

Failure to Persuade

The assessment "Least Cost Approaches to Reducing Emissions of Acid Pollutants," sponsored by the World Bank for Bulgaria, shared the policy objectives of the World Bank and the PHARE assessments for Poland. The World Bank assessment for Bulgaria was commissioned shortly after the signing of the Second Sulfur Protocol. It sought to provide a tool for discussions between industry and the government and ultimately to move the position of relevant actors toward agreement on policy change.

Despite their similar objectives, the structure of the World Bank assessment for Bulgaria was very different from the structure of the above-described assessments for Poland in that it relied entirely on international experts to produce the cost estimates and failed to involve relevant domestic actors in any meaningful way. The study was conducted by Coopers and Lybrand, a U.S. consultancy organization with solid experience in energy-sector issues and economic analysis. The Ministry of the Environment, which commissioned the study, saw it as a tool of persuasion rather than a mechanism to promote policy dialogue. The then deputy minister of the environment summarized the rationale behind this study: "We took the initiative and asked Coopers and Lybrand and the World Bank to do a study of the alternative strategies for SO_2 reduction, so that the energy sector will also hear the opinion of independent foreign experts, not only ours. All the energy sector had to do was to read this document, and to consider the options and alternative strategies as a basis for further political discussions."[14]

The Coopers and Lybrand assessment, however, failed to generate any interest on the part of the electricity sector in considering options for policy reform and in bringing industry to the negotiating table. The statement by the former minister of the environment continued: "Our efforts, however, were to no avail. The study was largely ignored by the National Electricity Company (NEC) and the Committee for Energy."[15]

As in Poland, the electricity sector in Bulgaria had strong economic incentives to oppose the adoption of EU and LRTAP sulfur emission standards and little immediate interest in considering implementation mechanisms. Presented with a cost assessment of compliance options, produced by an international organization, experts in the sector were quick to challenge the legitimacy of the results. The study was criticized for failing to take into consideration the specific circumstances of the industry and for proposing solutions that may sound good in theory but did not fit the circumstances of electricity generation in Bulgaria. Industry representatives argued that while the Coopers and Lybrand analysis was an abstract assessment of cost-efficient options, it should have been an analysis that started with local constraints and optimized options to fit these parameters. A representative of the National Electricity Company gave a specific example of the failure to consider the constraints faced by the industry: "The fact that the analysis recommends coal-to-gas conversion for the power generation sector as the best abatement strategy shows complete unfamiliarity with local conditions and problems."[16] Bulgaria imports more than 70 percent of its primary energy resources and has been unwilling for strategic reasons to diversify the basis of energy production away from local coal toward gas, which would increase its dependence on Russian imports (Andonova 2002).

The energy sector also criticized the World Bank Coopers and Lybrand study for the lack of technical credibility and analytic rigor: "A major difficulty with making economic estimates of the type presented in the World Bank study is that until you have a reasonably good energy-demand forecast, adequate country-based data on construction and operation costs of desulphurization technologies and on the cost of disposal of secondary products, it is very difficult to get good estimates."[17] The basis for challenging the technical quality of the assessment, despite the solid reputation of the Western consultant, was the failure to use industry-supplied data in the assessment process. Lack of adequate consultation implied that the scenarios were extrapolations of models based on U.S. data. As one industry representative stated, "Estimates based on data from Western countries are usually inadequate."[18] Attacks on the credibility of the Coopers and Lybrand assessment were used to undermine the study's influence in a social context, where the process by which the study was carried out lacked legitimacy.

As a consequence of these challenges, the World Bank study for Bulgaria, while very visible, remained ineffectual. It did not succeed in influencing the policy debate or the strategies of important domestic actors, much less did it have the intended policy effect. The government could not use the study to justify policy change because no policy change occurred. As a consequence of the continued opposition by the electricity sector, air pollution reforms were delayed considerably and specific air emission standards were not adopted until 1999.

Two important differences between the Polish and Bulgarian contexts are relevant to the analysis here. These differences have to do with the stronger technical capacity of Polish institutions for economic expertise and the existence in Poland's policy culture of a closer involvement of economists in environmental policymaking (Andersson 1999; HIID 1995). The existence of institutional capacity for linkages between political actors in the issue domain and highly reputable economic institutions facilitated the participatory structure of the World Bank and PHARE assessments in Poland. At the same time, however, it should be recognized that the lack of such capacity in Bulgaria did not necessarily mean that participatory aspects of assessments needed to be abandoned. Indeed, one way international assessment can truly affect environmental issue domains in societies with weaker expertise capacity is by involving participants in order to create or strengthen domestic capacity and the institutional linkages between experts and policy establishments.

Another illuminating example of an international cost assessment produced to enhance compliance with LRTAP and EU emission-reduction standards in Central and Eastern Europe is the study "Application of the Current EU Air Emission Standards to the Central and East European Countries. Integrated Assessment of Environmental Effects" (1997), sponsored by the EU and prepared by the International Institute for Applied Systems Analysis (IIASA). This assessment process was also centered at an international expert institution, IIASA, and established no mechanism of involvement of relevant audiences at the subnational levels. Despite the lack of a participatory mechanism in the structure of the assessment, however, the technical credibility of the assessment was never challenged either internationally or by domestic audiences. This reflected the high technical reputation of IIASA in Central and Eastern Europe as an institution that draws on data and expertise supplied by Central and Eastern European research organizations and experts. From the perspective of the European Commission, the IIASA study was considered one of the most credible cost assessments produced in the context of EU enlargement. A Commission report pointed out that "the IIASA study offers the best reference point" as it presents "the most complete set of costs of environmental approximation" (European Commission DG XI 1997, 58).

What constrained the influence of this assessment, however, was its limited salience and legitimacy with key actors such as industry and environmental groups. In Poland and Bulgaria, the study was known to the Ministries of the Environment but was not used in public discussions or in negotiating policy changes. Government officials regarded the study as technically sound, but as one that lacked salience in the domestic policy process, which ultimately leads to the formulation of a national strategy for compliance. Interviews conducted at the Polish Power Grid Company and in the National Electricity Company of Bulgaria showed no awareness of the study, let alone of its results.[19] Thus the IIASA assessment, like the World Bank study for Bulgaria, failed to influence the acid rain issue domain in Poland and Bulgaria despite the fact that the technical quality of expertise was never subject to scrutiny or challenge. The fact that the IIASA assessment, which was backed by the EU and conducted by a well-regarded institution for East-West scientific cooperation, did not generate much salience in either Poland or Bulgaria suggests that the structure of assessments matters for their influence even independently of the context of EU accession and the different levels of preparedness and expertise in each country.

It may be argued that the difference between the IIASA assessment and the other assessments considered here is not one of design but of focus. Possibly the low salience and legitimacy of the study was due to the fact that it covered all accession countries instead of focusing on a single state. There indeed may be some grounds for such an objection. However, one could also speculate that if this multicountry assessment had a participatory structure that used or created domestic institutional capacity to link transnational expertise and relevant domestic audiences, it could have achieved greater salience, legitimacy, and influence within each state. The U.S. Country Study Program for climate change, supported by the U.S. Department of Energy, provides convincing evidence to that effect. Like the IIASA study, the U.S. Country Study Program was an international assessment institution established to provide assistance to countries in transition, as well as developing countries, to evaluate the policy options for meeting the objectives of the Framework Convention for Climate Change. Unlike the IIASA assessment, however, the U.S. Country Study Program did not center the expertise process at a prominent international research organization, but linked domestic expertise establishments and created a strong network among these establishments, and between experts and relevant policy audiences. In large part as a consequence of its design, the information provided by the U.S. Country Study Program was extremely well received by relevant stakeholders in both Poland and Bulgaria. According to many interviews, the U.S. Country Study assessments had a clear imprint on the climate change policy debate in these countries, as well as on the policy programs adopted as a consequence of the close consultation process facilitated by the assessment, underlining once again the critical role of assessment design and the stakeholder involvement in the process.[20]

Conclusion

The study of the differential impact of international economic assessment on the acid rain issue domain in Poland and Bulgaria illuminates the significance of adequate political engagement in the structure of advisory institutions for the effective communication of international expertise and its influence on national policy agendas. This important lesson is also supported by other analyses of the structure of global environmental assessments and their influence across boundaries (see Biermann, chapter 4, this volume; Moser, chapter 8, this volume; Clark, Mitchell, and Cash, chapter 1, this volume). The cases presented in this chapter, furthermore, demonstrate that institutional structures that combine strong expertise and linkages to relevant political actors are likely to strengthen not only the salience and legitimacy of the assessment, but also its credibility. This is one of the central findings in this book. It is both counterintuitive and highly relevant for the effectiveness of international advisory institutions, since the assumed contradiction between political involvement and technical credibility often stands in the way of building assessments with strong outreach components. The analysis developed here shows that consultation of multiple actors can strengthen credibility by minimizing the opportunities for information bias in favor of one set of interests and by ensuring better access to data and local knowledge that may be crucial for more accurate technical analysis.

The argument does not discount the tensions that indeed exist between political representation and sound scientific judgment. It also recognizes that tensions between technical credibility and broader participation may be stronger across certain issue areas and contexts. Lessons drawn from the study of economic assessments may not fully apply to advisory institutions that examine different technical and scientific issues. However, this study points to broadly applicable mechanisms to alleviate tensions between political involvement and technical credibility. Examples of such mechanisms are embedding assessments in institutions that combine a high level of expert reputation established independently of the assessment process and institutional channels for stakeholder consultation, as well as drawing on multiple sources of data and knowledge that would enhance both the level of stakeholder involvement and the quality of information and analysis. The example of Bulgaria, furthermore, indicates that the capacity to achieve both a high level of participation and a high level of expertise is often lacking in many countries in transition or developing countries, and the establishment of assessment processes with adequate involvement of relevant actors may require conscious capacity-building and outreach efforts (VanDeveer, chapter 5, this volume). Moreover, the cases examined here and elsewhere in this book show that skewed political representation, which can be highly damaging to assessment credibility, should not be equated with a balanced stakeholder involvement, which builds on an institutional network that facilitates outreach while maintaining high professional standards. These findings apply directly to current and future efforts at transnational expertise building and facilitating cooperation on global environmental problems.

The structural argument developed in this chapter also has broader policy and theoretical implications for understanding the role of international institutions as information providers in world politics. An influential portion of the international relations literature explains the role of institutions in functionalist terms as efficient mechanisms for iterated bargaining, monitoring, and information sharing, which facilitate cooperative outcomes (Keohane 1984; Martin and Simmons 1998). Constructivist institutional theories also emphasize the role of information and knowledge communication in explaining institutional influence on actors' behavior (Haas 1992; Litfin 1994; Checkel 2001; Risse-Kappen, Ropp, and Sikkink 1999). Institutionalist theories highlight the importance of information credibility and the consensual acceptance of knowledge for its effect in international relations. This chapter and the volume as a whole contribute to the institutionalist literature by demonstrating that the structure of institutions, and more precisely the level of political representation, is an important and often overlooked determinant of information credibility in international relations. The argument thus identifies an important variable likely to determine the differential influence of institutions as information providers and implies that institutions intended to supply efficient and credible information in world affairs may fail in this function for reasons of design and structure.

The finding of the credibility-enhancing effect of participatory procedures of institutions thus helps us understand the frequent failure of well-intended international structures to affect the behavior of actors. International institutions that do not establish broadly participatory or consultative procedures are easily challenged for lack of legitimacy or credibility. Organizations such as the World Bank and the IMF have often been challenged by developing states or stakeholders for their failure to take into account local knowledge and information. By contrast, the information supplied by organizations such as Human Rights Watch or the Organization for Security Cooperation in Europe, which rely on a much more participatory institutional network, is more consistently perceived as credible and legitimate. The structure of assessments and other expertise-providing institutions, therefore, emerges as a critical variable for understanding the effects of such institutions not only in global environmental politics, but in many areas of international relations. This finding calls for concerted efforts in all areas of cooperation, and especially in areas where informational and scientific uncertainty is high, to establish more broadly participatory institutional processes and to strengthen the national and transnational expert capacity that is crucial for such structures.

Acknowledgments

I would like to thank Bill Clark and Nancy Dickson for their leadership and guidance of the project and the editors of the volume for their hard work and perseverance in realizing this project.

Notes

1. In this chapter, the terms *Central and Eastern European* and *Central and Eastern Europe* refer to the ten post-communist countries that applied for EU

membership during the 1990s: Bulgaria, the Czech Republic, Estonia, Hungary, Latvia, Lithuania, Poland, Romania, Slovakia, and Slovenia.

2. Environmental assessments are defined as processes by which expert knowledge related to a policy problem is organized, evaluated, integrated, and presented to inform policy and decision making.

3. The Large Combustion Plant Directive (88/609/EEC) was adopted in 1988. The Directive applies to combustion plants with thermal input of 50 MW or more. It specifies SO_2 and NO_x emission limits for new plants, national ceilings for total emissions from existing plants, and a requirement for Member States to draw and implement programs for the progressive reduction of annual emissions.

4. Interviews with the head of the EnergySys team; the Deputy Director of the International Relations Department of the Ministry of the Environment, Natural Resources and Forestry; and an air pollution specialist at the Institute for Sustainable Development. See also EkoFinanse 1997.

5. Interviews with the Chief of Staff of the Polish President, February 1998; Deputy Director of the Department of EU Integration and International Cooperation MOENRF, February 1998; Department for Environmental Protection, PPGC 1997 and 2000.

6. Interviews with the Deputy Director of the Department of EU Integration and International Cooperation MOENRF, February 1998; Department for Environmental Protection, PPGC 1998 and 2000; Director, Institute for Sustainable Development.

7. Interview, February 1998.

8. Interview, Tomasz Zylic, Department of Economics, Warsaw University, February 1998.

9. Interview at the Department for Environmental Protection, Polish Power Grid Company, February 1998.

10. Interviews at the Department for Environmental Protection, Polish Power Grid Company, February 1998, June 2000.

11. Interviews at the Department for Environmental Protection, Polish Power Grid Company, February 1998, June 2000.

12. Interviews at the Polish Power Grid Company and the Ministry of the Environment, Natural Resources and Forestry.

13. Interview, February 1998.

14. Interview with a former deputy minister of the environment, February 1998.

15. Interview with a former deputy minister of the environment, February 1998.

16. Interview at the Department for Environmental Protection, National Electricity Company, Bulgaria, February 1998.

17. Interview at the Department for Environmental Protection, National Electricity Company, Sofia, Bulgaria, February 1998.

18. Interview at the Department for Environmental Protection, National Electricity Company, Sofia, Bulgaria, February 1998.

19. Interviews at the Polish Power Grid Company and the Bulgarian National Electricity Company.

20. Interviews at the Ministry of the Environment of Bulgaria; at the Ministry of the Environment of Poland; with experts at Energoproek, Sofia; and at the Institute for Sustainable Development, Warsaw.

References

Alcamo, J., Shaw, R., and Hordijk, eds. 1990. *The RAINS Model of Acidification: Science and Strategies in Europe*. Boston: Kluwer Academic Publishers.

Andersson, M. 1999. *Change and Continuity in Poland's Environmental Policy*. Boston: Kluwer Academic Publishers.

Andonova, L. 2002. The challenges and opportunities for reforming Bulgaria's energy sector. *Environment* 44(10): 8–19.

Andonova, L. 2004. *Transnational Politics of the Environment: The EU and Environmental Policy in Central and Eastern Europe*. Cambridge, MA: MIT Press.

Botcheva, L. 2001. Expertise and international governance: Eastern Europe and the adoption of European Union environmental legislation. *Global Governance* 7: 197–224.

Checkel, J. 2001. Why comply? Social learning and European identity change. *International Organization* 55(3): 553–588.

Connolly, B., Gutner, T., and Bedarff, H. 1996. Organizational inertia and environmental assistance to Eastern Europe. In R. Keohane and M. Levy, eds., *Institutions for Environmental Aid: Pitfalls and Promise*. Cambridge, MA: MIT Press.

Council of Ministers of the Republic of Poland. 2000. *Poland's Position Paper in the Area of Environment for the Accession Negotiation with the European Union*. Warsaw: Council of Ministers of the Republic of Poland.

DISAE Facility. 1997a. *The Role of Costing in the Environmental Approximation Process*. Working paper. Brussels: DISAE Facility.

DISAE Facility. 1997b. *Using Costing as a Tool in Environmental Pre-Accession Activities*. Working paper. Brussels: DISAE Facility.

EkoFinanse. 1997, October. Ile Kostuje Unia? [What is the Price of EU Integration?] 7–10.

EnergySys. 1998. *Poland. Compliance with the European Union Air Pollution Emission Standards. Cost of Alternative Strategies for Reducing Sulfur Emissions*. Warsaw: EnergySys.

European Commission DGXI. 1997. *Compliance Costing for Approximation of EU Environmental Legislation in CEEC*. Report commissioned by the European Commission DGXI.

HIID. 1995. *The State of Environmental Economics and Training Needs in Central and Eastern Europe.* Cambridge, MA: HIID.

Jasanoff, S. 1990. *The Fifth Branch: Science Advisers as Policy-Makers.* Cambridge, MA: Harvard University Press.

Karaczun, Z. M. 1996. *Policy of Air Protection in Poland.* Warsaw: Institute for Sustainable Development.

Keohane, R. 1984. *After Hegemony: Cooperation and Discord in the World Political Economy.* Princeton, NJ: Princeton University Press.

Krakow Academy of Economics and Grontmij Consulting Engineers. 1996. *Development of Cost Methodologies and Evaluation of Cost-Effective Strategies for Achieving Harmonization with EC Environmental Standard.* Project PHARE EC/EPP/1/91/1.3.1.

Levy, M. 1993. East-West environmental politics after 1989: The case of air pollution. In R. Keohane, J. S. Nye, and S. Hoffmann, eds., *After the Cold War. International Institutions and State Strategies in Europe, 1989–1991.* Cambridge, MA: Harvard University Press.

Litfin, K. 1994. *Ozone Discourses: Science and Politics in Global Environmental Cooperation.* New York: Columbia University Press.

Martin, L., and Simmons, B. 1998. Theories and empirical studies of international institutions. *International Organization* 52(4): 729–759.

Peszko, G. 1997. *Estimation of Compliance Costs for the Approximation of EU Legislation in CEE States Guidelines for Country Study.* Opinion paper prepared for the Polish Ministry of the Environment, Natural Resource and Forests.

Risse-Kappen, T., Ropp, S., and Sikkink, K. 1999. *The Power of Human Rights: International Norms and Domestic Change.* New York: Cambridge University Press.

World Bank. 1994. *Environmental Action Programme for Central and Eastern Europe.* Washington, DC: World Bank.

World Bank. 1997. *Poland. Country Economic Memorandum. Reform and Growth on the Road to the EU.* Washington, DC: World Bank.

Zylicz, T. 1997. *Social and Economic Consequences of Approximation with the European Union (EU) in the Environmental Field.* Advisory note. Warsaw: Warsaw University, Economics Department.

7

From Regional to Global Information: Assessment of Persistent Organic Pollutants

Noelle Eckley Selin

Introduction

In May 2001, delegates and ministers from over 100 countries gathered in Stockholm for the signing of a global treaty on persistent organic pollutants (POPs). Merely twelve years earlier, a group of Canadian scientists struggled to raise international concern about these substances. POPs are organic chemicals that persist in the environment, bioaccumulate in living organisms, and pose a toxic risk to human health and the environment at locations far from the site of their use and release (Eckley 2001). International regulation of POPs (a category that includes the well-known chemicals DDT, PCBs, and dioxins) has undergone fundamental changes since the early 1990s, and information and assessments have had a high profile in policy discourse (Selin and Eckley 2003).

The Stockholm Convention, negotiated over three years under the auspices of the United Nations Environment Programme (UNEP), entered into force in May 2004.[1] The most significant precedent for UNEP action, and the forum where much relevant assessment was conducted, was the 1998 Århus protocol on POPs to the Convention on Long-Range Transboundary Air Pollution (LRTAP). The LRTAP Convention is a regional agreement under the United Nations Economic Commission for Europe (UNECE). Parties to LRTAP include European Union countries, Eastern European countries, the United States, Canada, and Russia.[2] LRTAP is a convention known for having a significant scientific component in many of its protocols, and the POPs protocol was no exception—it was preceded by a thorough assessment process (Eckley 1999, 2002).

During the global POPs assessment and negotiating process, LRTAP's assessment was used in various ways, with different results.

Despite the proliferation of POPs assessments in the 1990s, determining whether and how information had influence on POPs policy proves challenging. However, the progress of the POPs issue—from local assessments to global negotiations, via a regional agreement, in a short period of time—has several advantages as a case study. Much of the assessment work that was picked up in the global negotiating process was initially conducted in a regional forum. Therefore, many of the same assessments or assessment products were used in two different institutions with differing sets of rules and participants, and so comparative analysis can be made about the influence of the same information in two different institutional settings. The regional and global assessment processes addressed the same environmental issue—toxic chemicals—in similar ways at about the same time. Therefore, the power and interest configurations of the issue area are in this case relatively stable.

This case study explores the influence of assessments produced by this powerful region in a global forum, in order to identify whether and how information can be influential across groups of actors with very different interests. To do this, it looks at elements of the global POPs assessment process in which LRTAP assessments were used. By comparing the influence of global assessment on the issue of POPs, and the different attributions of assessments by regional and global participants, it is possible to draw more general conclusions about the ways information can influence global environmental policymaking.

The results of this investigation show that LRTAP-influenced assessments helped put POPs onto the global agenda and framed the issue; mobilized additional participants; and provided bargaining focal points and road maps to a global convention. This information became influential by being credible and legitimate to a broad range of parties. One surprising result from this case study is that ensuring the information's salience to those not involved in its production was far more difficult than ensuring its credibility or legitimacy. Though one might expect that a regional assessment produced by powerful actors would be unlikely to be deemed legitimate by others, this case illustrates how assessors and negotiators can address such concerns. Salience, however, seems to depend heavily on more substantive participation in the original assessment process. LRTAP-influenced assessments had significant influence despite their lack of salience to many parties, primarily because of the salience brought to these issues by other regional assessments.

Data for this investigation is based primarily on detailed, personal interviews conducted with LRTAP and UNEP assessors and negotiators, as well as examination of the assessments and relevant documents.[3] The analysis is structured as follows. The second section examines whether and how LRTAP's assessments influenced the global POPs assessment process, focusing in particular on changes in participation, institutions, decisions, and behaviors within the POPs issue area. The third section considers the idea that assessments are influential to the extent that they are deemed credible, salient, and legitimate by multiple audiences, by examining the attributions of LRTAP-influenced assessments by different participants in the global process, focusing on the issues of legitimacy and salience (which emerged as more important and controversial in this analysis than did credibility). The fourth section concludes by drawing specific lessons from this case about institutions and their design.

Influence of Information

If one were to examine the influence of the LRTAP POPs protocol in negotiations of the global POPs convention, as opposed to the influence of assessment information produced under its auspices, it is quite clear that many participants considered LRTAP to be a very important precedent. A senior representative of UNEP Chemicals said of its influence in a 1999 interview:

Probably the most important thing that LRTAP did is let us know that it's possible to reach a successful outcome. And when you're not doing something for the very first time it's a bit reassuring to know . . . that indeed we ought to be able to get a good treaty at the end of this, because the UNECE did.

LRTAP was indeed a significant factor in discussions. Whether the LRTAP *assessment* precedent had an influence on those contemplating and negotiating global action, however, is the question relevant here. LRTAP assessments influenced the global POPs assessment process in three important ways. First, LRTAP's assessment processes identified and defined the POPs problem, pushed the issue of POPs onto the global agenda, and set a dominant global framing of POPs as an international problem. Second, the global assessment processes, whose content was based heavily on information collected by LRTAP's assessments, mobilized a wider variety of actors, transforming the issue from one that included a few Northern scientists to a full-blown global issue with activists and participants from over 100 nations. Third, LRTAP-influenced assessments provided bargaining focal points and road maps in the global negotiations, forming a basis for negotiation and propelling the issue onto high-level political agendas.

Identifying the Problem and Framing the Issue

The influence of LRTAP and its assessments stretches back to the beginning of global interest in the POPs issue: if LRTAP had not addressed POPs, it is quite likely that the issue would not have been identified as a global problem, would not have been on global policy agendas, and would not have been framed as it was. The concept of a POP emerged virtually concurrently with the emergence of international assessments of toxic contamination from these substances, and scientific assessments done under the LRTAP process were instrumental in initial setting of the global agenda.

The impetus for an international agreement on persistent organic chemicals came in the late 1980s from Northern countries, particularly Canada, which found substances banned and restricted domestically were nevertheless accumulating in Northern biota, threatening wildlife and indigenous populations of the Arctic (AMAP 1998; Selin 2003).[4] In the late 1980s, the Canadians brought this emerging scientific evidence to the attention of several different international organizations, but there was little interest in establishing international controls. In an interview in September 1999, a Canadian delegate involved in the early scientific assessment work on POPs said of their effort:

At the time we couldn't get anybody interested. We couldn't get UNEP interested; we couldn't get WHO [the World Health Organization] interested. The only organization that showed any hint of an interest was the LRTAP Convention, and so between then and 1994 we put all of our energy into LRTAP. And that was in the form of providing scientific documentation, a convincing case that POPs from distant sources were a problem for health and safety in other places.

It was only after LRTAP's scientific work had resulted in a state-of-knowledge report and a decision to negotiate a protocol that global organizations began taking an interest in POPs. The State of Knowledge Report, the result of four years of assessment work under a LRTAP Task Force, was finalized in 1994 (UNECE 1994). In May 1995, the global POPs assessment process was initiated at UNEP's Governing Council meeting (UNEP 1995). UNEP's 1995 Governing Council decision invited an international organization, the Inter-Organization Programme for the Sound Management of Chemicals (IOMC), to work with two other international organizations, the International Programme on Chemical Safety (IPCS) and the Intergovernmental Forum on Chemical Safety (IFCS), in conducting an assessment process on twelve chemicals that were well-known toxic substances. At that time, the IFCS established an ad hoc working group on POPs, whose function was to provide information and make recommendations to UNEP on POPs (IFCS 1996a). As input to this effort, a background assessment report was conducted on the twelve POPs by a consultant to the IPCS (Ritter et al. 1995). The UNEP Governing Council explicitly asked that the background assessment process take into account information available from, among other sources, the UNECE process, and much of the information included had first been collected under LRTAP. However, the information was reviewed and collected under global auspices. This process occurred before negotiations commenced in the global process. After IFCS assessment activities in 1996, UNEP's Governing Council adopted another decision, establishing a mandate to begin negotiations on the twelve selected POPs (UNEP 1997a).

In addition to LRTAP's influence on identifying POPs as a problem and getting the issue onto the global agenda, the dominant framing of the problem—as a problem of persistent organic pollutants, as opposed to a problem of pesticides; of stockpiles of obsolete chemicals; of the need for technical assistance in chemicals-management activities; or of local problems from chemicals in international trade—reflected the influence of LRTAP's assessment process. The category of POPs per se is fairly unique. A number of efforts have regulated persistent, bioaccumulative toxic chemicals as a category, and several international agreements and organizations have addressed specific POP chemicals and contamination problems.[5] However, the category of POPs and its moniker "stuck" in international circles as a result of LRTAP.[6]

The term "POP" itself is a product of negotiation between scientists and policymakers, and is an example of an assessment-related product being used to frame the debate and set the agenda. A "POP" is neither purely a scientific category nor fully a political construct. While policymakers point to "scientific" definitions of criteria as defining POPs, scientists are more likely to view the category as a convenient policy construct around a class of particularly dangerous chemicals. In negotiating a global agreement on these substances, therefore, the category of POPs served to bound the scope of the discussion, and the existence of a LRTAP agreement on POPs helped this decision to be made without much controversy. Global action could have been framed around the issue of hazardous chemicals in general. Indeed, at the same time, the Nordic countries put forward a proposal for a framework convention on chemicals that was opposed by the United States, among others, which found the scope too broad, as a senior U.S. delegate indicated in a 1999 interview. The existence of the POP framing under LRTAP, which had been agreed to by both the United States and the European Union (and which had its origins in the initial LRTAP assessment work), allowed the framing of the global agreement to coalesce around something that had already been agreed to on a regional basis. In addition, the framing of the POPs problem as an issue of long-range transport of toxic substances carries through to the present as the dominant sort of description of POPs hazards.[7] While most official statements and communications emphasize the long-range risks of POPs, this is certainly not the only framing of the issue held by parties; the ramifications of this will be explored further in the next section.

Mobilizing Actors

A significant function of assessment-related information in the POPs issue domain was to mobilize additional actors around the issue, creating a shared cognitive account of the issue and forming a basis for further negotiation. In its initial assessment, the UNEP Governing Council decision explicitly directed the IFCS to "consolidate existing information available from IPCS, UNECE and other relevant sources, on the chemistry and toxicology of the substances concerned" as well as to analyze information about transport, sources, risks and benefits, costs, and response strategies related to POPs (UNEP 1995). Though the IFCS ad hoc working group reviewed UNECE information, it essentially conducted its own global assessment. Core information was quite similar to that used in the LRTAP process, including toxicological information and chemical and physical properties. These assessments, because they were conducted by globally representative institutions, brought the issue of POPs into a global forum, involving participants outside the UNECE region but making use of UNECE's assessments.

Other assessment processes, beyond those of LRTAP, also mobilized different actors. As part of the preparation and assessment in advance of the POPs negotiations, UNEP held a series of subregional workshops on POPs during 1997–1998. During these workshops, national decision makers presented case studies on POPs problems in their countries, and international experts participated. Eight such meetings were held in different regions, including Cartagena, Colombia; Lusaka, Zambia; St. Petersburg, Russia; and Bamako, Mali. This series of meetings functioned as an alternative regionally based assessment process for POPs. The holding of these meetings mobilized domestic actors by encouraging them to assess whether POPs were domestically regulated, and to conduct national scientific assessments of POPs. The proceedings of these meetings were published as information documents for POPs delegates (e.g., UNEP 1997b). The meetings also provided a forum in which chemicals regulators could meet their counterparts from other countries, with whom they would be negotiating the POPs treaty. It was in this forum that representatives of international chemicals organizations met some country representatives for the first time, as a senior UNEP Chemicals representative noted in a 1999 interview. This gave participants the opportunity to get to know each other, which later facilitated the negotiation and bargaining process.

Providing Bargaining Focal Points and Road Maps

The existence of LRTAP and its assessments provided bargaining focal points and road maps to the global negotiations. A substantive amount of previous scientific assessment work under the LRTAP agreement

formed a strong basis for action on the global level; because these conclusions achieved a degree of credibility and legitimacy among global
parties, scientific data central to the negotiations was not controversial
for the most part. Therefore, assessment-based conclusions that one
might expect would be areas of significant controversy in a global assessment process (for example, the selection of substances) proceeded rapidly
and without controversy in the global POPs negotiations.

Negotiations for a global POPs convention focused on twelve chemicals: nine pesticides (including DDT, Chlordane, and Mirex), two
byproducts (dioxins and furans), and a class of industrial chemicals
(PCBs). This list was established by UNEP's Governing Council in 1995,
and remained unchanged (UNEP 1995, 2001).[8] According to the UNEP
Governing Council decision, these twelve chemicals were chosen because
they were currently the list under negotiation in the UNECE forum,
under the LRTAP POPs protocol. The selection of substances for negotiation in the LRTAP process was preceded by a significant amount of
scientific input and discussion (Selin 2003). The LRTAP POPs protocol
eventually addressed four additional chemicals (UNECE 1998b).[9]
However, the UNEP list is a reasonable facsimile of the LRTAP list as it
existed in 1995.[10] Therefore, the products of a LRTAP assessment were
used here explicitly and without conscious modification, in a relatively
early policy stage.

The existence of substantive scientific assessments of POPs under
LRTAP allowed the early assessment work, and the selection of substances for agreement, to proceed with surprisingly little controversy.
One might expect the selection of substances for negotiation to be particularly controversial. Indeed, there were heated debates about which
chemicals should and should not be regulated during negotiation of the
LRTAP protocol, and the list was not finalized until the final days of the
negotiations. In the global process, partly due to the influence of LRTAP
and its assessment, the substance list was agreed on quickly and remained
the same throughout the negotiations. According to several negotiators
involved in the process, the UNECE substance list was passed around at
a UNEP Governing Council meeting, where it was circulated and agreed
to fairly rapidly at the ministerial level, with little if any domestic deliberation by countries not involved in the UNECE negotiations. In

addition, the fact that the United States and the European Union had already agreed to the list in the context of LRTAP certainly worked in favor of its adoption. To what extent the global agreement on substances was due to LRTAP's political influence, versus its scientific assessment tradition, is unclear. These chemicals were well-known substances, banned or severely restricted in most countries, so agreeing to the list was relatively easy for most. For this reason, it was likely more a political construct; however, it was a political construct with a good deal of scientific assessment behind it.

One might argue that one of the reasons the list was not controversial was that there was little at stake, because most countries had banned or severely restricted at least the ten commercially produced POPs listed among the twelve. The stakes for developing countries—and also for some developed countries—were, however, quite high in the POPs negotiating process. Few, if any, developing countries had taken action on the two byproducts on the list (dioxins and furans); they are required to do so by the agreement. The negotiations covered issues of trade and wastes, and a process for including other chemicals in the agreement. In all cases, developing countries are subject to significant requirements. In particular, the convention will require considerable restrictions on new sources of dioxin and furan emissions (e.g., waste incineration, pulp production, and certain metallurgical processes) to be implemented in accordance with national action plans. Further, had other chemicals been chosen, the stakes for all countries could have been even higher— and may be in the future, when such chemicals could be proposed for inclusion.

That scientific information on POPs had been collected and compiled for the LRTAP negotiations clearly allowed the IFCS assessment process to proceed as rapidly as it did. Because of the limited time frame authorized for the IFCS process—the entire assessment was to be conducted in eighteen months starting in May 1995—the work was not a peer-reviewed, scientific research endeavor, but a brief review consisting of a consultant's report and an expert meeting (Ritter et al. 1995; IFCS 1996b). This was in stark contrast to the type of assessments usually conducted under the auspices of IPCS, which are exhaustively peer-reviewed. Despite these time limitations, the results of this exercise were generally accepted as forming a scientific basis for further action (UNEP 1997a).

The influence of LRTAP's assessment precedent as a focal point in the global process was most evident in the deliberations of the Criteria Expert Group (CEG), which was set up by the Intergovernmental Negotiating Committee (INC) at its first meeting in June 1998. The CEG process set up criteria and a procedure for adding chemicals beyond the initial twelve to the POPs convention after its entry into force. The global POPs convention, like the LRTAP POPs protocol, is designed to be a flexible instrument. In both agreements, the procedure for adding substances is based on specified scientific criteria—threshold values of persistence and bioaccumulation, combined with a risk characterization—that establish that this chemical is of global concern. Such criteria are based on a combination of science and policy judgment (Rodan et al. 1999); that is, these threshold values could not be determined by scientists or policymakers alone, but involved assessing these values against those for known chemicals. The criteria and procedure for adding substances to the global POPs agreement were initially drafted by the CEG. Though the idea of such criteria came out of the LRTAP process, and LRTAP's assessments in this area were quite prominent, the global negotiations explicitly conducted their own complete process.

The result of the CEG's deliberations was a set of criteria for selecting POPs that looked very much like the LRTAP values, and by the end of the negotiation, the criteria numbers were exactly the same.[11] That the UNEP process came out with the LRTAP criteria was certainly not predestined by any clear scientific mandate; no clear scientific thresholds exist that separate POPs from non-POPs (Rodan et al. 1999). Why the similarity? The global process was conducted ostensibly as an independent exercise. However, according to participants, the LRTAP precedent played a large role, and provided a focal point around which negotiations could proceed, making it hard to sustain movement to any other criteria numbers. Indeed, LRTAP's values may also have been widely accepted because, as a compromise between the competing interests at the regional level, they served for many parties as a "best estimate" of where the global negotiations would end up anyway. In an interview in Washington, D.C., in 1999, a U.S. delegate described the process this way: "I guess you could say from a purist perspective that it independently got to the same place, but I think that the LRTAP criteria were seen by a lot of the parties as being in the ballpark of where you're likely to end up." A similar comment on the reasonability of the LRTAP values was made by a delegate from the EU: "Everybody was aware of the results of LRTAP because this LRTAP information was part of the basic information given to the participants for the first meeting, and it was just a question of debate between the experts, which resulted in that nobody really had good arguments to deviate from that."

Another impact of LRTAP assessment and negotiation that influenced the CEG process was the existence of previous assessment and agreement between the United States and the European Union, which served as a road map for their bargaining. One U.S. delegate spoke particularly about this:

The two squabbling . . . northern hemisphere large economic units didn't squabble as much as they would have. Especially at the first CEG. . . . Because there was an agreement to work on amongst certain countries, and there was also a history amongst those people in the negotiation of having gone through the squabbles.

The CEG meeting, by most accounts, was particularly harmonious, especially at its first session. Though there were questions and concerns raised by the influence of LRTAP, it was clear that LRTAP's influence was strong. On the matter of criteria, another U.S. delegate said of the areas of agreement and disagreement, "There's been a broad acceptance of the LRTAP model for UNEP. . . . We're basically haggling over a couple of threshold criteria but not over the basic approach, which is a flexible, parameter-based screening process." He indicated of this acceptance, "I was very surprised; I didn't expect LRTAP to be picked up necessarily in UNEP as easily as it was."

In several areas, therefore, LRTAP and its assessments provided global negotiations with bargaining focal points and road maps. Part of this was due to the political-level conclusions of a regional agreement, but particularly in the early assessments in the global process, a large part was due to the substantive assessments conducted as part of LRTAP's negotiations. As a strong assessment-based precedent for global negotiations, the results of the LRTAP agreement remained largely unchallenged by a larger set of participants: LRTAP's assessment-fueled conclusions made it through the global process with at least its scientific credibility and salience to the direct negotiating tasks intact. The influence of the United States and European Union, and the existence of agreement between these two strong negotiating powers, contributed to this. In an interview in Geneva in 2000, a representative of the LRTAP Convention noted that the global process "likely would have taken much more time had they tried to start from scratch." One delegate summed up the influence of LRTAP in his assessment of his experience of the global negotiations, with LRTAP providing a road map, at the time of the third negotiating committee meeting: "I'd hate to do this without LRTAP. I think LRTAP served a very valuable purpose, interestingly. . . . Would we have a better agreement if we didn't have LRTAP as a model? I doubt it. Where would we be now? Far behind where we are."

Pathways of Information Influence

Global assessments informed by LRTAP information were influential in shaping the issue domain of POPs—by identifying and framing the issue and setting the agenda, mobilizing actors, and providing bargaining focal points and road maps—because they were credible and legitimate to a broad range of parties in global negotiations. These assessments gained legitimacy beyond their original forum by making use of institutional strategies in applying this regional experience in a global forum, while their credibility was not much questioned (though it was critical in setting a basis for further action). These LRTAP-influenced global assessments managed to be influential despite being significantly less salient to those who were not involved in their production. However, this influence was facilitated by the existence of another concurrent set of assessments that were salient to global parties.

Legitimacy

As one might predict, legitimacy concerns were raised when LRTAP parties attempted to use LRTAP assessments in the global POPs assessment and negotiating processes. However, while global parties questioned the legitimacy of LRTAP's assessment in the global process, the degree to which this actually stalled negotiations was highly dependent on the strategies employed by LRTAP parties for applying LRTAP's experience in the global forum. In addition, regional assessments were more likely to be seen as legitimate in earlier policy stages, such as agenda setting and problem framing, and more likely to have their legitimacy questioned in later negotiating phases.

Those who sought to bring LRTAP's POPs assessments to the global negotiations became sensitized to legitimacy issues early on. Several delegates from LRTAP countries mentioned specifically the concern that LRTAP's assessment and results might not be seen as legitimate in the global process. In an interview in Washington, D.C., in 1999, a U.S. delegate said of this concern, "We and the EU were pretty careful not to be seen to be pushing LRTAP as the answer."

The most surprising finding from this case is that the list of substances—a clearly identified product of the LRTAP context—was not subject to controversy on the basis of legitimacy. The impacts of this lack of controversy on providing bargaining road maps for the global POPs agreement were examined in the previous section. However, the finding that this product of what was then an ongoing LRTAP assessment process avoided legitimacy concerns in a global process is unexpected. There are several reasons why this list might have been seen as legitimate enough in the global context. One hypothesis is that the weight-of-evidence assessment of the substances was so compelling that the countries were convinced of the need to address them. However, the degree of controversy *within LRTAP* over the substance list indicates that the weight of evidence was neither straightforward nor unproblematic. A UNEP representative posited that the list was agreed to because countries wanted an agreement more than they wanted to argue about what chemicals to include. The degree to which countries have haggled over other, less significant details of phaseouts and restrictions on substances, however, suggest this is not the case. The low level of contestation over the chemicals to include was in part a product of its framing—negotiations were limited to twelve well-regulated, well-known substances, and an explicit choice was made not to address more controversial ones.

The most convincing determinant of legitimacy was likely that the substances were agreed to on a political level first, and that this mandate was considered authoritative throughout the process. These chemicals were relatively easy to accept politically because they had already been banned or severely restricted by most nations involved. The list gained considerable legitimacy once it had the imprimatur of the UNEP Governing Council. It would have been difficult, for example, for a country delegate in the UNEP POPs process to question the UNEP mandate, given that its minister had officially agreed to the mandate in 1995. Therefore, by gaining legitimacy through such an international institution, the LRTAP-influenced assessment (that is, the original list circulated at the Governing Council meeting) became influential in global negotiations.

The importance of legitimacy is clearest in the Criteria Expert Group process, where legitimacy concerns were quite prominent. In its mandate, the CEG was tasked with considering the criteria and procedures for adding substances to the POPs convention, and it considered the UNECE procedure in its deliberations. The IFCS Ad Hoc Working Group on POPs had recommended in its report the establishment of an expert group to develop science-based criteria and a procedure for identifying POPs in addition to the twelve. The IFCS recommendation explicitly stated that the expert group should consider the criteria and procedure being considered by the UNECE (IFCS 1996a).

LRTAP's criteria, the result of much assessment and negotiation in the UNECE forum, were greeted with considerable controversy from the very start of the CEG discussions. One LRTAP country delegate said, in describing the first CEG, "Several times when people would raise LRTAP, eyes would roll, amongst other delegates from developing countries. . . . The LRTAP protocol was shown, and somewhat rejected by certain people, saying 'where do I sign' in a very sarcastic tone."

There was a great deal of sensitivity among LRTAP parties, however, in their citation of LRTAP's results. The way LRTAP information was considered in the global process indicates that delegates from LRTAP countries were paying particular attention to concerns about legitimacy in the CEG process. One LRTAP country delegate's view of how LRTAP was used in the CEG process was the following:

The LRTAP as such didn't play as a term of art, if you will, in the discussions. LRTAP would come up occasionally and the point would be made that this value was consistent with that which had been developed in LRTAP, but people were very careful not to be seen as advancing the view that merely because it was in LRTAP the case was closed.

Another LRTAP country delegate spoke of the hesitancy of LRTAP countries to put forward LRTAP's assessments, saying, "In the first meeting, when we started to discuss [the criteria] LRTAP people didn't dare to put forward this criteria, and other people didn't speak. So nobody would speak, because everybody was afraid to put forward the northern hemisphere data."

Despite this sensitivity, LRTAP's results were well known among delegates to the CEG. The LRTAP Executive Body decision establishing criteria for substance selection was translated and distributed to global participants.[12] In some cases, parties proposed LRTAP values without referring specifically to LRTAP. One example of such a proposal was a conference room paper (CRP) circulated by France at the first CEG. In its CRP, France proposed the LRTAP half-lives in air, water, soil, and sediment for selection criteria, but did not identify them as LRTAP's values (UNEP 1998). Once the LRTAP values were on the table, however, discussion coalesced around this precedent, and the numerical criteria values eventually agreed to in the CEG were quite similar to the LRTAP values. A LRTAP country delegate said that once the LRTAP criteria were on the table, "in the end then on the level of a contact group [LRTAP's criteria were] actually the basis for discussion, and . . . it was not challenged."

Several factors allowed the legitimacy of the LRTAP values to go essentially unchallenged. First, these values were perceived as "rational" on a scientific and political basis. Several delegates from LRTAP countries proposed that the LRTAP values were accepted because they were considered "rational"—that is, the selection of these criteria resulted in a sensible policy outcome regarding which chemicals were included or not. In a 1999 interview, one delegate from a LRTAP country credited this to the "scientific" nature of the LRTAP process, saying, "I think that many of the other parties . . . seemed to be of the view that the LRTAP process had a pretty fair scientific component behind it, and that the

LRTAP values were not . . . the result of a political process, that [they] in fact had a scientific foundation." Another delegate said of the perception of the LRTAP process by other countries, "The countries that weren't part of LRTAP looked at it and seemed to think, 'Oh yeah, this is the way it ought to be done.' Now is that science? Probably not. I mean, it's policy. But . . . it's based on certain scientific assumptions." Though the idea that the LRTAP results were considered particularly credible is not one that comes out strongly from statements by non-LRTAP country delegates, the LRTAP criteria did serve to isolate those chemicals that were widely agreed to be global problems. A representative of UNEP Chemicals said of the process, "I think a lot of experts looked at a set of relatively well-studied chemicals to see . . . if you used such and such a criteria for persistence, and such and such a criteria for bioaccumulation, what's in and what's out . . . on that sort of basis, you get a good sense of whether you're catching the right chemicals or not." Since it was generally accepted that the twelve UNEP POPs were of global concern, it is plausible that countries would see values that separated these chemicals from other organic chemicals of less concern to be rational or reasonable.

Second, the strategy employed by LRTAP parties of deemphasizing the LRTAP connection of their proposals helped legitimize the assessments they cited, and allowed LRTAP's assessments to be influential in shaping the global POPs negotiations. Though the eventual criteria ended up very similar to the LRTAP values, the global nature of the exercise seemed to allow delegates to accept this, because the process was ostensibly a fair one. An Australian delegate said of this concept, "We were aware of LRTAP but consciously put it aside because we weren't part of the process. We didn't want it actually affecting us. When [LRTAP and global] naturally coaligned, the various elements of . . . what we were doing, that was fine, it was supported." Thus, lack of participation, in his view, was a crucial element that meant that LRTAP's result was not legitimate to his country: they didn't want LRTAP actually affecting them.

Third, and more broadly, in the globalization of LRTAP assessment in the UNEP POPs process, avoiding problems of legitimacy became a matter of guaranteeing that the strategies for the application of LRTAP's assessment had enough questioning to ensure that the assessment was vetted globally. At the early stages of negotiation, in the selection of chemicals, review and approval by a global, political body was sufficiently rigorous for a LRTAP assessment product to be copied into the global forum. The background assessment, though fueled by LRTAP's assessment and science, needed a global review and reassessment. The CEG process ostensibly started from scratch, but was steered by LRTAP countries that were particularly sensitive about where and how they cited LRTAP's conclusions.

Salience

In the global POPs process, LRTAP assessments addressed Northern Hemisphere, largely developed-country concerns: their assessments had difficulty gaining salience with developing countries, tropical countries, and countries from the Southern Hemisphere. One LRTAP country delegate described the particular concerns in the early stages of the process:

The countries that had done the LRTAP assessment brought it to the global process. We very soon found, though, that we had to be extremely careful, because of an immediate reaction that there's a problem with high levels in northern temperate boreal and Arctic regions with POPs, and there isn't a problem in developing countries or in the southern hemisphere, and that the North wants to basically have the rest adopt . . . a protocol which has been designed in the North to meet northern needs. And that was a sensitivity that continues.

The sensitivity mentioned by this delegate is an indicator of a lack of salience of LRTAP's assessment in the global forum. One prime example of LRTAP's difficulty in gaining salience to a larger set of parties is in the framing of the POPs issue. LRTAP's framing of the POPs issue is that POPs are on the global agenda because they pose global risks due to long-range transport, tend to accumulate in remote areas, and pose risks to human health and the environment there. On the other hand, many developing countries, for example, look at POPs problems on a more local level. POPs are significant local pollutants for many countries. A number of countries have large stockpiles of obsolete POPs and contamination problems in local areas. Technical and financial assistance to deal with pesticides and chemicals is a priority for several countries.

LRTAP's assessments, which dealt with issues such as long-range transport, toxicology, and best techniques for reducing byproduct POPs, did not address what particularly developing-country users needed out of an assessment. This perspective can be seen from the statement of one delegate from a developing country, who emphasized that salient information would be an output of, rather than an input into, the POPs convention:

I think when the convention is in place is when you'll start to have more scientific effect that will be meaningful to the countries, rather than before the convention. So I believe the convention will trigger scientific effects that will trickle throughout the globe, rather than having scientific data that will be used for the convention. I think it will be the other way around, where the convention in fact will cause information to flow.

The sort of salient information that such countries are seeking is not the sort of information provided, for example, in the background assessment of POPs. Information on alternatives, management, and destruction to address the concerns of developing countries was not assessed in the LRTAP process. Significant gaps in understanding of POPs substances in tropical environments continue to exist. Most scientific investigations of POPs characteristics have been undertaken in the North, and values such as persistence have been evaluated in temperate or Arctic, but not tropical, environments. As one LRTAP country delegate noted,

There is a major gap in the science, and that is that we do know and understand reasonably well how POPs behave in the northern hemisphere, or at least the northern temperate hemisphere and further north. We have very little information for the rest of the world. So whether or not POPs are a problem elsewhere really and truly we don't know. . . . There is a lack of knowledge about significance in the south, or in tropical countries. And that is unfortunate in these negotiations, because we're not operating from a common information base.

If parties truly were not operating with a common information base, and if LRTAP assessments lacked salience to other parties in the global negotiation, then why was the negotiation able to proceed relatively harmoniously through the initial assessment and negotiation phase? Why were these assessments still able to influence the progress of the POPs issue? Clearly, something convinced delegates from non-LRTAP countries that they should be at the negotiating table. Was this purely a political decision, or did scientific assessments play a role?

Asked what convinced them that POPs were a problem, and that their countries should be involved in global POPs negotiations, delegates from developing countries did indeed cite scientific evidence as a key factor in their decision making. However, they were unlikely to cite the assessments of LRTAP countries or the global assessments that grew out of LRTAP. National and regional assessments, in which they had participated substantively, were much more likely to be salient to these parties. Among these were the UNEP-sponsored subregional workshops.

One advantage of the subregional workshops was that they allowed delegates to become familiar with locally and regionally produced assessments of POPs; delegates most often cited local and regional assessments as convincing them that they should negotiate a global instrument to address the POPs problem. Asked which scientific assessments he found particularly useful in negotiations, one developing-country delegate spoke of long-term monitoring of POPs done on a national basis, which showed contamination in breast milk and linkages to species extinction. Another delegate noted that he felt the information given to delegates was adequate, but that what information was not available internationally was supplied domestically. A delegate from southern Africa referred to consultation workshops held by the SADC countries, with invited experts from UNEP and the U.S. EPA, as particularly useful technical information.

In addressing POPs, delegates from developing countries looked toward practical information on local problems that might help enable better chemicals regulation. Though the globally produced information was credible, and many delegates mentioned that there was significant science that said that POPs were a problem, its utility to these countries was not as great as regional assessments in which they were active participants. Though a broad range of parties participated in global review of assessments such as the background assessment, and in the CEG process, it seemed that this sort of participation did not lead to the assessments' asking and answering the questions relevant to these parties— substantive participation was required. However, the existence of alternate assessments salient to these participants, in which they did participate substantively, allowed the LRTAP-influenced assessments to influence the development of the POPs issue at the global level, despite their own lack of salience to all participants.

Conclusion

Analysis of the POPs case reinforces the idea that assessments have influence to the extent that multiple audiences perceive them as credible, salient, and legitimate. Though LRTAP-influenced assessments lacked salience to most non-LRTAP parties to the global negotiations, they were influential because they were complemented by other assessments, which fulfilled information needs for those parties who had not been involved in the LRTAP process.

The issue of POPs represents a global environmental problem whose identification, framing, and existence were constructed by the influence of a regional assessment. While politics and power were significant, information and assessment played a critical role not only in establishing a basis for action and providing focal points, but also in creating the very concept—persistent organic pollutants—around which the issue domain revolved. Assessments played a significant role in constructing the issue of POPs, pushing the concept on the global agenda, and helping to create the issue domain. The assessments that succeeded in pushing the issue onto the global agenda, however, had limitations due to the fact that they were based on research conducted from Northern, developed-country perspectives. Other assessments were needed to advance the issue further, due to the lack of salience of these assessments to developing countries.

This case reinforces the critical role of participation in generating salient information from assessments. LRTAP assessments failed to be salient to countries outside Europe and North America because those countries had not participated in their formation and execution—and thus, the questions and concerns most important to their situations were not addressed.

For countries involved in global negotiations on POPs, there is quite a diversity of assessments and information available. Salient assessment information in the POPs negotiations comes not from one globally produced assessment intended to be useful and relevant to all parties, but from a patchwork of regional, subregional, and national efforts providing information on very different sorts of concerns.

This case also provides a model of assessment design for addressing the competing demands of making efficient use of existing precedents while addressing concerns of lack of salience. It is extraordinarily difficult for a regional assessment to gain salience to users outside the region conducting it. Such gaps in salience, however, can be made up for by the existence of alternate regional assessments. What occurred in the POPs case was that a dominant regional assessment provided the framing and road maps for the global negotiation process, and other regionally based assessments provided information that was lacking in the dominant assessment. This model of assessment, a combination of dominant and supplementary assessments, clearly made the POPs process more efficient. In contrast, the process might have tried to produce one assessment that provided a common base of credible, legitimate, *and* salient information to policymakers from all parties. In this case, if UNEP had chosen this route, assessors would likely still be arguing about this global framing and the information provided, due to the dramatically different framings of the issue held by different parties—and the process would have been delayed significantly. Both models have their advantages and drawbacks.

The trade-off between the "patchwork" model, with its risks to a common information base, and the "comprehensive" model, with its accompanying difficulties in constructing any assessment at all, is a difficult one. Must efficiency always come at the expense of salience? The model of distributed assessment systems proposed by Cash (2000) may in fact prove to be a third way, in constructing an integrated decision-support network that extends across multiscale interactions. At present, however, a growing number of regional assessments and actions indicate that globalizing regional precedents may become a significant strategy in making global environmental policy.

Notes

1. As of February 2006, the Stockhom Convention had 118 parties. See http://www.pops.int/documents/signature/signstatus.htm.

2. The Århus Protocol entered into force in October 2003. As of January 2006, it had 25 parties. See http://www.unece.org/env/lrtap/status/98pop_st.htm.

3. The interviews were conducted by the author at the third and fourth negotiating sessions for the global POPs agreement (Geneva, Switzerland, September 6–11, 1999; Bonn, Germany, March 20–27, 2000); and the LRTAP Convention's Executive Body Meeting, December 8–11, 1998. Additional interviews were conducted in Washington, D.C. (August 1999) and in Geneva, Switzerland (January 2000).

4. One of the peculiar properties of POP substances is their propensity to accumulate preferentially at higher latitudes; because they are semivolatile, they volatilize in warmer climates, condense in colder ones, and travel poleward in a cycle of volatilization and condensation termed the "grasshopper effect" (Wania and Mackay 1996).

5. Examples include the U.S. Environmental Protection Agency's Persistent Bioaccumulative Toxics (PBT) initiative, the Helsinki Commission (HELCOM), and the Paris Commission (PARCOM).

6. The terminology of POPs has an interesting history in the LRTAP process. The phrases "persistent organic contaminants," "persistent semivolatile bioaccumulating organic compounds," "persistent organic compounds," and "POC" were used to refer to POPs in several of the early assessments in the LRTAP process, before the term POP came into exclusive use.

7. The "dominant" description may be inferred by examining the press releases and information materials put together by UNEP, to provide information on the POPs convention. These materials often start with a description of POPs and their long-range transport hazards. One example is the UNEP press release on finalization of the POPs treaty (Johannesburg, December 10, 2000).

8. The twelve chemicals included in the Stockholm Convention are the pesticides Aldrin, Dieldrin, Endrin, Chlordane, Mirex, Toxaphene, Hexachlorobenzene (HCB), Heptachlor, and DDT; the industrial byproducts polychlorinated dibenzo-p-dioxins (PCDDs) and polychlorinated dibenzofurans (PCDFs); and the industrial chemicals polychlorinated biphenyls (PCBs). The unintentional generation of HCB and PCBs is also regulated by the convention.

9. The additional chemicals addressed under the LRTAP POPs protocol are the pesticides Chlordecone and Hexachlorocyclohexane (HCH, including Lindane, the γ-isomer); the industrial chemical Hexabromobiphenyl; and the byproducts polycyclic aromatic hydrocarbons (PAHs).

10. There was some confusion at the time of the UNEP Governing Council meeting about the exact status of the LRTAP protocol's chemical list; UNEP likely based their decision on a list that was not the current working document of LRTAP's assessment process. The most conspicuous discrepancy between the UNEP and LRTAP lists at the time was the chemical Heptachlor, which was later added to the LRTAP list. However, the UNEP Governing Council decision cites UNECE as the exclusive source of its list of twelve POPs.

11. The CEG, like LRTAP, set a threshold of a bioaccumulation/bioconcentration factor (BAF/BCF) of 5,000; a two-day persistence half-life in air; and a six-month persistence half-life in soil and sediment (UNECE 1998a; UNEP 1999). Later, in the negotiations, the final two criteria numbers (an octanol-water partition coefficient of 5, and a two-month persistence half-life in water) were agreed on in the global context; these were also the same numbers as LRTAP (UNEP 2001). The bioaccumulation/bioconcentration factor is a measure of how likely a chemical is to accumulate in biota. The octanol-water partition coefficient is a measure of lipid solubility and can be used as a proxy for potential bioaccumulation.

12. Working languages of the UNECE are English, French, and Russian. The UNEP negotiations are conducted in all six UN languages: English, French, Russian, Spanish, Chinese, and Arabic.

References

Arctic Monitoring and Assessment Programme (AMAP). 1998. *AMAP Assessment Report: Arctic Pollution Issues.* Oslo, Norway: AMAP.

Cash, D. W. 2000. Distributed assessment systems: An emerging paradigm of research, assessment, and decision-making for environmental change. *Global Environmental Change* 10: 241–244.

Eckley, N. 1999. *Drawing Lessons about Science-Policy Institutions: Persistent Organic Pollutants (POPs) under the LRTAP Convention.* Working paper. Cambridge, MA: Belfer Center for Science and International Affairs, Harvard University.

Eckley, N. 2001. Traveling toxics: The science, policy, and management of persistent organic pollutants. *Environment* 43(7): 24–36.

Eckley, N. 2002. Dependable dynamism: Lessons for designing assessment processes in consensus negotiations. *Global Environmental Change* 12(1): 15–23.

Intergovernmental Forum on Chemical Safety (IFCS). 1996a, June 17–19. *Persistent Organic Pollutants: Considerations for Global Action. IFCS Experts Meeting on POPs. Final Report.* Manila: Intergovernmental Forum on Chemical Safety.

Intergovernmental Forum on Chemical Safety (IFCS). 1996b, July 13. *IFCS Ad Hoc Working Group on Persistent Organic Pollutants Meeting: Final Report.* Manila: Intergovernmental Forum on Chemical Safety.

Ritter, L., K. R. Solomon, J. Forget, M. Sterneroff and C. O'Leary. 1995, December. *An Assessment Report on: DDT-Aldrin-Dieldrin-Endrin-Chlordane-Heptachlor-Hexachlorobenzene-Mirex-Toxaphene-Polychlorinated Biphenyls-Dioxins and Furans.* International Programme on Chemical Safety (IPCS) within the Framework of the Inter-Organization Programme for the Sound Management of Chemicals (IOMC). Guelph, Canada: IOMC/IPCS.

Rodan, B. D., D. W. Pennington, N. Eckley, and R. S. Boethling. 1999. Screening for persistent organic pollutants: Techniques to provide a scientific basis for POPs criteria in international negotiations. *Environmental Science and Technology* 33: 3482–3488.

Selin, H. 2003. Regional POPs policy: The UNECE CLRTAP POPs protocol. In D. L. Downie, ed., *Northern Lights against POPs: Combatting Toxic Threats in the Arctic*. Montreal: McGill-Queen's University Press.

Selin, H., and N. Eckley. 2003. Science, politics, and persistent organic pollutants: The role of scientific assessments in international environmental cooperation. *International Environmental Agreements: Politics, Law, and Economics* 3: 17–42.

United Nations Economic Commission for Europe (UNECE). 1994, June. *State of Knowledge Report of the UNECE Task Force on Persistent Organic Pollutants*. United Nations Economic Commission for Europe.

United Nations Economic Commission for Europe (UNECE). 1998a, June. *Executive Body Decision 1998/2 on Information to Be Submitted and the Procedure for Adding Substances to Annexes I, II or III to the Protocol on Persistent Organic Pollutants*. Århus, Denmark: United Nations Economic Commission for Europe.

United Nations Economic Commission for Europe (UNECE). 1998b. *Protocol to the 1979 Convention on Long-Range Transboundary Air Pollution on Heavy Metals and Executive Body Decision 1998/1 on the Criteria and Procedures for Adding Heavy Metals and Products to the Protocol on Heavy Metals*. Århus, Denmark: United Nations Economic Commission for Europe.

United Nations Environment Programme (UNEP). 1995, May 25. *Decision 18/32: Persistent Organic Pollutants*, UNEP Governing Council. Nairobi: United Nations Environment Programme.

United Nations Environment Programme (UNEP). 1997a, February 7. *Decision 19/13C: International Action to Protect Human Health and the Environment through Measures Which Will Reduce and/or Eliminate Emissions and Discharges of Persistent Organic Pollutants, Including the Development of an International Legally Binding Instrument*, UNEP Governing Council. Nairobi: United Nations Environment Programme.

United Nations Environment Programme (UNEP). 1997b, July 1–4. *Proceedings of the Subregional Meeting on Identification and Assessment of Releases of Persistent Organic Pollutants (POPs)*. St. Petersburg, Russian Federation, Inter-Organization Programme for the Sound Management of Chemicals. United Nations Environment Programme.

United Nations Environment Programme (UNEP). 1998, October 26. *Proposal by the Delegation of France: Strategy for the Selection, the Evaluation, and the Management of POPs*. Bangkok, Criteria Expert Group for Persistent Organic Pollutants, First Session. Bangkok: United Nations Environment Programme.

United Nations Environment Programme (UNEP). 1999, June 18. *Report of the Second Session of the Criteria Expert Group for Persistent Organic Pollutants.* Vienna: United Nations Environment Programme.

United Nations Environment Programme (UNEP). 2001, March 9. *Text of the Stockholm Convention on Persistent Organic Pollutants for Adoption by the Conference of Plenipotentiaries.* Stockholm, Conference of Plenipotentiaries on the Stockholm Convention on Persistent Organic Pollutants, 22–23 May 2001. Stockholm: United Nations Environment Programme.

Wania, F., and D. Mackay. 1996. Tracking the distribution of persistent organic pollutants. *Environmental Science and Technology* 30(9): A390–A396.

Interviews*

U.S. Scientific Adviser, Washington, D.C., August 17, 1999.

U.S. Delegate (1), Washington, D.C., August 19, 1999.

U.S. Delegate (2), Washington, D.C., August 20, 1999.

Delegate from Australia, Geneva, September 7, 1999.

German Delegate, Geneva, September 7, 1999.

Senior UNEP Chemical Representative, Geneva, September 8, 1999.

Canadian Delegate, Geneva, September 9, 1999.

Delegate from India, Geneva, September 10, 1999.

Senior U.S. Delegate to POPs INC-1, Venice, Italy, September 13, 1999.

Representative of LRTAP Convention, Geneva, January 29, 2000.

Delegate from the Caribbean Region, Bonn, March 20, 2000.

Developing-Country Delegate, Bonn, March 21, 2000.

Delegate from Southern Africa, Bonn, March 22, 2000.

* Interviewees were promised anonymity.

8

Climate Change and Sea-Level Rise in Maine and Hawai'i: The Changing Tides of an Issue Domain

Susanne C. Moser

Introduction

Sea-level rise (SLR) is evident at a variety of scales. Those producing and using information about it exist along the spectrum from the global to the local. Scientific assessments demonstrate a remarkable consensus on the potential for accelerating SLR due to anthropogenic climate change (Gregory et al. 2001, Intergovernmental Panel on Climate Change 2001a, 2001b; Nicholls and Lowe 2004; Oppenheimer and Alley 2004; Stive 2004; Zhang, Douglas, and Leatherman 2004; Meehl et al. 2005; Wigley 2005). Yet SLR is already occurring along much of the U.S. coastline—in some places at barely perceptible, in others at alarming rates (e.g., Boesch, Field, and Scavia 2000).

A rise in sea level and potential changes in storm climatology are of the utmost relevance to coastal zone policymaking, development, and management. Human welfare, high investments, and significant environmental resources intimately linked to human activities along the coast are at stake. Thus, it is all the more surprising that concern with global climatic and related environmental changes among U.S. coastal managers, especially at subnational levels, continues to be rather scant. Until the late 1990s, only a few U.S. coastal states had conducted assessments of SLR, and even fewer had made changes in their coastal policies or regulations. This suggests that coastal management exists largely separate from climate change and its impacts, including SLR.

The question arises then whether scientific assessments of global environmental risks—such as SLR—influence local decision making and management. If so, under what circumstances are different assessment designs and processes effective in supporting the management of cross-scale environmental risks? If salience, legitimacy, and credibility determine the influence scientific information has on decision making, then the question of how they are balanced in the context of cross-scale risk management should help us better understand effective information-decision-support systems.

I draw on case studies in Maine and Hawai'i to address these questions. At the heart of the case-study choice was an interesting conundrum: the island state Hawai'i is arguably more vulnerable to SLR and may have a greater need for useful SLR information, but as yet has not established any SLR-specific policy response. By contrast, the relatively less vulnerable Maine already has in place SLR-specific legislation. In examining the paradoxical relationship between these two states' vulnerability to SLR vis-à-vis their policy responses, I examined whether the quality and flow of information between scientists and decision makers influenced current local concern and policymaking on SLR. The study revealed two answers: one about the lack of immediate, or easily apparent, influence of assessments on policymaking and another about the much slower, more subtle, but no less important influences that alter the policy landscape and larger issue domain. In the latter case, how assessments are designed and conducted appears to make a difference.

In short, in single-level assessments, the challenge for assessors is to make the issue salient with nonparticipating audiences at other levels. The core challenge lies in forming connections between heretofore-separate issue domains where participant interests, frames, resources, and capacities differ radically. Once this connection is made, the issue domain of concern (e.g., climate change–induced SLR) has been altered to include participants from other issue domains (e.g., coastal hazards). In assessments that include participants from multiple levels, salience is more easily established. Here assessors must place more emphasis on legitimacy and credibility to ensure that participants feel their input matters and produces a desirable, fair, and defensible outcome. Once these basic procedural needs are met, participants may be more open to changing their beliefs, ways of framing an issue, and possibly their policy goals. Balancing credibility and legitimacy within the formal assessment process and beyond, as participants carry assessment inputs and outputs between their respective communities, becomes essential.

Multilevel Assessment Designs and Influence—the Research Approach

Assessment Outcomes

To ascertain the influence of assessment efforts on policymaking and issue domains, it is useful to recall the definition of *assessments*. The GEA Project defines them as more or less formalized efforts to assemble selected (e.g., expert) knowledge and to make it publicly available for use in policymaking and decision making (see chapter 1 and Global Environmental Assessment Project 1997). This broad definition views assessments as products and processes, and defies identifying a single measure of influence or effectiveness (see Cash, chapter 10, this volume, for examples of partial measures). In this study, I judge influence subjectively on the basis of empirically observed outcomes of assessments, not just in the narrow sense of producing policy changes, but also in the broader sense of contributing to a range of issue domain changes, including participation, awareness, understanding, framing, goals, and the attributed qualities—salience, credibility, and legitimacy—of information itself.

Assessments as Communicative Interactive Processes

The transfer of information and its application in practice is—while much facilitated and influenced by institutions and technology—fundamentally a communicative, interactive process between individuals. A better understanding of the role of assessments begs for an analysis of the information being transferred and transformed into active knowledge, the motivations behind information transfer, the actual and potential linkages among actors, and the quality and frequency of interactions among them and their institutions (Miller et al. 1997). These interactions are examined here in the context of institutions and formal and informal networks. Likewise, decision making at various scales most commonly occurs within the context of existing management structures, government programs, and established decision-making procedures

(Moser 1997). This assumption does not preclude the possibility of launching new initiatives or programs. They become embedded in or go beyond ongoing management efforts and institutions but must be legally consistent with existing programs.

This comparative case study investigated the role of perceived vulnerability and information need, the links among information producers and users, as well as political closeness between local, state, and federal institutions in affecting assessments and their influence on information exchange and decision making. Maine and Hawai'i share several similarities and differences, and thus make for a strong comparative research design.

The critical elements examined included

• The *players*: information producers, gatherers, disseminators, brokers, and users (including the quality of interaction among them)

• The *information transfer process*: "one-time" versus iterative exchange among new or repeatedly involved individuals and institutions

• The *degree of integration of the information* (or assessment) *in the decision-making process*

• The *degree of integration* of information and decision-making systems *across scales* and other boundaries

My research did not involve an explicit analysis of political-economic interests, but clearly these dynamics shape the context, motivations, behaviors, and interactions among issue-domain participants. Concerns over power and interests are thus implicitly examined in the context of information exchange and use in controversial policy- and decision-making settings.[1]

Information Sources
The analysis was largely based on interview and documentary evidence. Specifically, I drew on documents available at local to international levels, including assessments, coastal-management documents, and other information on climate change and variability, SLR, and its more visible manifestations—erosion and coastal storm impacts. These materials document some of the formal and informal bridges between scientists,

Table 8.1
Interviews conducted for study

Type of Interviewee	Hawai'i	Maine	Federal/ National	TOTAL
Researchers	7	6	6	19
Program directors	2	2	2	6
Planners	7	10	0	17
Hazard managers	2	1	1	4
Environmental specialists, engineers	3	5	2	10
Extension agents	5	1	0	6
Outreach specialists/ coordinators	1	4	0	5
NGO representatives	3	3	1	7
TOTAL	30	32	12	74

interested individuals, and decision makers. In addition, I conducted seventy-four face-to face interviews with key informants in state and federal offices, environmental NGOs, and research institutions (see table 8.1). Finally, I was a participant observer in state and federal assessment efforts.[2] The information obtained from these sources was validated through triangulation, then submitted to a qualitative, comparative analysis of the two states.

Contrasting Different Assessment Designs

There are two basic types of assessment designs for cross-scale information exchange. In one, assessments are conducted at one level, without involving participants from other levels. Assessors make no explicit attempt to directly capture the concerns, needs, and capacities of actors at other levels, but may assume that information coming out of the assessment affects decision makers at those levels. The IPCC climate change assessments are a good example. Research and experience consistently show that such expectations remain unfulfilled (e.g., Easterling 1997; Moser 2006), unless special efforts are made to downscale from global assessments to local decision-maker needs (see Patt's notion of "decision matching" in chapter 9 of this volume), and to involve players from those regions and subnational areas (see Biermann, chapter 4, this volume).

In the second type of assessments, assessors make an explicit effort to include participants from all levels deemed relevant to the issue, and thus to directly capture the concerns, capacities, and opportunities at those levels. The first *U.S. National Assessment of the Potential Consequences of Climate Variability and Change* (1997–2001) (hereafter *National Assessment*; see National Assessment Synthesis Team 2001) is an example of this design. Lessons from this unprecedented effort in designing and conducting an inclusive, participatory process are still being drawn (e.g., a study conducted by Carnegie Mellon University; see also MacCracken 2000; Fisher 2001; Moser, forthcoming), but several federal agencies and individuals are committed to finessing this approach (U.S. Global Change Research Program 2001).

In this study, examples of both assessment designs are examined. This allows me to examine the respective challenges and lessons for developing more effective assessment processes and information-decision-support systems.

Sea-Level Rise Concerns in Maine and Hawai'i

Maine and Hawai'i—while vastly different in geology and geography—stand to lose much from accelerated SLR. Both states already experience significant rates of SLR along their coastlines (figures 8.1 and 8.2). Both are at risk from severe storms and most of their populations, development, and economic activities are located in the coastal zone. By any measure, however, the island state is the more vulnerable: Hawai'i has a longer coastline exposed to more intense storms; over 90 percent of its population (versus ~70 percent in Maine) lives in a narrow coastal zone with inland areas too steep to retreat to; most resources must be imported across long distances or are limited to what can be captured, produced, and stored on the islands (e.g., water); and its tourism sector, predominantly dependent on the state's beaches, is to a larger degree than Maine's *the* driver of the state economy.

Interestingly, however, the less vulnerable state already institutionalized its concern with anthropogenic climate change–driven SLR in its

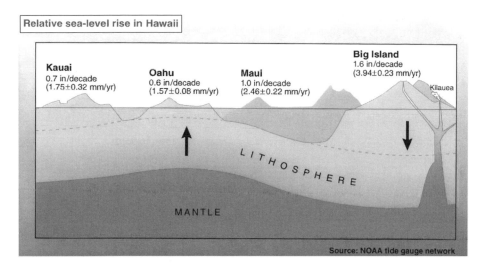

Kauai
0.7 in/decade
(1.75±0.32 mm/yr)

Oahu
0.6 in/decade
(1.57±0.08 mm/yr)

Maui
1.0 in/decade
(2.46±0.22 mm/yr)

Big Island
1.6 in/decade
(3.94±0.23 mm/yr)

Kilauea

LITHOSPHERE

MANTLE

Source: NOAA tide gauge network

Figure 8.1
Sea-level rise rates of main Hawaiian islands. *Source:* Graph by Chip Fletcher.
Reprinted with permission.

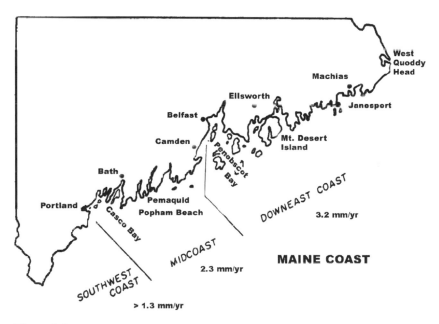

West
Quoddy
Head

Machias

Ellsworth

Janesport

Belfast

Camden

Mt. Desert
Island

Penobscot Bay

Bath

DOWNEAST COAST

Portland

Casco Bay

Pemaquid
Popham Beach

3.2 mm/yr

MIDCOAST

MAINE COAST

2.3 mm/yr

SOUTHWEST
COAST

> 1.3 mm/yr

Figure 8.2
Sea-level rise rates along Maine's coastline. *Source:* Adapted from Kendall, David
L. *Glaciers and Granite: A Guide to Maine's Landscape and Geology.* Unity, ME:
North Country Press, 1987, p. 50. Reprinted with permission from North
Country Press.

Table 8.2
Coastal zone management in Hawai'i and Maine

	Hawai'i	Maine
CZMP approved	1978	1978
Structure	Networked	Networked
Legal basis	Hawai'i Coastal Zone Management Act (1977)	13 different laws, especially Sand Dune Rules (SDR)
Home agency	State Planning Office	State Planning Office
Agencies involved	4 federal, 6 state (7 state NGOs)	4 federal, 7 state, 8 state NGOs officially integrated
Hazard priority?	Yes	Yes
SLR in law/regulations?	No	Yes (since 1988 even SLR due to global warming)

coastal laws in 1993, while there is no such policy in Hawai'i even now (table 8.2). One possible hypothesis holds that SLR assessments and cross-scale information exchange simply are more effective in Maine than in Hawai'i. If so, are there significant differences in design and process that can explain the paradox?

Sea-Level Rise Research and Assessments

National Context for Global Change Research and Assessments   This analysis begins at the national level, which is central to investigating information flow and decision making across scales. Since 1990, the plethora of global change research initiated and funded by federal agencies has been found under the umbrella of the U.S. Global Change Research Program (USGCRP) (now Climate Change Science Program, CCSP), whose mission is defined in the U.S. Global Change Research Act of 1990 (hereafter GCRA, as amended) (U.S. Congress 1990b). The GCRA mandates that the "development of effective policies to abate, mitigate and cope with global change will rely on greatly improved scientific understanding of global environmental processes" and that "an effective federal research program will require efficient interagency coordination, and coordination with the research activities of state, private and international entities." Coordinators of the USGCRP must "consult with actual and potential users of the results of the Program to ensure that such results are useful in developing national and international policy responses to global change" (Title I, secs. 101, 102).

The GCRA also requires that research results be made available to potential users through government dissemination services (Title I, sec. 104(d)). This has occurred since 1993 through the Global Change Research and Information Office (GCRIO). Interestingly, none of the subnational interviewees mentioned the GCRIO as a source for information on global change issues.[3] Interviews suggest that either the Office does not provide the kind of information its target audiences need and/or that there is insufficient effort by the GCRIO to consult with, and advertise its services to, potential users. So, while the GCRA establishes the framework for federal interagency cooperation, coordination, and communication of global change research across levels and constituencies, its success in reaching subnational information users is limited. One analyst predicted that "the program will likely produce 'good science' but fail to provide 'usable information' on which policy decisions relating to global change can be based" (Pielke 1994, 315) because no deliberate process was established to continuously assess "good science" and its usefulness in light of concrete policy problems and response options.[4]

Federally Sponsored, National and Regional Sea-Level Rise Assessments
Even before the passing of the GCRA, important SLR research and scientific assessments were conducted nationally (e.g., Hoffman, Keyes, and Titus 1983; Barth and Titus 1984; National Research Council 1987, 1990). Significant federal investments had been made in basic coastal science and SLR monitoring. Federal agencies also sponsored assessments and regional workshops on the potential impacts of SLR to raise awareness of the topic, educate subnational policymakers and coastal managers, and elicit input on information needs from the practitioner community (Mehta and Cushman 1989; Daniels et al. 1992; Gornitz et al. 1994; Rappa, Tomlinson, and Ziegler 1995).

Among the most visible federal SLR-related efforts is the research, assessment, and outreach conducted by the EPA since the early 1980s (e.g., Hoffman, Keyes, and Titus 1983; Barth and Titus 1984).[5] As part of a 1989 multivolume climate change impact assessment for the United States, the volume on SLR served as *the* reference on the topic for much of the 1990s (Smith and Tirpak 1989). The EPA's Jim Titus was instrumental in compiling this scientific assessment and bringing SLR to the attention of state and local stakeholders (Moser 1997).[6] EPA and NOAA continue to sponsor and conduct their own SLR research (e.g., Titus and Narayanan 1995).

In the 1990s, the EPA also offered funds to states to assess state-level SLR impacts and response options. This process rarely included a broad range of stakeholders. Rather, these studies involved interdisciplinary teams of researchers and, to a lesser extent, representatives of state agencies involved with coastal management. Interviews revealed that participation in such studies was the strongest predictor of subnational actors' awareness of these federally sponsored efforts, and of their knowledge about climate change and SLR. No evidence was found, however, that suggested these reports had any impact on subnational policymaking, or on the broader public awareness of the problem.

The *National Assessment* was the most comprehensive effort to reengage the question of climate change impacts on various sectors and regions. It remains the most explicit, federally sponsored attempt to design a multilevel, multistakeholder assessment process. Both Maine and Hawai'i were active in their respective regional assessments (see below), but no representatives from the two states were involved in the coastal sectoral assessment (Boesch, Field, and Scavia 2000). Finally, under the auspices of the U.S. Geological Survey (USGS), an unrelated effort got underway to assess the U.S. coastline's physical vulnerability to SLR (Thieler, Williams, and Hammar-Klose 2001).

State-Based Sea-Level Rise Research and Assessments in Maine   Maine has a well-established contingent of scientists, which for over three decades has investigated the sea-level history of the state, the ecological and economic impacts of SLR, and especially its most visible consequence—coastal erosion.

Maine's biggest assessment effort regarding climate change-induced SLR is a 1995 EPA-funded study conducted by the Maine State Planning

Office, the University of Maine's Marine Law Institute, and the Maine Geological Survey (Marine Law Institute/University of Maine School of Law, Maine State Planning Office, and Maine Geological Survey 1995). This study aimed to undertake "Maine's first systematic assessment of its vulnerability to a change in shoreline position as a result of accelerated SLR associated with global climate change" (p. S-1). The report, titled *Anticipatory Planning for Sea-Level Rise along the Coast of Maine*, is—in light of the general dearth of such studies at the subnational level— a remarkable document. It includes a physical-geographic analysis of SLR impacts (mainly based on past impacts of historical SLR in Maine and the development of scenarios), an economic vulnerability assessment and cost-benefit analysis of various response options, and a review of laws and regulations pertaining to the coastal zone that could be used to address SLR. The assessment uses low, medium, and high SLR projections and combines these with historical, locally measured rates of SLR.

The report builds on two basic premises: that "the state should protect and strengthen the ability of natural systems to adjust to changes in shoreline position, and that the state should prevent new development that is likely to interfere with the ability of natural systems to adjust to changes in shoreline position" (p. S-11). Assessors concluded that "meaningful preparations can take place now, despite scientific uncertainty, by carefully building upon what is already known" (p. S-2). The report also listed fifteen recommendations for planning and regulatory changes, research, and education.

Interview and documentary evidence suggests that no policy change resulted from that assessment. Experts continue to focus on the immediate (and growing) erosion problems without reference to future SLR. Interviewees reported little change in public awareness of SLR, and only few experts—either involved in it or close to the topic—even knew about the assessment. Neither finding is surprising since no significant outreach effort beyond a standard mailing and web announcement was undertaken. One private land trust used the findings to produce a video and attractive brochure for visitors to its land.

In 1997, Maine coastal experts were involved in a scoping workshop for the Northeast regional component of the *National Assessment.* In that workshop, impacts of extreme weather events and climate change impacts on coastal ecosystems were discussed, but did not rise to the level of a key concern for New England in the final assessment. Hence, SLR was not assessed in any detail, and after the scoping workshop, Maine coastal experts were no longer involved in the effort (New England Regional Assessment Group 2001).

State-Based Sea-Level Rise Research and Assessments in Hawai'i   SLR research on the Pacific islands dates back to the late 1940s, motivated by the desire to reconstruct the contested Holocene sea-level history of the Pacific Basin (Jones 1998; Nunn 1998). Other studies then and now focus on shorter-term sea-level variability associated with the El Niño–Southern Oscillation cycle because these variations are frequently larger, shorter in onset and duration, and thus more visible and of greater concern than the long-term changes expected with climate change (Lukas 1998). Mostly, however, coastal research was a stepchild of geology in Hawai'i in the face of the overriding interest in active volcanism.

Since the early 1990s, with coastal geologist Charles Fletcher joining the University of Hawai'i–Mānoa, geological research on Holocene sea-level changes took off with a more applied flavor. Studies on sediment deficiencies, shoreline change, erosion rates, and beach loss on each of the islands were intended "to make this knowledge available to governmental planners, decision makers and the public to better manage the coastal zone and ensure sustainability for future generations" (Coastal Geology Group 1997, 2001). In an attempt to establish a "scientific basis for evaluating current land management practices" in Hawai'i (Fletcher, Mullane, and Richmond 1997, 209), Fletcher is not only producing pertinent information, but also training a growing number of coastal experts at the University of Hawai'i. Ad hoc, site-specific research on the impacts of development on shoreline dynamics and coastal erosion is conducted by private-sector coastal engineers. All these efforts are improving information availability and expertise but, as one county official put it, "a big dearth of scientific information" on coastal processes still exists.

To achieve greater salience for coastal hazards, Hawai'i's experts—like their counterparts in Maine—focus on the immediate, visible beach erosion rather than on long-term SLR. In both states, experts occasionally use potentially accelerating SLR to augment arguments for changes in beach management (see also Fletcher and Hwang 1992b; Fletcher, Mullane, and Richmond 1997; Hawai'i Board of Land and Natural Resources 1998).

In 1998, a number of Hawaiian experts and stakeholders participated in the scoping workshop and later in the full assessment for the Pacific Island Region—another part of the *National Assessment*. In the workshop, participants showed great concern for sea-level variation, accelerated SLR and its associated hazards, and for their impacts on critical island resources and economies. Thus, the assessment strongly emphasized coastal issues (Pacific Islands Regional Assessment Group 2001). Moreover, local organizers of that assessment made an exemplary effort to involve state agencies and key private-sector representatives to initiate communication, and have been building on this initial effort ever since.[7]

Interestingly, federally sponsored assessment and information exchange efforts in Hawai'i face a challenge not found as prominently in Maine. Interviewees referred to the frequently tense relationship between Hawai'i, the U.S. mainland, and federal agencies, unless they have local offices and are staffed by local residents ("local feds"). These tensions are rooted in the political history of Hawai'i, the historical treatment of Native Hawaiians, the magnitude of the military's influence in local politics, and a basic distrust of "mainland" sources of information. Several interviewees spoke of the irrelevance of climate change information produced by mainland sources, because it does not account for special island challenges. Local information brokers and providers thus must present themselves as either independent of federal or mainland influences—even when such ties exist—or at least be unequivocal about their allegiances with Hawaiian concerns.

Policy Action in Maine and Hawai'i

The Federalist Approach to U.S. Coastal Zone Management The federal Coastal Zone Management Act (CZMA) of 1972 is the umbrella legislation for all state-based coastal-management programs and implementation of national coastal-management goals. Federal authorities review and approve state programs, but states have the freedom to achieve goals in ways they deem appropriate. In recent years, the CZMA has added mechanisms to increase state accountability to the federal sponsor.

In 1990, while global change figured high on the political agenda of the U.S. Congress, the CZMA was amended to include the following paragraph on global warming and its potential impacts on coastal areas:

Global warming could result in significant global sea level rise by 2050 resulting from ocean expansion, the melting of snow and ice, and the gradual melting of the polar ice cap. Sea level rise will result in the loss of natural resources and will contribute to the salinization of drinking water supplies. Sea level rise will also result in damage to properties, infrastructures, and public works. There is a growing need to plan for sea level rise. (U.S. Congress 1990a, sect. 6202)

Although such changes are legally nonbinding on states, they can raise awareness among state policymakers. Inserting the threat of SLR into the federal law, however, has had no discernible impact on state programs. Interviews in both Maine and Hawai'i gave no indication that inserting climate change and SLR into the CZMA evoked any state policy response. Few coastal managers were even aware of this change. Even within the Office of Ocean and Coastal Resource Management—the implementing branch of the federal Coastal Zone Management Program within NOAA—no programmatic shift occurred toward aiding states in taking SLR into account in implementing their coastal programs. With the passing of the GCRA and the amended CZMA, however, state coastal programs became eligible for federal funds earmarked for investigating global change and SLR impacts and for examining potential responses (an opportunity Maine, but not Hawai'i, took advantage of in its 1995 assessment).

Policy and Issue-Domain Changes in Maine   The case of Maine is peculiar in that a policy change occurred *before* the 1990 addition of SLR to the CZMA, before its comprehensive SLR assessment, and long before broader public awareness of the issue (Moser 1997). The policy history falls into three phases:

Late 1970s   This period saw the establishment of the state coastal program, in which historic SLR without reference to climate change was inserted in the legislative findings to justify the coastal-hazards focus of the program.

Late 1980s   In a landmark regulatory change to the state's Sand Dune Rules,[8] accelerated SLR due to anthropogenic climate change was used to strengthen hazards management, a move motivated opportunistically to justify, and provide the specific basis for, directing the development boom of the period in a preferred direction.

Late 1990s–Present   Slowly growing public awareness of global warming has expanded the climate change issue domain. While attention has primarily been focused on greenhouse gas emission reductions, a focus on adaptation has slowly emerged, opening the way to eventual integration of issue domains.

Recently, growing public concern about coastal erosion has led to the establishment of a multilevel, multisector Coastal Resources Stakeholder Task Force. Significant attention has gone to southern Maine's erosion problems and to regional beach-management schemes. Southern Maine's regional planning commission hired a "beach planner" to work with coastal communities on local beach-management plans that are integrated across municipal boundaries. The immediacy of erosion continues to dominate discussions, and local experts and key players in the debate see little value in focusing on the slow, imperceptible changes of SLR. At best, they use SLR as the "final nail in the coffin" to argue for improved coastal-management practices. For example, at the state level, the Sand Dune Rules were updated in 2004 (with a SLR projection over the next 100 years reduced from three to two feet), and outreach efforts are underway to strengthen stakeholder understanding of the value of restrictive regulations along beaches due to erosion (S.M. Dickson, personal communication, 2005). To date, key experts have rarely framed coastal hazards without reference to climate change.

Meanwhile, the combined impact of several regional conferences, increasing media attention, outreach efforts, research, and assessment activities by a variety of actors is changing discussions of climate change in Maine. In 2003, a state climate action plan, based entirely on voluntary measures, was replaced with one calling for an emission registry and mandatory targets and timetables for CO_2 emission reductions. More-over, the integration of climate change and coastal issues slowly contin-ues from the older state Climate Change Action Plan (Maine State Planning Office 2000). Both acknowledge the vulnerability of coastal areas to the impacts of climate change and recall the state's 1995 SLR assessment. A second indication is the regional New England–Eastern Canadian Climate Change Action Plan (Conference of New England Governors and Eastern Canadian Premiers 2001), which concentrates on mitigation, but also includes references to coastal adaptation.

In summary, Maine (compared to other coastal states; see Moser 1997) is one of the most progressive U.S. states in addressing SLR in its regu-lations (University of New Hampshire/Institute for the Study of Earth Oceans and Space 1997, 45; Maine Environmental Priorities Project 1996). There is considerable local pressure to address coastal erosion problems but experts and stakeholders alike make the link to SLR only if it strengthens their position. SLR impact assessments have only occa-sionally and opportunistically supported coastal-management efforts. More importantly, the concerted and persistent outreach and educational efforts of key players in the coastal-management issue domain have raised awareness of erosion problems and related hazards among the coastal citizenry.

Policy and Issue-Domain Changes in Hawai'i   Although Hawai'i has not yet formulated a policy response to SLR, climate change has not gone unnoticed in policymaking circles. In 1985, the Hawai'i Coastal Zone Management Program (HCZMP) produced a short report on the poten-tial "effects of a worldwide rise in sea level induced by the 'greenhouse effect'" (Hawai'i Coastal Zone Management Program 1985). This report—qualitative and typical for that time in its relatively simplistic approach—projected dire consequences under four different SLR sce-narios for Honolulu. These scenarios were alarming, if not outright catastrophic, and should have—given their focus on the political and economic center of Hawai'i—produced loud outcries among the intended audience. Maps showed several critical shorefront installations to become inundated under those SLR scenarios, including the Honolulu International Airport, major traffic arteries, and significant high-value properties in Honolulu's tourist center, Waikīkī. One nongovernmental but well-informed insider explained that for acute political reasons—the proposed expansion of the airport—this report vanished without receiving any publicity. It is unclear whether it was ever submitted to the state senate at all.

Unsurprisingly, the assessment had no discernible outcome, although it recommended (1) continuing to study SLR and its impacts on Hawai'i and revisiting the issue of SLR in 1989; and (2) developing a more comprehensive plan detailing how SLR should be addressed within planning, shoreline infrastructure development, existing regulations, and economic incentives to direct development away from hazardous areas (Hawai'i Coastal Zone Management Program 1985, 7–8).

The issue was not publicly revisited until the Regional Assessment (see below). Independently, the HCZMP has, however, financially supported the preparation of a Beach Management Plan (Fletcher and Hwang 1992a). The plan discusses current and projected rates of SLR for the major Hawaiian islands, taking island subsidence and accelerated SLR projections by the IPCC into account, and assesses available management options. No specific policy changes resulted from this plan, although proposals for planning and regulatory changes have been discussed. In the late 1990s, Fletcher's research group also conducted studies for each of the islands to provide shore-status baselines and identify beach-nourishment priorities. In a parallel effort, an interagency task force (MACZMAG, see below) is reviewing and streamlining beach-nourishment permitting procedures.

Other state-government publications occasionally mention SLR but have not resulted in any specific policy action.[9] Separately, several reports about climate change did not mention SLR—again a compartmentalization of issues that may have institutional and/or strategic motives, but that has resulted in independent framing of related issues.[10] In another instance—the state climate change action plan—SLR and climate change were mentioned simultanelously in one report, but the information had little local credibility. Initiated in 1997 through the EPA's State and Local Climate Change Partners Program, the plan (State of Hawai'i 1997c) incorporated an EPA pamphlet on climate change impacts on Hawai'i, including coastal impacts, but the information is uninformed and outdated—a good example of why Hawaiians frequently are skeptical of mainland information.

Over the past few years, several high-visibility climate change or coastal conferences in the region have addressed SLR, thus beginning to build a bridge between the climate and coastal-hazards issue domains.[11]

In the late 1990s, the HCZMP established a new statewide institution, the Marine and Coastal Zone Management Group (MACZMAG), to bring together a broad range of stakeholders to exchange views on, and discuss options for, coastal management. Interviewees considered this group critical to improving cross-agency, cross-scale, and cross-constituency information exchange and thus critical to improved decision making. One of its subcommittees—closely tied to the Coastal Geology Group—is exclusively focused on coastal erosion, but government interest in climate change–induced SLR remains low.

In short, while various state agencies have been involved in efforts to look at climate change and resulting impacts such as SLR, there is no indication yet that they have informed or led to specific policy or management changes. Those management changes that have been set in motion in recent years have been justified on the basis of tropical-storm and erosion-related hazards. However, these changes may be seen as fostering readiness to deal with SLR. According to interviewees, they contribute in a cumulative fashion to changes in awareness and policy changes over the long term. As in Maine, coastal managers return from such workshops to the daily pressures of more immediate erosion- and hazard-management challenges, pushing the long-term, less visible driving force again to the back burner. The strong strategic focus on beach erosion and replenishment that emerged in the late 1990s has resulted in research and outreach efforts. These have brought historical SLR to public and policymaker attention, although without any emphasis on future trends (Hawai'i Board of Land and Natural Resources 1998). Slowly, these efforts build a constituency "neighborhood association by neighborhood association" for alternative, regional and adaptive, learning-oriented approaches to beach management, according to a professor at the University of Hawai'i. They also slowly change the range of participants in the coastal-hazards issue domain and may be instrumental in integrating it with climate change–driven SLR.

Table 8.3
State responses to sea-level rise in comparison

	Hawai'i	Maine
Research	Some, accelerating in recent years	Significant research history
Assessments	1985, 1992 qualitative	1980–1990, 1995 quantitative
Programs/planning	1991–1992, 1997	1980–1990, 1995
Legislation	None for SLR Beach-management plans under development	Sand Dune Rules (1988, 1993) Beach-management plans instituted

Table 8.3 summarizes Maine and Hawai'i's scientific and policy responses to SLR. Below I examine in more detail the reasons behind these differences.

The Influence of Assessments in Issue-Domain Changes

The introduction to this volume argues that the qualities participants attribute to an assessment (salience, credibility, and legitimacy) largely determine its influence in an issue domain. Assessments influence the behaviors of actors and public policies by (1) changing the way people frame a problem, (2) mobilizing people to become participants in an issue domain, (3) altering people's knowledge about the issue and potential solutions, (4) affecting their goals, and (5) building their capacity to understand the science and/or deal with the problem (also see chapter 11).

The cases sketched above clearly suggest that there is no monolithic issue domain of climate change and (coastal) impacts linking the global with the local. Hence, achieving salience, credibility, and legitimacy across scales involves some interesting challenges. Experience in Hawai'i and Maine suggests that SLR assessments conducted at one level largely failed to become salient to scientists, policymakers, and decision makers at other levels. Coastal impact assessments by and large did not reach the broader coastal expert and management community. Interestingly, multilevel assessments, as the example of the regional or sectoral components of the *National Assessment* show, have no guarantee of doing so either, even though participation of the relevant stakeholders is more likely. The fact that multilevel participatory assessments are undertaken, however, despite the enormous time and resources required, marks a growing recognition of the importance of stakeholder input.

These findings suggest three fundamental conclusions. First, assessments of cross-scale environmental risks can fail to have an easily discernible influence on policymaking because those involved fail to deal effectively with the salience/credibility/legitimacy challenges involved. They may make strategic choices around participation, framing, and outreach that prevent such influence (see also Deelstra et al. 2003), or the assessments are conducted at a time in the issue domain's evolution when the policy environment is not yet primed for policy change. Second, if an effort is made to consciously design assessments of cross-scale environmental risks, the quantity and quality of relationships constituting the assessment process are of utmost importance to its outcome in terms of salience, credibility, and legitimacy. And third, understanding the dynamics between separate issue domains may help produce assessments that do reach the intended audience. Important differences in the quality and quantity of relationships between Maine and Hawai'i are delineated in table 8.4 and discussed in detail below.

To assess the extent to which the conduct of the various state-based assessments influenced outcomes, it helps to first eliminate some nonassessment factors, which also appear to have affected the observed differences in the policies of Hawai'i versus Maine. These are largely contextual factors, which assessment designers cannot influence directly, but also must not ignore if assessments are to be influential. Among these nonassessment factors are the state of the economy (as reflected, for example, in state budgets or development pressures on the coast); historical relationships between federal, state, and local decision makers; and the preassessment status of coastal and climate research, including the quality and extensiveness of the network of involved researchers and decision makers. Together, these factors appear to have made Maine more receptive *earlier* than Hawai'i to the issue of climate change–induced SLR.

Table 8.4
Comparison of information-exchange networks in Hawai'i and Maine

	Hawai'i	Maine
Multiactor networks	In place	Elaborate, well established
Frequency of interaction, communication	Issue-specific	High
Interagency relations (at same level)	Highly varied, competitive	Mostly congenial
Cross-scale relations		
State-local	Antagonistic	Collaborative
State-federal	Antagonistic	Collaborative
Science/policy relations (info producers/users)	Some existing, emerging and getting better	Established, strong
Satisfaction with interaction (generally, across all informants)	Low	High

Several differences, however, are less readily explained by these nonassessment factors and seem better explained by differences in features of the assessments themselves. They apparently made Maine decision makers more concerned with SLR than Hawaiians. They also all involve strategic decisions by assessment participants around salience, credibility, and legitimacy in light of the specific context: (1) to reframe the climate change issue in ways that "speak to" local decision makers, or to link local coastal issues to global change when doing so bolsters local policy goals; (2) to build a contingent of credible researchers as messengers of a complex, controversial issue, and to develop a transparent process of credibility assurance; and (3) to carefully design information-decision-support processes that involve participants who can provide the needed expertise, representation, and decision-making power, but also to skillfully tend to the interaction opportunities and challenges within multiactor networks. Each of these points is discussed in more detail below.

Salience: The Challenge of Separate Issue Domains
Salience refers to the level of interest and relevance information garners among potentially interested parties. In the cases presented here, there is ample evidence of separate issue domains that vary in salience: climate change and SLR apart from coastal-hazards management. Scientists and decision makers often fail to connect across the boundaries of these issue domains, even when logical, physical, and social connections exist. That such boundaries exist is precisely the power of framing and of the social networks and institutional arrangements involved in defining and maintaining them (Ancona and Caldwell 1992, 1990; Cash and Moser 2000; Fennell and Alexander 1987; Gieryn 1999, 1995; Guston 1999; Leifer and Delbecq 1978). In Maine and Hawai'i coastal management, there is a prevailing focus on present and near-term problems obvious to all stakeholders, especially after disasters. To address these issues, scientists—in Maine longer than in Hawai'i—have been working closely with coastal zone managers to fill critical information needs (e.g., on erosion and cliff recession rates, quantity and quality of sediment supplies for beach nourishment). The links between scientists and decision makers are now well established and information exchange within the coastal-management issue domain works reasonably well,[12] despite downsizing and fiscal constraints due to the cycles in state and national economies.

Outreach and stakeholder processes involving the larger public are a growing component of coastal management, but still often unsophisticated or only sporadic. Moreover, as coastal managers in both states contended, even the most pressing management challenges today continue to be addressed against a backdrop of little appreciation of coastal resources and a lack of understanding of shoreline dynamics.

In Hawai'i more so than in Maine, the climate change issue domain is still perceived as largely external to the concerns of coastal managers. Interviewees suggested that climate change–induced SLR—as framed—falls victim to everyone's limited attention span and burden of responsibilities. This lack of time and attention limits people's ability to educate themselves or others about it. Thus, they fail to examine the importance of the issue to their daily spheres of concern and responsibility. Moreover, doing so is typically not rewarded by a system of more narrowly defined agency missions and professional duties. Thus, if salience is the gateway to connect two previously separate issue domains, more than flashy information packages are needed to achieve resonance for SLR among potential information users. The challenge is to iteratively (re)frame and negotiate the meanings of an issue such that both sides can relate to it. In that way, frames become the doors through which previously uninvolved people step to become participants in a joint issue domain (see Gupta, chapter 3, this volume). Specifically, an effective frame would help people understand how day-to-day coastal management is affected by SLR; mobilize actors from one domain to become part of the other, too; and affect participants' understanding of management options and goals. Because existing issue frames often maintain issue-domain separation, additional resources and possibly new institutional structures could encourage communication among members of different domains, and in turn facilitate their eventual merging.

The study illustrates how in the United States, the federal government plays an important role in coastal management as well as in initiating and funding global change research and assessments. Through incentives (e.g., funding, program reviews) it can bring attention to otherwise-neglected issues at the state and local level. (By the same token, cessation of funding can bring the end to local efforts as well.)[13] Federal funds could also buy staff capacity to provide the human link between issue domains.

The two case studies also point to the importance of local, bottom-up interest in creating connections across issue domains. Both states' assessment and policy histories illustrate a mix of *strategic* choices among participants in one or both issue domains about when to link the climate/SLR issue with the more immediate erosion problems. Clearly, local actors understand how information can be used to connect issues, mobilize actors (or keep them at bay), and affect other parties' options and goals. Connecting issue domains is useful when it helps unite participants around decisions. It is counterproductive when such links would weaken an argument, invite additional (e.g., legal) challenges into the debate,[14] or draw resources and attention away from the other issue domain.

Because climate change is still scientifically uncertain and politically contentious, it adds elements to local decision making that require high skills of communication, discernment, and brokerage. Hard trade-offs between policy choices frequently weigh against adding the challenge of such vast, unwieldy problems perceived to be beyond local control. However, the fact that both states have witnessed bottom-up efforts to connect with the global problem also attests to the willingness, leadership, and commitment of individuals to overcome boundaries between issue domains. Structures and capacities can be used or created to foster a desire for the results of an assessment, thereby increasing its perceived usefulness (see Patt, chapter 9, this volume).

To create a desire or need for information points to a dimension of salience that interviewees alluded to repeatedly, one for which the issue of scale is particularly relevant. For local decision makers, the question is not only whether the issue of SLR is salient, but whether the information is actually relevant to the decisions a manager controls. Can that information be directly inserted into the decision-making process at his or her level? For example, accepting the reality of a rising sea level, a coastal planner will need to know how the accelerating SLR will change historical erosion rates in order to adjust setback requirements to provide adequate protection against future chronic and episodic erosion. Clearly, if assessors hold an expectation that local decision makers *should* respond to SLR, the assessment must produce information that is directly applicable to the decision they have control over. This typically only happens in the later stages of issue-domain development, yet it is essential to help a remote issue evolve into a routine, locally resonant one. In both states, decision-relevant information (erosion rates, cliff recession rates, sediment supplies, and so on) is now being produced, but in neither state do decision makers currently receive information about accelerated erosion rates due to climate change.

Credibility: The Interplay of Message and Messenger
In the two case studies, people rarely scrutinized the credibility of information as a means to decide about the fundamental validity of the climate change issue *before* they entered the issue domain. Rather, the lack of salience or the contentiousness of the issue—only in part based

on scientific uncertainty—deterred them from entering the issue domain. On the other hand, once people entered the issue domain and thus became participants, their interest in relevant information shifted beyond mere content and relevancy to matters of credibility. Interviewees did afford scientific knowledge a privileged, if not exclusive, status over other kinds of information. Thus, having such knowledge on one's side, and ensuring that it is produced in a credible, scientifically sound manner, is a strategic goal.

To the technical community (or communities), credibility means that the information is "true" or at least better than competing information and that it was derived via standard scientific methods and procedures (Steel et al. 2001). Participants in an issue domain without such technical expertise use "proxies" to assess "truth"—such as assurances about the scientific method, the source of information, or past performance, credentials and expertise of assessors, and so on (Steel et al. 2001). Of course, some communities (e.g., Native Hawaiians) may not afford science a privileged access to "truth," and standard scientific methods and procedures would thus not lead to greater credibility for them.

Interestingly, at subnational levels, where the number of involved players gets smaller—that is, where there is a fairly constant and limited pool of actors—the interplay between message and messengers (and their affiliations), or between truth and the trustworthiness of the information provider, becomes very important. The small pool of actors makes it possible to build familiar, trustful relationships with the messengers and habitually used information channels over time, unless personal conflicts create breakdowns in the communication (observed in both case studies).

The relationship between message and messenger is quite complex, especially when the information is uncertain or its implications are politically loaded and legally binding. For such information to be taken seriously, the information provider must build trust by offering credible, high-quality, and useful scientific information; follow through on contracts and promises; and serve as a noncondescending, accessible, and patient advisor. Equally important is the provider's willingness to work directly with communities and government agencies, and to hear managers' and coastal residents' concerns. Information users then express satisfaction with the access to information and the institutions and channels through which they express their information needs. If they encounter responsiveness, professionalism, and useful advice, trust grows and information, even about contentious issues outside their immediate sphere of responsibility (such as climate change), have a chance to be examined and absorbed.

The need for highly credible information and trustworthy messengers was only partially met in the multilevel regional component of the *National Assessment*. Two lessons for assessment designers can be drawn here. First, multilevel assessments find more fruitful soil when they tap into well-established, well-functioning networks and high-quality relationships among information providers and users. A more conscious effort in doing so and strategically choosing participants placed in leadership positions or at critical nodes in the information-decision system can enhance an assessment's influence. For assessments conducted only at one level, the implication is slightly different. To affect an issue domain at other levels, associated outreach efforts need to make use of existing networks. Interviews revealed differences between and within states, among NGOs as well as state agencies, suggesting that these networks were not used well and that not all outreach was conducted with equal skill or effort.[15]

Second, in situations where there are no or only small networks among information providers and users, credibility and trust cannot be obtained quickly and are easily lost if disregarded. Depending on the contentiousness of the issue and the quality of preexisting relationships, building trust and credibility may be of foremost importance in a multilevel assessment. Assessments conducted at a single level rarely have significant influence at other levels if there are no strong established networks. The historically contentious relationship between Hawai'i and the federal government exemplified this well. Both case studies uncovered instances where information was withheld—sometimes strategically—to maintain competitive advantage or entrenched antagonistic positions. Thus, if in the course of an assessment process trusted relationships are built, the process could be called a success, even if no immediate policy changes occur. Building trustful relationships means creating the precondition for effective information exchange (see Biermann, chapter 4, this volume).

Legitimacy: The Ultimate Obstacle to Moving Forward

Legitimacy in the context of an evolving issue domain refers to whether the assessment is perceived as fair, whether its participants or users believe that the assessment process respected the rules and norms of relevant institutions, whether it involved the right players, and whether their values and interests were adequately represented. The judgment over legitimacy and fairness has a different basis in a multilevel or single-level assessment. Evaluating legitimacy is also a function of personal involvement and—if available—the reading of the fine print on how and why the assessment was conducted in the first place.[16]

The case of Hawai'i illustrates vividly how the legitimacy of an assessment, or of technical information passing between levels of government, cannot be fully understood without considering the context of deeply engrained historical relationships between them and—at any one level—among the involved institutions and individuals. The greater distrust of the federal government in Hawai'i in part explains why that state is less responsive than Maine to SLR information. Apparently, legitimacy of any new assessment effort is judged against the background of such political "preexisting conditions." All too easily, it is the "politics that get in the way" of exchanging information and working collaboratively and effectively within assessment processes or with assessment outcomes in decision-support systems. While that is not a new finding, it is a fatal one to ignore.

Clearly, such "preexisting conditions" are outside the control of assessment designers or assessors. Assessors must be aware, however, that participants bring personal and institutional relationships—as well as cultural differences in some cases—to the issue domain. Moreover, contradictions in agency approaches and turf issues in cases of overlapping jurisdiction or expertise can help or hinder the assessment and information exchange. Similar issues of competition can arise across scale, such as local versus state authority in managing the immediate coastline. If the struggle for authority is aggravated by differences in goals—even if both authorities adequately adhere to the regulations they each administer—the legitimacy of an assessment process will come into question.

Assessment designers can work constructively with existing institutional arrangements (and baggage) by examining and working with the comparative strengths of potential players (see Cash, chapter 10, this volume). Again, it is a *strategic* decision to involve particular individuals or institutions since their participation can ensure a perception of greater legitimacy, and their satisfaction with the process can eliminate both internal and external challenges to legitimacy (see Andonova, chapter 6, this volume). Assessment coordinators of the Pacific Regional Assessment, for example, consciously weighed whether (1) to broaden the involvement of actors from agencies, academia, and the public to create more support and understanding for difficult CZM policies and decisions, or (2) to strategically reduce the number of players and— as one interviewee framed it—to "use the right tools and people for the right job" and to ensure that "the skill level and enthusiasm is high."

This and other regional assessments illustrate that in order to ensure legitimacy, some potential participants need to be enabled to legitimately participate and bring their insights and assets to the assessment process. Ensuring legitimacy by way of strategic choices around participation can mobilize relevant actors, and thus design effectiveness into an assessment or decision-support process. Typically, one-time mobilization alone will not suffice. As interviewees claimed and observation of the *National Assessment* process repeatedly showed, capacity building and maintenance are critical ingredients in designing legitimacy into an assessment process. Just "showing up" is not enough to make participation successful. Enabling participation and building capacity ensure that new players effectively add their insights and skills. In turn, this begins to shift the relative political weight of participants, and the coalitions they form, to affect policy change (Fisher 2001).

Conclusion

Viewing assessments as part and drivers of an issue domain is at once more fruitful and more challenging than previous approaches. The research reported here privileges the bottom-up view. Consequently, the complexity of this view puts assessments "in their place," appreciating the challenges they face and delineating the opportunities they afford in moving issues forward. The discussion of salience, credibility, and legitimacy highlights how the influence of assessments can range from little to significant depending on the strategic choices made to deal with the specific circumstances and challenges at any one level. While the efforts studied here produced little direct change in state or local policies, I uncovered opportunistic reactions to scientific SLR information: in Maine, the threat of global SLR was used to protect against certain forms of coastal development and to strengthen coastal erosion management. By contrast in Hawai'i, an early SLR impacts study was not publicized to avoid obstructing certain development goals, and more recently, SLR arguments are used only if they aid in advancing erosion-management efforts at the local level. It appears that assessments of cross-scale environmental risks fail to influence policymaking or decision making more strongly because those involved fail to deal effectively with the salience/credibility/legitimacy challenges involved, or because they make strategic choices around participation, framing, and outreach that prevent such influence.

What these studies also showed, however, is that the more important, albeit indirect, influence of assessments on issue domains relates to the process as opposed to the product per se. In both cases, assessments slowly affected the range of issue-domain participants, as well as their awareness and understanding of SLR, and thus—over time—the broader political landscape.

Somewhat counterintuitively, this chapter suggests that assessments intended as "purely scientific" might be more influential if their designers thought more strategically about the broader issue domain, its current stage of evolution, and thus about assessment design. Such choices, however, require the involvement of well-positioned and informed representatives from different levels, even if it is not a multilevel assessment. Single-level and multilevel assessments—if they want to be influential at any level at all—must be conducted with a politically savvy eye toward the context into which they will fall, lest they contribute to the growing number of shelves of dust-gathering reports.

Acknowledgments

This chapter is based on research conducted in 1997–1998 and summarized in Moser 1998. State and federal assessment and policy efforts were updated in early 2003. I wish to thank all my interviewees and informants for their generosity with time and information; several collaborators who influenced the development of this research, including Eileen Shea, David Cash, William Easterling, Tom Wilbanks, William C. Clark, and Sheila Jasanoff; and the participants of the Scale Working Group during a Summer Study at Bar Harbor, Maine (June 17–14, 1998), for constructive criticism and stimulating discussions and insights.

Notes

1. For the full detail on the two case studies, see appendices B and D in Moser 1998.

2. For a detailed interview protocol see Moser and Cash 1998. Interviews ranged from half an hour to two hours; the average length was just above one hour. About a half dozen of the interviews covered only selected issues of information exchange and decision making—for example, to obtain more detailed background on a particular study or education campaign.

   Interviewees in each state and at the federal level were selected through an iterative process and from a variety of sources, including prior contacts at the federal and state levels, institutional websites, scientific publications, and Coastlinks—a directory of Maine coastal organizations. Governmental interviewees included coastal program directors, planners, hazard managers, environmental specialists, engineers, extension agents, and outreach specialists and coordinators. Additional information and contacts for Hawai'i were obtained at the "Workshop on the Consequences of Climate Variability and Change for the Hawai'i-Pacific Region," held March 2–6, 1998, in Honolulu and at a public advisory committee (MACZMAG) meeting. At the national level, information was also gathered while participating at the "U.S. Climate Forum on the Consequences of Global Change for the Nation," held November 12–13, 1997 in Washington, D.C., as well as through continued access to information on the U.S. National Assessment process.

3. Some mused that they would search the Internet, which may open the door to this information clearinghouse.

4. The history of the Office of Technology Assessment (OTA) is instructive here. According to long-term observers of federal science policy, Congress abolished the OTA in 1995 because it was perceived to not produce enough "usable information" (although others believe there was significant political motivation

behind this judgment, if not the actual elimination of the OTA (see, e.g., Morgan, Houghton, and Gibbons 2001)). As a result, there is significant pressure on the USGCRP (and now the Climate Change Science Program) to produce policy-relevant science to keep the level of funding it has enjoyed in recent years ($1.742 billion requested in research in FY 2001) (Subcommittee on Global Change Research 2000). Researchers frequently interacting with federal agencies are acutely aware of the lack of cooperation within and across different divisions and agencies. In ongoing discussions about the Climate Change Science Program (the successor of the USGCRP), improvement of inter- and intraagency interaction is a central focus (U.S. Climate Change Science Program 2002).

5. Very shortly after the EPA published its first major global change assessment in 1983, the National Research Council brought forth its own assessment (National Research Council 1983). The two publications differed significantly in tone and assessment of the severity of the threat (with the NRC assessment being more skeptical of doomsday scenarios and more careful in pointing out the scientific uncertainties). Because of the differences and the odd timing of publication, the two reports received significant media attention at the time (Easterling, personal communication).

6. Neither of the two states considered here was the focus of any of these studies.

7. Publication of the regional assessment occurred well past this study. Thus examination of its impact, the ongoing outreach efforts following the assessment, and the influence on local policy and decision making require further follow-up.

8. The SDR are part of Maine's Coastal Wetlands Act, which—in 1988—was integrated with other legislation in the Natural Resources Protection Act. The SDR were not only remarkable in Maine but serve as a pioneering example to the nation. For details on the policy history, see Moser 1997. The SDR were updated in 2004 but are scheduled to "sunset" within two years, leaving Maine's coastal laws with no further regulation for shorefront development (S. M. Dickson, personal communication, March 31, 2005).

9. See, for example, Hawai'i Board of Land and Natural Resources 1998; Hawai'i Ocean and Marine Resources Council 1991a, 1991b; State of Hawai'i, DLNR 1998; State of Hawai'i, DBEDT, Office of Planning, HCZMP 1997; University of Hawai'i Sea Grant Extension Service and County of Maui Planning Department 1997. Interestingly, reference in these documents is to historical relative SLR only, not future projections of SLR.

10. See, for example, State of Hawai'i, DBEDT 1997; U.S. Army Corps of Engineers, Pacific Ocean Division 1997; U.S. Department of Energy, Office of Emergency Management 1996.

11. Examples include a workshop on Climate Change Implications and Adaptation Strategies for the Indo-Pacific Island Nations, held in September 1995 (Rappa, Tomlinson, and Ziegler 1995); or the 1998 scoping workshop that was part of the *National Assessment*). The HCZMP also cosponsored the First Regional Conference on Coastal Erosion Management in Hawai'i and Other

Pacific Islands held in April 1998, which addressed SLR and was attended by several state- and county-level government employees (University of Hawai'i Sea Grant 1998).

12. There are important exceptions to this general summary. For details see Moser and Cash 1998.

13. Examples in my case studies included EPA's funding for Maine's SLR impact assessment, Hawai'i's climate change action plan, and NOAA's cut of funding for Hawai'i's Sea Grant–based climate change education program.

14. In today's litigious climate surrounding coastal management, which frequently pits private property against public-domain rights, additional expensive legal challenges are a significant deterrent to local managers taking on complex issues.

15. The efforts in Hawai'i through coastal geologist Chip Fletcher and his group to produce relevant scientific information and spread it to a growing number of information users is a good example of building the necessary outreach network and capacity—one that simply was not available prior to his arrival. Similarly skillful efforts are underway in the Pacific region (essentially since the *Regional Assessment*) to build an information and decision-support network related to climate variability and change. It remains to be seen how these two networks get linked.

16. The move within EPA, NOAA, and other federal agencies toward greater stakeholder participation is at least in part a consequence of past information users questioning legitimacy (and issue salience) (U.S. Global Change Research Program 2001; U.S. Climate Change Science Program 2002).

References

Ancona, D. G., and D. Caldwell. 1990. Beyond boundary spanning: Managing external dependence in product development teams. *Journal of High Technology Management Research* 1(2): 119–135.

Ancona, D. G., and D. Caldwell. 1992. Bridging the boundary: External activity and performance in organizational teams. *Administrative Science Quarterly* 37: 634–665.

Barth, M. C., and J. G. Titus. 1984. *Greenhouse Effect and Sea-Level Rise: A Challenge for This Generation*. New York: Van Nostrand Reinhold.

Boesch, D. F., J. C. Field, and D. Scavia, eds. 2000. *The Potential Consequences of Climate Variability and Change on Coastal Areas and Marine Resources*. Report of the Coastal Areas and Marine Resources Sector Team. U.S. National Assessment. Silver Spring, MD: NOAA, Coastal Oceans Program.

Cash, D. W., and S. C. Moser. 2000. Linking global and local scales: Designing dynamic assessment and management processes. *Global Environmental Change* 10(2): 109–120.

Coastal Geology Group. 1997. *Current Research Projects.* Honolulu: SOEST, University of Hawai'i.

Coastal Geology Group. 2001. *Is Hawai'i's Coastal Zone Sustainable?* Powerpoint presentations available at http://www.soest.hawaii.edu/coasts/presentations/Coastalsustain.html.

Coastal Geology Group. 2003. Relative sea-level rise in Hawai'i. Graphic 7 in *Sea-Level Changes: Rising Seas, Past, Present and Future.* http://www.soest.hawaii.edu/coasts/presentations/sealevchang.html.

Conference of New England Governors and Eastern Canadian Premiers. 2001. *New England/Eastern Canadian Provinces' Climate Change Action Plan 2001.* Moncton, New Brunswick: Conference of New England Governors and Eastern Canadian Premiers.

Daniels, R. C., V. M. Gornitz, A. Mehta, S.-C. Lee, and R. M. Cushman. 1992. *Adapting to Sea-Level Rise in the U.S. Southeast: The Influence of Built Infrastructure and Biophysical Factors on the Inundation of Coastal Areas.* Oak Ridge, TN: Oak Ridge National Laboratories.

Deelstra, Y., S. G. Nooteboom, H. R. Kohlmann, J. van den Berg, and S. Innanen. 2003. Using knowledge for decision-making purposes in the context of large projects in The Netherlands. *Environmental Impact Assessment Review* 23(5): 517–541.

Easterling, W. E. 1997. Why regional studies are needed in the development of full-scale integrated assessment modeling of global change processes. *Global Environmental Change* 7: 337–356.

Fennell, M. L., and J. A. Alexander. 1987. Organizational boundary spanning in institutionalized environments. *Academy of Management Journal* 30: 456–476.

Fisher, A. 2001, June 19. *Workshop Summary.* Mid-Atlantic Regional Assessment Evaluation Workshop. University Park, PA: Pennsylvania State University.

Fletcher, C. H., and D. J. Hwang. 1992a. Beach management plan with beach management districts. In *Sea-Level Rise, Shoreline Hardening, and Beach Degradation in Hawai'i: Hearing Testimony, U.S. Senate Energy Committee,* 260–348. Honolulu: Hawai'i Coastal Zone Management Program, Office of State Planning.

Fletcher, C. H., and D. J. Hwang. 1992b. Sea-level rise, shoreline hardening, and beach degradation in Hawai'i. In C. H. Fletcher, ed., *Sea-Level Trends and Physical Consequences: Applications to the U.S. Shore.* Amsterdam: Elsevier Science.

Fletcher, C. H., R. A. Mullane, and B. M. Richmond. 1997. Beach loss along armored shorelines on O'ahu, Hawaiian Islands. *Journal of Coastal Research* 13: 209–215.

Gieryn, T. F. 1995. Boundaries of science. In S. Jasanoff, T. Pinch, J. C. Petersen, and G. E. Markle, eds., *Handbook of Science and Technology Studies,* 393–443. Thousand Oaks, CA: Sage.

Gieryn, T. F. 1999. *Cultural Boundaries of Science: Credibility on the Line.* Chicago: University of Chicago Press.

Global Environmental Assessment Project. 1997. A critical evaluation of global environmental assessment: The climate experience. A report of the First Workshop on Global Environmental Assessment and Public Policy. In *A Workshop Convened Jointly by the Committee on the Environment of Harvard University, the Center for the Application of Research on the Environment (CARE) of the Institute of Global Environment and Society, Inc., and the International Institute for Applied Systems Analysis.* Calverton, MD: CARE.

Gornitz, V. M., R. C. Daniels, T. W. White, and K. R. Birdwell. 1994. The development of a coastal risk assessment database: Vulnerability to SLR in the U.S. Southeast. *Journal of Coastal Research* (special issue: Coastal Hazards: Perception, Susceptibility, and Mitigation): 327–338.

Gregory, J. M., J. A. Church, G. J. Boer, K. W. Dixon, G. M. Flato, D. R. Jacket, J. A. Lowe, S. P. O'Farrell, E. Roeckner, G. L. Russell, R. J. Stouffer, and M. Winton. 2001. Comparison of results from several AOGCMs for global and regional sea-level change 1900–2100. *Climate Dynamics* 18: 225–240.

Guston, D. H. 1999. Stabilizing the boundary between politics and science: The role of the Office of Technology Transfer as a boundary organization. *Social Studies of Science* 29: 1–15.

Hawai'i Board of Land and Natural Resources. 1998. *Coastal Erosion Management Plan (COEMAP).* Honolulu: Department of Land and National Resources.

Hawai'i Coastal Zone Management Program. 1985. *Effects on Hawai'i of a Worldwide Rise in Sea Level Induced by the "Greenhouse Effect": A Report in Response to Senate Resolution 137, 1984.* Honolulu: State of Hawai'i, Department of Planning and Economic Development.

Hawai'i Ocean and Marine Resources Council. 1991a. *Hawai'i Ocean Resources Management Plan.* Honolulu: State of Hawai'i, DBEDT, HCZMP.

Hawai'i Ocean and Marine Resources Council. 1991b. *Hawai'i Ocean Resources Management Plan: Technical Supplement.* Honolulu: State of Hawai'i, DBEDT, HCZMP.

Hoffman, J. S., D. Keyes, and J. G. Titus. 1983. *Projecting Future Sea-Level Rise.* Washington, DC: U.S. EPA.

Intergovernmental Panel on Climate Change (IPCC). 2001a. *Climate Change 2001: Impacts, Adaptation, and Vulnerability.* Contribution of Working Group II to the Third Assessment Report of the Intergovernmental Panel on Climate Change. New York: Cambridge University Press.

Intergovernmental Panel on Climate Change (IPCC). 2001b. *Climate Change 2001: The Scientific Basis.* Contribution of Working Group I to the Third Assessment Report of the Intergovernmental Panel on Climate Change. New York: Cambridge University Press.

Jones, A. T. 1998. Late Holocene shoreline development in the Hawaiian Islands. *Journal of Coastal Research* 14: 3–9.

Kendall, D. L. 1987. *Glaciers and Granite: A Guide to Maine's Landscape and Geology*. Unity, ME: North Country Press.

Leifer, R., and A. Delbecq. 1978. Organizational/environmental interchange: A model of boundary spanning activity. *Academy of Management* Review 3(1): 40–50.

Lukas, R. 1998. El Niño: Seasonal-to-interannual climate variability. Paper presented at the Regional Workshop on the Consequences of Climate Variability and Change on the Hawai'i-Pacific Region. Honolulu, HI, March 2–6.

MacCracken, M. 2000, October 23–24. *Status Report and Some Initial Thoughts on Lessons Learned from the First Phase of the U.S. National Assessment on the Potential Consequences of Climate Variability and Change*. Prepared for discussion at a meeting of the Committee on Global Change Research, National Research Council, Washington, DC: NACO, USGCRP.

Maine Environmental Priorities Project. 1996. *Report from the Steering Committee, Consensus Ranking of Environmental Risks Facing Maine*. Augusta: MEPP.

Marine State Planning Office. 2000. *State of Maine Climate Change Action Plan*. Augusta, ME: Maine State Planning Office, http://mainegov-images.informe. org/spo/pubs/origpdf/pdf/ClimateReport.pdf [last accessed November 9, 2005].

Marine Law Institute/University of Maine School of Law, Maine State Planning Office, and Maine Geological Survey. 1995. *Anticipatory Planning for Sea-Level Rise along the Coast of Maine*. Washington, DC, and Augusta: U.S. EPA and MSPO.

Meehl, G. A., W. M. Washington, W. D. Collins, J. M. Arblaster, A. B. Hu, E. Lawrence, W. G. Strand, and H. Teng. 2005. How much more global warming and sea level rise? *Science* 307: 1769–1772.

Mehta, A. J., and R. M. Cushman, eds. 1989. *Workshop on Sea Level Rise and Coastal Processes*. Washington: U.S. Department of Energy.

Miller, C., S. Jasanoff, M. Long, W. C. Clark, N. Dickson, A. Iles, and T. Parris. 1997. Shaping knowledge, defining uncertainty: The dynamic role of assessments. In W. C. Clark, J. McCarthy, and E. Shea, eds., *A Critical Evaluation of Global Environmental Assessments*, 79–113. Cambridge, MA: Harvard University.

Morgan, M. G., A. Houghton, and J. H. Gibbons. 2001. Improving science and technology advice for Congress. *Science* 293: 1999–2000.

Moser, S. C. 1997. *Mapping the Territory of Uncertainty and Ignorance: Broadening Current Assessment and Policy Approaches to Sea-Level Rise*. Doctoral dissertation, Graduate School of Geography, Clark University.

Moser, S. C. 1998. *Talk Globally, Walk Locally: The Cross-Scale Influence of Global Change Information on Coastal Zone Management in Maine and Hawai'i.* Cambridge, MA: John F. Kennedy School of Government, Harvard University.

Moser, S. C. 2006. *Climate Scenarios and Projections: The Known, the Unknown, and the Unknowable as Applied to California.* Synthesis report of a workshop held at the Aspen Global Change Institute, March 11–14, 2004, in Aspen, Colorado. Aspen, CO: AGCI.

Moser, S. C. Forthcoming. *Stakeholder Involvement in the First U.S. National Assessment of the Potential Consequences of Climate Variability and Change: An Evaluation, Finally.* Draft report to the National Research Council, Human Dimensions of Global Change Committee's Study *Public Participation in Environmental Assessment and Decision-Making.* Boulder, CO: NCAR.

Moser, S. C., and D. W. Cash. 1998. Information and decision-making systems for the effective management of cross-scale environmental problems: A research protocol. Paper prepared for the workshop "Local Response to Global Change: Strategies of Information Transfer and Decision-Making for Cross-Scale Environmental Risks." Cambridge, MA: Belfer Center for Science and International Affairs, Harvard University.

National Assessment Synthesis Team. 2001. *Climate Change Impacts on the United States: The Potential Consequences of Climate Variability and Change.* Foundation report, USGCRP. New York: Cambridge University Press.

National Research Council. 1983. *Risk Assessment in the Federal Government: Managing the Process.* Washington, DC: National Academy Press.

National Research Council. 1987. *Responding to Changes in Sea Level: Engineering Implications.* Washington, DC: National Academy Press.

National Research Council. 1990. *Managing Coastal Erosion.* Washington, DC: National Academy Press.

New England Regional Assessment Group. 2001. *Preparing for a Changing Climate: The Potential Consequences of Climate Variability and Change—New England.* A report for the U.S. Global Change Research Program. Durham: Institute for the Study of Earth Oceans and Space, University of New Hampshire.

Nicholls, R. J., and J. A. Lowe. 2004. Benefits of mitigation of climate change for coastal areas. *Global Environmental Change* 14: 229–244.

Nunn, P. D. 1998. Consequences of sea-level change during the Holocene in the Pacific Basin: Introduction. *Journal of Coastal Research* 14: 1–2.

Oppenheimer, M., and R. B. Alley. 2004. The West Antarctic Ice Sheet and long term climate policy. *Climatic Change* 64: 1–10.

Pacific Islands Regional Assessment Group. 2001. *Preparing for a Changing Climate: The Potential Consequences of Climate Variability and Change—Pacific Islands.* A report for the U.S. Global Change Research Program. Honolulu: East-West Center.

Pielke, R. A. 1994. Scientific information and global change policy-making. Editorial essay. *Climatic Change* 28: 315–319.

Rappa, R., A. Tomlinson, and S. Ziegler, eds., 1995. Climate change implications and adaptation strategies for the Indo-Pacific island nations: Workshop proceedings, University of Hawai'i, Honolulu.

Smith, J. B., and D. Tirpak, eds. 1989. *The Potential Effects of Global Climate Change on the United States: Report to Congress.* Washington, DC: U.S. EPA.

State of Hawai'i, DBEDT. 1997a. *Hawai'i Greenhouse Gas Inventory.* Honolulu: DBEDT.

State of Hawai'i, DBEDT, Office of Planning, HCZMP. 1997b. *Hawai'i Coastal Zone Management Program: Section 309 Enhancement Area Grants Program: 1997 Assessment and Strategy.* Honolulu: HCZMP.

State of Hawai'i, DBEDT, Strategic Industries Division, 1997. *Hawai'i Climate Change Action Plan.* Honolulu: DBEDT. http://www.state.hi.us/dbedt/ert/ccap-toc.html [last accessed November 9, 2005].

State of Hawai'i, DLNR. 1998. *Coastal Erosion and Beach Loss in Hawai'i.* Honolulu: State of Hawai'i, DLNR.

Steel, B. S., D. Lach, P. List, and B. Shindler. 2001. The role of scientists in the natural resource policy process: A comparison of Canadian and American publics. *Journal of Environmental Systems* 28: 133–155.

Stive, M. J. F. 2004. How important is global warming for coastal erosion? *Climatic Change* 64: 27–39.

Subcommittee on Global Change Research. 2000. *Our Changing Planet: The FY 2001 US Global Change Research Program.* Washington, DC: Office of Science and Technology Policy. http://gcrio.org/ocp2001/ocp2001.pdf [last accessed November 9, 2005].

Thieler, E. R., J. Williams, and E. Hammar-Klose. 2001. *National Assessment of Coastal Vulnerability to Sea-Level Rise.* Woods Hole, MA: Woods Hole Field Center. http://woodshole.er.usgs.gov/project-pages/cvi/.

Titus, J. G., and V. K. Narayanan. 1995. *The Probability of Sea-Level Rise.* Washington, DC: U.S. EPA.

University of Hawai'i Sea Grant. 1998. *First Regional Conference on Coastal Erosion Management in Hawai'i and Other Pacific Islands.* University of Hawai'i–Sea Grant, Maui, HI.

University of Hawai'i Sea Grant Extension Service and County of Maui Planning Department. 1997. *Beach Management Plan for Maui.* University of Hawai'i–Sea Grant, Maui, HI.

University of New Hampshire/Institute for the Study of Earth Oceans and Space. 1997. Workshop summary report. In *New England Regional Climate Change Impacts Workshop.* Durham, NH: University of New Hampshire/Institute for the Study of Earth Oceans and Space.

U.S. Army Corps of Engineers, Pacific Ocean Division. 1997. *Coastal Hazard Mitigation Study for Energy and Lifeline Facilities: State of Hawai'i.* Ft. Shafter, HI: USACE.

U.S. Climate Change Science Program (CCSP). 2002. *Strategic Plan for the Climate Change Science Program, Review Draft, November 2002.* Washington, DC: CCSP. http://www.climatescience.gov/Library/stratplan2003/default.htm.

U.S. Congress. 1990a. *Coastal Zone Management Act of 1972.* 16 USC 1451–1464, Chapter 33; Public Law 92-583 (1972), as amended; Public Law 101-508 (1990). http://www.ocrm.nos.noaa.gov/czm/czm_act.html.

U.S. Congress. 1990b. *U.S. Global Change Research Act of 1990.* Public Law 101-606(11/16/90) 104 Stat. 3096–3104. http://www.gcrio.org/gcact1990.shtml.

U.S. Department of Energy, Office of Emergency Management. 1996. *Hawaiian Islands: Hazard Mitigation Report.* Honolulu: DOE, Office of Emergency Management for HI.

U.S. Global Change Research Program. 2001. *Draft Strategic Research Plan 2000–2010.* Washington, DC: USGCRP.

Wigley, T. M. L. 2005. The climate change commitment. *Science* 307: 1766–1769.

Zhang, K., B. Douglas, and S. Leatherman. 2004. Global warming and coastal erosion. *Climatic Change* 64: 41–58.

Selected Interviews

A. D. Challacombe, Chief, Environmental Review Branch, City and County of Honolulu, Department of Land Utilization, Honolulu, 1998.

S. M. Dickson, Marine Geologist, Certified Geologist, Department of Conservation, Maine Geological Survey, Augusta, 1998.

W. E. Easterling, The Penn State Institutes of the Environment, Pennsylvania State University, University Park, 1998.

A. Fisher, Department of Agricultural Economics and Rural Sociology, Pennsylvania State University, University Park, PA. February, 2001.

C. Fletcher, Professor, Department of Geology and Geophysics, University of Hawai'i, Honolulu, March 12, 1998.

J. Kelley, Professor of Coastal Geology, Certified Geologist, Maine Geological Survey, University of Maine–Department of Geology, Orono, various dates, 1998–1999.

S. J. Lemmo, Planner, Hawai'i Department of Land and Natural Resources, Land Division, Planning Branch, Honolulu, 1998.

E. Shea, Associate, Global Environmental Assessment Project, e-mail interview, Center for the Application of Research on the Environment (CARE) of the Institute of Global Environment and Society, 1998.

J. Walters, Planning and Policy Analyst, Coastal Zone Management Program, Honolulu, 1998.

Acronyms

CZMA	Coastal Zone Management Act (federal act of 1972)
CZMP	Coastal Zone Management Program(s) (at federal or state levels)
EPA	Environmental Protection Agency
GCRA	Global Change Research Act (federal act of 1990)
GCRIO	Global Change Research and Information Office
GEA	Global Environmental Assessment (project at Harvard University)
IPCC	Intergovernmental Panel on Climate Change
MACZMAG	Marine and Coastal Zone Management Group (Hawai'i)
NOAA	National Oceanic and Atmospheric Administration
OCRM	Office of Ocean and Coastal Resource Management (within NOAA)
SLR	Sea-level rise
USGCRP	U.S. Global Change Research Program
USGS	U.S. Geological Survey

9

Trust, Respect, Patience, and Sea-Surface Temperatures: Useful Climate Forecasting in Zimbabwe

Anthony G. Patt

Introduction

What does it take to make global information useful at the local level? Several other chapters in this volume examine this question. In chapter 10, for example, David Cash examines how distributed research, assessment, and decision-support systems in the American Midwest deal with problems existing on many scales. His most important lessons are the need for iterative interactions between scientists and information users, managed by boundary organizations that cut across several levels of scale. In chapter 8, Susanne Moser looks at how two American states, Maine and Hawai'i, interpret the issue of sea-level rise and its connections with global climate change. She suggests that when mechanisms for public participation are lacking, a major challenge of assessments is to deliver information that is actually salient—that is, useful for decision makers.

In this chapter, I highlight many of the same issues by examining seasonal climate forecasts for southern Africa, which grew out of an ability to predict the El Niño of 1997 in the tropical Pacific and its effects on weather patterns worldwide. I look at how different organizations brought the forecasts to a range of users in Zimbabwe: national policymakers, large-scale commercial farmers, and small-scale subsistence farmers. I identify the steps these organizations took, or failed to take, in order to make the forecasts salient and credible for their target audience. Beyond this, I examine what factors may have influenced each organization to take the steps they chose to take to enhance salience and credibility.

In this particular case, making the forecast salient meant translating it into terms that were useful for decisions being made on the ground. The regional (southern Africa) and national (Zimbabwe) forecasts contained valuable information about the chances of high, normal, or low rainfall. But these chances had a wide range of potential implications for different users, depending on their location, and the specific decisions (such as what crops to plant) they faced. Making the forecast credible meant, in large part, helping users understand the uncertainties associated with the predictions. The media picked up on the fact that El Niño was huge, and that El Niño meant drought for Zimbabwe, no ifs, ands, or buts. The official forecast for Zimbabwe, however, called for about a 50 percent chance of low rainfall—much higher than normal, but still far from certain. As the season progressed, starting with normal rains and then becoming erratic, the credibility of the forecast was tied in large part to users' perception of uncertainty.

This is a good case to study for several reasons. First, it shows us an assessment in search of an audience. It was up to the climate forecasters to make their product useful to decision makers, rather than responding to users' requests for information. This accentuated the need to sell the information as salient, while maintaining credibility. Second, it shows variance in how forecasters and boundary organizations went about this task. In Zimbabwe, agricultural information providers for the two main agricultural sectors—commercial and subsistence farming—made very different decisions about what to tell their audience, and how to tell them. Third, it shows variance in the results of their efforts. By and large, the commercial farmers used the new information, while the subsistence farmers did not, or used it poorly. Finding out why these events happened can teach us how and why boundary organizations function as they do, and let us design better institutions for the future.

Theoretical Issues: Building Salience and Credibility

The case studies throughout this volume suggest that assessment effectiveness can be explained by salience, credibility, and legitimacy. In the context of applying global information locally, salience is often problematic because it is unclear what implication information from afar can possibly have on local decisions. Credibility too can be an issue, not least because there may not be any relationship of trust between the information provider and the information user. In this section, I describe the reasons that issues of poor salience or credibility can arise in seasonal climate forecasting, and the things that institutions can do about it. Most important among these is putting in place an ongoing system for user participation in the development of the final forecast and response recommendations. The Zimbabwe case highlights how variance in public participation—arising for a variety of reasons—can produce vastly different levels of salience and credibility.

Salience

A salient assessment contains useful information geared to real-world decisions. Thus, it has to match the spatial and temporal scales at which decisions actually take place, and provide information that could be of sufficient magnitude and reliability to alter those decisions. Salience is a function of the information being assessed, the intended audience, and the efforts assessors make to connect the two. Climate forecasts fall into the type of blameless risk that McDaniels, Axelrod, and Slovic (1996) suggest often lacks salience. To make this information salient, an assessment would have to recognize what decisions might be affected by the information. A conscientious assessor must examine whether the new information is sufficiently different from prior beliefs to make a different decision outcome preferable. If we expect "bounded rationality" to rule the day in terms of most decision making, a salient assessment is one that either induces a boundedly rational agent to act, or that provides not only useful information but an analytic framework for evaluating it.

Scale As the National Research Council (1999, 81) states, effective climate forecasts "match informational messages to the characteristics and situation of the target group." Disparities of scale between the forecast and the response options can detract from salience, something also evident in this volume's chapters by Susanne Moser and David Cash. Cash, for instance, refers to "nested problems" in terms of scale. Easterling (1997) argues that most integrated assessment models study data and events at the global scale, and thus while useful to national and international decision makers, are not likely to prove useful at the local scale. In general, information that is clearly salient at the global scale should be less so at more local scales; although there are certain to be impacts *somewhere*, the information is unlikely to reveal to a particular decision maker whether her or his own village will suffer. Furthermore, local-scale users might lack the capacity to see information as salient, whereas national-level organizations can employ teams of analysts to hunt out salient elements in a particular assessment. Assessments aimed at local-scale audiences, speaking about issues not obviously relevant to them, can be made more salient through a special effort to operationalize the scientific information. I call this *decision matching*.

Decision Matching   Climate forecasts contain information relevant to many different users; perhaps the most important element in successful forecasting is departing from a "one size fits all" approach. Providing operational information to farmers requires identifying how *local* rainfall patterns are likely to change. It also requires matching it to actual or potential farmer decisions. Cash (chapter 10, this volume) calls this a "distributed research, assessment, and decision support system." Phillips, Cane, and Rosenzweig (1998) show the importance of this, having modeled the usefulness of El Niño–based forecast information for farmers in Zimbabwe. The researchers found that, contrary to conventional wisdom, farmers could most benefit by knowing when the probability of drought was *low*, rather than when it was *high*. Most farmers adopt a risk-averse strategy of planting drought-tolerant varieties of maize, because there is always a significant chance of drought. Telling the farmers that a particular year has a higher chance of drought than normal would not change that strategy. However, in a year that farmers learned the chances of drought were lower than normal, they may want to change their strategy, planting higher-yield but less drought-tolerant varieties. Unless assessors examine how decisions could change in response to information, they are likely to overlook such fine-scale phenomena. In the case of drought forecasting, this error would include communicating to farmers only in drought years—the years that national-level food planners need the information—even though for the farmers the information may be more relevant in the intervening wet years.

The choice of who engages in decision matching must be guided by the needs of the user, and not by the source of the information. In many GEAs, the users are national governments, and so the participation of governments and their agents is vital (Biermann, chapter 4, this volume; VanDeveer, chapter 5, this volume; Andonova, chapter 6, this volume). For local decisions, however, public participation is instrumental in matching information to decisions. Botcheva (1998) suggests that proper analysis requires such a wealth of information and observations that broader involvement is necessary. Experts can easily underestimate the complexity of the decisions that users face, and only through frequent meetings with the users can the two begin to learn what information is both useful and available (Wynne 1996; Patt and Gwata 2002). The process of public participation has to continue over time, not only to ensure that experts learn to ask and answer the right questions, but also to ensure that users learn to understand the information provided and how they can apply it to decisions they face (Kunreuther 1996, Kunreuther and Kleffner 1992). Collaboration between experts and users to discover what information helps to solve what problems requires iteration over many decision-making cycles to be successful (Cash, chapter 10, this volume). In many cases, users will be able to adapt their own operating procedures to include reliance on new information. As Orlove and Tosteson (1999) have demonstrated, the fit of a forecast results from the interaction over time between forecasters and users, in which users learn to expand their choice set in response to the availability of new information while forecasters adapt their information products to the changing capacity of users.

Credibility

A credible assessment is one that users believe and trust. As opposed to salience, credibility often depends less on the information transmitted than on characteristics of the communicator and the communication media, or *credibility by proxy*. Attribution of credibility in turn varies according to the user. Credibility comes easily when the communicator has built a successful track record of honesty, and when the audience has developed a habit of listening to and relying on scientific and technical information. Track records are difficult to build, often requiring flawless performance, since trust is hard to gain but easy to lose (Freudenburg 1996; Slovic 1993). Glantz (2001) describes the story in Brazil: people trusted the government drought forecast until the first time they perceived it as being wrong; thereafter they were reluctant to follow its advice. Obviously, one way to preserve that track record is never to be wrong. But in the Brazilian case, it was not that the forecast was absolutely wrong; rather, there was a drought that was less severe than the forecast had predicted. What is important is not to promise more with a piece of information than one can deliver.

Coping with Uncertainty   Not overselling salience—that is, not overstating the value of the information being provided—is easier said than done when there is significant uncertainty. First, most people find thinking in terms of probabilities difficult, especially for one-time events (Renn 1998; Weber 1997). They would rather know what will happen with certainty, and will ignore the messenger who tells them otherwise. Not wanting to be ignored, the media habitually portray future events as certain. Second, people often think in binary terms: an event is certain to occur (i.e., with a probability of 100 percent), or else is uncertain. For the latter, they tend to group all probabilities toward 50 percent. Thus, they overreact to the likelihood of low-probability events and underreact to the probability of high-likelihood events (Patt and Zeckhauser 2002). Third, they tend to correlate event likelihood with event magnitude, and are influenced by background probabilities. They will treat a forecasted 70 percent chance of rain in London as being more indicative of certainty than a 70 percent chance of rain in Madrid (Windschitl and Weber 1999). Thus, likelihoods are often either ignored or misinterpreted (Patt and Schrag 2003).

Forecasters have several strategies available to overcome these difficulties in communicating uncertainty. First, they can ignore the uncertainty altogether, not discussing low-probability events (Patt 1999). Although simple, this approach can result in surprises that reduce future credibility. Second, they can compare forecasted probabilities with other, more familiar, events, using risk ranking or risk comparison (Leiss 1996).

This approach is better, but still misses the problem people have separating probability from magnitude. Third, they can go through the elaborate process of public participation, making users partners in the process of developing and responding to risk information (Fischhoff 1996). This last participatory approach is time consuming and difficult, but ultimately may be necessary if users are fully to understand—and hence trust—the uncertainty associated with the information they are receiving.

Building Relationships   Credibility is also an attribution determined by characteristics of the audience and of the relationship between forecaster and audience. Many researchers have observed that audiences who are themselves empowered tend to trust experts more (Freudenburg 1996; Slovic 1997; Midmore and Whittaker 2000). Weber (1997) shows how existing sources of news influence people's receptivity to new information. She found that farmers who received their information from more sources, and for whom agricultural newspapers were one of those sources, were more likely to believe in global warming than farmers who relied on fewer media sources and sources generally limited to the popular media (e.g., daily newspapers, television, radio). Audiences can be empowered by participation. Frey and Stutzer (1999) found that the mere act of participation gives rise to more positive feelings about government. When users participate in the development of information, they will feel that they "own" it and can apply it to their unfolding decision-making needs, without further approval or sanctioning by experts—a point underscored by various contributors to this volume.

The case study of Zimbabwean climate forecasting highlights these issues. As I show at the end of the study, it also gives us some clues as to why some organizations would go to the trouble of salience and credibility building—primarily through public participation to build these relationships—while others would not.

Case Study

El Niño is one phase of the El Niño–Southern Oscillation (ENSO, see table 9.1 for abbreviations) phenomenon. During an El Niño event, surface water in the eastern tropical Pacific is warmer than usual, and ocean and atmospheric circulation patterns are different. The changes have predictable global repercussions (Mason et al. 1999; National Research Council 1996). In Zimbabwe, El Niño is associated with a high probability of drought (Watson et al. 1997; Rowlands 1998; Glantz 2001). This is important to Zimbabweans, close to 70 percent of whom are subsistence farmers on communally owned land and rely on rain-fed crops for their survival (National Economic Planning Commission 1999; Policy and Planning Division 1999).

In 1991–1992, a major drought caught the Zimbabwean government unprepared, and the process of importing large quantities of food at the last minute proved harrowing and costly (Scoones et al. 1996). The government came under criticism for failing to heed the warnings of climatologists, who had predicted the drought based on their El Niño modeling (Cane, Eshel, and Buckland 1994; Glantz, Betsill, and Crandall 1997). Between 1992 and 1997, the Zimbabwean government tried to coordinate its drought-management policies (National Economic Planning Commission 1999). When news of a possible upcoming El Niño started to appear in early 1997, many Zimbabwe institutions were more prepared, with formalized systems for responding to the information (Stack 1998).

Information Providers
The Zimbabwe Department of Meteorological Services (the Met Service) formed the heart of a network of organizations generating and interpreting climate information. The Met Service received information from a host of foreign organizations, exchanged information with the Drought Monitoring Centre for Southern Africa (DMC), and was in constant communication with the Southern African Development Community (SADC) Regional Remote Sensing Project (RRSP). The DMC and RRSP joined with all southern African met services, as well as the relevant foreign meteorological organizations (such as the U.S. National Oceanic and Atmospheric Administration, NOAA), to organize and fund the Southern African Regional Climate Outlook Forum (SARCOF). The first SARCOF occurred in September 1997, in Kadoma, Zimbabwe, and these forums have been held each year since. Meteorologists at SARCOF incor-

porated their separate predictions to negotiate a consensus forecast crossing national borders within the SADC region.

In close contact with the RRSP—and well represented at SARCOF—were several *early warning* organizations: the Famine Early Warning System (sponsored by the U.S. Agency for International Development, USAID), the Regional Early Warning System (sponsored by SADC), and the National Early Warning Unit (sponsored by the Zimbabwe Ministry of Agriculture and Lands). These can be viewed as *boundary organizations*, existing primarily to improve communication and interaction between scientists and policymakers. While the early warning organizations had traditionally monitored rainfall distribution and foliage and crop development during the growing season (Dilley 1997), beginning in 1997 they began paying attention to the seasonal climate forecast, treating it as an early warning of an early warning. If these indicators—poor crop development coupled with a forecast for light rainfall—were to show that food insecurity was likely, the early warning organizations would sound an alarm to national and international relief agencies. This alarm, it was hoped, would improve the chances of averting food insecurity, while reducing the cost through advance preparation.

It is worth noting that Zimbabwe was one of the leaders in developing and communicating seasonal climate forecasts. Compared to other southern African countries, and like South Africa, Zimbabwe has an extremely professional and competent Met Service. The SADC early warning organizations, including the DMC, are located in Harare, making the city the home base for the region's meteorological and forecasting community. While political factors have recently become important in the provision of information, food assistance, and other aid throughout the country, in 1997 this was not the case: the government in Harare appears to have been committed to doing what it could to help all farmers throughout the country.

Farmers and Boundary Organizations

While food-security organizations operate at the national scale, farmers make decisions at the local level. Agriculture was and is the biggest sector of Zimbabwe's economy. In the 1990s, farmers fell into three categories: communal land farmers, small-scale commercial farmers, and large-scale commercial farmers. For those familiar with Zimbabwe, it is worth keeping in mind that much has changed since 1997, and due to political and economic factors there are now very few large-scale commercial farmers. As of 1991–1992, there were 1.5 million communal land households cultivating 4.5 million of their 16.4 million hectares (Mudimu 1998). They are poor; most cultivate using draft animals, rather than tractors, and few can afford to apply fertilizer during the season. Small-scale commercial farmers owned a total of 1.2 million hectares, remain generally black, and face many of the same financial constraints as communal farmers. Together, communal farmers and small-scale commercial farmers comprise the *smallholder* farming sector.

Smallholder farmers' principal crop is maize, augmented by sorghum and millet in the driest regions of the country. Most of their grain goes for their own consumption, and what they do sell goes to cover the cost of inputs, such as seed. They round out food production by growing groundnuts, squash, soybeans, and sunflowers, as well as raising goats, cattle, and chickens. They grow a number of cash crops, such as cotton and paprika. Nonetheless, it is very difficult for these farmers completely to feed themselves, let alone sell enough cash crops to meet their financial wants and needs; most rely on remittances sent "home" from relatives working in the city or abroad (Scoones et al. 1996; Gundry et al. 1999).

In 1997, the Zimbabwe Farmers' Union (ZFU), based in Harare, was advocating for the smallholder farmers, but did not assist or advise them with respect to farming practices or climate forecasts. That responsibility fell on the agricultural extension service, now called Arex but in 1997 known as Agritex, within the Ministry of Lands and Agriculture. Within Agritex, information passed from the Harare office down a chain of command that included regional offices, district offices, and then local offices. The local offices were in larger villages and had a supervisor and one or more extension officers, who lived nearby. Most farmers, but not all, had occasional contact with an Agritex extension officer. For climate forecasts, the NEWU was located within the Agritex head office, and had made an effort to educate the regional directors on the causes and effects of ENSO, along with the uncertainties inherent in forecasting seasonal climate. As discussed below, such information generally did not reach the farmers themselves.

The characteristics of large-scale commercial farming allowed them to respond far more quickly to information. This sector of almost exclusively white-owned farms covered 11.2 million hectares. These farmers had greater access to capital, more tractors and other machinery, and more sources of news, including CNN, the Internet, Zimbabwean media, South African Weather Bureau forecasts, and agricultural magazines. Many had attended agricultural university in Zimbabwe or South Africa, and were receptive to new technologies. As a group, they were economically if not politically empowered. Commercial farmers had traditionally grown the same crops as smallholder farmers, as well as export crops such as cotton and tobacco.

Almost all commercial farmers were members of the Commercial Farmers' Union (CFU), based in Harare. The CFU took an active role in disseminating weather forecasts, and in 1997 extended that to include the seasonal climate forecasts. When they received the Met Service seasonal, monthly, and ten-day forecasts, they distributed them immediately to their membership. The 20 percent of farmers who had e-mail access received information directly. Others received it through regular ham radio broadcasts from CFU regional offices. The forecasts that the farmers received from the CFU office were the exact ones put out by the Met Service, with supplemental analysis based on information from other sources. The CFU also put out a monthly newsletter to its members, which contained the forecast information, and a monthly magazine, which contained more in-depth articles. In 1997, prior to the growing season, the CFU had made a special effort to educate member farmers about the forecasts, in particular their probabilistic character.

Because of Zimbabwe's heterogeneous climate and soil conditions (see figure 9.1) a single, national forecast will have very different implications across the country, since effects of high or low rainfall will depend on the normal amount of rain, the crops usually grown, and the specific agronomic practices, including crop type and irrigation availability, in different regions.

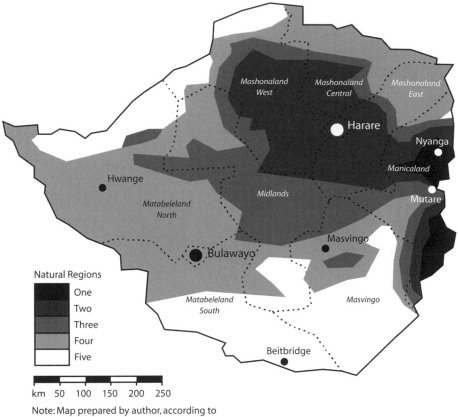

Figure 9.1
Zimbabwe natural regions. *Source:* Eakin 1998

1997 Forecasts and Response

A warm ENSO event (El Niño) became apparent in March 1997, and continued to grow for the next nine months. The effects of this ENSO, the largest of the century, were felt around the world for the next year. In southern Africa, however, heightened sea-surface temperatures in the southern Indian Ocean complicated the usual pattern of drought associated with ENSO warm events. Seasonal rainfall totals for much of Zimbabwe were near average, but the temporal rainfall distribution was far from normal. Most of the rain fell in a short period, causing extensive runoff and flooding rather than promoting healthy crop growth.

Preseason Forecast and Early Warning

Starting in April 1997, IRI climatologists communicated directly with scientists at the RRSP in Harare, expressing concern over the warming of the Pacific. The second-quarter REWU bulletin (SADC 1997a), published in May, did not report on the ENSO anomaly, and it was the June FEWS bulletin (FEWS 1997a) that first sounded the alarm for the early warning organizations. The bulletin devoted a page to describing ENSO and its teleconnections, and concluded by noting that "NOAA has now issued an ENSO advisory that a warm event is developing. Having started in the April–May period and having developed quite rapidly, this may be one of the stronger episodes. FEWS and other groups are monitoring this event carefully to track its development and determine its likely effect on weather and crops" (p. 1). By their July bulletin (FEWS 1997b), FEWS had begun to include a monthly "El Niño Update," and advised that countries in southern Africa "should be sure that structures are in place to anticipate and handle problems" (p. 1).

By mid-June, SADC had formed an ad hoc committee to monitor ENSO, made up of representatives from the REWU, FEWS, and DMC. That same month the REWU issued a statement addressed to the SADC ministers of agriculture, advising them to prepare for a likely ENSO-related drought. The June REWU quarterly food security bulletin (SADC 1997b) also warned of the developing ENSO warm event. In August a supplemental REWU bulletin (SADC 1997c) was devoted to ENSO effects. By September REWU and FEWS had collaborated in preparing an information packet for the SADC-member NEWUs, describing ENSO and its effects, and had organized a special training workshop (FEWS 1997c). Contemporaneously, the World Food Programme began cooperating with SADC and other regional institutions to plan for a possible drought. SADC and FEWS contracted with consultants to draw up contingency plans.

Within the Met Service, people were busy preparing for the first SARCOF, held in Kadoma, Zimbabwe, during the second week of September. Met Service representatives from eleven SADC countries attended, along with people from the DMC; the Universities of Witwatersrand, Zululand, and Zimbabwe; the World Meteorological

Organization; IRI; NOAA; USAID; the United Kingdom Meteorology Office; and the World Bank (NOAA 1999). SARCOF issued a consensus forecast for the entire SADC region, in general calling for above-normal rainfall in the north, normal to below normal in the central region, and below normal in the south. The definition of *normal* was rainfall within the range of the middle tercile of the past thirty years (i.e., the ten average years). The definition of *below normal* was rainfall amounts falling within or below the range of the lower tercile of those thirty years (i.e., the ten driest years). Likewise, the definition of *above normal* was rainfall in or above the range of the ten wettest years. Figure 9.2 shows the SARCOF probabilistic forecast for Zimbabwe, which the Met Service adopted and reissued as its own. The verbal forecast, accompanying the weather maps, indicated that Zimbabwe would likely receive near-normal rains early in the season, with a high likelihood of dry conditions late in the season.

Immediately following the September SARCOF, the Zimbabwe Met Service organized its own workshop to develop a Zimbabwe-specific forecast. Present at the Zimbabwe meeting were local stakeholders, the media, and political leaders. During the growing season, the Met Service issued ten-day forecasts to a long mailing list of users and the media, via

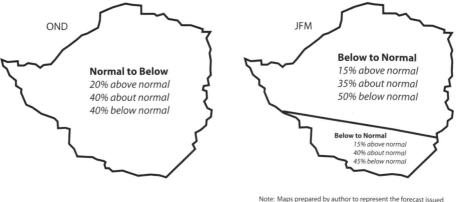

Note: Maps prepared by author to represent the forecast issued by the 1997 Southern African Regional Climate Outlook Forum and the Zimbabwe Department of Meteorological Services.

Figure 9.2
Zimbabwe early- and late-season forecasts for 1997–1998. *Source:* FEWS 1997c

fax and e-mail, and sent additional daily forecasts to the media and the airports. Representatives from the Met Service were available to meet with users directly.

Farmers' Response   The Commercial Farmers' Union (CFU) had been monitoring the media reports of a growing El Niño from the beginning, and so made a special effort to meet with forecasters from the Met Service to discuss implications, and to keep its members knowledgeable. During the winter months of July and August, the CFU incorporated discussions of El Niño into its "field-day" activities in the different regions, reinforcing the probabilistic nature of the prediction. Occurring in July and August, these deliberately coincided with times at which commercial farmers were buying their seed for the upcoming season. The general advice the CFU developed for its farmers, in coordination with the Met Service, was to plant early to take advantage of the predicted good early-season rains, and to plant short-season varieties to avoid the likely late-season drought. Farmers working with CFU agronomists at the field-day meetings generated location-specific recommendations about what particular varieties to plant. Most farmers incorporated these recommendations into their decisions.

Using the information was more difficult in the smallholder sector, especially among communal land farmers in drier regions of the country, where "below-normal" rainfall implied a high likelihood of crop failure. Modeling results (Phillips, Maudze, and Urganai 2001), and more recently field studies (Patt, Suarez, and Gwata 2005), show that the forecasts can be of value to farmers, by allowing them to optimize for the expected rainfall with a different mix of seed varieties and a staggered planting schedule. But as of 1997, except for a few people within the early warning unit (NEWU), most people had little idea what ENSO was, and how to interpret the seasonal forecasts. In July, Agritex organized a two-day workshop in Harare to discuss the use of seasonal forecasts with Met Service and RRSP personnel. One suggestion was to educate Agritex extension officers about El Niño, so that they could help farmers make better decisions. However, it took several months for this to happen.

Even though the workshops were late, Agritex did advise farmers prior to the normal planting time, soon after the release of the Met Service seasonal forecast in early October. Agritex instructed field staff to tell farmers that rainfall would be below normal. Agritex advised farmers to plant more drought-tolerant varieties of maize, or extremely drought-tolerant crops like sorghum and millet, to plant early (October instead of November), and to sell off draft animals, where possible. The communal farmers received this information in conjunction with the media reports. Both the media and the Agritex field staff compared the current year with 1991–1992, when there was a massive drought and even drought-tolerant crops had failed. Agritex deliberately tried to avoid conveying probabilistic forecasts down to the district and local level, out of a fear of confusing the farmers.

The workshops—planned in July—took place in eight provinces between November 18 and December 5 with representatives from the NEWU, Met Service, and DMC. Provincial Agritex staff attended, as did some district and local extension workers. This series of training sessions probably came too late to educate people for the 1997–1998 season, since they occurred after the time for early planting (October), and well after the time when communal farmers typically buy their seed (August and September). Furthermore, the vast majority of the local extension officers did not attend training sessions, and never learned about probabilistic forecasts associated with El Niño.

Communal farmers reacted in many different ways to the deterministic forecasts. Some, particularly among those in wetter areas of the country, did plant varieties of maize more drought tolerant than usual, and did plant early. Most communal land farmers did not change their behavior in response to the forecast, and very few sold their animals. Some farmers, particularly among those in the driest region, waited until December or January (i.e., late) to plant their millet, sorghum, or maize, after having seen early season rainfall turn out to be relatively normal. These farmers fared poorly when the rains ended early, as predicted. In total, the area of land the smallholder farmers planted was 21.3 percent lower than the year before, and the total harvest was 43.1 percent lower (Policy and Planning Division 1999). Those farmers who planted late suffered most.

Media and Government Response   The media extensively covered the ENSO event and corresponding forecasts of drought, and for many people was the only source of climate-related information. People in the meteorology, food-security, and agricultural sectors were highly critical of the coverage that the media devoted to the ENSO event, accusing them of blowing it out of proportion. The feeling among professionals was that the media hype contributed to a poor understanding of the uncertainties associated with ENSO. Because they felt that the media overplayed El Niño, many saw their own role as trying to downplay the significance of the ENSO warm event, urging people not to panic.

As the summer came to a close in March and April, the Met Service organized a postseason review meeting, where they reviewed with stakeholders the results of the forecasting effort during the season. The conclusion of the Met Service was that the forecast of normal to below normal had been accurate. What was not accurate, they said, were the stories in the media predicting a major drought from "the mother of all El Ninos," reports that most people in the country read and used in making their decisions.

Discussion: Building Salience and Credibility through Participation

In Zimbabwe, the 1997 forecast was quite salient to the SADC and national-level food planners. First, the spatial scale at which the forecast emerged from SARCOF—providing probabilities for the entire country and region—matched the level of decision making of these managers. Second, the costs of taking action in response to the forecast were low, consisting primarily of organizational meetings. There was a low threshold on information content needed in order to be relevant. Third, this audience was a sophisticated group of career analysts, who needed little help understanding what the information meant and how they could respond to it.

Building Salience for Farmers

The CFU also helped make the forecast salient to large-scale commercial farmers. Unlike the food-security planners, farmers operate at a fine scale—the individual farm—and face decisions that are costly if wrong. If a farmer believed that a drought was coming, he or she could plant a shorter-season variety. But if the rains turn out to be good, the farmer would have done better off by not changing crops, since under ideal conditions the shorter-season varieties have a lower output. The CFU provided farmers not only with the macrolevel SARCOF forecast, but interpreted it to make it useful at the local level. By incorporating the forecast into their crop workshops around the country, they were able to respond to individual farmers' concerns, and offer place-based guidance as to what crops to plant and why, recognizing the risks associated with changing behavior in response to the forecasts.

Communal farmers needed the same type of assistance, but did not receive it. Like the commercial farmers they faced fine-scale high-cost decisions, meaning that the SARCOF forecast without interpretation was not useful. The salience of the forecasts to communal farmers faced additional barriers: they were unlikely to understand the forecasts, especially the probabilistic one, and faced greater economic constraints that limited their decision options. Agritex, through local extension officers, gave uniform advice, such as planting more drought-tolerant varieties at wider spacing between rows. To avoid the problem of poor understanding of the forecast, Agritex gave a deterministic forecast, simply saying there would be a drought. Some farmers followed Agritex's advice. Many more did not find it useful, because it did not tell them what they felt they needed to know: when exactly to plant, what particular varieties to substitute, and whether the risks associated with changing their behavior were worth it.

Building Credibility

The original motivation for SARCOF and a consensus forecast had been to increase the forecasts' credibility. RRSP staff felt that the presence of multiple forecasts, predicting different weather patterns, not only added to people's lack of trust in climatologists' ability to predict the weather, but also gave policymakers an excuse for doing nothing in response. SADC climatologists decided that having a single forecast, even an imperfect one, would increase the forecasters' overall credibility, and make it more difficult for policymakers to avoid using the information.

There were still other forecasts available, developed by other forecasting institutions outside Zimbabwe, and available primarily on the Internet. As long as these forecasts were limited to the Internet, their presence was not a cause for concern. Those users who would access the forecasts in this manner—people such as commercial farmers with both an active interest in forecasts and an Internet connection—are precisely the ones who would be more likely to trust forecasts in general. Indeed, the presence of more avenues of information, telling similar stories, could actually lead these users to place greater faith in the potential reliability of forecasts.

However, the RRSP and Met Service did not have control over the news media, which reached a much wider audience. In 1997 this was significant for two main reasons. First, the media tended not to discuss the official forecast in probabilistic terms, especially during the spring season prior to the onset of heavy rains. Rather, the media treated the forecast as predicting a drought with a great deal of certainty, often in an alarmist manner. Thus, the forecast that the people on the street actually heard was not the SARCOF probabilistic one, but rather a deterministic translation. This was roughly the same as what Agritex told the communal farmers, namely that there *would be* a serious drought. Second, the fact that the popular understanding of the forecast was in these deterministic terms created an opportunity for the media to challenge the forecasters' credibility. Early in the season they discussed an additional forecast published on the Internet by Mark Jury of the University of Zululand, South Africa. This forecast was much more explicitly moderated in terms of probability. Later, when rains did actually fall in Zimbabwe, the media was able to say that the earlier forecast had been wrong. The inability of forecasters to convey the probabilistic forecast through the media led to the common perception that the forecast had been wrong, causing a loss in credibility.

The task fell on the CFU and Agritex to build credibility around the forecast. Those who had learned of the forecast not through the media, but rather through some other channel—such as the CFU—were able to understand that the forecast was not in fact wrong; the season's outcome was well within the range of the forecast's actual predictions.

Communal farmers, by contrast, learned nothing from Agritex not already available to them through newspapers and radio.

Explaining Variance in Salience and Credibility
Why did the CFU and the early warning organizations take steps to bolster the salience and credibility of the forecast information, whereas Agritex did not? First, the CFU and early warning organizations had in place institutional norms that promoted the participation between meteorologists, analysts, and end users. Agritex, by contrast, has never encouraged farmer participation. Second, the CFU and the early warning community trusts their audience to understand complicated information, whereas Agritex does not. This was reflected in the decision by Agritex to present a simplified, deterministic forecast to communal farmers, rather than the more accurate probabilistic version. Third, the CFU and early warning organizations faced competition, and hence a loss in legitimacy if they failed to deliver a valuable product. Agritex, by contrast, did not.

Preexisting Patterns of Participation   The CFU, as a member cooperative, has mechanisms for farmer participation. The organization publishes a monthly newsletter and magazine, to which members can contribute. Members serve on the board of directors on numerous committees, and as staff provincial offices. Each season, before planting, the CFU holds numerous "crop circuses," where farmers, agronomy consultants, and CFU staff members meet to discuss best farming practices. This tradition of communication and participatory decision making made it easy to involve farmers in the planning process surrounding the 1997 forecast. The main CFU meteorologist—Stephen Crawford—simply organized a series of meetings between CFU regional representatives and Met Service staff to develop an understanding of the implications of the forecast for commercial farmers. Then, at the crop circuses later in the winter, he organized workshops with the farmers in order to discuss the forecast and possible response strategies. At these meetings, he highlighted the uncertain nature of the forecast and stressed the need to not overreact.

By contrast, communal farmers do not participate in Agritex's analysis or decision making. Agritex sees its mission as educating farmers about proper, modern, growing techniques. This is not necessarily bad, because there are many farming practices—such as planting in rows perpendicular to the slope—that are not widely used, that Agritex encourages, and that likely would lead to preservation and enhancement of soil fertility and yields. Yet Agritex is a top-down organization, intent on educating farmers, rather than working with them and learning from them. Partly this reflects the belief within Agritex that farmers have little important knowledge to offer. In the field, complaints are heard that echo the disconnect often found between farmers and government scientists (e.g., Wynne 1996). Farmers complain that the advice Agritex offers them is insensitive to the constraints they face. Agritex complains that farmers neither respect nor listen to them. The result has been that only a small fraction of farmers follow Agritex's advice, Agritex devotes its attention to these farmers, and most farmers farm with little input from Agritex extension officers.

Trust and Respect of Users   The failure of Agritex to include farmers in participatory decision-making processes reflects the organization's hierarchical and bureaucratic history and Agritex's lack of trust in the capacity of their audience to understand complicated information. With climate forecasts, this manifests itself most obviously in the decision to provide deterministic, rather than probabilistic, information. Managers and analysts at Agritex did not believe farmers capable of understanding uncertainties associated with climate forecasts. As one said, "My father is a farmer, and there is no way he can understand a percentage likelihood of below normal rainfall." Given this belief, the only information that Agritex could provide to farmers was the news that there would be a drought. All discussion of forecast uncertainty stopped at the regional level; district Agritex officers received information that lacked any discussion of the probabilities of different rainfall quantities. In this view, public participation was unnecessary, and could actually confuse farmers, because it would inevitably identify the uncertainties in the forecast.

Recent research suggests this lack of trust and respect to be ill-founded. Patt (2001), through a set of psychology experiments, demonstrated that communal farmers had the skills necessary to understand probabilistic information. Using a series of betting games using a roulette wheel, Patt showed that farmers can understand probabilistic information with only minimal training and learned wise betting strategies quickly. This suggests that participatory assessment, carried out repeatedly, may be the best way to build experience in understanding probabilistic forecasts.

Competition from Other Organizations   Agritex may not have involved farmers in decision making simply because it did not have to. Communal farmers lack the resources to seek technical information from any other source. While the farmers did receive some seasonal forecast information from other sources—primarily through the media and from church leaders—none of these sources could be predicted to tell farmers information more salient or credible than that which Agritex provided. Developing systems of public participation, and learning that farmers have the capacity to understand complicated information, would require resources that could be used elsewhere. Agritex made the choice not to utilize these resources for the above purposes for the 1997–1998 season.

The competition that Agritex faced in 1997 stands in contrast to that within the food-security and commercial-farming sectors. The end users of climate information within the food-security sector are plugged into the Internet, and monitor climate information coming directly from outside organizations. If the early warning organizations failed to provide additional value through their interpretation of the forecast, there is no doubt that their funding would be cut, and the users would turn to the alternative sources of information. Likewise, commercial farmers have available to them sources of information other than the CFU. Most of these farmers have access to satellite television, and many to the Internet. The CFU main office monitors these alternative sources of information, and sees its role as providing the tools necessary to make sense of all of it. Stephen Crawford, the CFU's Research, Information, and Extension Executive, saw his role as adding value to the climate forecasts.

However, an argument based on competition incentives only goes so far. Even within Agritex, practices have changed in response to the 1997–1998 season. There was widespread agreement that Agritex had done a poor job of communicating the forecast to farmers, and they had not responded appropriately to the forecast (O'Brien et al. 2000). At workshops held in Harare in July 1999, and later in Kadoma in October 1999, Agritex began to explore the extent to which farmers relied on traditional rainfall indicators (UNSO 1999; Shumba 1999). Since then, Agritex has cooperated with researchers to institute pilot projects aimed at public participation, and the Drought Monitoring Centre has supervised a grant program, funded by NOAA, to foster pilot programs in this area. Agritex is changing, to include greater participation and trust of farmers, even though its status as sole technical information provider has not changed. Perhaps this is the beginning of an upward spiral of trust and respect, contrary to the downward spiral that Wynne (1996) shows can be so harmful.

Conclusion

This study illustrates the role of organizations and institutions in creating effective assessments. It provides evidence for this book's contention that salience and credibility are intermediate variables contributing to effectiveness. More importantly, however, it offers evidence as to why some organizations, but not others, seek to bolster the salience and credibility of their assessments. I identify three reasons: preexisting mechanisms for participation, trust in users, and competition for users' attention.

From this evidence come three lessons for institutions and organizations designing and conducting assessments. First, put in place mechanisms for participation before they are needed. By the time an emergency arises, as it did in Zimbabwe in 1997, it is too late to develop sound practices for public participation. Second, use the participation process to help understand and build the capacity of users to process difficult information and make decisions for themselves. All too often assessors underestimate users' abilities and potential to make valuable contributions (e.g., Orlove, Chiang, and Cane 2000). Third, pay attention to competition. For designers of assessment processes, such as the governments that fund the IPCC, consider being open to competing institutions as a way of stimulating hard work. Assessors themselves should realize that if they do not face competition now, they likely will in the future if their work does not respond directly to user's needs.

References

Botcheva, L. 1998. *Doing Is Believing: Participation and Use of Assessments in the Approximation of EU Environmental Legislation in Eastern Europe.* Belfer Center for Science and International Affairs (BCSIA) Discussion Paper E-98-13. Cambridge, MA: Environment and Natural Resources Program, Kennedy School of Government, Harvard University.

Cane, M., G. Eshel, and R. Buckland. 1994. Forecasting Zimbabwean maize yield using eastern equatorial Pacific sea surface temperature. *Nature* 370: 204–205.

Dilley, M. 1997. Warning and intervention: What kind of information does the response community need from the early warning community? *Internet Journal for African Studies* 2. http://www.brad.ac.uk/research/ijas.

Easterling, W. 1997. Why regional studies are needed in the development of full-scaled integrated assessment modeling of global change processes. *Global Environmental Change* 7(4): 337–356.

FEWS. 1997a, June 26. *FEWS Bulletin.* www.info.usaid.gov/fews/fb970626.

FEWS. 1997b, July 28. *FEWS Bulletin.* www.info.usaid.gov/fews/fb970728.

FEWS. 1997c, October 27. *FEWS Bulletin.* www.info.usaid.gov/fews/fb971027.

Fischhoff, B. 1996. Public values in risk research. *Annals of the American Academy of Political and Social Science* 545: 75–84.

Freudenburg, W. 1996. Risky thinking: Irrational fears about risk and society. *Annals of the American Academy of Political and Social Science* 545: 44–53.

Frey, B., and A. Stutzer. 1999. *Happiness, Economy, and Institutions.* Working paper. Zurich: University of Zurich.

Glantz, M. 2001. *Currents of Change: Impacts of El Niño and La Niña on Climate and Society.* 2nd ed. Cambridge: Cambridge University Press.

Glantz, M., M. Betsill, and K. Crandall. 1997. Food security in southern Africa: Assessing the use and value of ENSO information. Boulder, CO: National Center for Atmospheric Research.

Gundry, S., J. Wright, A. Ferro-Luzzi, G. Mudimu, and P. Vaze. 1999. *A Hierarchical Dimension to Food Security? The Multi-Level Structure of Spatial and Temporal Processes Influencing the Food and Nutrition System in a District of*

Zimbabwe. Working paper AEE 12/99. Harare: Department of Agricultural Economics and Extension, University of Zimbabwe.

Kunreuther, H. 1996. Mitigating disaster losses through insurance. *Journal of Risk and Uncertainty* 12 (2–3): 171–187.

Kunreuther, H. and A. Kleffner. 1992. Should earthquake mitigation measures be voluntary or required? *Journal of Regulatory Economics* 4(4): 321–333.

Leiss, W. 1996. Three phases in the evolution of risk communication practice. *Annals of the American Academy of Political and Social Science* 545: 85–94.

Mason, S., L. Goddard, N. Graham, E. Yulaeva, L. Sun, and P. Arkin. 1999. The IRI seasonal climate prediction system and the 1997/98 El Niño event. *Bulletin of the American Meteorological Society* 80(9): 1853–1873.

McDaniels, T., L. Axelrod, and P. Slovic. 1996. Perceived ecological risks of global change: A psychometric comparison of causes and consequences. *Global Environmental Change* 6(2): 159–171.

Midmore, P., and J. Whittaker. 2000. Economics for sustainable rural systems. *Ecological Economics* 35: 173–189.

Miller, C. 1998. *Extending Assessment Communities to Developing Countries.* Belfer Center for Science and International Affairs (BCSIA) Discussion Paper E-98-15. Cambridge, MA: Environment and Natural Resources Program, Kennedy School of Government, Harvard University.

Mudimu, G. 1998. *Population Growth Pressure and Environmental Degradation in Zimbabwe's Communal Lands: Trends and Implications for Common Property Resource Management.* Working paper AEE 7/98. Harare: Department of Agricultural Economics and Extension, University of Zimbabwe.

National Economic Planning Commission. 1999. *National Policy on Drought Management.* Harare: Government of Zimbabwe, Office of the President and Cabinet.

National Research Council. 1996. *Learning to Predict Climate Variations Associated with El Niño and the Southern Oscillation.* Washington, DC: National Academy Press.

National Research Council. 1999. *Making Climate Forecasts Matter.* Washington, DC: National Academy Press.

NOAA. 1999. *An Experiment in the Application of Climate Forecasts: NOAA-OGP Activities Related to the 1997–98 El Niño Event.* Boulder, CO: University Corporation for Atmospheric Research.

O'Brian, K., L. Sygna, L. Næss, R. Kingamkono, and B. Hochobeb. 2000. *Is Information Enough? User Responses to Seasonal Climate Forecasts in Southern Africa.* Report to the World Bank, AFTE1-ENVGC. Adaptation to Climate Change and Variability in Sub-Saharan Africa, Phase II. ISSN: 0804-4562.

Orlove, B., J. Chiang, and M. Cane. 2000. Forecasting Andean rainfall and crop yield from the influence of El Niño on Pleiades visibility. *Nature* 403: 68–71.

Orlove, B., and J. Tosteson. 1999. *The Application of Seasonal to Interannual Climate Forecasts Based on El Niño–Southern Oscillation (ENSO) Events: Lessons from Australia, Brazil, Ethiopia, Peru, and Zimbabwe.* Working Papers in Environmental Policy. Berkeley: Institute of International Studies, University of California.

Patt, A. 1999. Assessing extreme outcomes: The strategic treatment of low probability impacts in scientific assessment. *Risk Decision and Policy* 4(1): 1–15.

Patt, A. 2001. Understanding uncertainty: Forecasting seasonal climate for farmers in Zimbabwe. *Risk Decision and Policy* 6(2): 105–119.

Patt, A., and C. Gwata. 2002. Effective seasonal climate forecast applications: Examining constraints for subsistence farmers in Zimbabwe. *Global Environmental Change: Human and Policy Dimensions* 12: 185–195.

Patt, A., and D. Schrag. 2003. Using specific language to describe risk and probability. *Climatic Change* 61: 17–30.

Patt, A., P. Suarez, and C. Gwata. 2005. Effects of seasonal climate forecasts and participatory workshops among subsistence farmers in Zimbabwe. *Proceedings of the National Academy of Sciences of the United States of America* 102: 12673–12678.

Patt, A., and R. Zeckhauser. 2002. Behavioral perceptions and policies toward the environment. In R. Gowda and J. Fox, eds., *Judgments, Decisions, and Public Policy*, 265–302. Cambridge: Cambridge University Press.

Phillips, J., M. Cane, and C. Rosenzweig. 1998. ENSO, seasonal rainfall patterns and simulated maize yield variability in Zimbabwe. *Agricultural and Forest Meteorology* 90: 39–50.

Phillips, J., E. Makaudze, and L. Unganai. 2001. Current and potential use of climate forecasts for resource-poor farmers in Zimbabwe: Impacts of El Niño and climate variability on agriculture. *American Society of Agronomy Special Publication Series*, 63: 87–100.

Policy and Planning Division. 1999. *The Agricultural Sector of Zimbabwe Statistical Bulletin, March 1999.* Harare: Policy and Planning Division, Ministry of Lands and Agriculture, Government of Zimbabwe.

Renn, O. 1998. The role of risk communication and public dialogue for improving risk management. *Risk Decision and Policy* 3(1): 5–30.

Rowlands, I. 1998. Climate change cooperation in the global greenhouse. In I. Rowlands, ed., *Climate Change Cooperation in Southern Africa*, 1–26. London: Earthscan.

SADC. 1997a, April/May. *Food Security.* Harare, Zimbabwe: SADC Regional Early Warning Unit.

SADC. 1997b, June. *Food Security.* Harare, Zimbabwe: SADC Regional Early Warning Unit.

SADC. 1997c, August. *Food Security*. Harare, Zimbabwe: SADC Regional Early Warning Unit.

Scoones, I., C. Chibudu, S. Chikura, P. Jeranyama, D. Machaka, W. Machanja, B. Mavedzenge, B. Mombeshora, M. Mudhara, C. Mudziwo, F. Murimbarimba, and B. Zirereza. 1996. *Hazards and Opportunities: Farming Livelihoods in Dryland Africa: Lessons from Zimbabwe*. London: Zed Books.

Shumba, O. 1999. *Coping with Drought: Status of Integrating Contemporary and Indigenous Climate/Drought Forecasting in Communal Areas of Zimbabwe*. Country report prepared for the United Nations Development Programme / Office to Combat Desertification and Drought. Harare: Southern Alliance for Indigenous Resources.

Slovic, P. 1993. Perceived risk, trust, and democracy. *Risk Analysis* 13(6): 675–682.

Slovic, P. 1997. Trust, emotion, sex, politics, and science. In M. Bazerman, D. Messick, A. Tenbrunsel, and K. Wade-Benzoni, eds., *Environment, Ethics, and Behavior: The Psychology of Environmental Valuation and Degradation*, 277–313. San Franscisco: New Lexington Press.

Stack, J. 1998. Drought forecasts and warnings in Zimbabwe: Actors, linkages and information flows. Working paper AEE 2/98. Harare: Department of Agricultural Economics and Extension, University of Zimbabwe.

UNSO. 1999. *Report: Workshop to Enhance Farmer Use of Climate Forecasts*. October 4–6, 1999, Kadoma, Zimbabwe. Prepared by the United Nations Development Programme and the United Nations Office to Combat Desertification and Drought.

Watson, R., M. Zinyowera, R. Moss, and D. Dokken. 1997. *The Regional Impacts of Climate Change: An Assessment of Vulnerability*. Geneva: WMO and UNEP.

Weber, E. 1997. Perception and expectation of climate change: Precondition for economic and technological adaptation. In M. Bazerman, D. Messick, A. Tenbrunsel, and K. Wade-Benzoni, eds., *Environment, Ethics, and Behavior: The Psychology of Environmental Valuation and Degradation*, 314–341. San Francisco: New Lexington Press.

Windschitl, P., and E. Weber. 1999. The interpretation of "likely" depends on context, but "70%" is 70%—right? The influence of associative processes on perceptual certainty. *Journal of Experimental Psychology: Learning, Memory, and Cognition* 25(6): 1514–1533.

Wynne, B. 1996. Misunderstood misunderstandings: Social identities and public uptake of science. In A. Irwin and B. Wynne, eds., *Misunderstanding Science? The Reconstruction of Science and Technology*, 19–46. Cambridge: Cambridge University Press.

Interviews

Anonymous Farmers, Gwaii Forest, Matebleleland North, July 4, 1999.

Anonymous Farmers, Honde Valley, Manicaland, August 14, 1999.

Anonymous Farmers, Murewah District, Mashonaland East, July 29, 1999.

Anonymous Farmers, Whitewater District, Matabeleland South, August 6, 1999.

Stephen Crawford, Research, Information, and Extension Executive, Commercial Farmers' Union, Harare, July 26, 1999.

Graham Farmer, Chief Technical Advisor, Food and Agriculture Organization of the United Nations, Asmara, Eritrea, July 28, 1999.

John MacRobert, Agronomy Services, Seed Co Limited, Harare, July 27, 1999.

Ephias Makaudze, Lecturer, Department of Economics and Agricultural Extension, Harare, July 30, 1999.

Percy Malusalila, Extension Representative, Seed Co Limited, Harare, July 27, 1999.

Robert Mugwara, Director, Southern African Development Community Food Security Technical and Administrative Unit, Harare, July 27, 1999.

Veronica Mutikani, Director, National Early Warning Unit, Agritex, Harare, September 12, 1999.

Forman Sibanda, Agritex Supervisor for Tcholotcho North, Sipepa, Matebeleland North, July 12, 1999.

Caleb Tapfuma, Agricultural Manager, Standard Fire and General Insurance Company, Harare, April 27, 2000.

Isaac Tarakidzwa, Head of Agrometeorological Section, Department of Meteorological Services, Harare, September 14, 1999.

Leonard Unganai, Director, Climate Services Branch, Department of Meteorological Services, Harare, July 8, 1999.

Eliot Vhurumuku, Assistant Field Officer, United States Agency for International Development Famine Early Warning Project, Harare, July 28, 1999.

Acronyms

Agritex	Zimbabwe Agricultural Extension Service
CFU	Commercial Farmers' Union
DMC	Drought Monitoring Centre for Southern Africa
ENSO	El Niño–Southern Oscillation
FEWS	Famine Early Warning System
IPCC	Intergovernmental Panel on Climate Change
IRI	International Research Institute for Climate Prediction
Met Service	Zimbabwe Department of Meteorological Services

NEWU	National Early Warning Unit
NOAA	National Oceanic and Atmospheric Administration
RRSP	Regional Remote Sensing Project
SADC	Southern African Development Community
SARCOF	Southern African Regional Climate Outlook Forum
USAID	U.S. Agency for International Development
ZFU	Zimbabwe Farmers' Union

10

Mining Water, Drying Wells: Multilevel Assessment and Decision Making for Water Management

David W. Cash

Introduction

The study and practice of environmental assessment and management increasingly recognize the importance of scale and cross-scale dynamics in understanding and addressing environmental change (Ostrom et al. 2002). For many environmental issues, science communities, policymakers, and managers at all levels have begun to struggle with questions such as: How can we structure assessments of large-scale environmental change to influence local decision making? Who should participate in such activities to ensure salience for decision makers, scientific credibility, and political legitimacy? How should authority and responsibility to assess and manage environmental problems be apportioned at different levels? What are the implications for data collection, standardization, and analysis when information is produced and translated across multiple levels?

Numerous efforts to try to address these kinds of questions characterize the rapidly evolving landscape of environmental assessment practice and scholarship (Alcamo, Kreileman, and Leemans 1996; Carnegie Commission on Science, Technology, and Government 1992; Easterling, Weiss, and Hays 1998; Intergovernmental Panel on Climate Change 1996, 1998; Lins, Wolock, and McCabe, 1997; Millennium Assessment Secretariat 2000; Miller, Rhodes, and MacDonnell 1996; Wilbanks and Kates 1999). This volume represents a coordinated effort to address these questions, though mostly from an international-level perspective. This chapter complements the majority of cases in this volume by providing an initial way of thinking about and addressing the

challenges involved in integrating science and policy *across* multiple
levels. This contribution targets this gap. As such, the chapter presents
an empirical analysis of water management in the U.S. Great Plains, providing a deeper understanding of the interaction between assessment and
decision making in the context of multilevel environmental problems. It
asks: What are the characteristics of effective assessment and decision-
making systems that address multilevel environmental problems, and
how do such systems maintain salience, credibility, and legitimacy for
audiences at different levels?

This study finds that some systems have developed the ability to make
and enforce laws and regulations, design and implement a range of management tools, and change the behavior of water users, while other
systems have not. The effective systems can be characterized as distributed research, assessment, and decision-support systems (Cash 2000).
They integrate information and decision making through long-term iterated two-way interactions and institutional structures that foster informational credibility, legitimacy, and salience for decision makers at
multiple levels. These systems balance interests from different levels (e.g.,
the state and local level) and exploit comparative advantages in decision
making and information production that are specific to different nodes
in the network. Effective systems share three common institutionalized
features: (1) multiple coordinated connections between researchers and
decision makers at different levels (polyarchic networks) (Ostrom 1998);
(2) boundary organizations that mediate between information and
decision-making nodes and across levels (Cash 2001); and (3) long-lived
and adaptive organizations (Gunderson, Holling, and Light 1995), which
allow for iterated interactions between information producers and decision makers (a "science on retainer" model of interaction). In contrast,
ineffective systems are more centralized (not responsive to local context)
or too autonomous (fail to take advantage of expertise or capacities at
different levels), and coordinate less effectively between nodes in the
system.

Rationale for Studying Aquifer Depletion and Research Methods

As noted throughout this volume, numerous major international and
regional environmental treaties have been initiated in the last thirty years,

with most being top-down, centralized, and primarily focused on producing credible written scientific reports (Torrance, chapter 2, this volume; VanDeVeer, chapter 5, this volume). While this structure has effectively probed questions about large-scale phenomena and contributed to international negotiations, it has been poorly suited for identifying and describing regional and local vulnerabilities to large-scale phenomena, integrating and synthesizing data collected at multiple levels, linking the international assessments to local realities, and producing policy-relevant information for subnational decision makers (Jasanoff and Wynne 1998; Cash and Moser 2000).

A fundamental challenge for bridging levels is addressing the scale dependence of salience, credibility, and legitimacy. What is salient, credible, or legitimate to actors at one level might be different from (and even antithetical to) what is salient, credible, or legitimate to actors at other levels. This is clearly seen, for example, in the lack of legitimacy that U.S. federal agencies have in dealing with what are perceived as local issues in Hawai'i (Moser, chapter 8, this volume) or the lack of credibility that the national agricultural research institution (Agritex) in Zimbabwe has had with smallholder farmers (Patt, chapter 9, this volume).

The Case
What characteristics of assessment and decision-making systems ensure that information produced will be salient, credible, and legitimate at different levels simultaneously? To answer this question I examine depletion of the High Plains aquifer in the United States. Understanding and addressing this problem has implications at multiple organizational levels, and it has involved intensive use of scientific and technical information. From an analytic perspective, the case exhibits useful variance in information and decision-making institutions and their effectiveness, while controlling for many exogenous variables. Between 1940 and 2000, the High Plains aquifer (see figure 10.1), a major source of irrigation water underlying eight U.S. states in the semiarid Great Plains, declined in some areas by as much as 50 percent (McGuire 2003). Because irrigated agriculture is the economic foundation of this region, which supplies a significant portion of food and fiber products to U.S. and international markets, there has been considerable concern about

Figure 10.1
Extent of High Plains Aquifer in the central United States (in dark gray). *Source:*
V. L. McGuire et al. 2003. *Water in Storage and Approaches to Ground-Water
Management, High Plains Aquifer, 2000*. U.S. Geological Survey Circular 1243

the aquifer's decline among farmers, county officials, state agencies, and
federal politicians and administrators (Kromm and White 1992;
McGuire and Sharpe 1997). The interest in the issue of aquifer depletion has spawned an enormous array of hydrogeological, agricultural,
economic, and social research and assessment designed to aid and influence decision making at all of these levels.

Water-management regimes in Kansas, Nebraska, and Texas were
chosen as study sites. These states were chosen because they create a set
of comparative cases in which variables such as the characteristics of the
aquifer, risk of water depletion, and general economic characteristics are
held relatively constant, while specific institutional and management
variables vary.

While counties were a focus of analysis, the unit of analysis, or each
study site, can be more accurately described as the assessment and
decision-making system in which the county is embedded. This system
may include a range of local, state, and federal institutions with varying
boundaries and jurisdictions.

Evidence for the investigation include 80 semistructured interviews with those involved in or affected by aquifer use at all levels, a survey on involvement in collaborative efforts and multilevel linkages of 220 county agricultural agents in the three states, and technical reports, newsletters from water-management districts, fact sheets, and maps.

What Is to Be Explained: Effectiveness of Information and Decision-Making Systems

This study examines what contributes to the effectiveness of assessment and decision systems in addressing multiscale environmental risks. Although we would prefer to use the state of the aquifer as an indicator of effectiveness, data on the state of the aquifer is incomplete and the influence of management actions on the resource is difficult to identify given current levels of understanding regarding other hydrogeological and human influences. This study therefore looks "upstream" in the causal chain and focuses on three indicators of effectiveness (Haas, Keohane, and Levy 1994; Young 1999):

Management capacity The ability to make and enforce laws and regulations, and play an effective role in designing and implementing policy.

Management actions Including education, financial incentives/programs, regulations, monitoring, and enforcement.

Behavior change The adoption by farmers of highly efficient irrigation technology, including center-pivot irrigation systems.

Explanatory or Institutional Variables

Several variables might determine effectiveness of assessment and decision-making systems and provide insights into the relationship between institutions and outcomes as well as salience, credibility, and legitimacy. The most important of these include system organization, the existence of boundary organizations (Guston 1999), and the existence of adaptive institutions. Four general models of assessment and decision-making systems are found in the region:

Semicentralized Relatively centralized decision-making authority and information production situated largely in one node (e.g., a state capital or state land-grant college), coordinated across levels in a moderately dense network. Information and decision making are relatively well integrated. Utilize boundary organizations to some degree and show varying levels of adaptiveness.

Polyarchic   Multiple nodes in a dense network of information and decision making at multiple levels, none of which have overall primacy. These nodes are coordinated through institutional links. Decision making and information production are distributed. Utilize boundary organizations and show high levels of adaptiveness.

Autonomous   Multiple nodes at multiple levels with decision making generally at more local levels and information production distributed among nodes. This network is less dense and less well connected. Nodes are relatively uncoordinated. Information and decision making are not well integrated. Utilize boundary organizations infrequently and relatively little adaptiveness.

Semiautonomous   The locus of decision making is at the local level and information production is distributed. Coordination between nodes and across levels is more institutionalized than in the autonomous model, and information and decision making is more tightly linked. Utilize boundary organizations to some degree and show varying levels of adaptiveness

Comparison of Information and Decision-Making Institutions

Information and decision-making systems in Kansas, Nebraska, and Texas share many common nodes. All three are linked to the U.S. Department of Agriculture (USDA) and its conservation programs and requirements through the Natural Resource Conservation Service (NRCS), which has state offices, area offices that oversee programs in subregions of each state, and an office in every county. In addition, all three have state agencies that are tasked with addressing water-resource issues. The most important of these are the Kansas Division of Water Resources (KDWR), the Nebraska Department of Water Resources (NDWR), and the Texas Water Development Board (TWDB) (hereafter called state water agencies). In Kansas and Texas, water-management districts can be voluntarily formed through local petition and election that confers on these districts a variety of different rights and responsibilities. These districts can vary in size from one county to multiple counties. Such substate governments are Groundwater Management Districts in Kansas, and Underground Water Conservation Districts in Texas (hereafter called water-management districts (WMD)). In Nebraska, the state is divided into twenty-three multicounty Natural Resources Districts (NRDs). NRDs have responsibility for the management of a wide range of resources, including water (surface and underground), soil, forests, and wildlife.

The assessment systems in the three states also share features. The most important federal agency that has nodes in the region is the U.S. Geological Survey (USGS). In addition to a Great Plains office (located in Lincoln, Nebraska), each state has a USGS state office. USDA has a network of research centers from the Agricultural Research Service (ARS) in each of the three states, but more important, USDA is the coordinating federal agency for the Cooperative State Research, Education, and Extension Service (CSREES). The general organization of the CSREES system includes national administrative offices and research laboratories in Washington, D.C., and Maryland; a research/education/extension center housed in the state's land-grant college—Kansas State University (KSU), the University of Nebraska at Lincoln (UNL), and the University of Texas (UT); area research and extension offices throughout the state; and an elected advisory board and extension office in each county. In addition to the land-grant college and its associated substate research centers, each state has the equivalent of a state geological survey: Kansas Geological Survey (KGS); UNL's Conservation and Survey Division (CSD); and research divisions within the state water agency in Texas.

While the states share some common features, significant differences characterize the structure and function of the assessment and decision-making systems.

Kansas—Semicentralized Systems
While the state government has ultimate ownership of underground water, through locally elected boards of directors, WMDs have authority to adopt "reasonable standards and policies relating to the

conservation and management of groundwater" with approval from the state water agency (Kansas Statute 82a-1020-1040 1972). The ultimate arbiter of underground water rights is the agency's Chief Engineer. WMDs act as boundary organizations, coordinating state-local activity, translating information between levels, and connecting scientists from various state and federal nodes with WMD technical staff and farmers. This cross-boundary mediation is possible because of the accountability of WMDs to both the local constituents that elect it and to the state water agency and state legislature. The county agricultural extension office also acts as a boundary organization linking the multiple nodes from the KSU research and extension system, the USGS system, and local farmers. It also is accountable to a locally elected board that hires and fires staff, and to KSU.

Nebraska—Polyarchic Systems

The locus of decision making for groundwater management in Nebraska is distributed between the NRDs and the state regulatory agencies. As in Kansas, the state ultimately owns underground water, but this system is less hierarchical, with multiple nodes in the network sharing responsibilities. NRDs have broad regulatory, research, monitoring, and outreach authority, and integrate their management of groundwater quantity with management of surface water, water quality, soils, wildlife, and habitat conservation.

In addition, NRDs act as boundary organizations, linking local and state decision making through various institutional mechanisms. NRDs also have dual accountability to the electorate and state-level agencies. The county extension office plays a pivotal boundary organization role as well, linking NRD research and assessment with the UNL and the USGS activities and farmer demonstration projects.

Texas—Semiautonomous and Autonomous Systems

Groundwater management in Texas is governed by the absolute-ownership doctrine, which stipulates that landowners have full rights to underground water pumped from their property. No correlative right is associated with groundwater—rights to underground water on one property are not diminished even if pumping that water results in decreased groundwater availability on a neighbor's property. Thus, in Texas, the system is characterized by more local (individual and county-level) autonomy than in either Kansas or Nebraska. There is, however, variance in the degree of autonomy, conditioned on whether a county is within a WMD or not within a WMD.

Semiautonomous Systems   While WMD creation was enabled by state legislation, the day-to-day management activities of WMDs are not governed by state regulatory or legislative actions. WMDs can modify landowners' absolute right to groundwater, but except for well-spacing requirements there has never been an attempt to limit individual pumping. Primary WMD activities include education and research. The absolute-ownership doctrine limits state control of local water management to two avenues. The first involves engaging local WMDs in regional water-planning activities. The second involves conservation-incentive programs administered by the state water agency but coordinated by county and area NRCS offices and WMDs. The system is semiautonomous, with decision making residing primarily at the local (individual and management district) level, with a moderately dense network, and weak coupling with state-level decision making. As in Kansas and Nebraska, WMDs act as boundary organizations between local constituents and state policymakers, advocating on behalf of constituents and protecting them from encroachment by state regulatory agencies. Unlike in Kansas or Nebraska, WMDs' primary accountability is to local constituents, with little accountability to state agencies. As in Kansas and Nebraska, the county extension office functions as a boundary organization, facilitating the production of locally relevant information by coordinating research from the local to the area research and experiment stations. County extension agents in Texas are also dually accountable, answering to a locally elected board and the state land-grant college.

Autonomous Systems   Counties, and individuals, that are not within a WMD are governed by the full weight of the absolute-ownership doctrine. This results in decision making for water management being entirely at the individual level. The state water agency conservation-incentive programs apply only in areas within WMDs, making farmers in non-WMD counties ineligible. NRCS does make available some federal conservation monies, which act as the only link between local- and other-level decision making. The decision-making network is quite sparse. Agricultural extension offices in these counties are tied in to the state research and extension information system and act as boundary organizations between local farmers and area and state research and assessment efforts. The coordination between the county, area, and state levels is less well coordinated than for counties with WMDs, since the nodes associated with WMDs are missing. As in other counties in Texas, extension agents in non-WMD counties are dually accountable, answering to a locally elected board and the state land-grant college.

Effectiveness of Different Assessment and Decision-Making Systems

By examining indicators of management capacity, management actions, and behavior change, this section describes variation in management effectiveness.

Management Capacity

The most general indicator of effectiveness that I examine is management capacity. Management capacity, defined as the ability of actors in civil society to play an effective role in policymaking and implementation, is complex and multifaceted. One facet addresses decision-making capacity. High capacity can be indicated by the ability of managers to avoid legislative constraints on decision making at local levels. Lower capacity can be inferred from conflicts between decision makers at state and local levels, or actions at one of those levels that inhibit constructive management at the other level. This does not presume a primacy of "local" control, but instead focuses on how decisions at one level influence the capacity for decision making at other levels.

Management capacity is influenced by information capacity for several reasons. In addressing the local scale, the implications of changes in a large system like the aquifer require that different knowledge and expertise be available to understand the multilevel nature of the problem. Additionally, capacity to monitor the resource can improve the contractual environment, providing a means by which "shirkers" (overpumpers or wasters, in this case) can be identified.

In the High Plains region, management capacity varies among sites from high management capacity (consistent ability to craft, implement, and credibly enforce rules and produce and utilize information), to medium management capacity (high levels of capacity in some dimensions, and lower levels of capacity in others), to low management capacity (general inability to consistently craft, implement, and enforce rules and produce and utilize information).

High Management Capacity—Nebraska   The legal, political, and information institutions that manage groundwater in Nebraska create a management environment that supports rule making backed by credible enforcement and information provision. The existence of locally elected and empowered directors collaborating with active, transparent, and well-coordinated state agencies, all in a coherent legislative and judicial framework, produces a system that has high management capacity. Locally, it is politically legitimate yet responsive to state interests. This balance of local and state interests involves state ownership of the resource with delegation of management authority to the local level while retaining the threat of state control. The system has proven to be flexible: as new issues and concerns have arisen on the agendas at federal, state, and local levels, NRDs have been able to adapt their management strategies to respond to new problems.

The system in Nebraska attempts to build management capacity by exploiting decision-making expertise and political legitimacy at both state and local levels. Toward this end, the Nebraska legislature conferred a broad array of powers on NRDs. This expansive portfolio allows NRDs to experiment with, and develop, tools to address conservation issues. In addition to the kinds of authority that reside in NRDs, there is also a breadth of issue areas for which NRDs have responsibility. This integration of groundwater management into a larger natural resource management regime further builds capacity for NRDs to more holistically manage issues that are biogeophysically or socioeconomically linked (e.g., groundwater and surface water, or water quantity and water quality).

In addition to the NRDs' broad powers and mandate to manage multiple issues simultaneously, the state legislature, state agencies, and NRDs have been allocated clearly defined roles with relatively little ambiguity. Unlike in Kansas, NRDs enforce the rules they promulgate, with the knowledge that state agencies and courts will support their actions:

> There have not been so many litigations, but we have won all of them: the right to read meters; the right to cease and desist on overpumpers, [and they are] all based on scientific evidence. State law allowed monitoring, and we worked closely with the state legislature in working out legislation. . . . People think we'll enforce regulations. (NRD Manager)

Like the decision-making system, the information system contributes to high management capacity. In a distributed system of research, assessment, extension, and education, a network of nodes having different expertise is coordinated to transfer information and skills across levels and between agencies:

> We had done model surveys with USGS and CSD to show people what was happening. The model showed how long 'til it dried up. We used agronomic, rainfall, development information for the models. Models to show if we don't do anything, X will happen. We would generate these [models] at the board meeting, and we would generate a whole sheet of paper, and we'd sit half the night at these board meetings and we'd haggle and argue and debate. Everything we were doing had never been done before in Nebraska, never really been done anyplace, like we were doing it, so we were developing . . . we were breaking prairie, and still to a degree are. (Member, NRD Board of Directors)

The Nebraska resource management system has high management capacity. It involves careful, unambiguous, and distributed allocation of authority between state and local institutions and actors, and a structured information system that can provide useful information at multiple levels. These contribute to the capacity to design, experiment with, implement, and enforce an assortment of rules, regulations, incentives, and education programs.

Medium Management Capacity—WMDs in Kansas and Texas The two Kansas counties in this study are embedded in a management environment that is conducive to making decisions, creating rules and regulations, and implementing those rules. Statutes have vested the authority for some aspects of management in locally elected officials, while keeping ultimate control in the state water agency. The result is a system that generally has both local political legitimacy and state-level support. The underlying network structure allows for complementary actions that promote state goals while being tailored to local conditions (or at least the avoidance of conflicting state and local activities).

While ultimate control is at the state level, the system is not purely centralized—decision-making authority and responsibilities are distributed among different state agencies and between state agencies and more locally controlled WMDs. There is an attempt to allocate authority and responsibilities at the appropriate node in the system in an effort to balance the interests of the state and local landowners in conserving and protecting groundwater resources and economic development through irrigated agriculture. The WMDs and state water-agency offices coordinate well in general, but tend not to coordinate with respect to enforcement and local flexibility with water-rights trading, decreasing their management capacity. Although statute vests enforcement of WMD regulations with the state water agency, enforcement is often inconsistent and sometimes nonexistent:

The problem is that they [the state water agency] don't enforce their own work. We need enforcement from Topeka. We have three policies that have some enforcement: 1) the meter requirement; 2) overpumping regulations; and 3) waste of water . . . all three have enforcement provisions. . . . DWR makes it hard for us, because they don't enforce. (WMD Resource Conservationist)

In addition, WMDs have explored options for allowing trading of water rights within districts to encourage more efficient allocation of the resource. In general, there is strong local support for such policies, but state law has not enabled such trading in its strict interpretation of state ownership.

A similar structure is seen in the information arena. Overlapping networks of researchers and information providers that cross levels produce a rich and dynamic system responsive to the needs of irrigators and water managers at all levels. The structure capitalizes on existing expertise at different nodes (e.g., monitoring at local levels, modeling at higher levels) and transfers skills between nodes (e.g., transferring technical analyses from the Kansas Geologic Survey to WMDs).

Kansas has a moderate amount of management capacity, composed of high capacity in some arenas and lower capacity in others. Lamb County, Texas, and the High Plains Underground Water Conservation District (HPUWCD) also illustrate enormous capacity for information production and educational programming but limited capacity for regulatory experimentation and development. Carson County, Texas, and the Panhandle Underground Water Conservation District have high capacity in the education arena but have relatively little capacity to develop and utilize technical analysis to guide decision making.

Low Management Capacity—Non-WMD Counties, Texas   Swisher County in Texas is an example of an area that has relatively low management capacity. Mounting evidence about aquifer depletion, involving both scientific research and farmers' own observations of declining well levels, has raised concern. Yet citizens or those institutionally interested in water management (the extension and NRCS offices) have had few means of devising, let alone implementing, effective management policies. No level has adequate administrative, political, or information capacity to design and implement the kinds of policies that have been undertaken in other parts of the region.

From the state's perspective, there is little capacity to affect management choices in Swisher County. The absolute-ownership doctrine bars the state from imposing any kind of regulatory framework on water users. Nor is Swisher part of an Underground Water Conservation District (WMD), which would allow modification of this doctrine.

While the NRCS and extension offices rely on neighboring WMDs to supply some information, neither organization has the capacity to model or monitor the status of the aquifer. State agencies such as TWDB do not have the capacity to independently assess aquifer dynamics in the county, and USGS does not have an active state office in the panhandle region of Texas. Thus, at all levels with interests in management (local, county, and state), there is relatively little capacity in both decision-making and information production arenas.

Management Actions

Management capacity can provide information about potential solutions to aquifer depletion, giving insight into how able actors are to make and implement appropriate decisions. Analyzing management actions looks beyond decision making to implementation.

As with management capacity, management actions can be categorized as of low, medium, or high effectiveness. All else being equal, having a more diverse set of management tools produces more robust and effective management. In a system of complexity, uncertainty, and multiple interests, a large portfolio of actions increases the probability that decisions by individual farmers will conform to the goals of a district. Some might respond to cost-share incentives, others to educational efforts, others to the fear of enforcement. Thus redundancy in the system can foster greater compliance. A larger suite of actions also increases complementarity within the system. Enforceable regulations provide a stick for farmer decision making, but cost share, free irrigation evaluations, and training workshops provide carrots as well (see table 10.1 for a summary of management actions).

The descriptions below outline the variance in management actions throughout the study region.

High   Chase County, Nebraska, characterized by a diverse portfolio of management actions addressing education, financial tools, regulation, monitoring, and enforcement.

Medium   Finney and Sherman counties, Kansas; Box Butte County, Nebraska; and Lamb and Carson counties, Texas, characterized by variable portfolios of management actions, some being strong in education and weaker in regulation (Lamb), strong in education and weaker in financial tools and enforcement (Finney and Sherman), strong in education, moderate in regulations, and weaker in financial tools and monitoring (Box Butte), and strong in education but weaker in regulation and monitoring (Carson).

Low   Swisher County, Texas, characterized by some educational and financial actions but almost no regulatory, monitoring, or enforcement actions.

Behavior Change

The management actions described above are generally designed to encourage or compel farmers to make decisions about their own behavior that will contribute to aquifer conservation. Education programs seek

Table 10.1
Description of management actions used at the study sites

Management actions	Description
Education	
Outreach (newsletters, seminars, radio, TV, etc.)	There is communication with farmers through a variety of media about the agricultural practices, new techniques, etc.
PET	Potential Evapo-Transpiration information—information about soil moisture, weather conditions, and crop needs—that can be distributed to farmers on a daily basis and used to make irrigation scheduling decisions.
Status of the aquifer	There is communication with farmers through a variety of media about the status of the aquifer.
Aggregate water use and irrigation practices	There is communication with farmers through a variety of media about aggregate water-use and irrigation practices.
Irrigation evaluations for individual farmers	Evaluations of a farmer's irrigation system are provided to farmers.
Financial incentives/programs	
Cost-Share/Loans	Grants and loans provide funds for the adoption of water-efficient technologies.
Water "banking"	The transference of allocated water over time, either by farmers to themselves, or to a new landowner at the time of sale of the land.
Water "pooling"	The transference of allocated water over space. A farmer can "pool" various water allocations and distribute that allocation throughout all of his or her landholdings, depending on personal preferences.
Regulations	
Well-spacing requirements	Limit of distance between wells.
Permit for well	A permit is required for the drilling of a new well.
Moratoriums on new wells	Ban on new wells, usually in a specified area that has experienced excessive depletion.
Ban on tailwater waste	The banning of water that runs off a field after it has been irrigated.

Table 10.1
(continued)

Withdrawal limit	Limit placed on the quantity of water pumped for a individual landowner.
Depletion limit	Limit placed on the quantity of water pumped, aggregated over a particular area (e.g., township, or county) over a particular time.
Designation of critical areas	Designation of areas that are in critical need of management because of high levels of depletion (these areas may then be subject to stricter regulation).
Monitoring	
Meter requirement	Requirement of water meters on pumps.
Mandatory water-use reporting	Requirement of farmer to report water use at a regular interval.
Data collection	Organized collection, through well monitoring, of aquifer-related data.
Enforcement	
Cease-and-desist orders	Action that requires user to stop pumping.
Lawsuits	Legal action taken against violators.

to raise farmers' knowledge and concern about aquifer depletion and identify the benefits of using less water. Financial incentives seek to encourage farmers to switch to more water-efficient irrigation technology. Regulations seek to limit the amount of water available to farmers. Monitoring seeks to understand the status of the aquifer and efficacy of management programs to direct management resources appropriately. Enforcement strategies seek, in the near term, to compel farmers to follow regulations, and in the long term, to deter them from breaking rules.

Behavior change in response to these actions can include abandoning irrigated farming, switching to more efficient technologies, or changing on-farm management practices (e.g., switching to less water-intensive crops, employing conservation tillage, utilizing specific crop-fallow rotations that better retain moisture in a field, reallocating water resources to more efficient uses, or following the recommendations of Potential

Evapotranspiration Network outputs). Rates at which these kinds of behaviors occur can be one indicator of effectiveness.

Adoption of Center-Pivot Technology   To examine behavior change, I chose to investigate the adoption of one water-efficient technology—center-pivot systems. The superior water efficiency of center-pivot systems has made their innovation and adoption one of the most important developments for conservation of the High Plains Aquifer (Kromm and White 1992; Opie 1993). Center-pivot technology was developed in the late 1960s, and its adoption overlaps with the institutional changes in water management, allowing analysis of their interactions. Fortunately, county-level data on center-pivot adoption are relatively complete, allowing comparisons over time and across areas. The quantitative analysis that follows provides evidence of variation in the effectiveness of different management strategies and points to the institutional variables associated with that variation.

Comparison of Center-Pivot Use within WMDs and outside WMDs, Kansas   Data provided by the Kansas Water Office (KWO) on the proportion of irrigated acres using center-pivot systems from 1993 to 1996 allows comparison of areas within WMDs and outside of WMDs. Figure 10.2 shows the far greater adoption of center-pivot systems in areas with WMDs. Center-pivot use grew steadily within WMDs, increasing from 45 to 55 percent ($\triangle = +10\%$), while increasing only from 30 to 31 percent ($\triangle = +1\%$) outside of WMDs (after having dropped to 24 percent in 1994 and 1995).

Comparisons of Center-Pivot Use within WMDs and outside WMDs, Texas   Unlike in Kansas, accurate and systematic regionwide data has not been collected in Texas. Available data does allow the conduct of two analyses. First, comparing center-pivot adoption in Lamb County (within a WMD) and Swisher County (not within a WMD) shows that, between 1964 and 1994, center-pivot adoption increased steadily in Lamb County to 73 percent of irrigated acres but proceeded much more slowly in Swisher County, only reaching 19 percent of irrigated acres by 1994 (see figure 10.3).

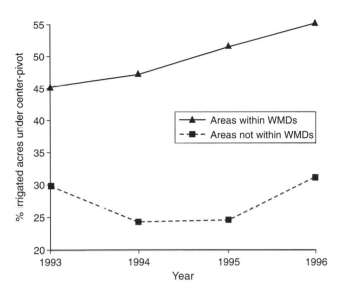

Figure 10.2
A comparison of irrigated acres under center-pivot systems in areas within and outside WMDs, western Kansas. *Source*: Compiled from data from the Kansas Water Office

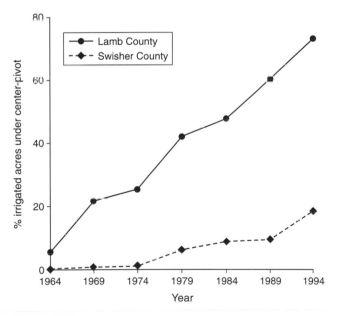

Figure 10.3
A comparison of irrigated acres under center-pivot systems in Lamb and Swisher counties, Texas. *Source*: Compiled from data from the Texas Water Development Board and the High Plains Underground Water Conservation District

Second, the Lamb County WMD has collected data for counties prior to when they joined the district. A dataset was created using county-level data on the number of center-pivot systems in 1986, 1990, 1993, 1995, and 1998 from thirteen of the fifteen counties in the district (two counties have an insignificant amount of irrigated acres and data was not available on irrigated acres using center-pivot systems). Since four of these counties joined the district between 1992 and 1994, we can compare *rates* of adoption of center-pivot systems before and after joining the district. To control for time effects, counties that were members of the WMD prior to 1986 were separated from those that joined in 1992–1994. Pooling of pre-1993 data and post-1993 data produced an annual percent increase in center-pivot systems in the two groups. The result, seen in figure 10.4, suggests that joining the WMD increases center-pivot adoption rates. Prior to 1992–1994, nonmembers show an annual rate of adoption of 11.9 percent. After joining the WMD, these counties' rate of adoption is 16.4 percent. During the same time period, counties that were already a part of the WMD keep roughly the same annual rate of adoption (13.9 percent, pre; 13.4 percent, post). Other variables that might explain such an increase (i.e., hydrological,

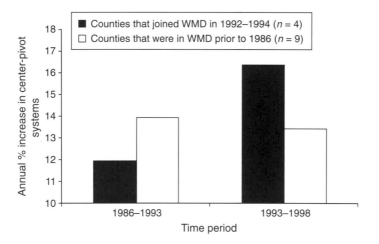

Figure 10.4
Effect of joining a WMD on rates of adoption of center-pivot systems. *Source*: Compiled from data from the High Plains Underground Water Conservation District

meteorological, economic, or agricultural) are relatively constant over time, and thus cannot effectively explain such a difference.

Cross-State Comparison of Center-Pivot Adoption   Data from several sources (NRC for Nebraska, KWO for Kansas, and WMDs and TWBD for Texas) allows comparison of center-pivot use among the seven sites at a single point in time. Analyzing variation across states complements and reinforces the preceding analysis of variation over time, illuminating how *overall* adoption of center-pivot systems compares across states. Figure 10.5 provides this comparison, charting the proportion of irrigated acres using center-pivot systems in 1995 across the seven study sites. Center-pivot adoption varies widely, from 19 percent in Swisher County to 90 percent in Chase County. Notably, the two "high-management-capacity" counties in Nebraska—Chase and Box Butte— have the highest rates in the group (90 percent and 81 percent, respec-

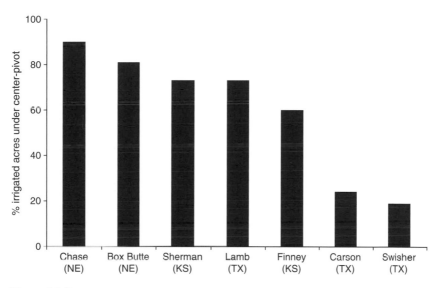

Figure 10.5
A comparison of irrigated acres under center-pivot systems across the seven study sites, 1995. *Source*: Compiled from data from the Nebraska Natural Resource Conservation Service, the Panhandle Underground Water Conservation District, the Kansas Water Office, the Texas Water Development Board, and the High Plains Underground Water Conservation District

tively), the Kansas counties (and Lamb County in Texas) show medium rates, and the other two Texas counties show the lowest rates.

Institutions and effectiveness

The preceding analysis illustrates four types of institutional structures: autonomous, semiautonomous, semicentralized, and polyarchic. A suite of indicators identify the seven counties as falling into three relative groupings:

Low effectiveness   Swisher County, Texas.

Medium effectiveness   Lamb and Carson counties, Texas; Finney and Sherman counties, Kansas.

High effectiveness   Chase County and Box Butte, Nebraska.

Does variation in institutional structure help explain this variance in effectiveness? If structure did not matter, the covariation of institutional variables with effectiveness that is illustrated in table 10.2 would not exist. The county that has an autonomous institutional structure, Swisher County, has the lowest effectiveness. Counties that are semiautonomous

Table 10.2
Relationship between institutional structure and effectiveness

Effectiveness					
High				Nebraska	
Medium			Texas (counties in WMDs)		Kansas
Low		Texas (counties not within WMDs)			
		Autonomous	Semiautonomous	Polyarchic	Semicentralized
		Institutional structure			

(Lamb and Carson) or semicentralized (Sherman and Finney) exhibit medium effectiveness. Finally, the polyarchic system in Nebraska (at neither extreme of the centralized or autonomous dichotomy) displays high levels of effectiveness.

Mediating between Institutions and Effectiveness: Salience, Credibility, and Legitimacy

What causal mechanisms underlie this correlation of institutional design with management effectiveness? More specifically, in the context of the present volume, what role do salience, credibility, and legitimacy play in the interaction of information and decision making across multiple levels of organization?

Table 10.2 provides a stylized picture of the correlation of institutions and effectiveness. It was derived by analyzing and comparing the seven counties to identify those sharing similar attributes. How are the characteristics of the institutions in each county linked to the outcomes we observe?

Polyarchic Systems and Salience, Credibility, and Legitimacy

We just have an absolute great relationship, I've been to many states and this is one of the most congenial systems here, across the board, from local through state and federal, and at the same time it's highly professional. (NRD Manager)

What contributes to this "great relationship ... from local through state and federal" levels, and how does that produce the effectiveness evident in these counties? What leads to development of the issue domain such that policies were made and implemented by managers and individual farmers to address aquifer depletion?

The enabling legislation for the Natural Resources Districts (NRDs) created a structure designed to distribute authority and responsibility to take advantage of each level's strengths while avoiding the state and local levels working at cross-purposes. Local groundwater managers and farmers need information and access to tools that are salient to that locale—to the climate, topography, characteristics of the aquifer, and political environment. The polyarchic nature of the system, as well as its attendant use of boundary organizations, encourages, constant and iter-ated two-way communication between decision making at multiple levels and scientists at multiple levels. Research conducted at UNL and CSD is seen as salient to state and local actors because they have helped set research agendas, and thus the questions that are important to them are addressed. Using institutional mechanisms (e.g., an advisory board for the county extension agent) ensures that needs are communicated to researchers, and findings are communicated in meaningful ways—whether this is for regulatory planning or for fine-tuning center-pivot technologies to local conditions. Such linkages also allow research and assessment that is simultaneously salient to actors at multiple levels. Analysis of the status of the aquifer is designed to capture both the local concerns of farmers and state-level concerns of generalized aquifer deple-tion (Cash 2001).

From a decision-making perspective, the apportionment of authority and responsibility to different nodes and levels (an apportionment that involved input from state, county, and local actors) is consistent with the federalist literature on establishing and maintaining political legitimacy. A similar construct works for the information system, which relies on symbiotic relationships between scientists and decision making at mul-tiple levels. State and federal scientists became legitimate sources of information because they are institutionally linked to local sources and engaged in producing outputs that require collaboration between local, state, and federal scientists. In Nebraska, comprehensive models of the aquifer that are useful to local and state decision makers cannot be con-structed with the data collection and monitoring done at the local level (USGS is ill-equipped to undertake this), the organization and standard-ization done by state agencies, and the technical resources and systemic view held by the USGS. None of these nodes could undertake such a venture without the other, and in this context, the actions and products of scientists at each level become legitimate in the eyes of actors at other levels. Such institutional linkages that encourage coproduction of models result in outputs that alter and broaden the universe of knowledge about options. In this case, these options relate to water conservation practices, management options, and policy, but we see altering of the knowledge of options in the stratospheric ozone case (Parson 2003), the Convention on Long-Range Transboundary Air Pollution's (LRTAP) case, and the Zimbabwe forecasting case (Patt, chapter 9, this volume).

Perhaps the most important institutional structure that encourages cross-scale credibility is the long-term and iterated nature of communication between decision makers and scientists. This structure helps build trust over time but benefits from other institutional structures that also foster the credibility of information produced and used at different levels. Researchers affiliated with UNL face an incentive structure that demands the production of peer-reviewed products. USGS analyses undergo extensive in-house and external peer-review processes. Area and county extension research projects, especially those that examine products from private industry (e.g., fertilizer trials, irrigation equipment, and so on) are transparent and go to great lengths to eliminate even the appearance of bias. An important element of building credibility is ground-truthing. In the networked system in Nebraska, farmers and managers, over a period of time, have many opportunities to test the credibility of research and assessment done at the area and state levels. On-farm demonstration trials, the farmers' own experience, and the farmers' use of private crop consultants to monitor farm practices all provide opportunities to test results. Ongoing monitoring of the aquifer, both individually and collectively at NRDs, provides continuous testing of the models and forecasts of USGS and CSD. USGS, CSD, and the area research centers have all, over time, built reputations for credible information production as farmers see their own well measurements being consistent with the published aquifer models, and UNL assessments of irrigation technology accurately predicting increases in productivity. At the same time, managers see models of the aquifer improving with changes in monitoring of the resource.

Semicentralized Systems

The system in Kansas shares many institutional features with that of Nebraska, with similar results. When the system does not work as effectively, it can be traced to institutional structures that diminish salience, credibility, and legitimacy. The more centralized nature of the decision-making system results in management options that are not as salient to local decision makers. Legislation, for example, that decreases the range of options that WMDs can explore decreases the toolbox from which managers can choose regulatory tools that best fit the local circumstances. This is seen, for instance, in the thwarted desire of WMDs to experiment with tradable water-rights schemes.

The ambiguity of roles in the network also contributes to decreased effectiveness by decreasing legitimacy and credibility across levels. The lack of clear authority raises questions of regulatory legitimacy, with the result that enforcement is severely limited. Likewise, unenforced regulations lead to a perception of decreased credibility for the state water agency.

Semiautonomous and Autonomous Systems

Where components of semiautonomous and autonomous systems are effective, they share similar institutional structures that enhance salience, credibility, and legitimacy in Kansas and Nebraska (e.g., cross-scale linkages and long-term iterated relationships). Where these systems fail, it can often be associated with institutional structures that decrease salience, credibility, or legitimacy, sometimes by increasing one at the expense of another.

The autonomous structure of parts of Texas, for example, is characterized by high levels of local political legitimacy. This is seen not just in the weak legitimacy granted to state-level decision making, but also in how information produced by state and federal agencies lacks both legitimacy and credibility. Granting political legitimacy almost exclusively to local actors comes, ironically, with a price of less salient information, resulting from a lack of linkage to multiple organizations at different levels:

There's gobs of work out there to do on the Ogallala [High Plains Aquifer], more than any one agency can do, so when they can cooperate and get together, you just have a bigger workforce to tackle the problem. More people and more expertise. (NRCS District Conservationist)

Where cross-scale cooperation is lacking (more autonomy), information that is systemically accurate and salient to local decision making is difficult to produce. Because there has been a lack of linkage with higher-level sources of aquifer analysis and information, local decision makers do not have the quality of information about the aquifer that farmers in Nebraska and Kansas have to help them make decisions. As a geologist in a WMD that only recently began coordinating with TWBD or USGS noted, "We're going to have to model the whole district, and it will be difficult to get the data. But we have to have good info to back us up and we won't know all that 'til we have the model" (WMD Geologist).

Institutions have not been in place to build the long-term credibility of state and federal scientists. Local decision makers are currently seeking to move their WMDs in particular regulatory directions (e.g., initiating pumping limits) but lack the credible science to support their decision making.

This also operates at the individual level, in decision making about center-pivot adoption. What can explain the lower adoption rates in more autonomous counties? Several factors that relate to the lack of cross-level coordination seem to be operating. First, poor coordination between state and local decision makers means that incentives and regulations are not structured to encourage center-pivot adoption and that salient information regarding the aquifer and technologies to slow its depletion are less available. The principal institutional structure that could provide the link across levels, both for decision making and assessment, is not present in Swisher County. As a neighboring county agricultural extension agent noted, "With a district, Swisher could double center-pivots overnight."

Links between Salience, Credibility, and Legitimacy

Salience, credibility, and legitimacy are not independent properties. Sometimes they reinforce one another, as when an effort to achieve political legitimacy through greater sensitivity to the views of previously excluded stakeholders results in an increase in salience of the resulting assessment to those groups. Sometimes there are trade-offs in increasing one of these attributes, as when an effort to increase political legitimacy through inclusion of multiple perspectives results in decreased scientific credibility (see table 10.3).

The multilevel nature of a problem like aquifer depletion brings these kinds of trade-offs into sharp focus because issues such as salience, credibility, and legitimacy exhibit strong scale dependence, and attribution

Table 10.3
Trade-offs and complementarities between salience, credibility, and legitimacy

Attempts to increase . . .	Influence salience	Influence credibility	Influence legitimacy
Salience	—	↓ by "tainting" science with politics; ↑ by including "place-based" knowledge	↑ or ↓ by increasing the inclusion of different decision makers
Credibility	↓ by isolating the science and removing decision maker input; ↑ by including different scientific disciplines that ask different questions	—	↓ by limiting participation and thus deceasing process legitimacy; ↑ by increasing inclusiveness of expertise from formally excluded groups
Legitimacy	↓ by changing the focus of the resulting information and therefore its usefulness to defined users; ↑ by increasing inclusiveness ∴ increasing participation of decision makers	↓ by "tainting" science with politics; ↑ by increasing the inclusion of different knowledges	—

of these three qualities can be relatively easily associated with specific levels: what is salient, credible, or legitimate to state-level actors often differs from and is antithetical to what is salient, credible, or legitimate to local actors. A state-level water plan that might be relevant to state actors ("aggregating over the state, this is how water can best be allocated"), might not be salient to local actors ("our concerns are not reflected in the state's overall plan"). Regulations set by a state's department of water resources, while legitimate to state actors ("after all, the state owns the water"), would not be legitimate actions in the eyes of local landowners ("we've had no input into rules that affect our livelihoods"). Assessment of the aquifer undertaken by a state's geological survey, while credible to state actors ("the state geological survey has the best geologists in the state, plus it's been peer reviewed"), would not be credible in the eyes of local landowners ("they don't understand the specific conditions here").

What can this study illuminate about the divergent attributions of salience, credibility, and legitimacy that arise from different perspectives at different levels?

First, information produced at more proximate levels is usually perceived as more credible and more salient. For a county agent (local level), information produced at the area research center is more credible and salient than information produced at the state land-grant college, which in turn is more credible and salient than information produced at federal research facilities (see figure 10.6).

Given the inverse relationship between proximity and level of credibility and salience, this research suggests that in systems with more tightly connected cross-scale links, information produced at one level will be more credible and salient at other levels than in systems without such links. The underlying notion is that long-term well-coordinated links, in effect, decrease the "distance" between nodes through building trust, increasing communication, and seeking common visions of the same problem.

A second potential connection between salience, credibility, legitimacy, and multilevel dynamics relates to the inherent negotiation-rich environment of a dense collaborative network. In such a network, actors are continually negotiating issues from scientific agendas to major legislation

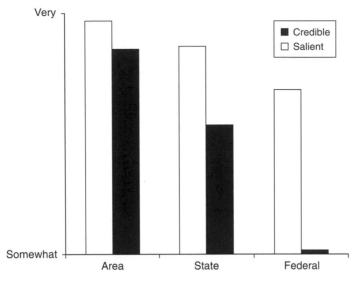

Figure 10.6
Comparison of credibility and salience of information produced at different levels
as perceived by county extension agents (self-report, $n = 169$). *Source*: Author's
survey data

to the allocation of responsibilities and authorities. In the counties that
demonstrated management effectiveness, this negotiation, mediated by
boundary organizations and supported by long-term relationships, was
routine. How does this relate to salience, credibility, and legitimacy?
Trade-offs between salience, credibility, and legitimacy partly exist
because of the different interests at each level. In a system in which negotiated balancing of interests is a fundamental part of operating, there is
space to minimize trade-offs between salience, credibility, and legitimacy
across levels by seeking ways to optimize this balancing. In a negotiated
networked system a conflict between those who say "the state geological survey has the best geologists in the state" and those who say "they
don't understand the specific conditions here" can be ameliorated by har-
nessing the "best geologists in the state" to study the "specific conditions
here." This has happened in parts of Nebraska, Kansas, and Texas, but
not in Swisher County, and only recently in Carson County. In an environment characterized by a negotiated network, increasing political

legitimacy through inclusion of multiple perspectives does not have to be mutually exclusive with maintaining scientific credibility. This has evolved in the model-building efforts described in this study, in which the roles of the farmers (raising political legitimacy and salience) have been clearly delimited through negotiation with scientists, brokered by extension agents so that the scientific credibility of the scientists' models cannot be questioned. Likewise, the roles of scientists have been clearly delimited through negotiation with farmers and brokered by extension agents so that a model's salience is generally high (see table 10.4 for trade-offs and potential solutions).

Conclusions

In an age of increasing globalization and increasing flows of information, decision makers and scientists are trying to better understand how to construct effective information and decision-making systems to address a range of multilevel problems. This volume contains analysis of what leads to effective global environmental assessments. One aspect of "what is effective" relates to how large-scale assessments link to assessment and decision making at different levels. This case study has attempted to illuminate this aspect. Water management in the U.S. Great Plains, a problem that spans multiple levels, demonstrates the effectiveness of polyarchic networks of collaborative information and decision making: distributed systems of research, assessment, and decision support. This study further proposes mechanisms that cause such systems to be effective, partly through balancing salience, credibility, and legitimacy: the use of boundary organizations to bridge science and decision making and across levels of scale, as well as long-term iterated communication that integrates science in the decision-making process.

Acknowledgments

This chapter is based on research supported in part by grants from the National Science Foundation (award BCS-0004236) with contributions from the National Oceanic and Atmospheric Administration's Office

Table 10.4
Cross-level trade-offs and potential solutions

	Trade-off	Institutional solution	Example
Salience between levels 1 and 2	Aggregation vs. disaggregation	x-scale networks with mechanism to simultaneously aggregate and be locally specific	USGS-CSD-NRD collaboration to build models of the aquifer that capture both system dynamics and local dynamics
Credibility between levels 1 and 2	Local knowledge vs. systemic knowledge	Mechanisms to integrate local knowledge into large-scale systems analysis	Using locally collected data, state coordination/ standardization, and rigorous peer-reviewed modeling by federal or state scientists
Legitimacy between levels 1 and 2	Centralized (efficiencies, public goods) vs. local control (local contingencies/ knowledge)	Institutions that facilitate the right participation, of the right people at the right time Appropriate allocation of authority across levels	Locally elected board of directors of NRDs, state agencies, USDA/NRCS offices

of Global Programs for the Research and Assessment Systems for Sustainability Project based at Harvard University, the National Science Foundation (award SBR-9521910) for the Global Environmental Assessment Project, Harvard University's Belfer Center for Science and International Affairs, the Center for International Earth Science Information Network at Columbia University, the U.S. Department of Energy, the Institute for the Study of World Politics, and the Center for Integrated Study of the Human Dimensions of Global Integrated Assessment Center at Carnegie Mellon University (National Science Foundation award no. SBR-9521914). I am indebted to the many people throughout the Great Plains—the agricultural extension agents, managers, local, state, and federal agency officials, university, agency, private scientists, and local elected officials—who contributed their time and thoughts in my interviews and in answering surveys.

References

Alcamo, J., E. Kreileman, and R. Leemans. 1996. Global models meet global policy: How can global and regional modellers connect with environmental policy-makers? What has hindered them? What has helped? *Global Environmental Change* 6(4): 255–259.

Carnegie Commission on Science, Technology, and Government. 1992. *International Environmental Research and Assessment: Proposals for Better Organization and Decision-Making*. New York: Carnegie Commission on Science, Technology, and Government.

Cash, D. W. 2000. Distributed assessment systems: An emerging paradigm of research, assessment and decision-making for environmental change. *Global Environmental Change* 10(4): 241–244.

Cash, D. W. 2001. "In order to aid in diffusing useful and practical information ...": Cross-scale boundary organizations and agricultural extension. *Science, Technology, and Human Values* 26(4): 431–453.

Cash, D. W., and S. C. Moser. 2000. Linking global and local scales: Designing dynamic assessment and management processes. *Global Environmental Change* 10(2): 109–120.

Easterling, W., A. Weiss, C. Hays, and L. Mearns. 1998. Optimum spatial scales of climate information for simulating the effects of climate change on agrosystem productivity: The case of the U.S. Great Plains. *Agric. For. Meteorol.* 90, 51–63.

Gunderson, L. H., C. S. Holling, and S. S. Light, eds. 1995. *Barriers and Bridges to the Renewal of Ecosystems and Institutions.* New York: Columbia University Press.

Guston, D. H. 1999. Stabilizing the boundary between politics and science: The role of the Office of Technology Transfer as a boundary organization. *Social Studies of Science* 29(1): 87–112.

Haas, P. M., R. O. Keohane, and M. A. Levy, eds. 1994. *Institutions for the Earth.* Cambridge, MA: MIT Press.

Intergovernmental Panel on Climate Change. 1996. *Climate Change 1995.* Cambridge: Cambridge University Press.

Intergovernmental Panel on Climate Change. 1998. *The Regional Impacts of Climate Change: An Assessment of Vulnerability.* Cambridge: Cambridge University Press.

Jasanoff, S., and B. Wynne. 1998. Science and decision-making. In S. Rayner and E. L. Malone, eds., *Human Choices and Climate Change.* Columbus, OH: Battelle Press.

Keohane, R. O., P. M. Haas, and M. A. Levy. 1994. The effectiveness of international environmental institutions. In P. M. Haas, R. O. Keohane, and M. A. Levy, eds., *Institutions for the Earth.* Cambridge, MA: MIT Press.

Kromm, D. E., and S. E. White, eds. 1992. *Groundwater Exploitation in the High Plains.* Lawrence: University Press of Kansas.

Lins, H. F., D. M. Wolock, and G. J. McCabe. 1997. Scale and modeling issues in water resources planning. *Climatic Change* 37(1): 63–88.

McGuire, V. L. 2003. *Water-Level Changes in the High Plains Aquifer, Predevelopment to 2001, 1999 to 2000, and 2000 to 2001.* Denver: U.S. Geological Survey.

McGuire, V. L., and J. B. Sharpe. 1997. *Water-Level Changes in the High Plains Aquifer—Predevelopment to 1995.* WRIR 97-4081. Denver: U.S. Geological Survey.

Millennium Assessment Secretariat. 2000. *Millennium Ecosystem Assessment: Strengthening Capacity to Manage Ecosystems Sustainably for Human Well-Being.* Washington, DC: Global Environment Facility, United National Foundation, World Bank.

Miller, K. A., S. L. Rhodes, and L. J. MacDonnell. 1996. Global change in microcosm: The case of U.S. water institutions. *Policy Sciences* 29: 271–290.

Opie, J. 1993. *Ogallala: Water for a Dry Land.* Lincoln: University of Nebraska Press.

Ostrom, E. 1998. Scales, polycentricity, and incentives: Designing complexity to govern complexity. In L. D. Guruswamy and J. A. McNeely, eds., *Protection of Biodiversity: Converging Strategies,* 149–167. Durham: Duke University Press.

Ostrom, E., T. Dietz, N. Dolsak, P. C. Stern, S. Stonich, and E. U. Weber. 2002. *The Drama of the Commons*. National Research Council. Washington, DC: National Academy Press.

Parson, E. A. 2003. *Protecting the Ozone Layer: Science and Strategy*. Oxford: Oxford University Press.

Wilbanks, T. J., and R. W. Kates. 1999. Global change in local places: How scale matters. *Climatic Change* 43(3): 601–628.

Young, O. 1999. *The Effectiveness of International Regimes*. Ithaca, NY: Cornell University Press.

11
Information and Influence

Ronald B. Mitchell, William C. Clark, and David W. Cash

Introduction

Scientific assessments have become increasingly common in the landscape of global environmental affairs, at least in part, due to the tantalizing prospect that better and more widely shared information fosters better management of complex, transnational interactions between humans and nature. According to proponents, global environmental assessments (GEAs) can evaluate the state of knowledge about the world, improve our understanding of the probabilities and risks of various scenarios, and illuminate the expected costs and benefits of alternative policies. The hope has been that better understanding of the environmental impact of human actions, decisions, policies, and behaviors, and of the options for mitigating those impacts, will help political, social, and economic decision makers discern and pursue their own self-interest in a more enlightened manner. More ambitiously, scientific assessments can foster collective efforts to address global environmental problems, providing tools scientists, stakeholders, or policymakers can use to persuade others (Benedick 1998; Watson 1994; Walsh 2004; Harrison and Bryner 2004; Wilkening 2004).

These hopes for scientific assessment are not without foundation. Internationally shared scientific and technical knowledge—developed at least in part through GEAs—has clearly facilitated progress in managing environmental risks such as acid rain and stratospheric ozone depletion. Other assessments, however, have had few discernible impacts. Indeed, scholars have identified many reasons that scientific research that seeks to influence policy fails to do so (see, for example, Pulwarty and

Melis 2001; Pulwarty and Redmond 1997; Pielke and Conant 2003; Lemos and Morehouse 2005). It is precisely the question of "Why do some assessments have more influence than others?" that this book seeks to address. Here, we delineate findings and conclusions derived from the range of cases analyzed in the preceding chapters.

The first section of this chapter reviews major findings regarding the sources of GEA influence that are supported by evidence from most or all of our cases. As noted in the introduction, our initial research led to two propositions that we sought to evaluate systematically across our cases, namely that (1) GEAs are better conceptualized as social processes rather than published products, and (2) to be influential, potential users must view a GEA as salient and legitimate as well as credible. In addition, this section delineates other, more detailed, propositions that were evident when looking across our chapters but that were not propositions that chapter authors systematically sought to evaluate. By identifying such patterns of GEA influence that emerge from most or all of our cases, we hope to help guide those interested in GEA influence toward promising areas for future research.

The next section of this chapter looks across our cases for other, less expected, insights into the conditions, factors, and processes by which GEAs wield influence. Unlike the insights supported by most of our cases, we believe it is worth reporting several insights that are supported by only a few of our chapters and in which we, therefore, have less confidence. We believe such insights also provide interesting clues regarding new questions and new trajectories for research.

We end with a short set of "considerations for practitioners." Other research related to the larger project of which this book was a part, much more directly and explicitly sought to identify what design choices assessors can make to improve assessment influence—including initial choices regarding what issues to address, what types of actors to involve in assessments, how to bridge the science-policy interface, and how to treat uncertainty and dissent (Farrell and Jäger 2005). Yet our efforts to determine when assessments have influence also identified several insights that can help make the many currently underway or upcoming GEAs be more effective and influential. We do not intend these considerations as specific design principles for assessment but as broader, higher-level recommendations regarding how assessors should think about assessments in order to enhance their influence. We delineate those lessons here in the hope that our efforts can inform future global environmental assessments.

Major Findings

Our study leads to five major conclusions. First, assessments vary both in what type of influence they have and in how much influence they have. Second, assessment influence is relational—we cannot evaluate an assessment's influence in general but only its influence with different potential audiences. Third, assessment influence with any audience depends on that audience seeing the assessment as salient, credible, and legitimate. Fourth, audiences tend to see those assessments as salient, credible, and legitimate in which they have been able to participate, a process of coproduction of knowledge. Fifth, assessments gain influence by addressing incapacity problems, whether those are incapacities that inhibit full participation as a producer of assessments or incapacities that inhibit full understanding as a user of assessments.

Assessments Vary in Type, as Well as Amount, of Influence

As expected, we found considerable evidence that people are more responsive to some assessments than to others. But, less expectedly, we found that assessments prompt many changes that both differ from—and are sometimes contrary to—those that assessment producers sought. In part, this finding reflects our initial choice to look for assessment influence in an expansively defined issue domain rather than only in policy and behavior changes (see the introductory chapter). One important result of our research has been to identify, verify, and document the variety of intended and unintended ways in which audiences respond to assessments and thus alter an issue domain. Thus, we have come to replace our earlier sense that some assessments have an influence and others do not with a more subtle understanding of the variation in the type and amount of influence assessments may have.

The impact of an assessment depends at least partly on when they are conducted, relative to an issue domain's development. Those conducted at early stages are unlikely to lead to immediate and direct policy change; those conducted at more mature stages in an issue's development are unlikely to transform fundamentally the ways in which various audiences conceptualize an environmental problem. Early on, different audiences can use an assessment to prompt scientific, public, and political debate about a previously undiscussed environmental problem. Audiences are more likely to accept an assessment's framing of an issue that has received little previous attention. As an issue develops, however, various stakeholders may succeed in promoting alternative framings that highlight different environmental, economic, social, or political facets of the problem, perhaps doing so through assessments. As discussion of an issue shifts from identifying and defining the problem to developing and debating possible responses, some societal actors may respond to assessment processes by seeing how their interests are (or are not) at stake, becoming correspondingly more (or less) engaged. At later stages, policymakers and stakeholders may see assessments as useful resources in identifying, evaluating, or supporting particular policy options. Assessments can have these and many other influences on an issue domain. And, as our cases show, assessments may also fail to have any influence or may have influence that is difficult to discern because it is small or because of the researcher's limited ability to detect subtle changes in the issue domain and/or to demonstrate that such changes are due to an assessment.

Assessments sometimes directly influence behaviors that affect the environment. Parson's (2003) account of how scientific assessments fostered global action that slowed ozone-layer depletion provides a powerful example. Policymakers in the Convention on Long-Range Transboundary Air Pollution (LRTAP) used improved scientific understandings not only to shift acid precipitation regulation from flat-rate emission standards to "critical-load" criteria but also from common obligations to politically more challenging differentiated ones (VanDeveer, chapter 5, this volume). Polish electricity producers negotiated industry-government agreements on how to achieve sulfur emission reductions in response to participatory assessments of alternative policies (Andonova, chapter 6, this volume). Global negotiators of rules regarding persistent organic pollutants (POPs) would have moved more slowly and would have been unlikely to select those chemicals and criteria that they did were it not for earlier LRTAP-related assessments of POPs (Selin, chapter 7, this volume). Commercial farmers in Zimbabwe and farmers in Nebraska adopted practices that would have been unlikely in the absence of processes for gaining their acceptance of drought forecasts and information on methods for mitigating aquifer depletion (Patt, chapter 9, this volume; Cash, chapter 10, this volume).

Assessments often influence issue development in more subtle or time-delayed ways that make their effects harder to isolate. Many political, economic, and other forces influence policy choice, directly or indirectly (Andonova, chapter 6, this volume). The Villach climate assessment did not lead directly and immediately to negotiation of a climate change convention and the boost it gave to international policy actors promoting global action on climate change was highly contingent on other factors, most notably success on ozone loss, having created receptive audiences for its claims (Torrance, chapter 2, this volume). Assessments may influence an issue domain by engaging scientists in ways that make them both more interested in and more capable of studying particular issues.

Both our work and that of other researchers has identified numerous cases in which assessments had no discernible or immediate influence. The lack of influence of some assessment processes seems virtually global in extent, as in the Swedish assessment of acid rain presented at the 1972 Stockholm Conference on Human Environment, the 1975 assessment of supersonic-transport threats to the ozone layer, the various pre-Villach assessments of climate change, and the 1995 Global Biodiversity Assessment (Social Learning Group 2001a, 2001b; Torrance, chapter 2, this volume; Cash and Clark 2001). In other cases, assessments that some actors have readily accepted have been ignored or rejected by others. In India, not only the generally uninfluential Global Biodiversity Assessment but also the Villach and subsequent climate assessments had little influence (Biermann, chapter 4, this volume). Aquifer-related science was quite influential in some American counties but had almost no influence in many parts of Texas (Cash, chapter 10, this volume).

Because different actors respond to assessments in ways that reflect their concerns, interests, and policy preferences, assessments may influence an issue domain by evoking counterintuitive, skeptical, or oppositional responses. Skepticism that assessments of POPs conducted in Europe and North America would have findings applicable to other regions prompted new assessment efforts in those regions (Selin, chapter 7, this volume). Similarly, scientists in developing countries responded to climate change and biodiversity assessments by initiating "counterassessments" that identified inaccuracies in the science of prior assessments and rejected their policy implications (Biermann, chapter 4, this volume). Our findings that assessments often influence issue development without leading directly to behavior change are consistent with evidence that society's attention to, and management of, most issues typically exhibits long periods of relative stability punctuated by shorter episodes of rapid change (Baumgartner and Jones 1993), and that new ideas must often "incubate" for a decade or more before they have much influence on behavior (Weiss 1975; Sabatier 1993).

We were also struck by cases in which an assessment induced little if any response even from actors we would have expected to be receptive to it. Assessments of climate change and sea-level rise had no immediately discernible influence on coastal zone managers in Maine and Hawai'i, who used it simply to justify previous policy choices that had nothing to do with sea-level rise (Moser, chapter 8, this volume). Many assessments of acid rain, including one by the International Institute for Applied Systems Analysis (IIASA)—whose assessments have frequently been central to acid rain politics in Western Europe—have been ignored in public discussions and negotiation of policy changes in Poland and Bulgaria (Andonova, chapter 6, this volume).

We should not be surprised that assessments differ in the type of influence they have or whether they have any readily discernible influence at all. Indeed, it would be naive to think that scientific findings can replace or be divorced from the fundamentally political and normative conflicts whose resolution they seek to promote (Jasanoff 1990, 2004). As Gupta demonstrates with respect to biosafety negotiations, fundamentally normative and political conflicts regarding the nature of an environmental problem and its appropriate resolution cannot be resolved by reference to science that is merely technically credible (Gupta, chapter 3, this volume). Rather, in such areas, perceptions of technical credibility are themselves closely intertwined with the normative conflicts. To be influential, assessments must grapple with this complex reality, balancing the need for getting the science right with the need for "political engagement" (Andonova, chapter 6, this volume; Herrick and Jamieson 1995; Lemos and Morehouse 2005; Pielke 1995).

Influence Depends on the Assessment-Audience Relationship

A second insight of our cases is that assessment influence is relational. Since multiple audiences evaluate any given assessment, a claim that an assessment is influential can only be understood if we know "with whom." Some assessments tend to be accepted by a wide range of audiences; others are given little credence even by those who produced them. Most assessments have influence with some audiences but not others. Thus, the Commercial Farmers' Union (CFU) helped large-scale farmers in Zimbabwe make use of drought forecasts in ways that small-scale and communal farmers could not (Patt, chapter 9, this volume). Publics and policymakers were far more interested in and receptive to climate change assessments in Europe than they were in India (Biermann, chapter 4, this volume). Assessments that convinced many European and North American policymakers of the value of global POPs regulations had to be carefully adapted to convince Asian, African, and Latin American policymakers (Selin, chapter 7, this volume).

The relational character of assessment influence poses a special challenge for assessments intended for use in transnational or global contexts. The concerns, perspectives, knowledges, data, and assumptions of groups (e.g., nations) initiating a global environmental assessment often differ markedly from those of other groups whose cooperation is needed to address an environmental problem. The power and interests of the countries and substate actors involved in any environmental problem affect both the policy agenda and the assessment agenda. The responses of Central and Eastern European states on acid precipitation issues, of India on biodiversity and climate issues, of developing states on biosafety issues, and of Hawaiian industry on reports of sea-level rise all demonstrate that whether findings from an assessment are accepted by a given audience depends on a range of "nonscientific" political, social, and economic factors.

The Attributions That Determine Influence

Our study found considerable evidence of our second proposition, that GEAs have influence with audiences that see them as salient and legitimate as well as credible. As noted in the introduction, salience, credibility, and legitimacy are attributions that potential users make about the assessment. Audiences or potential users of an assessment that differ in their goals, interests, beliefs, strategies, and resources are also likely to differ in whether they perceive an assessment as salient, credible, and legitimate and, therefore, to differ in whether and how they respond to the assessment. As the more detailed results below attest, an assessment's failure to influence particular audiences most often reflects a failure to address salience, credibility, and legitimacy in ways that are convincing to those on the other side of the North-South divide, the scientist-policymaker divide, or the global-local divide.

Salience   The notion that an assessment must be salient—that is, relevant—to potential users in order to be influential with them seems obvious. Yet many assessments lack influence with potential users because they fail to produce information with an eye toward "what decisions might be affected by the information" (Patt, chapter 9, this volume). Information must be responsive to local conditions and concerns, must link to issues on which decision makers focus and over which they have control, and must be timely, coming before—but not too long before—relevant decisions get made.

Even audiences who we would expect to find a particular assessment salient may ignore or reject it if it fails to define a problem or discuss its impacts in ways that resonate with that audience or fails to identify actions that that audience can take to mitigate or adapt to the problem. Sea-level rise has important implications in Hawai'i and Maine, yet assessments of sea-level rise related to climate change have generally been ignored because they failed to identify erosion or flood information in ways that coastal zone managers could incorporate in their regular management decisions (Moser, chapter 8, this volume). Small-scale farmers in Zimbabwe have often been unresponsive to drought predictions, not because droughts are not salient, but because these farmers are risk averse and tend to plant drought-tolerant crops. Forecasts would be more influential if they predicted abnormally wet years in which farmers would face minimal risk from planting crops that provide higher-than-average yields in wet years but do poorly in dry years (Patt, chapter 9, this volume). Options for minimizing acid rain reduction costs in Bulgaria were ignored because those conducting the assessment misunderstood the decisions faced by, and circumstances of, electricity producers (Andonova, chapter 6, this volume).

Ensuring an assessment's salience proves particularly challenging when an assessment seeks to influence multiple audiences. Many of our cases lacked salience with "additional" audiences that were not initially demanding, involved in, or an intended audience of the assessment. International assessments often are initiated by "leader" states concerned about an issue (Sprinz and Vaahtoranta 1994; DeSombre 2000). Not surprisingly, such assessments tend to define and frame the problem, undertake science, and propose solutions in ways that are salient for people in those states but are inattentive to the concerns of states that subsequently become involved. Scandinavians saw acid rain as a "chemical war" against the Scandinavians, and states like Germany became more invested in assessments only after they recognized acid rain's impacts on their own forests (VanDeveer, chapter 5, this volume). People in India (and presumably other developing countries) failed to be persuaded by the Global Biodiversity Assessment (GBA) because it framed the problem as one of flora-and-fauna protection, overlooking developing countries' concerns with equity and development and the dramatic ways in which preservation policies influence the lives and livelihoods of "people living in the centers of biodiversity" (Biermann, chapter 4, this volume). Negotiations over what information to exchange regarding genetically modified organisms demonstrate how much what is salient varies across audiences: GMO-exporting countries were concerned about trade restrictions on GMOs, European states wanted to control imports to address domestic political concerns, and developing countries sought to prevent the spread of novel hazards (Gupta, chapter 3, this volume).

Salience depends on "framing"—that is, on defining an environmental problem, its impacts, and its potential solutions in ways that highlight certain aspects and downplay others. This is clearly evident in the biosafety negotiations, where conflicts over problem framing were center stage. As Gupta shows, how the problem is framed in this global arena is key to the perceived salience of the biosafety assessments to be shared via this global regime (Gupta, chapter 3, this volume). Efforts to mobilize international action on POPs because of problems of long-range transport and bioaccumulation resonated in developed countries; developing countries became more engaged only after regional assessments helped identify the local health impacts of POPs (Selin, chapter 7, this volume). Efforts to help Zimbabwean farmers understand drought forecasts, to produce regional assessments of POPs salient to developing countries, or to identify a wide range of impacts in a climate assessment all reflect assessors finding aspects of an environmental problem that make it salient to new audiences.

Salience also depends on decision matching: ensuring that the scale and timing of information meets the needs of decision makers. Potential users are apt to ignore assessments that get the scale of informational resolution wrong. Global-scale data, knowledge, and models relevant to international and national decisions are often simply not useful to the day-to-day decisions of farmers, aquifer users, or coastal zone managers. Assessments gain influence with lower-scale decision makers by "localizing" their knowledge, reframing findings in terms that are more relevant to national and/or local decision makers (Jasanoff and Martello 2004). National food planners need long-term, national rainfall forecasts to plan crop purchases far enough in advance to avert famine; farmers need local-scale, shorter-term forecasts regarding where, how much, and when rain will fall (Patt, chapter 9, this volume). Decision matching also requires information that is responsive to "decision calendars" (Pulwarty and Melis 2001; Pulwarty and Redmond 1997). Initial workshops conducted by agricultural extension services in Zimbabwe had little impact because they occurred only after farmers had purchased their seed and finished their early plantings (Patt, chapter 9, this volume).

Salience can be fostered through different mechanisms. Ongoing, explicit, and self-conscious processes that encourage participation by, and are responsive to, decision makers are particularly important to fostering salience (Farrell and Jäger 2005). Acid rain assessments by IIASA are "explicitly linked to state-controlled policymaking authority" and are often responses to specific requests from LRTAP policymaking bodies (VanDeveer, chapter 5, this volume). Water networks in Nebraska involve farmers and other local-level actors in setting research agendas so that research findings address the questions and concerns of water users (Cash, chapter 10, this volume). Salience can also be fostered by explicit efforts to bring in local knowledge and concerns, as illustrated by the greater influence of regional and subregional assessments of POPs (Selin, chapter 7, this volume). Salience can also be promoted by information brokers who self-consciously recognize and redress the disconnect between large-scale assessments and local-level decisions, as evident in the Zimbabwean Commercial Farmers' Union translating national drought forecasts into place-based information on what crops to plant and why (Patt, chapter 9, this volume).

Finally, salience often depends on factors and conditions beyond the assessment's control. Assessments have an inherently more difficult task if they address environmental problems whose impacts are gradual, diffuse, off in the future, uncertain, or have unclear causes. Environmental assessments often will be less salient to developing countries and economies in transition (Biermann, chapter 4, this volume; Gupta, chapter 3, this volume; VanDeveer, chapter 5, this volume). Assessments can fall victim to bad timing, arriving "too early" or "too late." The Villach climate change assessment had little new scientific content but was looked to by more policy advocates and policymakers than earlier assessments because of the "window of opportunity" opened by recent governance successes on ozone-depleting substances (Torrance, chapter 2, this volume). Likewise, LRTAP assessments regarding acid rain controls became salient to Central and Eastern European states only after EU accession became a possibility.

Credibility   Assessment influence also depends on credibility—that is, on convincing actors that the facts, theories, ideas, models, causal beliefs, and options contained in an assessment are "true," or at least a better guide to how the world works than competing information. Assessors usually expend considerable effort to make GEAs credible—at least with other scientists "like" those performing the assessment (Jäger et al.

2001). But, as noted above, assessments address multiple audiences and those audiences often evaluate credibility using quite different criteria than do the community of scientists from which assessment participants are drawn.

Before incorporating an assessment's findings and claims into their decisions, potential users seek assurance that the assessment reflects an unbiased effort to determine how the world is, rather than how self-interested actors would like the world to be. Technical credibility might seem the easiest of our three attributions to achieve. But assessments are usually undertaken in arenas of uncertainty in which most audiences cannot independently judge the information and claims being made (Haas 1992). Some countries have the capacity to evaluate international assessments independently before accepting their results. Thus, the administration of President George W. Bush requested that the U.S. National Academy of Sciences review the results of the Intergovernmental Panel on Climate Change's (IPCC) Third Assessment. More often, however, policymakers and other audiences cannot evaluate message content and must assess credibility through the proxies of credentials and process (Slater and Rouner 1996; Osgood and Tannenbaum 1955). Audiences differ in their views of what constitute "credible" credentials but tend to trust sources that have provided accurate information in the past and that have expertise (i.e., the training to identify accurate information) and are trustworthy (i.e., will report that information honestly) (Hurwitz, Miron, and Johnson 1992).

Our cases illustrate the need for "local credibility" that comes from ensuring that higher-scale findings fit the local context (Jasanoff and Martello 2004). Audiences frequently dismiss scientists and scientific groups with the best scientific credentials because those individuals or groups lack local expertise, in the sense of understanding local concerns and decisions and being able to integrate local knowledge and data into larger-scale analyses. Many of our case authors independently identified the importance of tapping into existing networks of expertise. Assessments of sea-level rise and of aquifer depletion had more influence when they tapped into "well-established, well-functioning networks . . . among information providers and users" (Moser, chapter 8, this volume; Cash, chapter 10, this volume). Commercial farmers in Zimbabwe found

El Niño–Southern Oscillation (ENSO) forecasts more credible because they were both interpreted by and vouched for through trusted, local scientists working with the CFU (Patt, chapter 9, this volume). Polish policymakers accepted findings regarding sulfur reduction options (even those conducted by Americans) more readily than did Bulgarian policymakers because those assessments involved and cited respected Polish scientists in "domestic expertise establishments" who already had credibility with those policymakers (Andonova, chapter 6, this volume).

For local audiences to view an assessment as credible, it also must take into account, and be seen as taking into account, local conditions. Developing countries often assume that "data from the North are easily misleading if merely extrapolated to the South" (Biermann, chapter 4, this volume), as evident in tropical countries questioning findings in POPs assessments that derived exclusively from research in temperate and Arctic climes (Selin, chapter 7, this volume). Even involving partisan stakeholders in assessment processes can increase credibility if those stakeholders bring with them otherwise-unavailable data. Central and Eastern European scientists and policymakers gave little credence to early acid rain assessments because they estimated emissions rather than requesting data (VanDeveer, chapter 5, this volume). They saw later assessments as more credible because they involved Eastern European industry representatives who brought better data to the table (Andonova, chapter 6, this volume).

The availability of alternative sources of information also affects the credibility that various audiences give to an assessment. The nongovernmental Villach assessments lost credibility rapidly once governments established the intergovernmental IPCC—even though many of the same scientists contributed to both assessments (Torrance, chapter 2, this volume). LRTAP's influence on acid precipitants in Eastern Europe (VanDeveer, chapter 5, this volume) and on POPs in global negotiations (Selin, chapter 7, this volume) appears to have depended considerably on the absence of other sources of information on these problems. One unintended influence of assessments that appears not uncommon is to prompt audiences with which a given assessment has little credibility to fill the informational gap with a "counterassessment" (Franz 1998)—a

1990 U.S. Environmental Protection Agency (EPA) study that attributed one-third of global methane emissions to India prompted an Indian assessment that showed these estimates to be off by a factor of ten (Biermann, chapter 4, this volume). What was initially a reactive assessment has promoted a more general increase in "communication and cooperation among Indian scientists on climate-related issues" (Biermann, chapter 4, this volume).

Lastly, our cases confirm the importance of assessment processes, with credibility having to be developed over time. IIASA's assessments and models gained credibility slowly and steadily over time by doing careful science that involves relevant stakeholders who contribute local data and insights while gaining better understandings of "the science" (VanDeveer, chapter 5, this volume). Although not examined in this volume, the four IPCC assessments have gained credibility with increasing numbers of audiences as the IPCC process has become more inclusive and transparent and as their findings have gained support from other independent studies. As Patt (chapter 9, this volume) notes, communicators that build a track record of honesty can gain credibility as audiences develop the habit of listening to and relying on the information they provide, but such track records are difficult to build. Assessment credibility is fostered by ensuring that potential users understand underlying data, methods, and models sufficiently well to replace "credibility by proxy" with "credibility through understanding" (Moser, chapter 8, this volume). This type of understanding often entails building local capacity, a point developed below.

Legitimacy   An unexpected finding of our study has been the importance of legitimacy to assessment influence. Legitimacy involves the perception by relevant audiences of an assessment process as "fair," having considered the values, concerns, and perspectives of that audience. Environmental problems often embody highly complex biophysical and human-environment interactions, and assessments cannot analyze the full variety of causes, impacts, and policy options relevant to their resolution. The choices that must be made regarding what to analyze and what to omit—and the implications of those choices—are inherently, if not always explicitly, political. Not surprisingly, then, audiences evaluate an assessment's legitimacy before accepting its claims.

Central to legitimacy is the notion that if assessments are conducted in support of policy, then those affected by those policies should be involved in the assessment process. Relevant stakeholders that are not included view such assessments as illegitimate, since such assessments tend to ignore or misidentify core concerns and tend to define problems, their causes, and responsibility for their resolution in ways that such audiences are unwilling to accept. Climate change assessments that imputed lower values to human life in developing than developed countries; that equated emissions from automobiles, airplane travel, and air-conditioners with emissions from food production; and that saw developing countries as equally responsible for climate change were, not surprisingly, viewed as illegitimate by those in developing countries (Biermann, chapter 4, this volume). Precisely because assessments identify and categorize the causes of problems and options for resolution, they also, if often implicitly, allocate blame and responsibility in a way that raises political issues of legitimacy.

Audiences judge legitimacy based on who participated and who did not, the processes for making choices, and how information was produced, vetted, and disseminated. Potential users often reject assessments that lack legitimacy as "not invented here." As noted with respect to salience and credibility, "localizing" knowledge is important (Jasanoff and Martello 2004). Unlike their Polish counterparts, Bulgarians rejected assessments of sulfur-reduction alternatives that were credible but lacked legitimacy because consultants and international institutions conducted them (Andonova, chapter 6, this volume). Proponents of global POPs regulations used LRTAP values and criteria but were extremely careful not to reference their LRTAP origins, so as to avoid resistance from countries that would have questioned the legitimacy of findings from assessments that had not included their representatives, concerns, or perspectives (Selin, chapter 7, this volume). As with salience, audiences frequently question the legitimacy of assessments originally undertaken by leaders to address their own concerns. Precisely because those actors not initially concerned about a problem are unlikely to want to be involved in early assessments, their concerns and perspectives on the problem are unlikely to be reflected in those assessments, and they will, therefore, tend to question the legitimacy of those assessments. Including representatives of different audiences promotes legitimacy by ensuring that the assessment incorporates those audiences' views, goals, interests, and concerns and that those audiences perceive it as having done so.

An assessment's legitimacy can also founder because of deep, preexisting distrust between assessment producers and potential users. The historical context of North-South relations leads many developing countries to be skeptical that GEAs reflect their interests and perspectives, whether they relate to climate change, GMOs, or POPs (Biermann, chapter 4, this volume; Gupta, chapter 3, this volume; Selin, chapter 7, this volume). Hawaiian policymakers have a "basic distrust" of federal assessments of sea-level rise due to the "political history of Hawaiʻi . . . [and] the magnitude of the military's presence and influence in local politics" (Moser, chapter 8, this volume). Similar dynamics—related to the Cold War rather than colonialism and development—affect the legitimacy that Eastern European audiences give to many GEAs (Andonova, chapter 6, this volume; VanDeveer, chapter 5, this volume).

For an assessment to overcome such distrust and mistrust requires considerable time, attention, and effort. Building trust requires extended interactions with assessment producers that reassure potential users that the assessment process is not simply the "continuation of policy by other means" (Clausewitz 1982, 119). Particularly in highly contested arenas, as in North-South negotiations over biosafety, climate change, or biodiversity, legitimacy is simultaneously crucial yet hard to achieve. The biosafety negotiations on GMOs were dominated not by questions of credibility but by normative conflicts over whether the information to be exchanged would reflect the socioeconomic and human health risks that concerned developing countries (Gupta, chapter 3, this volume). Governments established the IPCC as an alternative to the Advisory Group on Greenhouse Gases (AGGG), presumably because they felt an intergovernmental assessment process would reflect their views and concerns more accurately than a nongovernmental one (Torrance, chapter 2, this volume).

The Trade-Offs among Attributions Our two final findings about salience, credibility, and legitimacy were that tactics adopted to promote one attribution often undermine another but that opportunities to promote different attributions simultaneously do exist. Assessments, particularly those organized by scientists, often try to maximize credibility by involving only the most respected scientists and attempting to isolate the process from political influence. Such an approach, predictably, will have little influence since it will have ignored the questions most salient to policymakers and stakeholders. The reverse can occur when efforts to answer salient questions require that the scientific community provide tentative or premature results, thereby bringing the assessment's credibility into question. Efforts by the initial Climatic Impact Assessment Program (CIAP) to estimate the global costs and benefits of protecting the ozone layer lacked influence because they promised more than they could deliver (U.S. Department of Transportation 1975; Social Learning Group 2001a, 292; Glantz, Robinson, and Krenz 1982; Clark and Dickson 2001). Similarly, some assessments seek to foster legitimacy by including stakeholders or scientists who are brought in because they can represent the views and concerns of audiences that assessors hope to influence; in so doing, however, they may decrease the scientific credibility of the assessment, at least with other scientists and potentially with other decision makers.

Efforts to design assessments to promote their influence do not always involve such trade-offs in fostering attributions of salience, credibility, and legitimacy with different audiences. Efforts to "downscale" global climate models to support local decision makers have sometimes proved successful, as evident in the case of Zimbabwean farmers presented by Patt (chapter 9, this volume) and in Indonesia rice production (Naylor et al. 2001). As evidence from the acid rain (Andonova, chapter 6, this volume) and POPs cases (Selin, chapter 7, this volume) illustrates, increasing participation that is intended to increase salience and legitimacy can also increase credibility by providing access to local knowledge and to anecdotal and systematic data that would otherwise be unavailable. If stakeholders are involved, scientists can ensure that their models of environmental problems and human-environment interactions better represent local conditions. Equally important, participation helps stakeholders better understand the foundations of assessment findings, thereby increasing the extent to which they find them to be credible.

Assessments as a Process of Coproduction of Knowledge through Participation

The research presented in the foregoing chapters strongly supports our initial finding (see chapter 1) that suggested an assessment's influence flows from the process by which it creates knowledge rather than from the reports it may produce. The content and form of assessment reports are poor predictors of their influence. What matters is how the assessment process was conducted, from initial efforts to define the problem and the questions to ask to ongoing efforts to help users understand and incorporate new information into their decisions. The effectiveness of assessment processes depends on a process of coproduction of knowledge between assessment producers and potential assessment user groups in which the boundaries among these groups are bridged so that they can develop reciprocal understandings of what salient, credible, and legitimate mean to the others involved (Jasanoff and Martello 2004; Jasanoff and Wynne 1998).

A traditional model of assessment sees scientists as generating the "best" possible science and communicating it to decision makers. Assessments lack influence because scientists do not communicate their findings clearly or policymakers do not pay attention to the science that is done. Our study suggests that a more accurate model recognizes that assessments have influence to the extent that they involve long-term dialogues and interactions in which potential users of an assessment educate scientists about their concerns, values, priorities, resources, and knowledge of the problem while scientists educate potential users about the nature, causes, consequences, and alternatives for resolution of the problem at hand as well as the ways such knowledge is arrived at. Coproduction implies that assessments are influential to the extent that they are bidirectional, with science shaping politics but also politics shaping science.

Decision makers tend to listen to the findings of assessments in which they were involved and that they therefore find salient, credible, and legitimate. Stakeholder participation creates a sense of informational "ownership" (Patt, chapter 9, this volume). At a deeper level, who participates in the coproduction of an assessment shapes what knowledge gets produced. As scientists better understand decision makers' concerns, they can conduct and communicate research in ways that fit into the day-to-day decisions of policymakers, coastal zone managers, power plant operators, or farmers. As laypeople better understand scientific procedures (such as confidence intervals and peer review), their mistrust of science declines and their capacity to comprehend findings deepens. Scientists gain access to local knowledge that ensures that models and analyses reflect local conditions. By involving stakeholders with competing interests and reassuring nonparticipants that competing views were listened to, participatory assessments can reduce the chances that those divergent interests simply ignore assessment findings (Andonova, chapter 6, this volume; Gupta, chapter 3, this volume).

Influential assessments are those that eschew one-way communication from scientists to decision makers in favor of coproduction of knowledge—that is, when producers and potential users of an assessment have long-term interactions that foster communication and mutual understanding (Cash, chapter 10, this volume). Scientists can simply conduct research on topics they view as important and present the results to policymakers, but such exercises are unlikely to be persuasive. Stakeholder participation fosters salience, since decision-maker participation is crucial to matching the information assessments produced to the decisions being faced (Patt, chapter 9, this volume). Stakeholder participation fosters credibility, since assessments often must involve those responsible for a problem because they have data and evidence needed to understand it and because their involvement fosters their understanding, and reduces their distrust, of the knowledge the assessment produces. Stakeholder participation fosters legitimacy, since ongoing interactions among scientists and potential users reassure the latter that their perspectives and concerns are fully understood and accounted for in the models and analyses that scientists undertake.

Ongoing and iterative relationships between those "doing the science" and those "using the science" provide a way to incorporate stakeholder views into an assessment and to demonstrate that scientists have listened to stakeholders who did not participate (thereby fostering legitimacy).

These relationships also help scientists understand users' needs and decisions so they can frame and answer questions in ways that are relevant to potential users (thereby fostering salience). Further, a collaborative approach helps users gain an understanding of assessment methods and models sufficiently to believe in them and helps scientists gain access to users' knowledge of local conditions (thereby fostering credibility). Participation explains much of the variation in the influence of our assessments. Initial biodiversity and climate assessments had few immediate, visible, or intended affects on policymaking in India in no small part because they failed to involve Southern participants. IPCC assessments have slowly gained influence in India as initially token participation by developing-country scientists has become more substantive and substantial (Biermann, chapter 4, this volume). Involving Polish academics and electricity companies in cost-assessment processes garnered Western-initiated assessments far more influence than similar assessments in Bulgaria that lacked such stakeholder involvement (Andonova, chapter 6, this volume). In relation to American aquifer depletion, state and federal scientists became "legitimate sources of information" when they worked with local scientists and local farmers in "on-farm demonstration trials" and other joint efforts that fostered scientists' understanding of farmer concerns and constraints and farmers' understanding of scientific conclusions and recommendations (Cash, chapter 10, this volume).

When successful, relationships and networks can bridge across scale as in the polyarchic networks in the American Midwest (Cash, chapter 10, this volume) and the CFU's communication of drought forecasts to commercial farmers (Patt, chapter 9, this volume), across regions as in the LRTAP POPs and acid rain cases (Selin, chapter 7, this volume; Andonova, chapter 6, this volume; VanDeveer, chapter 5, this volume), or between scientists and policymakers as in the climate case (Torrance, chapter 2, this volume). When such relationships are absent or do not function well, they can inhibit assessment influence as evident in global biosafety negotiations (Gupta, chapter 3, this volume), Indian responses to climate change and biodiversity assessments (Biermann, chapter 4, this volume), and Hawaiian responses to sea-level rise assessments (Moser, chapter 8, this volume).

Understanding assessments as processes also highlights that the assessment process does not end once scientists have reached some set of conclusions. It may take considerable effort to help decision makers and stakeholders understand and accept the validity and relevance of scientific findings to their decisions. Commercial and smallholder farmers in Zimbabwe needed help in converting weather forecasts into planting guidance (Patt, chapter 9, this volume). Global acceptance of LRTAP POPs assessments depended on conducting subsequent regional assessments that developed further knowledge and fostered acceptance of that knowledge (Selin, chapter 7, this volume). Educating potential users is rarely effective when viewed as "dissemination" to be undertaken once an assessment is complete but works best when viewed as integral to the assessment process.

Of course, participation is not a panacea. As noted above, trade-offs exist among salience, credibility, and legitimacy. Indeed, many scientists believe that assessment processes should be kept relatively, or even completely, free of nonscientist policymakers, stakeholders, and interested parties. For these scientists, promoting legitimacy and salience eviscerates credibility. And, certainly, participation by self-interested actors can lead audiences to question the expertise and trustworthiness on which credibility with those audiences depend.

This study, however, confirms the view of the "social studies of science" literature that science rarely achieves the impartial detachment from politics that many consider crucial to the influence of scientific information (Jasanoff and Wynne 1998). But our research goes further and demonstrates that efforts to achieve such objectivity and neutrality often inhibit informational influence. Stakeholder involvement is not antithetical to credibility and it is almost essential for stakeholders to incorporate information from assessments into their decisions. Effective participation requires involving stakeholders in ways that shape what questions get asked and how the answers to those questions are framed, delivered, and understood without allowing that involvement to dictate the answers produced. As the unwillingness of various audiences to accept initial IPCC reports, LRTAP POPs assessments, proposals regarding GMO information exchanges, or federal assessments of sea-level rise illustrates, focusing on credibility alone all but ensures that the assessment will have less influence than it might. Equally important, our cases show how assessors have involved stakeholders and relevant decision makers in ways and at points that have increased salience and legitimacy while either not undermining or actually increasing credibility (on these issues of assessment design, see Farrell and Jäger 2005; Farrell, VanDeveer, and Jäger 2001).

Capacity Building

A final finding in many of our cases was the value of building the capacity of various actors to be involved in producing assessments and to understand the findings of assessments. Because scientific infrastructures and expertise tend to be concentrated in developed countries, developing-country scientists have often participated only in token ways, if at all. Assessment processes have gained influence with wider audiences, however, by establishing a long-term goal and process to enhance the capacity of a range of scientists to participate substantively in assessments, thereby mitigating trade-offs among credibility, salience, and legitimacy. Building capacity among assessment producers and assessment users expands the group of people who see and know the world in similar ways and fosters the coproduction just mentioned by developing common ways to interpret information about the environment, politics, economics, and the other factors involved in resolving environmental problems (for recent reviews of capacity building, see Sagar and VanDeveer 2005; VanDeveer and Sagar 2005).

Investments in building scientific capacity expand the range of scientists involved in scientific research on a given environmental problem, increasing the legitimacy of assessments among stakeholder groups that view themselves as represented by those scientists but also increasing the credibility of assessments by bringing in knowledge, data, and perspectives that would not otherwise be available. As Andonova notes, an important way that assessments gain influence comes from involving participants and thereby helping "strengthen domestic capacity and the institutional linkages between experts and policy establishments" (Andonova, chapter 6, this volume). The IPCC made such efforts and, after fifteen years, that investment is evident in developing-country scientists having considerably more influence on IPCC analyses, and in those analyses having increasing influence in developing countries (Biermann, chapter 4, this volume). For decades, IIASA ran workshops and training sessions for Central and Eastern European scientists and policymakers and ensured that computer models could run on less capable computers (VanDeveer, chapter 5, this volume). Beyond allowing researchers to contribute meaningfully to IIASA research, these efforts produced a network of IIASA and RAINS alumni that helps IIASA assessments gain acceptance because members of that network can understand and vouch for their credibility and legitimacy and because those members have credibility and legitimacy with their own policymakers (VanDeveer, chapter 5, this volume; Andonova, chapter 6, this volume).

As the IIASA case illustrates, capacity building among potential users is as important as among assessment producers. The ability to understand and interpret scientific information may be lacking in countries that are most likely to be affected by particular problems. In the biosafety negotiations, significant and ongoing capacity building will be needed to help GMO-importing countries access, process, and understand the information on the risks of such imports that will be provided through the clearinghouse mechanism (Gupta, chapter 3, this volume). Poland had "a great deal of scientific expertise but little experience in environmental management or in the open use of information as a basis of decision making," and involving government and corporate stakeholders in acid rain cost assessments helped "facilitate the adoption of European acid rain standards in Eastern Europe" (Andonova, chapter 6, this volume). Both commercial and smallholder farmers in Zimbabwe required training, whether by the CFU or Agritex, in how to understand drought forecasts as well as the implications of those forecasts for their planting decisions (Patt, chapter 9, this volume). In Maine, geologists expended considerable effort to help local decision makers understand coastal processes, slowly building a management and policymaking network that is knowledgeable about, and in the future may become willing to address, sea-level rise directly (Moser, chapter 8, this volume). By directly involving stakeholders in assessment processes—whether it involves farmers conducting experiments on their farms or policymakers and industry representatives helping scientists develop scenarios for acid precipitation models—stakeholders build the capacity to understand and trust the results of those assessments.

Areas for Future Research

Our research has uncovered several additional insights that were evident in only one or a few of our cases but that deserve further study by those interested in the influence of GEAs.

First, the characteristics of the institution that sponsors or undertakes an assessment affect how much influence that assessment will have. Undertaking initial assessments on acid precipitation through the Organization for Economic Cooperation and Development (OECD) helped increase attention to those issues among Western European states but inhibited those assessments' influence among Central and Eastern European states that were not OECD members (VanDeveer, chapter 5, this volume). Much of the variation in the use made of information about aquifer depletion and water use in the American Midwest can be explained by looking at which institutions conducted those assessments, particularly their preexisting linkages with water managers and farmers (Cash, chapter 10, this volume). Climate change assessments conducted by the intergovernmental IPCC have been much more influential among the world's governments than nongovernmental efforts, even when many of the same scientists have been involved (Torrance, chapter 2, this volume).

Second, attributions of salience, credibility, and legitimacy have particular difficulty traveling across scales. Assessments that various national- or international-level audiences view as salient, credible, and legitimate are often viewed differently by local-level audiences. In assessments, "one size does not fit all" and disconnects often emerge between the aggregate, large-scale, low-resolution data needed by those trying to understand the environmental problem and the disaggregated, small-scale, high-resolution analyses needed by those making decisions among the options available to them. Various scenarios of average global temperature that motivate international climate negotiators frustrate those national policymakers concerned about the impacts on their country under each scenario. Careful management can, however, help convince audiences at one scale to accept assessments that were conducted to support decisions at another scale. Ideas from European assessments had influence in global POPs negotiations only because promoters of those negotiations recognized the need to keep the European provenance of the assessments in the background (Selin, chapter 7, this volume). In Zimbabwe, regional rain forecasts were used by farmers only because the CFU translated these forecasts into knowledge that matched their day-to-day decisions (Patt, chapter 9, this volume).

Third, an assessment's influence depends on the informational environment into which it enters, particularly the degree of informational competition. One source of the influence of IIASA's assessment and modeling of acid precipitation in Europe or the POPs assessments internationally is the absence of alternative sources of information on these issues (Andonova, chapter 6, this volume; VanDeveer, chapter 5, this volume; Selin, chapter 7, this volume). The nongovernmental Villach assessment's influence declined precipitously once the IPCC was established (Torrance, chapter 2, this volume). Nor is the informational environment static: as noted, assessments can generate their own competition by prompting counterassessments such as the responses of Indian scientists to American assessments of methane emissions (Biermann, chapter 4, this volume) and of climate skeptics to IPCC reports (Franz 1998).

Finally, and fortunately, our cases demonstrate that assessors can improve assessments over time. The IPCC has gained increasing acceptance with more audiences by ensuring that developing-country scientists are increasingly, if still under-, represented in the IPCC process (Biermann, chapter 4, this volume). The Millennium Ecosystem Assessment has learned from the failures of the Global Biodiversity Assessment and involved a more geographically diverse set of scientists and located their headquarters in Malaysia (Biermann, chapter 4, this volume). The Zimbabwean agriculture extension service (Agritex), recognizing prior mistakes, has increased public participation and stakeholder education and has redesigned drought forecasts to make them more timely and more useful to farmers (Patt, chapter 9, this volume). The influence of LRTAP assessments on acidification and POPs reflects years of using past experience to refine assessment processes (VanDeveer, chapter 5, this volume; Andonova, chapter 6, this volume).

The foregoing chapters present many other insights into when and how assessments gain influence with different audiences as well as into the many obstacles to such influence. We hope that those undertaking further research on GEAs will use the wealth of ideas identified in those chapters to shape that research.

Considerations for Practitioners

Our findings suggest several lessons for those actually involved in designing and carrying out global environmental assessments. Although many more, and more refined, lessons are delineated in the associated volume by Farrell and Jäger (2005), we delineate those most closely related to our findings here.

Focus on the Process, Not the Report

Our most important lesson for practitioners is that the conduct of an assessment determines its influence more than its conclusions do. Decision makers are more likely to incorporate the knowledge of assessments if that knowledge comes through iterative, two-way communication with assessment producers rather than from reading a report. Equally important, assessments prove more effective when assessment producers also see them as involving mutual education and coproduction of knowledge rather than as scientists aggregating and disseminating information to policymakers and decision makers.

Focus on Salience and Legitimacy as Well as Credibility

Assessors too often focus exclusively on ensuring an assessment's scientific credibility. Credibility is important but assessment influence also depends on audiences viewing the assessment process and products as salient and legitimate. Accurate information that is irrelevant to decision makers' needs or that disregards their concerns, perspectives, and values is as likely to be dismissed as inaccurate information is. Fostering assessment influence requires promoting attributions of salience, credibility, and legitimacy through assessment processes that mitigate the frequent trade-offs among these attributions while taking advantage of potential synergies among them.

Assess with Multiple Audiences in Mind

Assessment influence declines the greater the "distance" of assessment producers from potential users. For GEAs to contribute to the resolution of the problems they address, they must influence numerous, diverse audiences. Each audience will evaluate the salience, credibility, and legitimacy of an assessment on terms that reflect that audience's unique set of interests, perceptions, knowledge, and beliefs. People in different countries, at different scales, or with different training or values will not all accept an assessment's findings unless assessors make conscious efforts to make the assessment salient, credible, and legitimate to all of those audiences.

Involve Stakeholders and Connect with Existing Networks

It is tempting to identify rules of thumb by which assessments can promote salience, credibility, and legitimacy with multiple audiences. Yet our study shows that the most effective path to influence involves promoting substantive and substantial participation by potential users. Participation fosters salience by ensuring that the problem definition, the research agenda, the menu of options, and the criteria for choosing among options match the concerns and decision needs of potential users. Participation fosters credibility by ensuring that no single stakeholder dominates the assessment process, by maximizing access to relevant data, and by helping potential users understand and trust the methods by which assessment conclusions are derived. Participation fosters legitimacy by ensuring that the interests and values of affected actors are taken into account and addressed in the assessment. Engaging existing networks of scientists, decision makers, and policymakers allows assessments to bring the expertise, knowledge, and data of these actors into the assessment while taking advantage of the preexisting salience, credibility, and legitimacy that actors in these networks have with important audiences.

Develop Influence over Time

Assessments rarely gain significant influence with multiple audiences overnight. Understandably, most audiences will not change their policies and practices immediately in response to new information. Influence often takes time to develop, varies over time, and may take time to reveal itself. The influence that IIASA assessments have had on acid rain and POPs regulation owes much to sustained and conscious efforts to engage stakeholders (Andonova, chapter 6, this volume; VanDeveer, chapter 5, this volume; Selin, chapter 7, this volume). IIASA, the IPCC, and other assessment processes become salient, credible, and legitimate with various audiences not only by getting particular assessments "right" but through an extended effort to build a reputation for producing assessments that audiences believe they should take into account in their decisions. Investments in building capacity, both of scientists and stakeholders to participate and of potential users to understand assessment findings, take time to pay dividends (Biermann, chapter 4, this volume; Patt, chapter 9, this volume; Andonova, chapter 6, this volume). Finally, assessments also may benefit from independent changes in how interested governments and decision makers are in an environmental problem—the influence of the Villach climate assessment and the LRTAP acidification assessments increased due to the success of ozone negotiations and the possibility of EU accession, respectively (Torrance, chapter 2, this volume; VanDeveer, chapter 5, this volume). It takes time to build a reputation for understanding the decisions and constraints that stakeholders face; for providing unbiased, reliable, and understandable information; and for taking account of the values, interests, and views of stakeholders—and through that reputation to gain influence.

Conclusion

Global environmental assessments can and do change how many people consider human impacts on the environment to be a problem, how and how well they understand those problems, and whether and what action is warranted to address it. However, achieving these impacts poses challenging tasks that require overcoming numerous obstacles. This book has demonstrated that an assessment's influence depends far more on its conduct than its content and that significant influence requires using assessment processes to convince not one but multiple audiences of the salience, credibility, and legitimacy of the information in an assessment. Those producing GEAs are usually separated from potential users by numerous boundaries to effective communication, including those dividing science from policy, those isolating certain nations and groups of nations from others, and those conducting science and those making decisions at different scales on the international-regional-national-local spectrum. Overcoming these boundaries to the uptake of scientific ideas requires avoiding the assumption that assessment influence depends only on scientific credibility. Those conducting assessments are most successful when they recognize assessments as social processes aimed at the coproduction of knowledge, foster the participation of a wide range of stakeholders, and build the capacity of scientists to participate in assessments and of potential users to understand and trust those assessments. We hope our research helps scholars and practitioners learn from the experiences of the assessments analyzed here so that future assessments can make greater contributions to the resolution of the myriad global environmental problems we face.

Acknowledgments

We would like to thank Frank Alcock and Lisa Martin for major efforts in developing this chapter. We would also like to thank Frank Biermann, Susanne Moser, Noelle Eckley Selin, and Stacy VanDeveer for helpful comments on earlier drafts of the chapter.

References

Baumgartner, F. R., and B. D. Jones. 1993. *Agendas and Instability in American Politics*. Chicago: University of Chicago Press.

Benedick, Richard Elliot. 1998. *Ozone Diplomacy: New Directions in Safeguarding the Planet*. Cambridge, MA: Harvard University Press.

Cash, David W., and William Clark. 2001. *From Science to Policy: Assessing the Assessment Process*. John F. Kennedy School of Government Faculty Research Working Papers Series RWP01-045. Cambridge, MA: Harvard University.

Clark, William C., and Nancy M. Dickson. 2001. Civic science: America's encounter with global environmental risks. In Social Learning Group, ed., *Learning to Manage Global Environmental Risks, Volume 1: A Comparative History of Social Responses to Climate Change, Ozone Depletion, and Acid Rain,* 259–294. Cambridge, MA: MIT Press.

Clausewitz, Carl von. 1982. *On War.* New York: Penguin Books.

DeSombre, Elizabeth R. 2000. *Domestic Sources of International Environmental Policy: Industry, Environmentalists, and U.S. Power.* Cambridge, MA: MIT Press.

Farrell, Alex, Stacy VanDeveer, and Jill Jäger. 2001. Environmental assessment: Four under-appreciated elements of design. *Global Environmental Change* 11: 311–333.

Farrell, Alexander E., and Jill Jäger, eds. 2005. *Assessments of Regional and Global Environmental Risks: Designing Processes for the Effective Use of Science in Decisionmaking.* Washington, DC: Resources for the Future.

Franz, Wendy. 1998. *Science, Skeptics, and Non-State Actors in the Greenhouse.* Discussion Paper E-98-18. Cambridge, MA: Belfer Center for Science and International Affairs, Harvard University.

Freudenburg, W. 1996. Risky thinking: Irrational fears about risk and society. *Annals of the American Academy of Political and Social Science* 545: 44–53.

Glantz, Michael H., J. Robinson, and M. E. Krenz. 1982. Climate-related impact studies: A review of past experiences. In William C. Clark, ed., *Carbon Dioxide Review: 1982,* 55–92. New York: Oxford University Press.

Haas, Peter M., ed. 1992. *Knowledge, Power, and International Policy Coordination.* Columbia: University of South Carolina Press.

Harrison, Neil E., and Gary C. Bryner. 2004. *Science and Politics in the International Environment.* Lanham, MD: Rowman & Littlefield.

Herrick, C., and Dale Jamieson. 1995. The social construction of acid rain: Some implications for policy assessment. *Global Environmental Change* 5: 105–112.

Hurwitz, Steven D., Murray S. Miron, and Blair T. Johnson. 1992. Source credibility and the language of expert testimony. *Journal of Applied Social Psychology* 22(24): 1909–1939.

Jäger, Jill, with Jeannine Cavender-Bares, Nancy M. Dickson, Adam Fenech, Edward A. Parson, Vassily Sokolov, Ferenc L. Tóth, Claire Waterton, Jeroen van der Sluijs, and Josee van Eijndhoven. 2001. Risk assessment in the management of global environmental risks. In Social Learning Group, ed., *Learning to Manage Global Environmental Risks, Volume 2: A Functional Analysis of Social Responses to Climate Change, Ozone Depletion, and Acid Rain.* Cambridge, MA: MIT Press.

Jasanoff, Sheila. 1990. *The Fifth Branch: Science Advisers as Policy-Makers.* Cambridge, MA: Harvard University Press.

Jasanoff, Sheila. 2004. *States of Knowledge: The Co-production of Science and Social Order.* New York: Routledge.

Jasanoff, Sheila, and Marybeth Long Martello, eds. 2004. *Earthly Politics: Local and Global in Environmental Governance.* Cambridge, MA: MIT Press.

Jasanoff, Sheila, and Brian Wynne. 1998. Science and Decisionmaking. In S. Rayner and E. Malone, eds., *Human Choice and Climate Change: The Societal Framework.* Columbus, OH: Battelle Press.

Lemos, Maria Carmen, and B. J. Morehouse. 2005. The co-production of science and policy in integrated climate assessments. *Global Environmental Change* 15: 57–68.

Naylor, Rosamond L., Walter P. Falcon, Daniel Rochberg, and Nikolas Wada. 2001. Using El Niño/Southern Oscillation climate data to predict rice production in Indonesia. *Climate Change* 50: 255–265.

Osgood, C. E., and Percy H. Tannenbaum. 1955. The principle of congruity in the prediction of attitude change. *Psychological Review* 62: 42–55.

Parson, Edward A. 2003. *Protecting the Ozone Layer: Science and Strategy.* Oxford: Oxford University Press.

Pielke, Robert Jr. 1995. Usable information for policy: An appraisal of the U. S. Global Change Research Program. *Policy Sciences* 28: 39–77.

Pielke, Robert Jr., and R. T. Conant. 2003. Best practices in prediction for decision-making: Lessons from the atmospheric and earth sciences. *Ecology* 84: 1351–1358.

Pulwarty, Roger S., and Ted Melis. 2001. Climate extremes and adaptive management on the Colorado River: Lessons from the 1997–1998 ENSO event. *Journal of Environmental Management* 63: 307–324.

Pulwarty, Roger S., and Kelly Redmond. 1997. Climate and salmon restoration in the Columbia River basin: The role and usability of seasonal forecasts. *Bulletin of the American Meteorological Society* 78(3): 381–397.

Sabatier, Paul A. 1993. Policy change over a decade or more. In P. A. Sabatier and H. C. Jenkins-Smith, eds., *Policy Change and Learning: An Advocacy Coalition Approach.* Boulder, CO: Westview Press.

Sagar, Ambuj D., and Stacy D. VanDeveer. 2005. Capacity development for the environment: Broadening the focus. *Global Environmental Politics* 5(3): 14–22.

Slater, Michael D., and Donna Rouner. 1996. How message evaluation and source attributes may influence credibility assessment and belief change. *Journalism and Mass Communication Quarterly* 73(4): 974–991.

Slovic, Paul. 1993. Perceived risk, trust, and democracy. *Risk Analysis* 13(6): 675–682.

Social Learning Group, ed. 2001a. *Learning to Manage Global Environmental Risks, Volume 1: A Comparative History of Social Responses to Climate Change, Ozone Depletion, and Acid Rain.* Cambridge, MA: MIT Press.

Social Learning Group, ed. 2001b. *Learning to Manage Global Environmental Risks, Volume 2: A Functional Analysis of Social Responses to Climate Change, Ozone Depletion, and Acid Rain.* Cambridge, MA: MIT Press.

Sprinz, Detlef, and Tapani Vaahtoranta. 1994. The interest-based explanation of international environmental policy. *International Organization* 48(1): 77–105.

U.S. Department of Transportation, Climatic Impact Assessment Program. 1975. *Impacts of Climatic Change on the Biosphere, Final Report.* Washington, DC: U.S. Department of Transportation.

VanDeveer, Stacy, and Ambuj Sagar. 2005. Capacity building for the environment: North and south. In A. C. Kallhauge and G. Sjöstedt, eds., *Furthering Consensus: Meeting the Challenges of Sustainable Development Beyond 2002.* London: Greenleaf.

Walsh, Virginia M. 2004. *Global Institutions and Social Knowledge: Generating Research at the Scripps Institution and the Inter-American Tropical Tuna Commission 1900s–1990s.* Cambridge, MA: MIT Press.

Watson, Robert T. 1994. The stratospheric ozone debate: Global research that led to achieving scientific consensus. *Abstracts of Papers of the American Chemical Society* 208, part 1: 172.

Weiss, Carol H. 1975. Evaluation research in the political context. In E. S. Struening and M. Gutentag, eds., *Handbook of Evaluation Research.* London: Sage.

Wilkening, Kenneth E. 2004. *Acid Rain Science and Politics in Japan: A History of Knowledge and Action toward Sustainability.* Cambridge, MA: MIT Press.

Index

Global Environmental Accord: Strategies for Sustainability and Institutional Innovation

Nazli Choucri, series editor